INSIDERS' GUIDE® TO
SEATTLE

HELP US KEEP THIS GUIDE UP-TO-DATE

We would love to hear from you concerning your experiences with this guide and how you feel it could be improved and kept up-to-date. Please send your comments and suggestions to:

editorial@GlobePequot.com

Thanks for your input, and happy travels!

INSIDERS' GUIDE® SERIES

INSIDERS' GUIDE® TO

SEATTLE

FIRST EDITION

SHELLEY SEALE

INSIDERS' GUIDE

GUILFORD, CONNECTICUT
AN IMPRINT OF GLOBE PEQUOT PRESS

All the information in this guidebook is subject to change. We recommend that you call ahead to obtain current information before traveling.

To buy books in quantity for corporate use or incentives, call **(800) 962–0973** or e-mail **premiums@GlobePequot.com.**

INSIDERS' GUIDE ®

Editor: Amy Lyons
Project Editor: Kristen Mellitt
Layout Artist: Kevin Mak
Text Design: Sheryl Kober
Maps: Daniel Lloyd © Morris Book Publishing, LLC

Library of Congress Cataloging-in-Publication Data is available on file.
ISBN 978-0-7627-5544-8

Printed in the United States of America
10 9 8 7 6 5 4 3 2 1

CONTENTS

Directory of Maps

ABOUT THE AUTHOR

Shelley Seale was born in Dallas, Texas, grew up in a neighboring suburb, and got to the cool, irreverent city of Austin as fast as she could. A few years ago she moved to Seattle and began splitting her time between Seattle and Austin—two simpatico cities that share a love of quirkiness, thriving music and art scenes, a healthy respect for individuality, and very funky vibes. Perhaps these commonalities were what caused this Austinite to feel so at home in, and fall totally in love with, Seattle.

Before writing the *Insiders' Guide to Seattle,* Seale published a nonfiction narrative called The *Weight of Silence: Invisible Children of India*. This book chronicles her journey over three years in India and tells the stories of some of the real-life children behind such fiction as the movie *Slumdog Millionaire*. Seale is also a contributing author to *The Voluntary Traveler, A Cup of Comfort for a Better World,* and *A Century of Hospitality*. Her writing has appeared in *National Geographic*'s GeoTourism MapGuides and on its Intelligent Travel blog, the *Seattle Times, Outdoors NW* magazine, *Andrew Harper Traveler, Washington* magazine, and many others.

Although she is a freelance writer by trade, Seale is really a vagabond by nature. Her absolute favorite thing to do is travel, and she loves exploring—and even getting lost in—new and foreign places. She is passionate about sustainable travel and traveling with a purpose, attempting as much as possible to immerse herself in the cultural identities of the places she visits and supporting local businesses there, as opposed to outside corporations—in other words, trying to travel in a way that's not simply embodying a consumerist mentality.

Some of the odder things Seale has done include singing karaoke in a Qingdao, China, KTV bar, night snorkeling with manta rays in Hawaii, performing a catch on the flying trapeze, and getting robbed by a monkey in Nepal.

The irony of writing her own bio in the third person, knowing full well that you astute readers are not fooled for one second, is not lost on Seale.

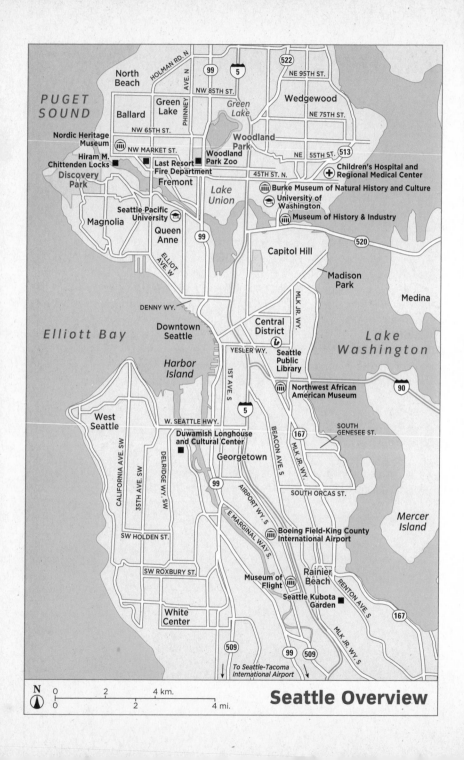

Seattle Overview

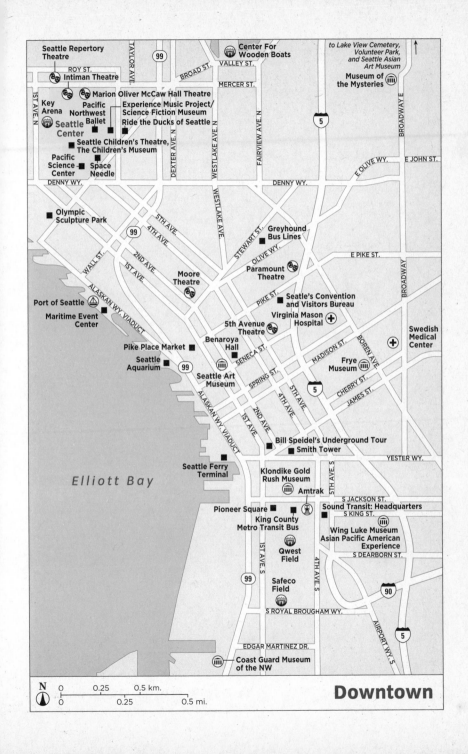

Seattle Repertory Theatre

ROY ST.
Intiman Theatre

Center For Wooden Boats

VALLEY ST.

to Lake View Cemetery, Volunteer Park, and Seattle Asian Art Museum

MERCER ST.

Museum of the Mysteries

1ST AVE. N
Key Arena

TAYLOR AVE.
99

BROAD ST.

Marion Oliver McCaw Hall Theatre
Pacific Northwest Ballet

Experience Music Project/ Science Fiction Museum
Ride the Ducks of Seattle

FAIRVIEW AVE. N

5

BROADWAY E

Seattle Center

Seattle Children's Theatre, The Children's Museum

DEXTER AVE. N

WESTLAKE AVE. N

E OLIVE WY.

E JOHN ST.

Pacific Science Center
Space Needle

DENNY WY.

DENNY WY.

DENNY WY.

Olympic Sculpture Park

5TH AVE.

4TH AVE.

99

WESTLAKE AVE.

STEWART ST.

Greyhound Bus Lines

OLIVE WY.

E PIKE ST.

WALL ST.

2ND AVE.

1ST AVE.

Moore Theatre

Paramount Theatre

BROADWAY

Port of Seattle

ALASKAN WY. VIADUCT

Maritime Event Center

PIKE ST.

Seattle's Convention and Visitors Bureau

Virginia Mason Hospital

Swedish Medical Center

Pike Place Market

5th Avenue Theatre

Benaroya Hall

SENECA ST.

MADISON ST.

BOREN AVE.

Frye Museum

Seattle Aquarium

99

Seattle Art Museum

SPRING ST.

2ND AVE.

1ST AVE.

4TH AVE.

5TH AVE.

5

CHERRY ST.

JAMES ST.

Elliott Bay

ALASKAN WY. VIADUCT

Bill Speidel's Underground Tour
Smith Tower

YESTER WY.

Seattle Ferry Terminal

Klondike Gold Rush Museum

Amtrak

5TH AVE. S

S JACKSON ST.

Pioneer Square

King County Metro Transit Bus

Sound Transit: Headquarters

S KING ST.

Wing Luke Museum Asian Pacific American Experience

S DEARBORN ST.

1ST AVE. S

Qwest Field

4TH AVE. S

99

Safeco Field

90

5

S ROYAL BROUGHAM WY.

AIRPORT WY. S

EDGAR MARTINEZ DR.

Coast Guard Museum of the NW

N

0   0.25   0.5 km.

0   0.25   0.5 mi.

Downtown

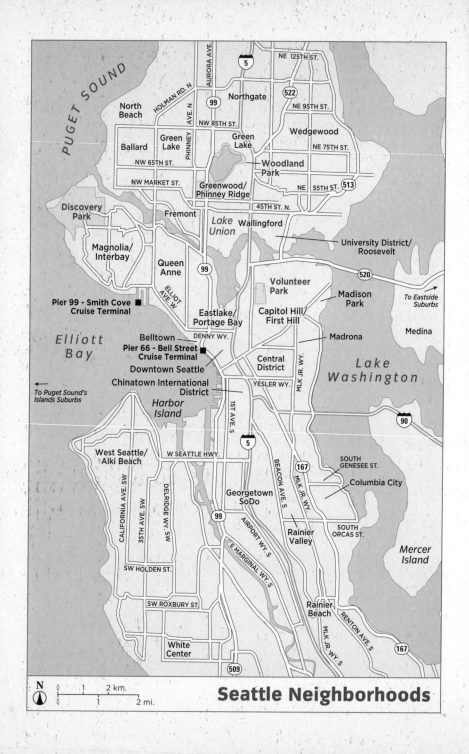

Seattle Neighborhoods

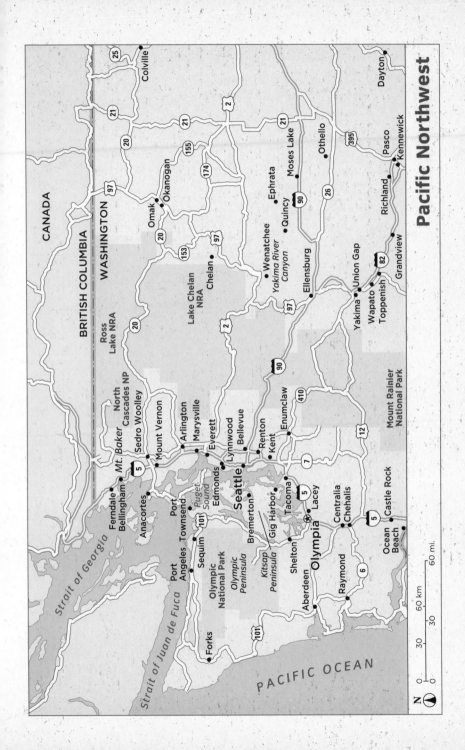

Pacific Northwest

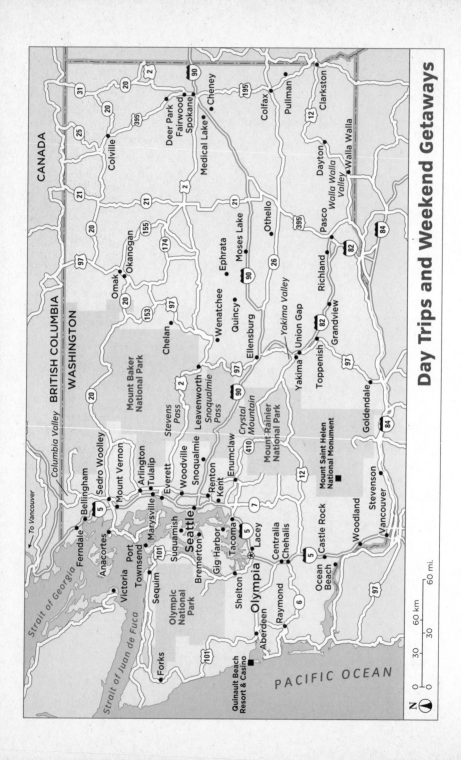

Day Trips and Weekend Getaways

PREFACE

Thoughts of Seattle typically begin with a few things: the Space Needle, coffee culture, grunge music, and a liberal, tree-hugging, outdoors-oriented populace. Though these things are indeed part of Seattle's culture and charm, they are far from the only aspects of this sophisticated, diverse place known as the "Emerald City," set in the middle of the magnificent Pacific Northwest.

Seattle is a study in dichotomy. It's an epicenter for tech and business, yet it also has a delightfully quirky, irreverent side. By the weekend, the same people wearing suits in high-rise office buildings on a weekday afternoon may be found in the crowds at the Summer Solstice Parade where completely naked—but painted—bicyclists and dancers make their way down the streets of Fremont. In any given coffee shop or music club you will find the tattooed and pierced side by side with the preppy and those wearing haute couture. Men walk around in kilts or sarongs—more often than you may think—and no one looks twice. The ethnic melting pot is refreshing and vibrant; there seem to be more languages, more dreadlocks, more eccentric people, and more interaction between them all than in many other places.

It's a sophisticated city full of five-star restaurants and power couples attending the opera, yet the entire populace seems to exude a down-home, casual attitude and live-and-let-live philosophy. These are all good reasons why Seattle was voted #2 in America's Best Cities 2009 by *Outside Magazine* (just behind Colorado Springs) and #4 on *Forbes'* list of Best Cities for Singles. It was also ranked by the Census Bureau as the best-educated big city in America.

People here are known for being very polite. It's just a . . . well, nice place. Without crossing over into that annoying, overly effusive friendliness, Seattleites are generally very pleasant and helpful. Almost everyone who moves here or visits for long soon acquires a "people are so nice" story to tell. For me, it was the moment I realized that wherever I walked, drivers would stop the second I neared the curb, waiting for me to enter the street. Even if I was only pausing or looking around—when I wasn't even at a corner or didn't have the right-of-way to walk—they would smile from behind the wheel and gesture for me to go ahead in front of them as the cars behind all waited patiently.

This behavior was disconcerting to a pedestrian used to not only waiting for the light to change, but first looking both ways to make sure an impatient driver wasn't making a run for it. I can only imagine how New Yorkers must react to this. Polite driving is sort of a running joke here; the "oh no, please, after you" merging mentality of the highways sometimes seems to create the traffic jams. But you will likely encounter the same helpfulness from waitstaff, at the market, or with a retail sales clerk. In fact, the late etiquette author Marjabelle Young Stewart named Seattle the third most well-mannered in the country, based on reports from visitors tickled to find that Seattleites don't honk or scream at them.

PREFACE

The bottom line is that although Seattle has grown and changed plenty over the past 20 years, it is a relaxed place where you will find friendly locals obsessed with the outdoors, green living, and coffee. It is a place with a strong sense of community and a healthy appreciation for the bizarre; where uniqueness and individuality are prized; where a cast of vastly different characters coexist peacefully; and above all, it is a city of breathtaking beauty. Welcome to Seattle—and prepare to be enchanted.

HOW TO USE THIS BOOK

You undoubtedly picked up this book because you have arrived in Seattle, are planning a trip there, or are relocating to the city. Whether you stay in the Emerald City for a day or the rest of your life, my goal in writing this Insiders' Guide is to provide you with indispensible facts and insights, as well as personal and fun glimpses into the heart of this wonderful place.

The categories the book has been organized into are meant to make it easy to find the relevant information you are most interested in. My hope is that this guide will soon be high-lighted, dog-eared, scribbled in, and carted around to the point that it's nearly unpresentable. However, this *is* Seattle, so digging a grubby, well-worn book from the bottom of your bag to peruse in a coffee shop will really only make you seem more at home here.

The book is broken into chapters and sections that do not require reading in sequential order, and that will allow you to most easily find the specific information you are looking for at any given time. Some things will cross-reference each other; for example, a site in the Attractions chapter may also be appreciated by families and may also be mentioned in the Kidstuff chapter as well. Likewise, a city park in the Parks & Recreation chapter may also have a great beach that should be mentioned in that section. In all of these cases, a full overview with details is given in just one part of the book, with notations in other applicable sections on where to find that information.

Throughout the book you will find Insiders' Tips **i** that will let you in on a local secret, reveal a helpful resource, or give a special insight. You will also find fun sidebars that are full of interesting tidbits about the sorts of things that make Seattle so quirky.

The Area Overview will introduce you to the greater Seattle and Puget Sound region, as well as the personalities of individual neighborhoods throughout the city. For simplicity's sake, I have broken down the city into North, Central, and South sections (as outlined on the map) so that as you read, you will be able to have an immediate idea of the general part of the city where something mentioned is located. The Area Overview also gives a lot of the data and statistics that are often useful when visiting or moving to a city, and a historical timeline of the region.

Getting Here, Getting Around is a chapter that is self-explanatory, giving you all the information you need to navigate Seattle. Next, the History chapter delves into how this place came to be Seattle, and the frontier town's early history through its modern development as an urban city.

In the Accommodations chapter you will find detailed listings on places to stay of all sorts, from the fanciest high-rise hotel to trendy boutique hotels; from basic family accommoda-tions with kitchenettes and hostels to historic bed-and-breakfast inns. These are arranged first by the type of accommodation, and then by geographical area. Restaurants are similarly laid out, categorized by the type of cuisine and with the geographical area given in parentheses.

The Nightlife chapter will introduce you to all the fun and fantastic things you can do in Seattle at night, from the low-key, such as movies and cocktail lounges, to the outrageous, such as burlesque or drag shows. If Shopping is your thing, you'll find an overview of the shopping styles in different parts of town and what you'll find there, followed by a shopping guide of great stores under myriad categories.

Of course, when you visit Seattle you'll want to get out and see everything this fabulous city has to offer. The Attractions chapter lays it all out for you, with details on museums of all kinds, science centers, landmarks, significant architecture, cultural and maritime centers, tours of the city to meet any sort of specialized interest, and a helpful sidebar giving five great rainy-day itineraries. In addition, there are a number of tips for saving money while sightseeing, including a comprehensive "Seattle on a Shoestring" list of 37 awesome things you can do in Seattle that are completely free or cost next to nothing.

Seattle is home to a great mix of classical arts and cutting-edge, modern art; the Arts chapter tells you all about it. Art walks take place one night a month in neighborhoods all over the city, and the areas of Belltown and Pioneer Square in particular are brimming with galleries. By the way, *Sleepless in Seattle* is far from the only movie set in the Emerald City; check out the fun list of more than three dozen other movies set or filmed here.

If you are visiting Seattle as a family, you won't want to miss the Kidstuff chapter. Listing everything from amusement parks and arcades to museums and tours that kids will love, this chapter also tells you how to get the most out of your family vacation. Want to know the best restaurants to go to with children, or what kid-oriented festivals are happening during your trip? You'll find it here.

The next chapter will give you a complete listing of Annual Events & Festivals, in chronological order. Besides the biggies like Bumbershoot and Seafair, Seattle has a host of cultural celebrations of all kinds, as well as some of the oddest festivals around. Ever heard of the Moisture Festival, Summer Solstice Parade, or the Erotic Arts Festival? Read all about these wacky days of fun here.

An *Insiders' Guide to Seattle* could not have been written without special attention given to the majestic bounty of the Pacific Northwest. This chapter gives an overview of the beauty and natural resources found in the entire region, from the mountains to the water. You'll also find a sidebar of sustainable travel tips for those who like to go green, and a look at some of the Northwest's fascinating mountain-climbing legends. This regional overview leads into the following chapter, Parks & Recreation, which focuses specifically on Seattle and the city's recreational options, including beaches, boating and fishing, cycling, hiking, golf, and more. Spectator Sports will give you the inside scoop on the city's professional, minor-league, and collegiate games that you may want to check out.

When you want to explore outside of Seattle, the Day Trips & Weekend Getaways chapter is your resource. Here you can find great information on destinations such as the nearby towns, islands, spas, cruises, casinos, ski resorts, and wineries that can be easily visited from Seattle. There's even a section on British Columbia—there's no better place to combine a trip to western Canada. Moving to Seattle or already live here? The blue-tabbed section at the back of the book, **Living Here,** gives special information for newcomers and those relocating to Seattle. Here you will find a wealth of data on area neighborhoods, real estate, schools, health care, and more.

Every effort has been made to provide the most accurate, up-to-date information possible, but of course, details change continually. If you discover an error or something that's been missed, or you simply have a different opinion about something written here, please don't hesitate to contact us at Globe Pequot Press, P.O. Box 480, Guilford, CT 06437-0480 or at editorial@globepequot.com.

AREA OVERVIEW

The Emerald City is a glimmering jewel surrounded by water, and these waterways make up a good part of Seattle's appeal and character. It is the core city of the Pacific Northwest, midway between Portland, Oregon, to the south and Vancouver, British Columbia, to the north. To the east lies Puget Sound, which connects with the Pacific Ocean about 150 miles north of Seattle. As the Sound reaches Seattle, it feeds into Elliott Bay, on which downtown Seattle sits. On the east side of the city is massive Lake Washington, a glacial lake that is the second largest in the state. Meandering within the city are Lake Union, Green Lake, and the Chittenden Locks, a network of working canals. All told, the city has more than 190 miles of waterfront. Life evolved in Seattle around the water, and its early fishing and seafaring communities existed because of it. Today, Seattleites love the water as much as ever and sports such as sailing, kayaking, fishing, and water-skiing are extremely popular.

SEATTLE LIFESTYLE

The location amid the spectacular natural resources and beauty of the Pacific Northwest means that the Seattle lifestyle is also very much steeped in outdoor recreation, from hiking and birding to alpine sports such as mountaineering, snow skiing, and snowshoeing. Mount Rainier, Mount St. Helens, and the Cascade and Olympic mountain ranges provide nearly endless adventures in summer and winter. Locals are passionate about their city and the bounty the Pacific Northwest offers, from sports to nature to food. Such a close affinity and appreciation for the natural wonders of the area have led Seattleites to be early pioneers in environmental sustainability; it is one of the greenest cities in the country and an early proponent of technologies such as renewable energy. Littering is one offense that is taken very seriously here.

But far from being a population focused only on health or the outdoors, Seattleites are an extremely intellectual bunch as well. The city has one of the highest percentages of population over age 25 who have graduated from high school (more than 91 percent compared to the national average of 70 percent), as well as those who have obtained at least a four-year college degree (more than 52 percent compared to a 27 percent national average). There seems to be a bookstore on every corner, and educational/intellectual pursuits are valued highly by residents here. This combination creates what is, to me, a delightfully charming mix of physical fitness and geekiness.

Seattle enjoys a relatively strong economy and is a prominent technology center of the United States, largely thanks to Bill Gates and Microsoft. The Northwest has more Internet firms per capita than any other place in the world. Other industries with a strong presence in the area include aerospace, biotech, health care, and research institutions. The city's largest employer is the University of Washington, which employs more than 28,000. School systems are highly rated and the healthy housing market escaped the drastic downturn that many regions throughout the country have experienced in recent years. It's not all completely rosy in the Emerald City, however—a large contingent of homeless people are found throughout downtown, sleeping and asking passersby for change. There is little crime associated with the homeless, however, and many service centers are downtown, around which they tend to congregate. The relatively large homeless population may exist here because Seattle refuses to criminalize it. Simply exercise the same caution you would anywhere, about avoiding parks and secluded areas late at night.

CLIMATE

The climate is relatively mild, as Seattle benefits from the warm Pacific water and weather patterns, and is protected by the Olympic Mountains from colder easterly weather. Winter averages around 46 degrees Fahrenheit and the city sees snow only a few days a year. Spring is very nice, though a bit soggy, and the summers are glorious, dry with little humidity and plenty of warmth and sunshine. Summer days usually hover around the pleasant high 70s.

Of course, what Seattle is really known for is the rain, even among those who have never been here. Or perhaps *especially* among those, because Seattleites know that it doesn't actually rain very hard all that much—it just threatens to rain a lot. Seattle receives around 37 inches of precipitation a year—Houston, Miami, Atlanta, and New York all get at least 10 inches more. What creates the image of the Emerald City as the Rainy City—and what is the hardest for most residents to deal with—is the nearly constant overcast grayness between October and March.

Although rainfall itself is not more abundant than in many other cities, for days and even weeks on end the skies can remain cloudy, and a misty drizzle seems to keep Seattle almost constantly wet and gray in the winter. Summers arrive late, and the anticipation of its sunny warmth is a source of constant discussion from April on; therefore, it can be quite disappointing to walk outside in May and find the same damp, cool, overcast day that you had in January. But, as we tell ourselves, it is this very weather that creates the stunning green landscape of the Pacific Northwest.

i If you don't want to look like a tourist, forget the umbrella. You'll rarely see a Seattleite carrying one unless it's really pouring. Opt for a hat or hooded jacket instead. And if you really want to fit in, just wear shorts and flip-flops in the winter, and a stocking cap in the summer.

NEIGHBORHOODS AT A GLANCE

The city proper of Seattle is home to dozens of neighborhood areas. As early European settlers originally began to establish the area, unique autonomous townships formed in a hasty and loosely zoned manner, widely scattered at the time and each operating independently and developing its own flavor and personality. Eventually, as the city grew and spread, these towns became enveloped into the larger city of Seattle and turned into distinct neighborhoods, retaining their individuality.

These delightfully different neighborhoods are, in fact, a large part of the charm of today's Seattle. Each separate one can feel like its own small town, almost unrelated to the others. But they can also be a bit confusing, as boundaries meld into one another in an ambiguous manner. No official neighborhood boundaries have existed in the city since 1910, leaving the neighborhood system informal and subjective. Boundaries are not fixed and thus often disputed, with sections of town being referred to by different names depending on who is doing the naming.

For the purpose and ease of this book, we will divide Seattle up into three broad sections: North, Central, and South.

North Seattle

I have defined the North section of Seattle as everything north of the waterways that connect Puget Sound with Lake Washington, just to the north of downtown—namely, Salmon Bay, Lake Union, Portage Bay, and Union Bay.

These northern neighborhoods of Seattle are possibly the most eclectic. Ballard has its roots as an early outpost for Scandinavian shipbuilding and fishing, and much of its personality and cultural appeal still come from these Nordic seafaring roots. It also feels a bit like a small New England town, with pretty tree-lined streets of restored two- and three-story brick buildings that now house trendy restaurants, antiques stores, and clothing boutiques—never more so than in the fall, when orange and red maple leaves scatter across the historic sidewalks.

Next-door Fremont has a completely different vibe. Bohemian and hippie, Fremont definitely dances to the beat of its own drummer and calls itself, in a refreshingly unself-conscious way, the "Center of the Universe." Here you'll find funky vintage shops instead of Ballard's high-end antiques, along with tattoo parlors, music studios, public art installations, and the famous Fremont Sunday Market. The neighborhood is also home to some beloved, though often inexplicable, Seattle landmarks, such as the Lenin Statue and Fremont Troll.

Adjacent to Fremont is family-friendly Wallingford, with its Craftsman-style homes and wide boulevards full of sidewalk cafes in restored character buildings. The result is a place so Americana that it almost feels as if it belongs in a movie, yet there's a healthy mix of cultural fusion in its retail offerings and some of the city's top ethnic restaurants. Just to the west of Wallingford lies the University District, a haven for students and a slightly postcollegiate crowd. University Way—or simply The Ave, as it's known to locals—has a laid-back vibe, full of astrology and meditation centers as well as yoga and massage studios. Bookstores, galleries, and inexpensive eateries are also a mainstay both in the University District and the slightly more grown-up Roosevelt community just to the north.

North of these areas lies Green Lake, a 50,000-year-old glacial lake surrounded by public parks and nearly 3 miles of paths. Seattle's equivalent of Central Park, Green Lake is enjoyed by residents on all but the worst weather days. The surrounding neighborhoods of Greenlake and Greenwood have a bit more of a sprawling, suburban feel than others in North Seattle, along with a cohesive sense of community. A high concentration of the city's athletic and recreational stores can be found here, as well as the Woodland

Park Zoo and a nice mixture of single-family homes, apartments and condominiums, and affordable housing developments.

Ravenna, named by its early settlers after a seaside district in northern Italy, shows glimpses of its Italian heritage in a down-to-earth community. Its wholesome sensibility is pervasive; you will rarely find people out past 10 p.m., and there is a noticeable lack of the tattoo parlors and sex shops that dot some of Seattle's funkier neighborhoods.

Central Seattle

The Central section of Seattle encompasses everything from the Puget Sound–to–Lake Washington waterways, south to I-90 and Safeco Field.

While downtown Seattle is the city's central business and visitors' district, it also has several thriving residential neighborhoods. Belltown is a lively entertainment area, a place to see and be seen at many of the city's trendiest bars and restaurants, that was reborn from a rather seedy previous incarnation. It's also home to a lot of young, hipster professionals who enjoy incredible skyline and Puget Sound views from their high-rise condos. Don't fret about gentrification, though; Belltown's location in the heart of downtown means that a gritty urban scene is still intermixed with the boutiques, art galleries, and sushi joints.

The parallel streets of Pike and Pine are the figurative heart of Seattle, and the surrounding blocks offer many residential buildings as well as some of the top visitor attractions in the city. The best-known of these is the century-old Pike Place Market; more than just throwing fish, the market and surrounding streets are full of restaurants and street performers, as well as a seemingly equal mix of tourists and locals. Slightly more bohemian than Belltown, but with a similarly high hipster-sighting scale, the Pike/Pine area offers more vintage shops, coffeehouses, and tattoo parlors, along with an equally happening nightlife.

To the south is Pioneer Square, the historic birthplace of Seattle. The first downtown was destroyed in the 1889 fire but was quickly rebuilt; It is now a charming trip through yesteryear with mostly original, refurbished buildings. The Romanesque architecture houses beloved favorites such as the Elliott Bay Book Company, Smith Tower, and the Underground Tours through eerie subterranean tunnels. A generous smattering of old-fashioned pubs and taverns makes Pioneer Square a place with plenty to do from early in the day to the wee hours of the morning.

Heading east from the waterfront and downtown you encounter First Hill, so named because it was where Seattle's first families built their homes, near the mercantile/business center of Pioneer Square. Stately homes and gardens still dot the neighborhood, although it is known today more for the hospitals and medical research institutions located here, giving the area its nickname of "Pill Hill."

At the southern end of downtown is Seattle's Chinatown, also known as the International District (or I.D.). Here the city's early Asian immigrants first arrived, and a jumbling mix of Chinese, Filipino, Vietnamese, Cambodian, and Japanese businesses of every kind defines the I.D. today. The diversity of cuisines, goods, and cultural flavors creates an exciting destination where a number of festivals and holidays are celebrated by residents of all backgrounds. The I.D. may not be the prettiest part of the city, but it's certainly one of the most authentic.

Vital Statistics

Founded: 1853; incorporated 1865

Mayor/governor: Mike McGinn, Christine Gregoire

Size: 83.9 square miles

Population: Approximately 600,000

Median resident age: 35.4 years

Visitors: 9.4 million annually

Airport: Seattle-Tacoma International (SEA)

Sales tax: 8.8 percent

Hotel tax: 12 percent

State income tax: None

Median household income: $61,786

Median per capita income: $43,012

Median home price: $491,600

Median gross rent: $940

Cost of living index: 126.5 (compared to 100 average for U.S.)

Climate: Mild combination of Oceanic and Mediterranean

Average annual temperature: 52.4°F

Annual precipitation: 36.6 inches

Number of sunny days: 71

Average elevation: 350 feet

Major attractions: Seattle Center and the Space Needle, Pike Place Market, the Hiram Chittenden Locks, Woodland Park Zoo, Tillicum Indian Village, Seattle Aquarium, waterfront, lakeside and sound beaches, Pioneer Square, International District, and local wineries and breweries

Major sports: Seattle Mariners, Seattle Seahawks

Major universities: University of Washington, Seattle University, Seattle Pacific University

Percentage with high school diploma: 91.9

Percentage with B.A. or higher: 52.7

Major employers: University of Washington, Microsoft, Costco, Defense Department, Boeing, Washington Mutual, Weyerhaeuser, Amazon, Nordstrom, Starbucks

Major interstates: I-5, I-90, I-405, Freeway 520, WA 618, SR 99/Alaska Way Viaduct

Daily newspaper: *Seattle Times*

Weekly newspapers: *The Stranger, Seattle Weekly*

Chamber of commerce: 1301 5th Ave., Suite 2500, 98101, (206) 389-7200, www.seattle chamber.com

Convention and visitor bureau: 701 Pike St., Suite 800, 98101, (206) 461-5800, www.visit seattle.org

Famous people of Seattle*: Patrick Allen, Paul Allen, Bob Barker, Glenn Beck, Jeff Bezos, Josie Bissett, William Boeing, Max Brand, Aaron Brooks, Terry Brooks, Linda Buck, Nate Burleson, Dyan Cannon, Jerry Cantrell, Richard Carey, Neko Case, Jim Caviezel, Carol Channing, Charlie Chong, Erika Christensen, Kurt Cobain, Judy Collins, Chris Cornell, Fred Couples, Bing Crosby, John Elway, Frances Farmer, Kenny G, Bill Gates, Cameron Joslin Gigandet, Richard Gordon Jr., Tom Gorman, Alex Haley, Leland Hartwell, Jimi Hendrix, Frank Herbert Jr., Peter Horton, Frederick Hutchinson, Quincy Jones, Hank Ketcham, Gary Larson, Bruce Lee, Gypsy Rose Lee, Kenny Loggins, Kyle MacLachlan, Phil Mahre, Dave Matthews, Mary McCarthy, Rose McGowan, Alfred Moen, Apolo Ohno, Stacie Orrico, Jeff Probst, Ron Reagan, Tom Robbins, Ron Santo, Francis (Dick) Scobee, Sir Mix-a-Lot, Tom Skerrit, Jean Smart, Jeff Smith, John Stockton, Julia Sweeney, Blair Underwood, Eddie Vedder, Jennifer Warnes, Adam West, Lou Whittaker, Jim Whittaker, Marcus Williams, Ann Wilson, Nancy Wilson, Rainn Wilson

* Born or grew up in the greater Seattle or surrounding area, or have made their homes here for a significant period of time.

Crossing the main thoroughfare of I-5 and heading a little north, the large and vibrant Capitol Hill promises an experience that is uniquely Seattle. This is the place where grunge began, and the alternative music sound that sprung up in the early '90s with bands such as Nirvana and Soundgarden got its start here. Music is still very much a part of Capitol Hill, but the neighborhood is such an eclectic mix that it's hard to define it as one thing. It is home to the largest gay community in this extremely gay-friendly city, and rainbow flags flutter along the main drag of Broadway. The boutiques and coffeehouses are also filled with professionals, young families, and yes, tattooed and pierced musicians.

To the west of Capitol Hill you'll find a much more staid scene. Madison Valley, Madison Park, and Madrona are homey places with plenty of parks and day-care centers for the baby boom that seems to be happening here. Real estate prices have escalated as these neighborhoods are revitalized from a much more down-and-out recent history. There are even gated communities on the shores of Lake Washington, something that is almost unheard of inside city limits. Still, these neighborhoods embrace Seattle's accepting mind-set, and old-money matrons eat and shop right alongside gay homesteading couples and struggling artists.

At the eastern end of the city's central section lie Queen Anne and Magnolia. Queen Anne was rated as the most desirable neighborhood by *Seattle* magazine in 2009, and it's not hard to see why. Its location up on a hill just outside downtown gives it some of the most remarkable views of the city, and the historic Victorian mansions are worth spending a couple of hours simply driving through. Queen Anne is also, not surprisingly, some of the most expensive real estate in the city. In-demand restaurants such as How to Cook a Wolf are located here, along with new boutiques and art galleries as well as longtime favorites such as Queen Anne Books.

At the western tip jutting out into Puget Sound is Magnolia, quieter and with lots less attitude. Streets here are unpretentious, and it's a haven for outdoors lovers. Majestic views of the water and 500-acre Discovery Park come with the neighborhood, and you can easily forget that you are in the middle of a large metropolis.

South Seattle

I have defined the South region of Seattle as everything south of I-90 and Safeco Field. One thing to mention so that you won't be confused—there is a neighborhood called West Seattle. You will see it mentioned in this book and probably come across it other places as well. West Seattle is indeed west of I-5, though not nearly the westernmost points that Queen Anne or Discovery Park are. However, because West Seattle lies to the south of the boundary line I have used, it will be classified under the broad reference area of South Seattle.

The southern section of Seattle proper is worlds away from the central and northern neighborhoods. Once you cross I-90 to the south or the West Seattle Bridge into West Seattle, you find yourself in either industrial wastelands or neighborhoods with a much more suburban feel. Between I-5 and Boeing Field is one of the industrial, warehouse areas that has just recently begun a comeback as the urban enclaves known as SoDo (for South of Downtown) and Georgetown. Against the train and airplane noise, refurbished warehouse spaces and single-family homes coexist along with bars, gas stations, and nondescript commercial buildings. More townhomes are constantly being built here, which is likely to cause most of the creative urban pioneers who call it home to flee to grittier pastures.

Travel over the monstrous West Seattle Freeway Bridge into Alki and Delridge, two charming areas. Alki Avenue, which follows the water along Alki Beach, has the look and feel of a Southern California beach town. Casual eateries and taverns line the street across from the sandy sunbathing areas and parks. The intersection of Alaskan Way and California Avenue, known to locals simply as the Junction, is a hip little corner of shops and restaurants in historic landmarks. Delridge, on the other hand, seems stuck in the '50s in a good way with a fun midcentury aesthetic, and a mixture of longtime elderly residents next to young families who are moving in. The area's blue-collar profile is slowly giving way to modern new condos. The classic "across the water" views of downtown Seattle made popular by TV shows like *Grey's Anatomy* and *Frasier* are from this vantage point, accessible via Harbor Avenue or Admiral Way.

At its southernmost, Seattle neighborhoods like Columbia City, Seward Park, and Rainier Valley are melting pots that offer everything from Ethiopian restaurants to Vietnamese groceries, hair braiding salons to orthodox synagogues, and school populations that speak more than a dozen different languages.

WHEN TO GO

The best time by far to visit Seattle is from the late spring through summer. While much of the rest of the country swelters, Seattle enjoys gorgeous weather with mildly warm temperatures that rarely get above the low to mid 80s, and are usually in the perfect 70s with plenty of sunshine. June to September are peak tourism months. Lots of great festivals are held during summer, including Seafair in late July and Bumbershoot Music & Arts Festival in September. Of course, this is also the time when most tourists descend on the area, as well as the period when locals crowd parks, lakes, and outdoor recreational areas.

If you don't mind overcast skies and a little drizzle, the fall and early spring shoulder seasons—even winter—can still make for an excellent trip. Because thunderstorms are rare and it doesn't often rain hard (or for very long), and winter temperatures are relatively mild, visiting Seattle between October and March can be a great option for avoiding the masses.

According to the Washington, D.C.-based Americans for the Arts, Seattle ranks within the top five U.S. cities for the arts. The city offers an abundance of indoor attractions from world-class galleries and museums to performing arts and one of the best live music scenes in the country. Bring a hat and lightweight water-resistant coat; about the only things you'll miss at this time of year will be some of the summertime outdoor activities, but winter in the Pacific Northwest offers its own equally amazing adventures and gorgeous scenery.

GETTING HERE, GETTING AROUND

Seattle is a haven for people who like to use bikes and their own two feet to get around; here people walk more and drive less. The city was rated the sixth most walkable in the country by WalkScore.com. Fitness-oriented Seattle is extremely pedestrian, and cyclist, friendly and offers a pretty decent public transportation system to boot, for a western city. Downtown and central neighborhoods are compact and easy to navigate, although walkers should be aware of steep San Francisco–like hills in many areas, and remember that what goes down probably has to be hiked back up. The good news is that a bus is almost guaranteed to come along if you wear out or accumulate too many bags, and in the "Ride Free Area" of downtown you don't even have to pay!

As a rule, residents are friendly and helpful, so don't hesitate to ask a shopkeeper or other local for help; they actually seem to relish giving directions here. Seattle drivers are generally a pretty laid-back and polite bunch, but traffic congestion during rush hours is bad, especially along I-5. Parking is also scarce and expensive—something you may keep in mind if you're considering renting a car. For the short-term visitor who will stay mainly in the central areas of the city, using public transportation and your own horsepower may be easier. You can always rent that car just to head out of Seattle for a day trip.

GETTING HERE

Airports

SEATTLE-TACOMA INTERNATIONAL AIRPORT (SEA)
17801 Pacific Hwy. South
Just off I-5 at the intersection of WA 518, WA 99, and WA 509
13 miles south of downtown
(206) 787-5906, (800) 544-1965
www.portseattle.org/seatac
Seattle-Tacoma International Airport, known as Sea-Tac, is run by the Port of Seattle and is a major gateway that links the United States to Asia and Europe. The airport is served by 28 airlines, and more than 32 million passengers a year come through Sea-Tac, making it the 17th-busiest airport in the country. There are three terminals: North Satellite Terminal, with 14 gates; South Satellite Terminal, with 13 gates; and Central Terminal, which houses Concourse A (14 gates), Concourse B (11 gates), Concourse C (11 gates), and Concourse D (11 gates). A shuttle train loops between the terminals and concourses to transport passengers.

Sea-Tac is a hub for Alaska Airlines and Horizon Air. In the continental United States, Sea-Tac is the closest airport to Asia and is approximately nine hours by air from either Tokyo or London. There are more than 45 scheduled flights to international destinations each week.

Modern and clean, Sea-Tac offers plenty of high-quality vendors. The airport has added more than 35 new restaurants and stores recently and now offers services such as frozen food storage, manicures, and massages. Sea-Tac has recently unveiled a number of useful, convenient tools for travelers. Free Wi-Fi service is now available throughout the terminals and public areas. Passenger services include ATM and change machines, currency exchange, e-mail services, and "Laptop Lane" in the North Satellite terminal, providing online access for computers, phones, fax machines, photocopying, and more. Other services include mailboxes and postal centers, notary services, send-it-home kiosks, storage, and Regus Business Centers Express.

Like many aspects of Seattle, the airport is one of the greenest in the country. Sea-Tac took first place for the Best Green Concessions Practice among North American airports, by recycling more than 1,200 tons of concessions material annually—an amount equal to the weight of six Boeing 747 planes. Concessionaires also generate revenue through rebates on recyclables, and donated food that served 8,000 meals to the needy in 2008. The airport also used U.S. Department of Energy funds to add electric charging stations and replaced 200 gas and diesel ground support vehicles with electric ones.

One enjoyable and unique aspect of the Seattle-Tacoma airport is its public art displays. As you make your way down the terminals and corridors, you can't miss the collection of magnificent artwork installed throughout. The public art project at the airport features some of the region's finest contemporary work in painting, photography, sculpture, and glass by artists such as Frank Stella, Robert Rauschenberg, and Louise Nevelson. The collection not only is inspiring, but also lends a very Seattle vibe to an otherwise practical structure.

Getting To And Leaving The Airport

Seattle-Tacoma International Airport is 13 miles south of the central business district. To reach the airport from downtown, drive south on I-5 to exit 154B, taking WA 518 west. From there you will follow the signs to the Sea-Tac Airport Exit. From northbound I-5 you will take the same exit. From the east take Interstate 405, which turns into WA 518, to the Sea-Tac Airport exit. The drive to downtown Seattle from Sea-Tac Airport will take 20–30 minutes—depending on the traffic. A trip to downtown Seattle from the airport on public transportation takes 30–40 minutes.

Getting to and from the airport is much easier since December 2009, when the new Link light rail line opened linking downtown to the Sea-Tac/Airport station, connected to the fourth floor of the airport parking garage. If you drive to the airport and are flying one of five airlines—Alaska, Continental, Delta, Horizon, or United—you can check in and print your boarding pass at parking garage kiosks. The parking garages are connected to the main terminal via sky bridges on the fourth floor, and new simplified parking rates and payment options were recently introduced. Hourly and long-term reduced parking rates are available, and parking services include wheelchair-accessible and motorcycle parking spaces, electric vehicle plug-in stations, and premier corporate programs.

Airport drives are for passenger dropoff and pickup only; parking and waiting are not allowed. Sea-Tac has a cell phone waiting lot, where drivers who are picking up arrivals can wait until passengers have deplaned, collected baggage, and are curbside. The lot can be reached by turning onto the Air Cargo Road from Airport Expressway or International Boulevard. Several ground transportation options are available for getting into Seattle from the airport:

i To obtain updated flight information on your cell phone, you can text your airline and flight number to FlySEA (or 359732). Within seconds, you'll receive the latest real-time information, including the flight number, departure or arrival time, gate number, and flight status.

Link Light Rail

The SeaTac/Airport Station is connected to the fourth floor of the airport garage. Link light rail service runs from 5 a.m. to 1 a.m. Mon through Sat, and 6 a.m. to midnight Sun. Trains arrive and depart every 7½ to 15 minutes, varying by time of day. Depending on the area of Seattle you are coming from or going to, Link fare ranges from $1.75 to $2.50, with discounted senior/disabled and youth fares. For complete information, visit www.soundtransit.org.

King County Metro Bus Service

Public transit buses arrive at and leave from the far south end of the baggage claim area, outside door number 2. Departure times are shown on signs at the bus stop. You also can pick up printed bus timetables at the ground transportation information booth on the baggage-claim level near door number 16 (across from baggage carousel 12). Bus fares range from $2 to $2.75 depending on how many zones you will travel through, with reduced youth, senior, and disabled fares. For complete information, maps, and schedules, visit http://metro.kingcounty.gov.

Shuttles and Shared-Ride Service

Numerous shared-ride shuttles and vans run almost continuously around the clock, with scheduled departure and arrival times. The ground transportation information booth and pickup areas are on the third floor of the parking garage. You can also dial 55 from any travelers' information board at the base of the baggage-claim escalators for ground transportation information. These services will cost anywhere from $10 to $40 on average, one-way, depending on the service used and how far you are going.

Shuttle Express offers door-to-door shared-ride service to the following cities: Auburn, Bellevue, Bothell, Everett, Federal Way, Fife, Issaquah, Kent, Kirkland, Lakewood, Mercer Island, Puyallup, Redmond, Renton, Seattle, Steilacoom, Tacoma, Totem Lake, and Woodinville. Call (425) 981-7000 for reservations, or visit www.shuttleexpress.com.

Airporter Services pick up and drop off passengers in the parking lot at the south end of Baggage Claim, outside Door 00. The Gray Line Downtown Airporter departs twice an hour to and from major downtown Seattle hotels for $10.25 one-way and is the best shuttle service if you're going downtown. The Airporter Shuttle goes to the ferry terminals and other areas outside

Seattle. Other airports such as Bremerton-Kitsap, Capital, Olympic, and Whidbey take passengers to destinations outside Seattle. Check the "ground transportation" link of the Sea-Tac Web site for a full list, destinations, and schedules.

Courtesy vehicles for hotels, rental car facilities, and off-site parking lots pick up and drop off passengers on the third floor of the parking garage, at Islands 1 and 3.

Rental Cars

Nine rental car companies have information counters in the baggage-claim area, and several companies offer car pickup and dropoff on the first floor of the garage across from the main terminal. Off-site rental car companies will pick up customers in a shuttle at Islands 1 and 3 on the parking garage's third floor.

Taxis and Limos

Taxis are available on the third floor of the parking garage. Curbside phones for taxi service are available at Baggage Claim, or you can call (206) 246-9999. A taxi from Sea-Tac to downtown Seattle will cost a flat fare of $29 (including the new $1 fuel surcharge). Elsewhere, taxi rates are set at $2.50 for the meter drop, $2 per mile, and 50 cents for each rider beyond two passengers. STILA limousine service is stationed at the airport and offers town cars, SUVs, and stretch limos at the curb outside Baggage Claim and on the third floor of the parking garage. You can also access ground transportation using the touch screen on the travelers' information board in Baggage Claim. All limousine and taxi drivers at the airport are required to be credentialed.

Nearby Alternative Airports

BOEING FIELD/KING COUNTY INTER-NATIONAL AIRPORT
7277 Perimeter Rd. South
(206) 296-7380
www.kingcounty.gov/transportation/ kcdot/Airport.aspx

This regional airport is one of the busiest primary non-hub airports in the nation. Located 5 miles south of downtown Seattle, it averages more than 300,000 takeoffs and landings each year. In 2001, it was selected by the National Air Transportation Association as one of the "100 Most Needed Airports" in the United States. It receives no general tax revenues, as it is financed by tenant and customer fees. Boeing Field/King County serves small commercial passenger airlines, cargo carriers, private aircraft, helicopters, corporate jets, and military and other aircraft. It is also home to the interesting Museum of Flight, with a wide variety of aircraft and exhibits showcasing aviation history.

Seaplane Ports

Due to its location on the water and proximity to nearby islands such as the San Juans and Victoria, British Columbia, Seattle has several seaplane companies and ports. The largest of these is **Kenmore Air,** the largest seaplane operator in the United States. Kenmore Air's fleet consists of more than 20 seaplanes and a few wheeled planes, and in addition to providing flights between destinations, the company also offers sightseeing flights that return to the original departure port, as well as pilot lessons. Kenmore operates from seaports at Lake Washington and Lake Union, as well as five other harbors in the Northwest. Kenmore Air can be reached at (866) 435-9524 or www.kenmoreair.com.

Other seaplane companies flying out of seaports in or around Seattle include **Northwest Seaplanes** and **Seattle Seaplanes,** which both offer charter and sightseeing flights as well as flight instruction.

Cruises and Ferries

PORT OF SEATTLE
Pier 91/Smith Cove Cruise Terminal
2001 W. Garfield
Pier 66/Bell St. Pier
2225 Alaskan Way
(206) 787-3000
www.portseattle.org/seaport
Due to Seattle's location on Puget Sound, it is a hub for both cruise ships and ferries. Many visitors to Seattle arrive via one of these modes of transportation, mainly from Alaska, British Columbia, and Puget Sound islands. Two downtown cruise terminals and convenient air travel connections at the airport make cruising easy.

The Port of Seattle, which runs Sea-Tac Airport, also runs Seattle's ports, both for maritime trade and leisure activities. Holland America Line, Princess Cruises, and Royal Caribbean home port at the new cruise terminal at Pier 91, located at the north end of the waterfront. Norwegian Cruise Line and Celebrity Cruises depart from the Bell Street Pier Cruise Terminal, an 11-acre complex at Pier 66. Bus, taxi, and shuttle connections, as well as rental car kiosks, are available at both piers to get you to your Seattle destination. Other passenger services include luggage storage, parking garages, shuttles to the cruise terminals, and onboard airline check-in.

All of downtown Seattle is easily accessible from the waterfront, a mile and a half

north–south stretch along the west side of the city, facing Elliott Bay. A major feature of the waterfront area is the Alaska Way Viaduct/SR 99, an elevated roadway you will need to cross under to get to the rest of downtown Seattle. Be prepared for hills and steps if you decide to walk up into the city.

ℹ️ In 2010, an estimated 846,000 passengers sailed aboard 222 cruise ships bound for Alaska from Seattle.

Train and Bus Service

AMTRAK
303 S. Jackson St.
King Street Station
(800) USA-RAIL (800-872-7245)
www.amtrak.com
If you are interested in taking a train to get to Seattle, Amtrak provides service all along the west coast, from stations in Oregon and California to the south, and from British Columbia to the north. Amtrak trains stop at King Street Station, which is located just south of downtown near Safeco Field.

One of Amtrak's most beautiful routes is the Amtrak Cascades train, which runs three times a day between Eugene, Oregon, and Vancouver, British Columbia, with a stop in Seattle about two-thirds from the southern end of the journey. The Cascades train features panoramic windows designed to showcase the excellent views of the spectacular scenery along this Pacific Northwest passage. The cars on the Cascades route are European-style and extremely comfortable, and are also eco-friendly with low emissions and aerodynamic engineering. The Amtrak Cascades is also highly recommended for traveling from Seattle to Canada or Portland, or for taking a day trip from the city. Note that a valid U.S. passport and photo identification are required to enter Canada.

> ℹ️ In 2008, 774,421 passengers rode Amtrak *Cascades*—a 14.4 percent increase over 2007. Ridership for 2008 was the highest since the inception of the service 10 years before.

GREYHOUND BUS LINE
811 Stewart St.
(206) 628-5526, (800) 231-2222
www.greyhound.com

For transportation to Seattle by bus, Greyhound provides cross-country service. The terminal is at the northeast edge of downtown Seattle. You can buy tickets online, over the phone, or at a Greyhound terminal. No reservations are necessary. If you know the departure schedule, simply arrive at the terminal at least an hour before departure to purchase your ticket. Boarding generally begins 15 to 30 minutes before departure. Seating is on a first-come, first-served basis and advance-purchase tickets do not guarantee a seat.

GETTING AROUND
Driving

The street system is relatively easy to figure out for first-time drivers, especially if you know up front about a few oddities to the roadways. North- and southbound roadways in Seattle are labeled "avenues," while east- and westbound roadways are labeled "streets." You may also hear the word "arterial"—Seattleites use this term to mean any main thoroughfare through town. Although the street system is laid out in a general grid pattern, because the city is bordered by several bodies of water and

has an often hilly topography, many streets wind, curve, and extend at odd angles. Outside downtown, pay close attention to the directional designation of addresses (NE, SW, and so on). Many opportunities exist for getting lost or driving the wrong way if you are going to, say, 1400 45th but neglect to pay attention to the NE designation. If you end up at 1400 45th SW instead, you are in a completely different part of town.

Seattleites tend to follow the rules of the road, signal, seldom honk, and rarely exceed the speed limit. Even with this good driving behavior, however, the city's traffic is only marginally better than that of Los Angeles. Partly due to the terrain and numerous bridges—some of them drawbridges—and partly due to the huge influx of new residents, Seattle's traffic congestion is nearly legendary. I-5 in particular seems to always be bottlenecked; the average commuting speed is 22 mph.

The major roadways are I-5, I-90, I-405, Freeway 520, WA 618, and SR 99/Alaska Way Viaduct. Try to avoid driving on these arteries during the rush hours of 7 to 9 a.m. and 3 to 7 p.m.—especially I-5. Also be aware that the two major sports stadiums, Qwest Field and Safeco Field, are located at the southern end of downtown near the intersection of 99 and WA 519. If there is a game or event at one of these stadiums, traffic will likely be extremely heavy for hours in the area.

HOV Lanes

If you must drive on the interstates during high-traffic hours and two or more people are in the vehicle, get into the express HOV lanes if possible. HOV lanes are reserved for people who share the ride in buses, van pools, or carpools; motorcycles and emergency vehicles are also allowed. The required number of people on most HOV lanes is two, including the driver, except for SR 520, west of I-405, which requires three or more. HOV lanes on the west side of Lake Washington operate 24 hours a day, seven days a week. HOV lanes on eastside freeways are open to all drivers at night.

Freeway HOV lanes are generally inside (left) lanes and are identified by signs along the freeway and diamond symbols painted on the pavement. They are typically separated from the other lanes on the freeway by a solid white line. Vehicles carrying the required number of people may enter or exit an HOV lane wherever there is a single line separating the HOV lane from the lane next to it. Vehicles may not cross double lines. The traffic flow in HOV lanes is toward downtown in the morning, away from downtown in the afternoon, but keep in mind that there are fewer exits from the HOV lanes, so they aren't a good option for shorter commutes.

Child Seat Laws

Washington state's child car-seat laws require children to sit in car and booster seats until they are eight years old, or 4 feet 9 inches tall. Babies must ride in rear-facing infant seats until they are a year old and weigh 20 pounds. The fine is $112 for each improperly buckled child, and placing a shoulder strap under an arm or behind a back is illegal.

Cell Phone Laws

As far as cell phones are concerned, Governor Christine Gregoire signed a law into effect as of July 2008, prohibiting drivers to text message or to talk on a cell phone without a hands-free device. Fines are $124 for each offense. An exception is made if the wireless communication device is being used to report illegal activity, summon medical or other emergency help, or to prevent injury to a person or property. Legislators are looking at toughening the "distracted driving" law, from a secondary to a primary offense. The best bet for safety is to simply refrain altogether from using a cell phone or PDA while operating a vehicle.

Drinking And Driving

Driving under the influence (DUI) refers to operating a motor vehicle while affected by alcohol, drugs, or both. This applies to both legal and illegal drugs, including prescription medication and over-the-counter drugs. In Washington state, drivers are cited for DUI if the breath or blood test returns an amount of alcohol in the blood of .08 or higher (.02 or higher for minors under 21). If a suspected driver refuses to take a test for blood alcohol level, his or her license will be revoked. Under Washington's Implied Consent law, simply operating a motor vehicle automatically gives consent to have your breath or blood tested if a law enforcement officer suspects you of driving while under the influence. For drivers with out-of-state licenses, the offense is recorded on their Washington state driving record, license privileges are suspended or revoked, and a copy of the citation is forwarded to the licensing state.

Weather

The Pacific Northwest climate also plays a part in Seattle driving. If you are not accustomed to driving in a rainy climate, now is the time to learn. The most important thing to remember is that stopping times are much longer for vehicles on wet surfaces. You need to be aware of this not only when driving and coming to a stop behind other cars, but also when approaching pedestrians, bike riders, intersections, and stop or yield signs.

Public Transportation

SOUND TRANSIT

401 S. Jackson St.

(206) 398-5000, (800) 201-4900

www.soundtransit.org

Sound Transit (ST) operates the bus and light-rail public transportation system throughout Seattle and the Central Puget Sound area, as well as a commuter train between Seattle and Tacoma. Sound Transit operates out of the King Street Station south of downtown, close to Safeco Field, and has lines that run from Everett in the north to Tacoma in the south. ST has a great trip planner on its Web site, where you can input your starting and ending locations and receive exact trip information and details.

ST Express bus fares are $1.50 for one zone, $2.50 for two zones, and $3 for three zones, for a single-ride ticket (transfers are allowed). The zones are broken up by the city limit borders, so if you are staying in Seattle proper you will be in only one zone. ST Link light rail fares are based on distance traveled, ranging from $1.75 to $2.50. For Sounder commuter rail, the base fare is $2.55 and goes up to $4.75 depending on the length of trip and destination.

Discounted fares are available for youth ages 6–18, senior citizens age 65 and up, and disabled riders on all Sound Transit systems. Ticket vending machines are available at all rail stations, and tickets must be purchased before boarding the train. For buses, you can pay the driver when you board (exact change required) or use a pass. Monthly PugetPass cards provide a savings for high use over a month or longer, or consider getting a prepaid ORCA card, which can be used on any bus, train, or ferry in the area.

i Don't overlook the Ride Free Area (RFA). This zone of downtown Seattle permits everyone to ride for free between 6 a.m. and 7 p.m. The boundaries are roughly Elliot Bay on the west side of downtown, I-5 to the east, Battery Street on the north, and Jackson Street on the south. The bus operator will announce the last stop in the RFA so you are prepared if your further journey will require a ticket. The Tacoma Link light rail commuter train is also free for all passengers.

KING COUNTY METRO TRANSIT

201 S. Jackson St.

(206) 553-3000

http://metro.kingcounty.gov

Metro Transit is another major local bus operator in the Seattle area. In keeping with the city's ecologically responsible mind-set, King County's transit system has 236 hybrid buses, one of the largest such fleets in North America.

Fares range from $2 to $2.75 depending on peak and off-peak travel times, and whether you are traveling within one zone or two (within the city limits constitutes one zone). Discounted youth, disabled, and senior fares are available, and children five years old and under ride free. Metro Transit also offers a "Family Plan" on Sundays and holidays that allows up to four children age 18 and under to ride free with a paying adult. All Metro bus travel within the downtown RFA is free of charge, and the ORCA card works on Metro buses as well. You can also pay as you board the bus, and remember that the drivers do not make change. It's important when traveling by bus to double-check the route number displayed on the front and side of the bus before boarding, as several different routes come through the same bus stops. The Metro Transit Web site offers an interactive trip planner to help you find your way.

Streetcars And Monorail

Metro Transit also runs streetcars and water taxis (information in Boats and Ferries section that follows). There was a **Waterfront Streetcar Line,** which ran along the downtown waterfront area; however, that service has currently been suspended due to construction in the area, and although King County Metro has plans to restore the vintage streetcars to active service, no date in the near future has been announced. These routes are currently served by Metro Transit buses.

The **South Lake Union Street Car** runs a limited route downtown from Pacific Place Station at Westlake and Olive Way to Fairview and Campus Drive at South Lake Union. Streetcars come along every 15 minutes, and the $2 fare can be purchased at the vending machines located at each trolley stop, or on board. Several new routes are in the works, including the neighborhoods of First Hill (due to open in 2013), Capitol Hill, Pioneer Square, and the International District.

The **Seattle Center Monorail** provides a quick trip between downtown Seattle and Seattle Center, which includes the Space Needle, Pacific Science Center, and the Experience Music Project. It's really more of an attraction than a way to get around, as the monorail goes only from Point A to Point B on a 1-mile, two-minute trip. The monorail was built for the 1962 World's Fair and was the first such system in the country. Originally plans were to expand the line, but that never happened. The monorail departs every 10 minutes from the Seattle Center station and the Westlake Center Mall station

at Fifth and Pine. Round-trip fares are $4 for adults, $1.50 for children 5–12 (4 and under ride free), and $2 for seniors and disabled passengers. One-way tickets can be purchased for half of those prices.

i If you hear a local talk about "riding the slut," don't immediately be offended. An interesting and humorous tidbit about the streetcar is its original name, which was the South Lake Union Trolley—bearing the unfortunate acronym SLUT, apparently unnoticed by anyone until the streetcar line opened. "Ride the SLUT" soon became a running joke in Seattle, and Metro Transit quickly changed the name. Seattleites still fondly call it the SLUT, however, with T-shirts and a http://ride theslut.com Web site springing up. The T-shirts and other SLUT merchandise can be purchased at Inner Chapters bookstore at 419 Fairview Ave. North. Robin Williams has even been spotted sporting a SLUT T-shirt around Seattle!

Taxis

Due to the high-quality public transit system and the fact that most residents own vehicles, Seattle isn't a place where you can get around by just jumping in and out of taxis. In the central downtown core you will find taxis plentiful during the weekdays and early evening at major hotels and on the main streets; veer just a few blocks away and you're not likely to find a cab cruising for passengers. Most people tend to call for a taxi in advance rather than hailing one; if you are in a hurry or outside the major downtown thoroughfares, or it's late at night, your best bet is to call ahead as well (at least 10 minutes in advance is recommended).

The City of Seattle regulates taxis and sets rates within the city limits, through a government ordinance. The fare starts at a $2.50 flat rate, with an additional $2 per mile and 50 cents for each additional passenger (excluding children). There is also a charge of 50 cents per minute that the taxi driver must wait. The flat rate from downtown hotels to Sea-Tac Airport is $32.

A company called **Green Cab** offers an all-hybrid fleet of taxis—contact them at (206) 575-4040. Other taxi companies include:

- **Farwest Taxi:** (425) 454-5055
- **Orange Cab:** (206) 905-4212
- **Graytop Cab:** (206) 622-4800
- **Green Cab:** (206) 575-4040
- **Redtop Cab:** (206) 789-4949
- **Yellow Cab:** (206) 622-6500

i A nifty service called Taxi Fare Finder enables you to input your travel information and calculate cab fare. The site also provides a map of your trip. Check it out at www.taxi farefinder.com/main.php?city=Seattle.

Boats and Ferries

KING COUNTY WATER TAXI
(206) 684-1551
**www.kingcounty.gov/transportation/
kcdot/Marine/WaterTaxi.aspx**
Metro Transit operates the King County Water Taxi, which provides a weekday commuter route between Pier 50 downtown and Vashon Island ($4.50), and a seasonal route between downtown and the Seacrest Dock in West Seattle ($3.50). ORCA cards are accepted on the King County Water Taxi.

WASHINGTON STATE FERRIES
2901 Third Ave., Suite 500
(206) 464-6400, (888) 808-7977
www.wsdot.wa.gov/ferries

The Washington State Department of Transportation runs the largest ferry system in the world. State ferries depart from the Colman Dock (Pier 52) and from Pier 50 just to the south, to destinations such as Bainbridge Island, Bremerton, and Vashon Island, with connections to other destinations all around Puget Sound. There are street connections to taxis and buses just outside the Colman Dock ferry terminal. The Washington State Ferries to Bainbridge Island and Bremerton take both auto and walk-on passengers, and the Vashon Island ferry is for walk-on passengers only. It is suggested that you make a reservation online for a vehicle, especially during the peak summer travel season.

Fares are based on the ferry route, the size of your vehicle if you are boarding with one, as well as the length of time you will be on board. Fares are also calculated based on the age or disability of each passenger and are collected either for round-trip or one-way travel, depending on the departure terminal. Seniors, persons with disabilities, and passengers with proof of Medicare eligibility can travel at half the regular passenger fare. You can buy ferry tickets online, at terminal kiosks, or vehicle tollbooths. ORCA cards are also accepted on the Washington State Ferries.

Other ferry and boat services along the waterfront include **Argosy Cruises,** offering many different leisure cruises from Piers 55 and 56 on the waterfront, and the *Victoria Clipper,* with popular runs to the San Juan Islands and Victoria, British Columbia, from Pier 69 on the waterfront. And be sure to remember that if you take a ferry or boat across international lines into Canada, you will be required to present a valid passport and photo identification.

Bicycles

As mentioned before, getting around on a bike is a popular option for Seattle residents, so you may consider giving it a try! In Washington state, bicycle commuting has increased more than 75 percent over the past ten years; there is even a bicycle patrol of the Seattle Police Department. The main thing for visitors to keep in mind is the hilly terrain, which can create a quite challenging ride for inexperienced cyclists.

Most areas of the city are safe for cyclists, with bike-friendly streets and crossings, but of course exercise caution when cycling on busy streets or in downtown traffic. Cyclists are not required by law to wear helmets or ride in the bike lanes, but of course both are highly recommended. Even when traveling in the bike lanes or on bike paths, be alert for other traffic such as pedestrians, skaters, pets, and other cyclists. Communicate with all vehicles and other traffic using standard signals. All city buses are equipped with free bike racks, making it easy to combine cycling with public transportation. Bicycles are also permitted on state ferries and streetcars.

Outside of city transportation, Seattle is an excellent place for trail riding and bicycle touring, with about 270 miles of bike trails. The state has been recognized as a leader in trail development and provides some of the best spots in and around Seattle for riding. The Burke-Gilman Trail is one of the most popular, providing an extremely scenic ride over 16.5 miles of mostly flat terrain, as well as an efficient artery through the city. The trail extends from Ballard to the University of Washington, through Gas Works Park and then over either the Fremont or Ballard Bridge into downtown.

i Pick up your free copy of the City of Seattle's *Seattle Bicycling Guide Map* at bike shops, by calling (206) 684-7583, or online at www.seattle .gov/transportation/bikemaps.htm.

Other top bike trails include the 2.5-mile Elliott Bay Trail along the downtown waterfront and the 8 mile Alki Trail in West Seattle. For more details on bicycle recreation and places to rent a bike, check out the Cycling and Mountain Biking section of the Parks and Recreation chapter, on p. 227.

HISTORY

A look at the historical timeline of Seattle, even long before it was Seattle, shows a rich legacy. Its well-positioned port location in the teeming Pacific Northwest waters made it prime real estate in ancient as well as in modern times. From early Native American tribes who made their homes in its beauty and lived off the abundant land to the settlers who built and grew the city, Seattle has in many ways been a "boom and bust" sort of town. Since its founding in 1851, relatively late in U.S. history, there have been gold rushes and labor strikes, business peaks and valleys, fires and earthquakes, but always steady growth. Over the years Seattle has quietly grown from being a far-flung port town to being nationally recognized as one of the most livable cities in the United States.

PREHISTORY AND EARLY EXPLORATION

About 100 million years ago, in the late Mesozoic Era, the microcontinent of Okanogan collided with the landmass that is now North America, docking there and extending the coastline of the Pacific Northwest by about 50 miles westward. This collision, along with tremendous glacial volcanic activity, created the Puget Sound landmass, where the city of Seattle sits today.

For thousands of years, the Puget Sound area was home to Native American tribes, the ancestors of today's First Nations people. Archaeological sites here date back more than 10,000 years and are found throughout the landscape, from high in the Cascade Mountains to lowland rivers and beaches. Around 1725 the first recorded sighting of Europeans in the Pacific Northwest occurred. The Clatsop tribe discovered a shipwreck and its four stranded sailors along the Pacific coast at about the Washington/Oregon state line. The Clatsops called these bearded,

"bearlike" strangers *tlehonnipts*, meaning "those who drift ashore." These Europeans introduced metals previously unknown in the region, and the Clatsop took one of the sailors as a slave, to convert these metals into useful tools. This man became known as Konapee the Iron Maker, and he and the other Europeans eventually married into local Native American tribes.

In August 1774 Spanish explorer Juan Perez sailed past what is now Washington state, sighting Mount Olympus on his voyage. Perez christened the mountain Cerro Nevada de Santa Rosalia (it was renamed four years later by the British) before continuing north. Although Perez did not land or explore the region at that time, his expedition represents the first official European discovery and exploration of the Pacific Northwest.

Less than a year later, in July 1775, Perez returned with Bruno de Hezeta and Bodega y Quadro, landing at what is now Grenville Bay and claiming Washington and the Pacific Northwest for Spain. Because the expedition had set sail from Mexico and much of the crew were Mexican, the claimed land was officially considered part of both Mexico and Spain. However, the victory was short-lived. As the explorers retreated to their two ships, a party of seven was sent ashore to gather firewood and fresh water. There, the men were confronted and massacred by Quinault warriors while the captains watched through spyglasses in horror.

Contact with the foreigners, and those to come after, was also devastating for the Native Americans. From the 1770s through the next hundred years, smallpox contracted from these outsiders wiped out an estimated 30 percent of the native population, killing more than 11,000 western Washington tribespeople. Measles, influenza, and other diseases also played their parts, resulting in an estimated 28,000 Native American deaths over the century.

EUROPEAN TRADERS AND SETTLERS

Although Spain had claimed the Pacific Northwest, Great Britain disputed the claim. Fur trading had grown immensely popular and profitable after Captain James Cook's search for the Northwest Passage in 1778. Although Cook failed to discover the passage, he did trade sea otter furs with the Nootka Indians and sent back news of the wealth available in the Northwest. Traders from England, as well as Russian traders and American colonists from the East Coast, continually ignored Spain's claim to sovereignty as they frequented Northwest trading centers. The dispute came to a head in 1789, when Spanish Captain Esteban Jose

Martinez seized four English trading ships and took the captain and crew prisoner. Great Britain threatened war, and in October 1790 the two countries signed the Nootka Convention, which abandoned all nations' claims and gave every country the right to navigate, trade, and establish settlements in the region.

In May 1792 the first permanent European settlement was completed at Neah Bay by Spanish and Mexican settlers. That same month, British Captain George Vancouver dropped anchor off present-day Seattle and sent Peter Puget and Joseph Whidbey to conduct detailed surveys of the waters and islands of what was named Puget Sound. Whidbey Island would later be named for Joseph Whidbey, after he circumnavigated it the following month.

On October 10, 1805, perhaps the most famous Northwest explorers entered Washington state. Meriwether Lewis and William Clark crossed the Snake River from Idaho into Washington, partially led by Sacagawea, the young Shoshone guide. Lewis and Clark were also attempting to find the elusive Northwest Passage that would provide a water route across the continent. Instead, they ran into more formidable mountains and hardships than they had ever imagined, and by the time the expedition reached the Pacific Ocean on November 15, exhausted and starving, the explorers were convinced that a Northwest Passage did not exist.

FOUNDING OF SEATTLE

The first Europeans to establish a permanent settlement in present-day Seattle arrived at Alki Point on November 13, 1851. The group of 10 adults and 12 children came ashore on a schooner called *Exact*, led by city founder Arthur Denny, who had originally had his eye on the Oregon Territory. At the time, Portland was already a thriving town with a lot of publicity, while Puget Sound was a rain-sodden wilderness that attracted little interest. Perhaps a more pioneering spirit drove Denny, but he later wrote about his landing at Alki, "It dawned upon me that I had made a desperate venture."

Joined by Henry Yesler and David "Doc" Maynard, the settlers soon moved to a more hospitable patch of land a few miles away—what is now the Pioneer Square Historic District in downtown. The indigent Duwamish Indians and their leader, Chief Sealth, aided the settlers and largely contributed to their success. The Duwamish largely outnumbered the newcomers and felt they had nothing to fear, not knowing that soon they would be displaced and banned from their own land, their homes burned down. Much of the Native American land was ceded to the U.S. government, and despite the Duwamish cooperation, the settlers were attacked several times by Indians upset at their loss of land and forced relocation. Other indigenous tribes that called the Seattle area home included the Suquamish, Muckleshoot, Snoqualmie, Tulalip, and Puyallup Nations. Numerous skirmishes, gun battles, and lynchings occurred during the early years of the settlement's struggle for establishment. To this day, the Duwamish are not federally recognized and are the only local indigenous tribe without a reservation.

Lumber was the settlement's first export and quickly became a major industry—largely to rebuild San Francisco after its devastating fire of 1851. A post office was established, the Washington Territorial University was founded in 1861 (today the University of Washington), and in 1863 the town's first newspaper, the *Gazette,* rolled off the presses. By 1870 the population of Seattle was just over 1,100, a figure that tripled over the following decade.

The fledgling city was met with its own disaster, however, when the Great Seattle Fire swept through Pioneer Square on June 6, 1889. More than 25 blocks were left in smoldering ruins, a seemingly cruel twist of fate for the city that had largely grown from supplying lumber to San Francisco's postfire rebuilding efforts. There were no confirmed deaths, however, and new construction began immediately. Downtown Seattle rose from the ashes with mostly brick and stone buildings that were largely completed within a year. By 1890 the population had reached 42,000, an incredible 12-fold increase from 1880 that was due in large part to the transcontinental railway and the port that now served the city. Yet even greater growth was still to come.

THE GOLD RUSH AND SEATTLE'S GROWTH

By 1897 steamships from Alaska were docking in Elliott Bay, carrying prospectors along with their stores of gold and tales of wild success. The Klondike gold rush in Canada's Yukon Territory was in full swing and gold fever had struck—even Seattle's mayor quit to join the stampede. Seattle merchants quickly exploited their location as the northernmost U.S. departure point for Dawson City, the heart of the gold rush. Food, clothing, supplies, and transportation were arranged in Seattle for 7 out of 10 prospectors heading to the Yukon, and the city enjoyed another boom, which doubled the population between 1890 and 1900.

This economic and population growth largely continued throughout the next

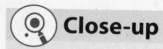

Close-up

Historic Timeline of Seattle

1851: (Nov 13) First settlers land at Alki Point

1852: (Apr 3) Settlers move across Elliott Bay to present-day downtown

(Dec 22) King County is incorporated

1855: (Jan 22) Point Elliott Treaty is signed, ceding most Native American land in western Washington to the U.S. government

1866: (June 7) Chief Sealth dies

1869: (Dec 2) The city of Seattle is incorporated

1882: (Dec) The first trans-Pacific steamship departs from Seattle

1889: (June 6) The Great Seattle Fire consumes more than 25 blocks of downtown Seattle

(Nov 11) Washington Territory becomes a U.S. state

1890: (Jan 7) The first transcontinental train arrives in Seattle

1897: (July 17) The steamship *Portland* docks in Seattle loaded with gold, setting off the Klondike gold rush

1901: The Wallin & Nordstrom store opens, forerunner of retail giant Nordstrom

1907: (Aug 17) Pike Place Market opens

1909: (June 1) The World's Fair, named the Alaska-Yukon-Pacific Exposition, opens in Seattle

1910: (Nov 8) Washington state grants women the right to vote

1911: The Port of Seattle is established

1916: William Boeing launches his first airplane from Lake Union

1917: (May 8) Lake Washington Ship Canal and Hiram Chittenden Locks are completed

1919: (Feb 6) First general strike in U.S. history begins with 60,000 Seattle workers refusing to show up for work

century, with only an occasional downturn. At the turn of the twentieth century, Seattle began to focus on an aspect of the city that has been front and center ever since: public parks. In 1903 the city council hired the famed Olmsted Brothers, stepsons of Frederick Olmsted, who designed Central Park in New York, to design and landscape Seattle parks. Olmsted's master plan laid out a 20-mile-long system of parks strung along scenic boulevards throughout the city, and a few years later this "emerald necklace" was expanded by 30 additional miles. Within a decade, Seattle boasted a park system that few cities could match, and public green spaces, parks, and natural reserves have

1926: (May 9) Bertha Landes, the first female mayor of a major U.S. city, is elected

1940: (June 5) The Lake Washington Floating Bridge opens

1942: (Apr 21) Japanese Americans are ordered to evacuate Seattle, resulting in more than 12,000 being placed in relocation centers

1949: (July 9) Seattle-Tacoma International Airport opens

1960: (Jan 1) The University of Washington football teams wins the Rose Bowl

1962: (Apr 21) The World's Fair opens, and the Space Needle along with it

1970: (May) Pioneer Square is designated as the city's first historic district

1971: (Apr) Starbucks opens its first coffeehouse in Pike Place Market

(Nov 24) D. B. Cooper hijacks a Northwest Airlines flight bound for Seattle, collecting $200,000 and jumping out over southwest Washington and is never heard from again

1977: (Apr 6) The Mariners baseball team plays its first game

1978: Microsoft establishes its campus in Bellevue, a Seattle suburb

1979: (June 1) The Supersonics basketball team wins the NBA championship

1982: (July 15) The Green River killer's first of 49 victims, Wendy Lee Coffield, is found

1983: (Feb 18) Three Hong Kong immigrants open fire at a gambling parlor in Chinatown, killing 13 people in the state's worst mass murder

1990: Seattle's population tops half a million

1999: (Nov 29 to Dec 3) The World Trade Organization meeting erupts in rioting, with nearly 600 arrests

2000: (June 23) The Experience Music Project opens

2001: (Feb 28) The most powerful earthquake in more than half a century causes more than $2 billion in damages, much of it to historic buildings

remained important parts of the Seattle landscape.

Seattle's growth and prosperity, as well as its part in the Klondike gold rush, led it to be the site of the 1909 World's Fair. Called the Alaska-Yukon-Pacific Exposition, it was held on the University of Washington campus and drew more than three million visitors, giving the city international recognition for the first time. The fair incorporated aspects of Canada and the Pacific Rim into its exhibits—both Japan and Canada erected their own buildings as exhibit pavilions for the 138-day exposition. The Woman's Building emphasized the role of women in pioneering the American West.

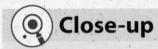 **Close-up**

Lake View Cemetery: Repository for Seattle's Founders

If you want to visit the graves of some of the city's most noted founders and shapers, head to **Lake View Cemetery (**1554 15th Ave. East, 206-322-1582, www .lakeviewcemeteryassociation.com) in Capitol Hill, near Volunteer Park.

Many pioneers of the Northwest are buried here, and a stroll through the weathered headstones provides a glimpse into the history of Seattle itself. Some of the inscriptions are touching and prophetic; others are whimsical and even humorous. You'll find the Denny family, the Mercers, shipbuilder and one-time Seattle mayor Robert Moran, and John Pike, designer of the University of Washington. Henry Yesler rests in eternal peace here, as well as Princess Angeline, the daughter of Chief Sealth. At her request, the Duwamish princess was buried near Yesler, who was her friend and protector.

One of the most moving memorials is the 20-foot-high monument dedicated to the American soldiers of Japanese ancestry from the Seattle area, who died in the service of their country in World War II. Inscribed beneath the names of some 60 men is a quote from President Franklin D. Roosevelt that reads, "Americanism is a matter of the mind and heart. Americanism is not, and never was, a matter of race or ancestry."

In addition to Seattle's founding fathers and war heroes, father and son Bruce and Brandon Lee are buried side by side. The martial arts and movie stars' graves get the most attention, with people coming from all over the world to visit them.

Established in 1872, the 40-acre cemetery also has one of the best views in the city, spanning Puget Sound to the Olympic Mountains, Cascade Mountains, and Lake Washington. Lake View Cemetery is open from 9 a.m. to dusk daily; office hours are 9 a.m. to 4:30 p.m. Mon through Fri, and Sat by appointment. Here you can pick up a map showing the locations of noteworthy gravesites.

Shipbuilding and fishing became major industries in the early 20th century, largely assisted by the completion of the Lake Washington Ship Canal and the Hiram Chittenden Locks. The growth of these industries was accompanied by a large influx of Scandinavians who worked mainly in the shipyards. During this time, immigrants also arrived in large numbers from Japan, China, the Philippines, and Italy. Shipbuilding grew during World War I, as Seattle produced 20 percent of the nation's wartime ship tonnage. At the end of the war, shipyard workers went on strike to maintain their high wages. Soon afterward the city came under a general labor strike, and many unions were formed and more strikes held in the following decades, partly giving Seattle its reputation for political radicalism.

POSTWAR AEROSPACE AND TECHNOLOGY

Both the shipbuilding and lumber trades were hit hard in the years following World War I and the Great Depression, but the

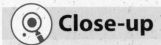

Close-up

Eccentric Seattle Residents

- **Wyatt Earp**—The famed Wild West sheriff once operated a gambling house on Second Avenue, around 1900.

- **Lou Graham**—This madam was a German immigrant whose high-end brothels made her one of the city's most successful businesspeople. She contributed more money to educating Seattle's children than all other prominent early citizens combined. The astute, wealthy madam also saved many banks and prestigious families from bankruptcy.

- **Ivar Haglund**—A folk singer, radio personality, and restaurateur, Ivar was a local character who most famously opened the first aquarium and fish-and-chips stand on Pier 54 in 1938. Lovable Ivar was known as the "Mayor of the Waterfront" and pulled off many crazy publicity stunts. This expanded into Ivar's Acres of Clams and an empire of seafood eateries, and he eventually bought Pier 54. Ivar died of a heart attack in 1985, but you can still get a bowl of his famous clam chowder at several Ivar's locations around Seattle.

- **Asa Shinn Mercer**—The first president of the University of Washington (then Territorial University) and its sole instructor, by virtue of his being the only college graduate in Seattle in the 1860s. Mercer realized that while Seattle was attracting hordes of men to the timber and fishing industries, there were few marriageable women. In 1864 Mercer traveled to Massachusetts to recruit single women, bringing 11 young ladies known as the "Mercer girls" back to Seattle, and 34 more the following year—one of whom he married.

- **Roy Olmstead**—During Prohibition in the 1920s, this former police lieutenant became one of Seattle's most successful bootleggers, eventually growing into one of the largest employers in Puget Sound.

- **J.P. Patches**—Real name Chris Wedes, J.P. was a much-loved clown character who starred in the *J.P. Patches Show* for 23 years beginning in 1958. J.P. lived in the city dump, where he welcomed a wide variety of guests on his show, such as the Harlem Globetrotters, Angus Young of AC/DC, Jacques Cousteau, and Tiny Tim. There were also many well-known "Patches Pals," including Bill Gates, Matt Groening, who created *The Simpsons,* and the mayor and governor. In August 2008 a statue of J.P. Patches was unveiled at Solstice Plaza in Fremont.

Second World War sparked a rebound. The Boeing Company also flourished; founded in 1916, it had been moderately successful but saw its annual sales skyrocket from $10 million to $600 million during the World War II years. The "Space Race" was under way worldwide, and Boeing put Seattle on the map as a major player. In 1954 the Boeing 707 took off on its first flight, becoming the first successful passenger jet in the world.

The year 1962 saw the second World's Fair to be held in Seattle, with a focus on space, science, and the future. Called the Century 21 Exposition, it forever changed both Seattle's skyline and the image most people have of the city, with the construction of the

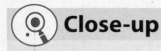

Close-up

Interesting Seattle Factoids

- Before the city was named Seattle in late 1852, it was called Duwamps.

- The name Seattle comes from Noah Sealth, chief of the Duwamish and Suquamish Native American tribes.

- The term "skid row," referring to a seedy section of town, originated from Seattle's early lumber business. Woodcutters used greased "skid roads" to send logs to the sawmill; the term came to refer to the lack of respectability that defined the lumber mills and the flophouses that sprang up around them.

- Washington state attempted to give women the right to vote long before it was U.S. law. An 1854 women's suffrage proposal by city founder Arthur Denny failed by one vote; Seattle women were finally granted the right to vote in 1883, although it was ruled unconstitutional by a higher federal court.

- The Great Seattle Fire of 1889 destroyed most of the original downtown. It was rebuilt within a year, on raised street levels right on top of the ruins—some of which remain underneath.

- Reginald H. Thomson, who became city engineer in 1892, forever changed Seattle's landscape with his aggressive leveling and regrading of the area's substantial hills, believing that commercial growth needed flat land. While he did not succeed in completely flattening the city, the amount of dirt displaced during this time would completely fill in the Panama Canal.

- The city played a major role in the Klondike gold rush of the late 1890s, as the northernmost U.S. departure point for the Yukon. Merchants advertised Seattle as the "Gateway to the Gold Fields," and some 70 percent of stampeders stopped first in Seattle to stock up on provisions.

landmark Space Needle for the event. At the time, the Space Needle was the tallest structure west of the Mississippi River, at 605 feet (about 60 stories), with elevators to the top, an observation deck, and a revolving restaurant. The monorail, science center, and numerous sports and performing arts venues were also built, eventually turning the area into what is now called Seattle Center. The fair was hugely popular, drawing nearly 10 million people during its six months and providing the setting for the Elvis Presley movie *It Happened at the World's Fair*. Many people largely credit the 1962 exposition with revitalizing the city's

economic and cultural life, and since that time the population has remained stable at around the half-million mark.

The rest of the 1960s continued a building boom, with several skyscrapers, highways, sports arenas, and floating bridges completed; Seattle acquired professional sports franchises with the Sonics basketball team and the Pilots baseball team. Boeing and the aerospace industry, however, began a decline that started in 1970 when Congress killed the Super Sonic Transport project. Known as the "Boeing Bust," employment levels at Boeing dropped from 95,000

- The world's first gasoline service station was opened on Holgate Street in 1907.

- Progressive Seattle was the first major American city to elect a female mayor. Bertha Knight Landes led the city for one term, from 1926 to 1928, but remained an active civic leader and role model for many years.

- The landmark Camlin Hotel in downtown Seattle was built using embezzled funds. Bankers Adolph Linden and Edmund Campbell used around $2 million in bank funds to open the hotel in 1926; the two men were imprisoned, but the Camlin Hotel enjoyed success for many years.

- In 1939 Seattle opened the first racially integrated public housing in the United States at Yesler Terrace.

- These liberal racial policies did not, however, prevent the city from ordering Japanese Americans to evacuate during World War II. More than 12,000 U.S. citizens of Japanese ancestry from King County were held in relocation centers during the war.

- Seattle had its own Red Scare in the 1940s, several years before the McCarthy hearings. Washington state Representative Albert Canwell doggedly pursued numerous alleged Communists, destroying the careers of several University of Washington professors in the process.

- Wing Luke became the first Chinese-American to hold a major public office in the United States when he was elected to the city council in 1961.

- Two Seattle heritage museums are the only ones of their kind in the country: the Nordic Heritage Museum, showcasing five Nordic countries, and the Wing Luke Museum, devoted to Asian American history.

to 38,000 and created a depression in the local economy. The company would end up moving its headquarters to Chicago in 2001.

However, a new industry would keep Seattle at the forefront of business: technology. In 1975 a company called Micro-Soft opened. Originally founded by Bill Gates and Paul Allen in Albuquerque, the company moved back to Gates and Allen's native Seattle area in 1978 and removed the hyphen from its name, becoming Microsoft Corporation. Bringing both jobs and wealth, Microsoft led the way in Seattle's becoming a worldwide hub for computer technology and software.

By 1995 the company had become the world's most profitable and led the way for many other Internet and tech firms in what was called the Silicon Valley of the North.

Other milestones for the city during this period included the first Starbucks to open, in Pike Place Market in 1971, starting a major coffee culture, as well as the arrival of the Seahawks football team, Supersonics basketball, and Mariners baseball. Research institutions, particularly at the University of Washington, and defense work contributed to Seattle's growth, largely due to Senators Warren Magnuson and Henry Jackson.

MODERN-DAY SEATTLE

Air and sea trade with Alaska, Asia, and the North Pacific continued to grow tremendously. From the 1970s through today, the Port of Seattle evolved into a major enterprise; however, the city's waterways were not without their mishaps. In 1978 a freighter hit the West Seattle Bridge, putting it out of commission for seven years, and in 1990 the floating bridge across Lake Washington that was part of I-90 sank in a storm (it reopened in 1993).

By the 1980s Seattle began evolving from an entrepreneurial though hardly avant-garde city into one with a thriving creative class. In the space of one generation the population nearly doubled, and with it emerged a community of artists, musicians, writers, and philosophers. Seattle began to develop its reputation as a hotbed for live music and new recording acts, largely due to the grunge movement that was born here and changed music forever.

Independent record label Sub Pop, formed in 1986, signed then-unknown local bands Mudhoney, Nirvana, and Soundgarden, among others. The label almost went bankrupt before releasing Nirvana's *Nevermind* album in 1991, which almost single-handedly put this new Seattle sound on the map. Although many grunge bands disbanded by the late 1990s, their influence continues to impact music today, and Seattle remains a city with a vibrant live music scene and the highest per-capita music and dance attendance in the country.

The city's reputation for other performing arts grew as well. The nearly century-old Seattle Symphony Orchestra was boosted by new world-class performance venues such as Benaroya Hall, the Seattle Opera, Pacific Northwest Ballet, Intiman Theaters, and McCaw Hall. The Bumbershoot music festival at Labor Day and Seattle International Film Festival in May and June draw audiences from around the world.

Seattle's political activism gained worldwide attention during the World Trade Organization meetings in November 1999. Protestors and demonstrators rioted in the streets resulting in police confrontations and nearly 600 arrests in what was dubbed the "Battle of Seattle." Today, Seattle continues to be known for its progressive politics, active civic involvement, and commitment to the environment.

ACCOMMODATIONS

Seattle is a city with a huge range of options for accommodations, from the most luxurious four- and five-star hotels to kitschy motor lodges; quaint bed-and-breakfasts to comfortable hostels; and trendy boutique hotels to floating rental homes. There is truly something for every personality, traveling style, and type of trip.

Perhaps the main criterion to begin your search for lodging should be the area of town in which you wish to stay, or plan to spend the most time in. The downtown neighborhoods and central business district are, of course, the main areas for hotels—keep in mind that parking is a major hassle and very expensive in these areas, so if you have a car or plan to rent one, staying slightly outside downtown may be a better option. Lodging is also at a premium in the summer months, between the high tourist season, numerous conventions and festivals in the city, and filled-to-capacity cruise ships that dock in Elliott Bay each week. You will pay the highest rates in the summertime, and booking early (as well as considering going outside of downtown) is advised. Many hotels on the outskirts of downtown provide free shuttles to major locations such as Pike Place Market, Westlake Center, and the Space Needle.

OVERVIEW

In the traditional off-season between November and March, excellent deals can be had. The Seattle Convention and Visitors Bureau has sponsored a long-running promotion called the Seattle Super Saver program, offering discounts of up to 50 percent at participating hotels and a coupon book with reservations that provides great savings on local restaurants, attractions, and shopping. Seattle Super Saver promises the best available rate at more than 80 hotels, with no booking or hidden fees, no prepayment or change fees, no cancellation fee until 24 hours prior to arrival, and the best available room promised at check-in.

The accommodations listings are categorized by type of property (hotels, bed-and-breakfasts, home rentals, etc.), and within each lodging category the accommodations are further organized by area of town. The price range is based on the published rack rates provided by each property, and of course depending on deals, discounts, coupons, and time of year, you may well be able to get a lower rate than what we have listed.

The amenities offered by each property are listed, along with pet acceptance policies (if applicable). Every listed property accepts major credit cards unless otherwise noted and offers guest rooms with accessible features that comply with the Americans with Disabilities Act. Hotels are exempt from the state smoking ban; however, most Seattle hotels are completely nonsmoking nevertheless. An accommodations listing will specify if the property offers any smoking rooms or exceptions to this general rule. Due to the mild summer weather, a few hotels do not come equipped with air conditioning in some or all guest rooms, particularly some historic properties. Although it rarely gets hot enough in the area to make A/C a necessity, hotels that are not fully air-conditioned are noted. Complimentary Wi-Fi service is standard in most Seattle hotels now, so unless a charge is noted, each accommodation does offer free high-speed Internet access.

We have included a quick index before the main listings for added convenience.

Price Code

The following price code represents the average published double-occupancy room rate during peak season. Prices do not include hotel tax, which is 12 percent.

$................. **Less than $100**
$$ .... **$100 to $150**
$$$ .... **$151 to $200**
$$$$ .... **More than $200**

ACCOMMODATIONS

HOTELS AND MOTELS

Downtown/Central

ACE HOTEL   **$–$$**
2423 1st Ave.
(206) 448-4721
www.acehotel/seattle

The Ace is an ultrahip, modern small hotel in Seattle's vibrant, eclectic Belltown neighborhood, putting its in-the-know clientele square in the middle of the city's most happening scene. Yet these trendy digs are amazingly affordable, partly because of the hotel's youthful vibe and combination of private and shared baths. Just 28 rooms offer a refreshingly clean design aesthetic, with a bohemian edge evidenced in the vintage furnishings. There is plenty of fun and funky artwork throughout the hotel and in guest rooms. Standard rooms are crisp and white, with low platform beds and an in-room vanity but a shared bathroom down the hall. Deluxe rooms have their own private bathrooms, king- or queen-size beds, and air conditioning. Some have partial water views. All rooms offer large windows with an abundance of natural light, high loftlike ceilings, hardwood floors, cable television, and a minibar. The historic building has incorporated many sustainable, eco-friendly elements in keeping with the times. Cyclops Café and the Panther Room bar are located directly downstairs, serving food and drinks until late hours. The Ace is also dog-friendly.

ALEXIS HOTEL   **$$$–$$$$**
1007 1st Ave.
(206) 624-4844
www.alexishotel.com

The Alexis is a luxury boutique hotel that recently completed a $10 million renovation. The hotel is dedicated to the local arts community, displaying original works throughout public areas and guest rooms. The location is excellent, within easy walking distance of Pike Place Market, Pioneer Square, and the waterfront, as well as numerous galleries and museums. The 121 rooms are a combination of king and queen rooms, as well as suites and one-bedroom apartment suites. Hotel amenities include concierge services, complimentary overnight shoe-shine service, 24-hour room service, fitness center with steam room, a day spa, and a nightly wine reception. Wi-Fi access is complimentary for Kimpton InTouch Guest Loyalty members (no cost to join) and $10/day for nonmembers, but wired Internet is always free. The Library Bistro and Bookstore Bar offer meals and drinks in a nice atmosphere. The only parking option is valet, at $36/night with a 50 percent discount for hybrid vehicles. Special KimptonKids packages for children are offered, making this an excellent choice for families. Pets are accepted without size or weight restriction, and there is no additional charge; in fact, guest pets are provided a designer doggie bed, water bowl, and treats during their stay.

i Take advantage of the Seattle Super Saver program by calling (800) 535-7071 or visiting www .seattlesupersaver.com to see a list of participating hotels and to book online.

BELLTOWN INN   **$$**
2301 3rd Ave.
(206) 529-3700, (866) 525-4704
www.belltown-inn.com

In a central, hip Belltown location, this clean and comfortable inn offers 174 new studio guest rooms with kitchenettes. Rooms offer a full- or queen-size bed and weekly housekeeping, but the rates are very reasonable, especially for this part of town. Nightly, weekly, and monthly stays are available. Other amenities include a business center, rooftop deck, courtyard, and guest laundry. There is a daily charge for Internet service.

BEST WESTERN EXECUTIVE INN $$
200 Taylor Ave. North
(206) 448-9444, (800) 351-9444
www.bestwestern.com/
   executiveinnseattle

This is primarily a convention hotel, located right next to the Space Needle and Seattle Convention Center. The 123 guest rooms offer cable satellite television, microwave, and minifridge. It is, of course, very business-friendly with meeting facilities that will accommodate up to 275, a business center, and audiovisual equipment available. Other features include a 24-hour exercise facility and hot tub. A complimentary hot breakfast buffet is served each morning, and the hotel also offers Brella's restaurant and lounge. On-site parking is $15/day.

BEST WESTERN LOYAL INN $$
2301 8th Ave.
(206) 682-0200
www.bestwestern.com/loyalinn

This centrally located Best Western is across the street from Denny Park, and a five-minute walk to the Space Needle and Seattle Center. Each of the 91 guest rooms features a king-size bed, microwave, and minifridge. An updated exercise facility and sauna, spa, eco-friendly rooms, complimentary hot breakfast buffet, and business services round out the amenities. On-site parking is $10/night.

BEST WESTERN
PIONEER SQUARE $$$
77 Yesler Way
(206) 340-1234, (800) 800-5514
www.pioneersquare.com

This Best Western is situated in a beautiful, restored turn-of-the-twentieth-century building in the heart of historic Pioneer Square. This is the only working hotel in the Pioneer Square district, set amid the rich architecture and cobblestone streets and close to Seattle's major downtown attractions. The 75 rooms offer your choice of king, queen, or two double beds and are decorated in period decor. Complimentary hot breakfast is also offered, and parking is available in a nearby garage for $20/night. Al Boccalino's award-winning Italian restaurant is next door and will provide room service.

COMFORT SUITES DOWNTOWN
SEATTLE CENTER $$
601 Roy St.
(206) 282-2600, (800) 517-4000
www.comfortsuites-seattle.com

This hotel provides comfortable accommodations in the heart of downtown, walking distance to the Space Needle and Seattle Center. The 158 guest rooms and suites offer in-room microwaves and refrigerators and satellite television with free HBO. Suites also include a separate living area and two-line telephones. Hotel features include 1,200 square feet of meeting space, exercise facilities, laundry rooms, business center, complimentary breakfast buffet, and free secure underground parking—a rare amenity downtown.

COURTYARD BY MARRIOTT—DOWNTOWN SEATTLE LAKE UNION $$$
925 Westlake Ave. North
(206) 213-0100, (800) 321-2211
www.marriott.com/seacd

This location in the South Lake Union neighborhood is just on the edge of downtown Seattle and provides a nice water's-edge accommodation that is still very near the main attractions in the city center; the streetcar stops just across the street. The 250 rooms offer picturesque views of either Lake Union or the Seattle skyline. Each room has either a king or two double beds; the king rooms include a pull-out sofa that can accommodate a child or third guest without extra charge. Hotel amenities include a pool, whirlpool, fitness center, and the Lamontagne Restaurant. On-site parking is available for $20/day.

COURTYARD BY MARRIOTT SEATTLE DOWNTOWN PIONEER SQUARE $$$
612 2nd Ave.
(206) 625-1111
www.courtyardpioneersquare.com

This Courtyard by Marriott is located in the beautiful 1904 Alaska Building, making an adaptive reuse of the first steel building in Washington state. The excellent location is 1 block from Sound Transit's Pioneer Square station and within walking distance of Safeco and Qwest Fields, and boasts water views of Elliott Bay. The on-site Starbucks and Courtyard Bistro restaurant are nice touches, and the hotel offers valet parking at $26/day. There are 262 rooms total, including two-room suites and a studio apartment; and 55 rooms on floors 9–15 have Elliott Bay views. There are also nine meeting rooms that provide 4,500 square feet of meeting space.

CROWNE PLAZA HOTEL SEATTLE $$$$
1113 6th Ave.
(206) 464-1980, (800) 521-2762
www.cphotelseattle.com

The Crowne Plaza is a 34-story hotel just off I-5, within walking distance of the convention center. Many of the 415 renovated guest rooms and suites have city or Puget Sound views, and provide their trademark Sleep Advantage Beds with plush duvets, quiet-zone floors, sound-effect CD players with sleep CDs, and a guaranteed wake-up call, virtually ensuring a great night's sleep. Club Floor rooms also offer complimentary continental breakfast and evening hors d'oeuvres, and Executive Guest Suites have a separate living room and sofa bed. Pets are allowed at Crowne Plaza; please inquire about policies and fees. Hotel amenities include full-service meeting facilities, Regatta Bar & Grille, 24-hour fitness center, a parking garage at $32/night, and valet parking for an additional fee. Smoking rooms are available.

DOUBLETREE ARCTIC CLUB HOTEL $$$$
700 3rd Ave.
(206) 340-0340, (800) 222-TREE
www.arcticclubseattledowntown
.doubletree.com

The Doubletree is a beautiful, recently renovated hotel that aims to pamper its guests. The 120 rooms feature one king or two queen beds, and some have sofa beds and whirlpool baths. The suites are spectacular, with rooftop terraces and gorgeous city views. Doubletree is known for its Sweet Dreams plush-top beds that come with five jumbo hypoallergenic pillows. Other room amenities include 32-inch HDTV and DVD player, CD stereo player with MP3 docking station, Starbucks in-room coffee service, great work space, and rainfall showerheads. The JUNO Restaurant is extremely good, and the lobby Polar Bar is a be-seen place with exquisite cocktails and absinthe fountain. Other on-site offerings include a lounge, fitness center, business center with complimentary printing, pool table, gift shop, convenience store, and laundry service. At the Doubletree, pets are not only welcomed, but also pampered, guests (maximum weight of 30 pounds). Valet parking is offered at $32/day.

EASTLAKE INN $$
2215 Eastlake Ave. East
(206) 322-7726
www.theeastlakeinn.com
This small neighborhood inn is just north of downtown, in the quiet and charming Lake Union area. The minisuite accommodations offer kitchenettes and cable television, with views of the Space Needle and skyline, at extremely reasonable rates. Twelve rooms feature a queen or two double beds and dining areas, some with full refrigerator and stove. Two one-bedroom suites are also available, featuring four double beds total, private entrances, and full kitchenette. Free on-site parking is included.

EDGEWATER HOTEL $$$$
2411 Alaskan Way (Pier 67)
(206) 728-7000, (800) 624-0670
www.edgewaterhotel.com
The Edgewater is a Seattle classic on the waterfront, with the shimmering city behind it and Elliott Bay at its doors. Edgewater achieves a Pacific Northwest lodge feel, with knotty-pine furniture and river-rock fireplaces, that is still modern and edgy. The hotel made *Conde Nast Traveler*'s Gold List in

2008 and has been recognized worldwide for its eco-friendly practices, which go far beyond those of many hotels. Half of the 223 rooms overlook Elliott Bay, while the others offer dramatic city views. All feature custom knotty-pine furniture, custom bedding with down blankets and pillows, refrigerator, and sitting area with overstuffed chairs, ottoman, and rustic gas fireplace. A selection of king, queen, and double rooms are available, as well as four suites including the incredible Penthouse Suite, and the Beatles Suite—yes, the band stayed here while touring the United States in 1964. The bathrooms are all European luxury, with amber quartz slate flooring, claw-foot slipper tubs, and garnet walls. The excellent Six Seven restaurant is located here, featuring inspired Pacific Northwest cuisine crafted with local ingredients and regional seafood with a backdrop of breathtaking views. There is a very nice boutique on-site, as well as a fitness center, concierge services, business center, and valet parking ($33/night). Edgewater provides complimentary shuttle service within 2 miles of the hotel between 8 a.m. and 9 p.m. Conference and event spaces are also available. Wi-Fi access is available for $9.95/day (waived for members of the AvantEdge Program, and available at no cost in the business center). The Edgewater is pet-friendly, with no deposit or fees required.

EMERALD CITY SUITES $$$$
2nd Avenue and Wall Street
(206) 856-9100
www.emeraldcitysuites.com
These beautifully furnished apartments are located in the vibrant Belltown section, within walking distance to Pike Place Market and a plethora of dining, shopping, and gallery locations. The professionally decorated

one- and two-bedroom suites are fully furnished right down to the martini glasses, and
each has a private balcony with excellent
city views. On-site amenities include a gym,
indoor pool, jetted spa, sauna, business center, clubroom, and secured garage parking
for one car (included in rates). There is also a
stunning, award-winning garden courtyard
with fountains. Nightly and monthly rates
are available. Emerald City Suites charges a
$75 cleaning fee on each stay of five nights
or less (waived for more than five nights).

EXECUTIVE HOTEL PACIFIC $$$
400 Spring St.
(206) 777-7106, (888) 388-3932
www.executivehotels.net/seattle
Although virtually every Seattle hotel is now
nonsmoking, this was the first completely
smoke-free hotel in the city. The Executive
Hotel's pitch is offering a five-star location
and four-star service, for three-star prices.
The location is certainly excellent, in a premier downtown location within walking
distance of many top attractions, including
Pike Place Market and dozens of restaurants, shops, and theater/cultural venues.
The building is gorgeous, built in 1928 and
with a very European style and feel to it.
Yet the facilities are renovated and modern,
including the addition of meeting rooms,
business center, fitness center, and the
LaBou Salon and Spa. There is also a Seattle's
Best Coffee shop right in the lobby, free
continental breakfast is included, and the
Asian-European fusion Jasmine Restaurant
is very good. The 152 rooms (and one suite)
are elegant yet understated, with a Eurasian
decor of rich cherry wood and gold and
green tones. Your choice of a king, queen, or
two double beds has been upgraded with
pillowtop mattresses, luxury duvets, and

five pillows for comfort. Parking is available
for $18/day, and pets are accepted up to
30 pounds and stay free. Interesting side
note—the staff speak Japanese!

FAIRMONT OLYMPIC HOTEL $$$$
411 University St.
(206) 621-1700, (800) 257-7544
www.fairmont.com/seattle
This incredible Italian Renaissance style hotel
originally opened in 1924 and is listed on
the National Register of Historic Places. A
true Seattle treasure, the courtyard gardens
and entrance lobby are spectacular. Located
in the heart of downtown, the Olympic
offers 450 well-appointed guest rooms, and
suites feature a king, queen, or two twin
beds, CD players, and Sony PlayStations. In-
room computers, DVD players, microwaves,
and minifridges are available if you request
them in advance. Some suites have sofa
beds and decorative fireplaces. Hotel amenities include meeting and event spaces,
business center, a full-service health club,
indoor swimming pool, whirlpool, concierge,
gift shop, laundry service, and children's
amenities. Three dining or lounging options
are available, from the elegant Georgian
Restaurant to Shuckers pub or The Terrace
piano bar. Self-parking is available for $26/
day and valet parking for $36. Pets up to 15
pounds are welcome at the Fairmont Olympic. Smoking rooms are also available.

FOUR SEASONS HOTEL $$$$
99 Union St.
(206) 749-7000, (800) 819-5053
www.fourseasons.com/seattle
The Four Seasons brand is long known for
being the epitome of luxury, and the Four
Seasons in Seattle is no exception. The entire
hotel and 147 guest rooms are elegantly

furnished with an urban sophistication using Pacific Northwest materials, with works by local artists displayed throughout and unbelievable views. The most spectacular vantage point can be had from the pool terrace level, which features a Zen garden and hot tub along with the infinity pool, and an outdoor fire pit facing the scenery of Elliott Bay and the Olympic Mountains. Rooms feature extra-deep marble soaking tubs, rain showers, pillowtop beds with luxury linens, 42-inch plasma televisions, and floor-to-ceiling windows. DVD players and MP3 docking stations are also provided. Thirteen suites are also available. A state-of-the-art fitness center includes a whirlpool and steam room, and a fully equipped business center is also available. The service, of course, is signature subtle-yet-doting Four Seasons style. The restaurant serves exquisite Pacific Northwest cuisine using many locally sourced and organic ingredients, and the ART Restaurant and Lounge is another place to enjoy great food and signature cocktails. The luxurious spa offers all the pampering and packages a guest could want in a peaceful sanctuary.

GRAND HYATT SEATTLE $$$$
721 Pine St.
(206) 774-1234
www.grandseattle.hyatt.com
Located in the heart of Seattle's theater district and best retail shopping, the distinctive Grand Hyatt offers sophisticated flair with a laid-back Northwest attitude. Excellent service from the top-notch staff along with the modern, stylish decor and magnificent original artwork complete the ambience here. The 425 guest rooms and suites offer the Hyatt's trademark king-size Grand Beds, iHome stereo system with iPod dock, blackout curtains, soaking tubs, and gorgeous

city and Puget Sound views. Hotel amenities include 24-hour business and fitness centers, whirlpool, steam room, sauna, the Elaia Spa, more than 25,000 feet of event/meeting space including high-tech amphitheater, concierge services, and valet parking ($33/night). Self-parking in the adjacent garage is available for $28/night. Ruth's Chris Steakhouse and Ruth's Chris Lounge are located here, as well as a Starbucks coffee shop. Some smoking rooms are available.

HAMPTON INN & SUITES $$$
700 5th Ave. North
(206) 282-7700, (800) 321-3232
www.hamptoninnseattle.com
This Hilton Family hotel offers a unique and charming location in the desirable Queen Anne neighborhood, up on a hill overlooking downtown Seattle. The location is within walking distance of Seattle Center and the Space Needle, and a short bus or taxi ride to other downtown attractions. The 198 rooms offer a choice of a king or two double beds, and one- or two-bedroom suites with full kitchens are also available. Most, but not all, of the suites also have fireplaces and balconies, making them perfect for family travel. The satellite televisions include HBO, and a free breakfast buffet is served each morning. Other amenities include an exercise center, laundry facilities, business center and meeting facilities, and gated underground parking.

HILTON SEATTLE $$$
1301 6th Ave.
(206) 624-0500, (800) HILTONS
www.seattlehilton.com
With a good location 1.5 blocks from the convention center, the Hilton Seattle offers 237 standard rooms, executive rooms, and suites with a king or two double beds. The

32-inch HD televisions come with Lodgenet service, which includes Web TV, music channels, pay movies, and Nintendo gaming system. Property amenities include a fitness center and meeting spaces; laundry and babysitting services are also available. The Top of the Hilton restaurant on the 29th floor has a breathtaking panorama of the city and bay, with an eclectic Northwest menu. Covered self-parking is available for $28/night, and Internet access is $10.95 per 24-hour period.

HOLIDAY INN EXPRESS
HOTEL & SUITES $$$
226 Aurora Ave. North
(206) 441-7222, (877) 865-6578
www.hiexpress.com/seattlecenter
On the north side of downtown with easy access to Seattle Center, this hotel is a good choice for families or extended-stay travelers because of the suite units offered at a reasonable rate. The 195 rooms and suites come with a king or two queen beds, and the suites also have a microwave and minifridge. Other on-site amenities include a 24-hour fitness center, heated indoor pool, business center, and 861-square-foot meeting room. A complimentary breakfast bar is served each morning, and parking is available for $10/night. Smoking rooms are available.

HOLIDAY INN SEATTLE CENTER $$$
211 Dexter Ave. North
(206) 728-8123
www.holidayinn.com/seattlewa
The downtown Seattle Holiday Inn is located on the north side of the city's center, just a few blocks from Seattle Center. It is on the corner of Denny Park, which can be a bit sketchy at night due to the vagrants who sleep here. The 196 total guest rooms include

23 suites, 117 rooms with two double beds, and 79 rooms with king-size beds; 14 rooms are smoking. All rooms include refrigerators, microwaves, plates and glassware, in-room video games, and work space. The hotel provides complimentary breakfast and a Kids Eat Free program, at the on-site Emerald Grill Restaurant. A business center and fitness center are also available; laundry and travel services are provided upon request.

HOMEWOOD SUITES BY
HILTON SEATTLE $$$$
1011 Pike St.
(206) 682-8282, (800) CALL-HOME
www.seattleconventioncenterpikestreet
.homewoodsuites.com
Located down the street from Pike Place Market, this all-suite hotel is in the midst of the theater and shopping districts downtown, and is a popular option for corporate housing and extended-stay guests. Each of the 195 individually designed studio, one-, and two-bedroom suites features separate living and sleeping areas, king or queen beds, and a fully equipped kitchen with full-size refrigerator, microwave, stove, and dishwasher. Two televisions and two telephones are also provided in each suite. Enjoy the complimentary hot breakfast daily, and evening reception Mon through Thurs offering food, beer, and wine. Homewood Suites offers a free shuttle to area medical facilities and other locations, as well as a 24-hour fitness center, business center, and billiards room with a 50-inch LCD television. Valet parking is available for $25/night. The hotel offers seven smoking suites. There is also another Homewood Suites nearby, at 206 Western Ave. north of downtown; this one accepts pets up to 50 pounds for an additional $20/day.

HOTEL 1000 $$$$
1000 1st Ave.
(206) 957-1000, (877) 315-1088
www.hotel1000seattle.com

This is possibly Seattle's hippest, most luxurious, most happening hotel right now. It has been selected as one of the top hotels in the world by numerous magazines, including *Travel + Leisure*, the *Robb Report*, and *Conde Nast Reserve List*. The wildly popular BOKA Kitchen + Bar is located here, a vibrant fusion of lounge, bar, and restaurant that serves urban American food alongside handcrafted cocktails and a stellar wine list. The lobby includes Studio 1000, a sanctuary with dramatic back-lit onyx and dark brown leather-wrapped walls surrounding a steel and concrete open fire pit. Studio 1000 is a perfect spot for relaxing with coffee or a drink, and offers a terrific speaker series in conjunction with the Seattle Art Museum. Hotel 1000 also offers a virtual reality golf experience, full-service spa, fitness zone with dry saunas, and business center. Event and meeting spaces are available, as well as valet parking ($32/night) and Les Clefs d'Or concierge service. Pets under 40 pounds are welcomed with custom treats from a local pet bakery, as well as beds, bowls, litter boxes, and toys ($40 pet fee per stay). Hotel 1000 offers some of the best high-tech suites around, with ultra-high-speed Wi-Fi, smart technology temperature control in the rooms, 40-inch HDTV in each room, media hubs with connectivity for MP3 players, DVD player, laptops, and more, and a touch screen VOIP telephone where you can check flight information and make restaurant reservations. Other cool amenities in the 120 rooms and suites include a two-person pedestal tub that fills from the ceiling, Thai silk bed linens, and that widely disappearing art of the nightly turndown. For the ultimate in decadence, go for the 2,000-square-foot Grand Suite with double-sided fireplace and amazing water view.

HOTEL ANDRA $$$$
2000 4th Ave.
(206) 694-7260, (877) 448-8600
www.hotelandra.com

Hotel Andra is a bastion of urban luxury, in the hip Belltown neighborhood. This boutique hotel is a serene, sophisticated oasis in the midst of the art, dining, and club scene all around it. Originally built in 1926, the classic building was renovated in 2004 to create Hotel Andra, with Scandinavian design influences and Northwest building elements of wood and stone. The lobby welcomes you with distressed plank floors, cool Arne Jacobsen chairs in bright orange, and minimalist accent lighting. A steel-wrapped plasma screen projects an always-changing collection of electronic images. Floating above this living area is an exposed loft, a haven for reading and quiet socializing. The 119 rooms and suites feature dark wood furniture, warm walls, and brushed stainless accents for a rich ambience. Bathrooms are designed in a cool Icelandic blue, and towels and linens are all Frette. The suites feature beds that are truly incredible—handcrafted Swedish Hastens made of natural materials that contour to the body's shape. The in-room coffee service is Starbucks and each room has a private bar and Tivoli clock radio with iPod dock. In-room massage and spa services can be arranged, and hotel amenities include business and concierge services, meeting rooms, valet parking, and on-site fitness center as well as affiliations with nearby yoga studios and gyms. Lola, the restaurant by renowned chef Tom Douglas, is a happening spot for visitors and locals alike; Assaggio provides a second hotel restaurant.

HOTEL MAX $$$
620 Stewart St.
(206) 728-6299, (866) 833-6299
www.hotelmaxseattle.com

If you are an art lover, you simply have to check out Hotel Max. It is a celebration of local, original artists—*Continental Airlines Magazine* says that the Seattle Art Museum has competition from the Max. Hotel Max offers up a blank canvas for both established and emerging Seattle artists and photographers. More than 350 original paintings and photographs are found throughout the public spaces and guest rooms. The decor of the 163 rooms doesn't compete with the artwork, but rather provides an understated elegance that shows it off. Choose from rooms with one or two double beds, a queen or king bed, all with pillowtop mattresses and your choice of pillow types. Hotel Max is run by Provenance Hotels, which offers the unique "You Got It" phone menu. A mere press of the button enables guests to order up their specific pillow preference, religious book of choice from the "spiritual menu," music playlists, and a host of other items. Hotel amenities include a 24-hour fitness center and business center, pet-friendly rooms (fee required), and the Red Fin restaurant, offering eclectic Asian fusion dishes. Note that there is a daily fee here for Internet access.

HOTEL MONACO $$$$
1101 4th Ave.
(206) 621-1770, (800) 715-6513
www.monaco-seattle.com

Luxury, boutique Hotel Monaco enjoys an excellent location in the heart of downtown, within easy walking distance of Pike Place Market and Pioneer Square. The decor is reminiscent of Greek seaports, with white stucco and azure-blue accents, hand-blown glass, and frescoes inspired by the Palace of Knossos. The 189 guest rooms and suites are decorated in crimson with yellow and charcoal accents, or vibrant yellows with raspberry and cream accents, all in fun and whimsical patterns. Pillowtop beds with Frette linens, LCD televisions with DVD players, and CD stereos are all designed to provide maximum comfort. Suites include sofa beds and two-person Fuji jet tubs. The hotel provides complimentary shoe shine, same-day laundry and dry cleaning (fee-based), in-room spa services, fitness facility and affiliation with nearby athletic club, and business and concierge services. Hotel Monaco accepts pets with no size restriction or extra fees; in fact, the hotel indulges guest pets and can arrange pet-sitting services. Wi-Fi access is complimentary for Kimpton InTouch Guest Loyalty members (no cost to join) and $10/day for nonmembers. KimptonKids packages are great for travelers with children. Valet parking is $36–$39/night, with a 50 percent discount for hybrid cars. Sazerac Restaurant is located adjacent and is one of Seattle's hippest dining spots. The hosted wine hour for guests each Fri evening is a nice touch, and there is also a fortune-teller in the lobby every Wed and Sat. The hotel will even provide you with a goldfish companion during your stay!

HOTEL VINTAGE PARK $$$
1100 5th Ave.
(206) 624-8000, (800) 853-3914
www.hotelvintagepark.com

This uniquely themed boutique hotel celebrates Washington Wine Country by dedicating each of its 125 rooms to a local winery and vineyard. The European-style hotel also hosts a wine tasting each evening and provides a popular venue for weddings. Rooms come with either a king or queen bed, two queens, or two doubles, and some have sofa sleepers. The Chateau St. Michelle suite has a double-sided fireplace, two-person jetted tub, television in the bathroom, DVD player, and fully stocked private bar. Wi-Fi access is complimentary for Kimpton InTouch Guest Loyalty members (no cost to join) and $10/day for nonmembers. Other hotel amenities include a fitness center, "Mind Body Spa" in-room exercise programs, business center, laundry service, complimentary shoe shine, and a pet-friendly policy that has no size restrictions or additional fees. Like all Klimpton properties, Hotel Vintage Park provides extras for guest pets and can arrange for pet-sitting. Each Wed you can find complimentary hand massages in the lobby, and the Tulio Italian restaurant is on-site. Valet parking is $30/night, with a 50 percent savings for hybrid vehicles.

HYATT AT OLIVE 8 $$$$
1635 8th Ave.
(206) 695-1234, (800) 492-8804
www.olive8.hyatt.com
Seattle's downtown Hyatt has a sleek, modern design, and the distinction of being the first LEED-certified green hotel in the city. Puget Sound, Pike Place Market, and the heart of the city are within blocks of the front doors. The 346 luxurious rooms with king or queen beds (and two suites) feature 37-inch flat-panel televisions, deluxe beds and baths, refrigerator, and an iHome stereo system with iPod dock. Hyatt takes fitness to a new level, offering not only a 24-hour state-of-the-art gym, but also a fitness concierge

and YogaAway program. The eco-friendly Elaia spa is for pampering, and the hotel also offers concierge and dry-cleaning services, child-sitting arrangements, valet parking ($33/night), a lobby cafe, and the Urbane restaurant and bar, with a farm-to-table concept serving local, organic food. A ballroom and 12,000 square feet of meeting space are available. Wi-Fi access is available for an additional fee.

INN AT EL GAUCHO $$$–$$$$
2505 1st Ave.
(206) 728-1133, (866) 354-2824
www.inn.elgaucho.com/inn.elgaucho
Now, this is truly a unique Seattle stay. This luxury urban inn with only 18 guest suites is located above the renowned El Gaucho steakhouse, in the hip Belltown district. The swank, retro fifties decor includes handmade furnishings in the rooms, combined with modern amenities such as plasma televisions with high-definition premium cable channels, Bose Wave sound systems, and Wi-Fi access. The colors are rich and warm, and the entire feel is that of an insider VIP secret that only you, and a few other select guests, know about. Luxury touches, such as Anichini linens on the featherbeds and L'Occitane and Philip B products, are also found, and of course personal attention is high, with 24-hour concierge services. Room service comes from the exquisite El Gaucho restaurant. The inn has also partnered with nearby merchants to offer additional services, such as gym facilities at the Seattle Athletic Club, spa services, valet parking, and town car service. Note that the front desk and lobby are located on the second floor, above the restaurant, and accessible only by stairway. This hotel is not wheelchair accessible.

INN AT HARBOR STEPS $$$$
1221 1st Ave.
(206) 748-0973, (888) 728-8910
www.innatharborsteps.com

Nestled in the glamorous, urban Harbor Steps Park, this small boutique inn is located in the heart of the arts and business district. A member of the prestigious Four Sisters group, this wonderful little gem blends sophisticated luxury with the traditional architecture and personal service of a B&B. With only 28 king and queen guest rooms, rates include a full breakfast each morning, afternoon tea and hors d'oeuvres, and afternoon wine hour. Other nice, old-fashioned touches include fresh-baked cookies, evening turndown service with chocolates, and a library of movies, books, and CDs at the front desk. Some rooms have a private patio, while others include a gas fireplace. The Deluxe King Spa Guestroom features a fireplace, Juliet balcony, oversize jetted spa tub, and wet bar with refrigerator. There is also an indoor lap pool, fitness room, and basketball court. Concierge services are available, and adjacent garage parking for $18/night.

INN AT QUEEN ANNE $$
505 1st Ave. North
(206) 282-7357, (800) 952-5043
www.innatqueenanne.com

Located in the historic and charming Queen Anne neighborhood, minutes from downtown, this small 1930s hotel provides a charming atmosphere with old-world courtyards and lobbies with Tiffany lamps. The 68 guest rooms are furnished in European style and are simple, yet clean and stylish. Standard and deluxe rooms come with one queen bed, a queen/twin bed combination, or two twin beds. Junior suites feature a queen bed, DVD player, and eat-in kitchen, and the inn also offers a one-bedroom suite with a queen bed, separate living room with twin pull-out sofa, two televisions, and a DVD player. All rooms come with a kitchenette including refrigerator, microwave, cooktop, and utensils/cookware. The hotel offers a complimentary minimal continental breakfast bar, same-day laundry service and guest laundry facilities, and on-site parking (inquire about current parking fees). The Inn at Queen Anne is not wheelchair accessible and does not have an elevator, due to the building's historic nature. Also, not all rooms have air conditioning (although they do all have ceiling fans, and A/C is rarely essential in Seattle).

INN AT THE MARKET $$$$
86 Pine St.
(206) 443-3600, (800) 446-4484
www.innatthemarket.com

Inn at the Market, a true boutique hotel, is the only hotel located in downtown Seattle's beloved Pike Place Market. Slip into the ivy-covered courtyard and discover a tranquil hideaway from the vibrancy of Pike Place Market. Enjoy the cozy ambience of the lobby fireplace and the inn's unique collection of original regional artwork. One of the nicest features of this original boutique hotel is the rooftop deck, offering one-of-a-kind water views. Inn at the Market is designed with Northwest style and comfort, and home to one of Seattle's most acclaimed restaurants, Campagne, as well as the more casual bistro, Café Campagne. Both are very popular with locals. The rooms are elegant and comfortable, with floor-to-ceiling windows that open, Nintendo gaming system on the television, and Seattle's Best Coffee in-room. Inn at the Market offers a complimentary business center for guests, and valet parking. The staff are extremely atten-tive; other services available include in-room massage, Shine in the Market Salon in the hotel courtyard, and guest privileges to the prestigious Seattle Athletic Club in Pike Place Market for the length of your stay.

INN AT THE WAC $$$$
1325 6th Ave.
(206) 464-3055, (800) 275-3775
www.wac.net/default.aspx?id=inn

The gorgeous, historic Washington Athletic Club may not be a place that you think of for hotel accommodations—but you should. The Inn at the WAC is a masterpiece of warm, subtle, hip decor that is graced with works of art from notable Northwest artists. The Lobby Lounge is home to the Chihuly Alcove, a stunning display of works by Dale Chihuly, the renowned Seattle glass artisan. Since 1930 the WAC has been a downtown Seattle institution, and the inn has been part of that since the beginning. The 109 guest rooms are appointed with modern designer touches, sophisticated fabrics, and beautiful art. Each comes with a flat-screen plasma television with MP3 integration, Sealy Palatial plush bed with 300-thread-count Egyptian cotton sheets, a smart occupant-sensing thermostat, newly remodeled bathrooms with multiple-spray showers and L'Occitane bath amenities, and a CD player complete with relaxation CDs for your enjoyment. Little old-fashioned touches such as evening turndown service are nice. There are 12 pre-mier rooms with wet bars and oversize two-person bathtubs, as well as nine luxury suites that come with two televisions, wine refrig-erator, separate living room, and sweeping views. On-site amenities feature, of course, the athletic club that provides five floors of the most comprehensive facilities in the

Northwest, as well as a pool, sports courts, The Spa at the WAC, concierge services, same-day laundry service, and valet parking. Complimentary use of the WAC parking facil-ities is also available. Dining options include Torchy's fine dining restaurant with Wash-ington nouvelle cuisine, Hagerty's Sports Bar, and the 8th Floor Sports Café. Room rates are available at a discount for WAC members.

INN AT VIRGINIA MASON $$
1006 Spring St.
(206) 583-6453, (800) 283-6453
www.innatvirginiamason.com

This warm, stylish midsize hotel enjoys a nice residential location on First Hill that is still very convenient to downtown Seattle. Originally built in the 1920s as the Rho-dodendron Apartments, the building was later purchased by Virginia Mason Hospital, from which the inn gets its name. The inn provides housing for visiting doctors and families of patients, and donates a portion of its profits to medical research. The 79 rooms offer a choice of king, queen, or double twin beds, and many retain historic architectural elements such as arched entryways and crown molding. Some of the larger rooms include sleeper sofas and refrigerators. Select suites also feature wood-burning fireplaces, microwaves, whirlpool baths, and excellent city views. Guest parking is available for a reasonable fee. Don't miss the exquisite roof garden with gorgeous views.

KING'S INN $
2106 5th Ave.
(206) 441-8833
http://kingsinnseattle.com

King's Inn is a basic hotel offering one of the few budget options downtown, located in the excellent Belltown neighborhood. The hotel offers free parking—a rarity downtown—and 68 clean, simple rooms with one queen or two twin beds, and cable television. Suite rooms also offer coffeemakers, refrigerators, and microwaves.

LA QUINTA INN AND SUITES $$$
2224 8th Ave.
(206) 624-6820, (800) 753-3757
www.lq.com

This centrally located downtown hotel is 8 blocks from the convention center and walking distance to the Space Needle. The 72 rooms, including 12 suites, come with king or queen beds as well as microwaves and premium cable channels. Some rooms have a sofa sleeper, and suites come with kitchenettes. On-site amenities include limited free parking, complimentary morning breakfast, business and fitness centers, and guest laundry facilities. La Quinta accepts pets; inquire about policies and fees.

MARQUEEN HOTEL $$$$
600 Queen Anne Ave. North
(206) 282-7407, (888) 445-3076
www.marqueen.com

This historic boutique hotel offers romantic charm and personal hospitality, as well as some of the best hilltop views of the city. Built in 1918 as the Seattle Engineering School, the Queen Anne landmark is a hidden treasure characteristic of the neighborhood's architecture, with beveled glass doors and a grand staircase leading from the foyer. Although the 58 guest rooms and suites have an old-world ambience that includes hardwood flooring and period-inspired furnishings, they are complete with modern amenities. All include kitchens with microwave, refrigerator, and seating area, and some also have a stove. A king or two

queen beds are available, and suites offer a sofa bed and DVD player. The on-site Jull Bucy European day spa is heavenly, and there is also a fitness center, Caffe Ladro espresso bar and bakery, and Ten Mercer Restaurant. Additional amenities include overnight shoe-shine service, turndown service, wine receptions on select evenings, and valet parking (fee applies).

MARRIOTT SPRINGHILL SUITES $$$
1800 Yale Ave.
(206) 254-0500, (888) 236-2427
www.springhillseattle.com

Tucked between the shopping/sightseeing district and South Lake Union, this all-suite hotel offers 234 guest rooms with one king or two double beds, minifridge, microwave, and premium cable channels. Complimentary hot breakfast buffet, fitness facilities, indoor pool and whirlpool, a restaurant, bar and courtesy shuttle are also provided to guests. Complimentary Wi-Fi access available in lobby and suites; free wired Internet access in guest rooms. Meeting space is available, as well as valet parking ($20/night).

MARRIOTT WATERFRONT $$$$
2100 Alaskan Way
(206) 443-5000, (800) 455-8254
www.seattlemarriottwaterfront.com

On the Seattle waterfront, this Marriott offers breathtaking mountain and water views. Its location right across from the cruise terminal at Pier 66 and near Pike Place Market is exceptional for cruise travelers. The 2100 Bistro and Bar offers a culinary experience drawn from coastal cultures around the world. Half of the hotel's 358 guest rooms have private balconies, and all include luxury bedding on king or double beds, 42-inch LCD television, CD player, minifridge, and iPod docking stations (on concierge level). Junior suites are waterfront-facing corner rooms with separate living areas and sofa beds. Other amenities include business services, meeting space, complimentary shoe shine, laundry facilities and valet dry cleaning, 24-hour fitness center, and the Trolley Café & Gift Shop, serving Starbucks coffee. Wireless Internet access is available for $12.95/day. Valet parking is offered for $40/day and off-site self-parking is $18.

MAXWELL HOTEL $$
300 Roy St.
(206) 286-0629
www.themaxwellhotel.com

One of Seattle's newest hotels, the Maxwell opened in Mar 2010 in an excellent location near Seattle Center. Its interior decor is a bit midcentury modern meets Paris in a funky style, and the hotel aims to combine style with affordability to delight the senses. The architecture and interior design elements capture the movement, color, and fun of our vibrant performing arts neighborhood. The 139 king or queen rooms feature a 42-inch flat-panel television, DVD player, premium cable channels, iPod docking station, refrigerator, and microwave. Most rooms feature a shower only, although a few spa tub rooms are available. On-site amenities include a heated indoor pool, fitness facility, laundry facilities, lobby espresso bar, business center, and meeting facilities for small groups. Garage parking is also offered free—a rare beast in downtown hotels. There is a very nice outdoor seating area and courtyards with climbing vines and nice planters that create an oasis, as well as a privacy screen from the lively urban surroundings. Loaner bicycles are available for guests, another nice touch. Dogs are accepted with a fee of $50.

MAYFLOWER PARK HOTEL $$$
405 Olive Way
(206) 623-8700, (800) 426-5100
www.mayflowerpark.com

The historic Mayflower Park Hotel was originally built in 1927 and is now a lovingly restored, independently owned masterpiece whose period antiques and crystal chandeliers offer a European elegance. The hotel opens directly into Westlake Center, the large shopping district in the heart of downtown, and home to the monorail and light rail stations. The 161 elegant guest rooms include 29 luxury suites, with individually designed artwork, original tile floors in bathrooms, extra-deep tubs, and king or queen beds. The Mayflower also features the award-winning Andaluca Mediterranean restaurant and Oliver's Lounge. A complimentary wine reception is held each Wed, and other amenities include same-day laundry service, a fitness studio, business services, Les Clef d'Or concierge services, and valet parking ($20/day). The Mayflower is a member of Historic Hotels of America and is the longest continuously running hotel in Seattle. Many employees have been there for one or two decades, and three staff members have become official hotel historians.

MEDITERRANEAN INN $$$
425 Queen Anne Ave. North
(206) 428-4700, (866) 525-4700
www.mediterranean-inn.com

The Mediterranean is a new hotel located 1 block west of the Space Needle, at the base of the vibrant Queen Anne neighborhood. It is an all-suite property, featuring studio apartments with kitchenettes that offer nightly, weekly, and monthly rates. The 180 suites are furnished with warm cherrywood furniture, granite countertops, and nice roomy work desks with ergonomic chairs. The majority of the rooms have functional, opening windows, and only a portion are air-conditioned, so if this is important to you, be sure to specify that you want an A/C room. Amenities include an exercise room, business center and meeting rooms, garage parking (inquire about pricing), Starbucks in the lobby, and 24-hour guest laundry facilities.

MOORE HOTEL $
1926 2nd Ave.
(206) 448-4851, (800) 421-5508
www.moorehotel.com
The Moore Hotel is a landmark of downtown Seattle, built in 1907 and located near Belltown, 2 blocks from Pike Place Market. The original architecture includes restored marble, tiles, and decorative molding. The Moore isn't fancy, but it's home to the famous Moore Theater and offers an incredible history, as well as one of the best deals in downtown hotels. The 120 rooms each have a queen bed, private bathroom, cable TV, and a phone. The building is completely nonsmoking and promotes itself as a green hotel—including one major energy-conserving feature of a complete lack of air conditioning. This is rarely a problem in Seattle, but if you are booking for July or Aug, it is something to be aware of.

PAN PACIFIC HOTEL $$$$
2125 Terry Ave.
(206) 654-5010, (877) 324-4856
www.panpacific.com/seattle
The Pan Pacific is a luxury high-rise hotel very convenient to Seattle Center and the shopping and attractions downtown, yet in a slightly more residential neighborhood near South Lake Union. Designed by the Hirsch Bedner firm, this sleek urban oasis

has a modern style throughout, with zebra-wood furnishings and muted hues of taupe, slate, and cream. The 160 well-appointed rooms feature king or queen beds with fine Egyptian bedding, 32-inch plasma televisions with premium cable channels, Internet radio, and oversize tubs. Many rooms have spectacular Space Needle views. The Pan Pacific also features a 24-hour fitness center and exceptional eateries including the Seastar Restaurant and Raw Bar. Half a dozen meeting and event rooms are available, as well as the luxurious Vida Spa. Valet parking is available for a fee. The hotel's location in the 2200 Westlake Center offers a Whole Foods Market and many upscale shops.

PANAMA HOTEL $-$$
605½ S. Main St.
(206) 223-9242
www.panamahotelseattle.com
This boutique hotel is a time capsule of Japanese culture, located in the Japantown section of the historic International District. The hotel is on the third floor walk-up of a 1910 building, which has served throughout the years as home to Japanese immigrants, fishermen, and international travelers. The only remaining, intact Sento (traditional Japanese bathhouse) in the United States is here at the Panama. It is no longer a working bathhouse but has remained preserved just as it was when it closed in 1950, and tours offer a fascinating glimpse into another world. The 50 guest rooms are small, with one or two double beds and personal sinks en suite, but bathrooms are shared among approximately five rooms (separated by men's and women's baths). The hotel offers educational history walking tours and was named the best teahouse in the city by *Seattle* magazine. Free continental breakfast is offered.

PARAMOUNT HOTEL $$$
725 Pine St.
(206) 292-9500, (800) 663-1144
www.paramounthotelseattle.com

Located next to the historic Paramount Theater on the east side of downtown close to I-5, the Paramount is recently renovated and offers a European-style boutique hotel atmosphere. The 146 rooms offer a king or queen bed, premium cable channels, Nintendo gaming system, and MP3 docking station. Some feature city views, and executive rooms also include a soaking tub. Grand Suites offer a separate dining/conference room, sitting area with double-sided fireplace, wet bar, and soaking tub. On-site amenities include a business center, meeting facilities, fitness center, laundry service, concierge service, and valet parking for $27/day. Wi-Fi service is $9.95/day. The Dragonfish Asian Café offers innovative pan-Asian cuisine with an exhibition kitchen, terrific happy hours, and Sushi & Sake Sundays.

RAMADA INN
DOWNTOWN SEATTLE $$
2200 5th Ave.
(206) 441-9785, (800) 272-6232
www.the.ramada.com/00015

The Ramada is located on the northern end of downtown, near the waterfront and the monorail. A recent remodel has upgraded the furnishings and public areas, as well as added a business center. The 120 guest rooms offer a view of either the Space Needle or downtown Seattle, and include queen or king beds. Other amenities include a fitness center, meeting facilities, on-site parking for $12/night, Max's Café, and a 24-hour convenience store.

RED LION HOTEL $$$$
1415 5th Ave.
(206) 971-8000
www.seattleredlionfifthavenue.com

The Red Lion is located along 5th Avenue, in between the office/business district and the waterfront and tourist attractions. It offers one of the largest ballrooms in Seattle, the Emerald Ballroom, making it popular for business travel and events, and recently underwent a renovation. With a new Northwest decor and modern furnishings, the Red Lion's 297 guest rooms (including 10 suites) now feature plush pillowtop beds, refrigerators, 37-inch plasma flat-screen televisions and iPod docking stations. Most rooms enjoy spectacular waterfront, city, or mountain views. Two restaurants, the Terrace Garden and Lounge and the Elephant & Castle Pub, offer distinctly different experiences. The hotel has 15,000 square feet of flexible, high-tech event space. Other on-site amenities include a fully equipped fitness center, business center, same-day dry cleaning, concierge staff, and secure underground parking ($30/night). The Red Lion is also pet-friendly, offering a complimentary goodie bag, pet pillows, and food/water tray. There is a $20 cleaning fee per stay, but even that is waived if you are a member of the Red Lion R&R Club program.

RENAISSANCE HOTEL $$$–$$$$
515 Madison St.
(206) 583-0300, (800) 546-9184
www.marriott.com

This luxury hotel is a member of the Marriott family and bills itself as the body of a full-service hotel with the soul of a boutique inn. The colorful lobby displays works by local artists, and most of the hotel boasts stunning views. The 553 rooms include five spacious suites and come with a king or two double pillowtop beds, premium movie channels, and a minifridge. Amenities include a fitness center, indoor pool, Maxwell's restaurant, Visions Lounge, and a one-of-a-kind event space on the 28th floor. Self-parking is available for $30/day, or valet for $36/day. Other guest services include concierge, babysitting arrangements, shoe-shine stand, valet dry-cleaning service, business center, beauty shop and meeting rooms. Wi-Fi is available in the meeting rooms and public areas, while for $12.95/day, guests receive high-speed Internet and unlimited local or long distance calls from their room. Pets are allowed at the Renaissance, with a $100 nonrefundable fee.

ROOSEVELT HOTEL $$$
1531 7th Ave.
(206) 621-1200, (800) 663-1144
www.roosevelthotel.com

This Seattle landmark was built in 1929 and named after President Theodore Roosevelt, with its distinctive and iconic pink neon rooftop sign still glowing over the city. After going through several incarnations since then and being closed for several years during the 1980s, the Roosevelt reopened in 1989. The hotel is in the live theater district, near the Paramount and ACT, a half-block from the convention center, and surrounded by the city's finest shopping. The 151 rooms are cozy and spacious, featuring a choice of double, queen, or king beds. Whirlpool suites include a two-person jetted tub, and the Roosevelt Suite is the largest room with separate seating area. Wi-Fi is available for $9.95/day. On-site amenities include a fitness room, meeting rooms, and parking for $26/night. The Roosevelt is pet-friendly, accepting two dogs per room up to 50 pounds, for a $50 nonrefundable fee per dog.

SEATTLE PACIFIC HOTEL $$
325 Aurora Ave. North
(206) 441-0400, (888) 451-0400
www.seattlepacifichotel.com

This simple midrange hotel a few blocks from Seattle Center offers 59 newly decorated rooms with a queen or two double beds, microwave, and minifridge. Larger, family-friendly rooms are available with three double beds and a full-size refrigerator; a two-bedroom suite features a kitchenette. California king–bed rooms are also offered poolside. The hotel accepts pets. Additional amenities include free continental breakfast, outdoor pool, Jacuzzi, laundry facilities, on-site parking, and a computer station in the lobby for guest use. Smoking is allowed in 5 percent of the rooms.

SHERATON HOTEL $$$–$$$$
1400 6th Ave.
(206) 621-9000, (800) 325-3535
www.sheraton.com/seattle

This is the largest of Seattle's hotels, with 1,258 rooms. Luxurious Sweet Sleeper king or double beds are in all rooms, as well as a flat-screen television with premium cable channels, video games, ergonomic work space, and original artwork by renowned glass artist Dale Chihuly. Suites are also available on floors 25–33, with separate living and dining area, wet bar, and terrific views. Guests in Sheraton Club rooms are also treated to upgraded amenities and complimentary breakfast and afternoon hors d'oeuvres in the Club Lounge. Additional services include a full-service business center, flexible meeting space, Link@Sheraton with Microsoft computer stations in the lobby, fitness center, indoor lap pool, Jacuzzi, concierge services, gift shop, and on-site floral service. Internet access is available for

$10.95/day (free for Club members). The Daily Grill restaurant and Lobby Lounge offer food and drink; "grab and go" snacks are also available from In Short Order, adjacent to the lobby. The Sheraton is pet-friendly, accepting dogs up to 80 pounds (must be approved in advance) and providing a welcome kit with dog bed and bowls. Valet parking is offered at $40/day, and bike racks are also available.

SILVER CLOUD HOTEL
BROADWAY $$$
1100 Broadway
(206) 325-1400, (800) 590-1801
www.silvercloud.com

The Silver Cloud is located in the eclectic, vibrant Capitol Hill neighborhood. A local area shuttle is also available to take guests downtown and to nearby attractions. The 179 rooms with king or queen beds offer microwaves, refrigerators, and 42-inch plasma televisions with premium cable channels. Some rooms also include wet bars, Jacuzzi tubs, electric fireplaces, and sofa sleepers. Other amenities include an indoor pool, hot tub, fitness center, concierge, gift shop, conference rooms, and business center. Guest laundry facilities are available at no charge, and dry-cleaning services are also offered. The Broadway opened a brand-new restaurant in June 2010 called Jimmy's. Covered secure parking is available for $16/day.

SILVER CLOUD HOTEL STADIUM $$$$
1046 1st Ave. South
(206) 204-9800, (800) 497-1261
www.silvercloud.com

This Silver Cloud is located right across the street from Safeco Field, and adjacent to Qwest Field. Pioneer Square is within walking distance, and free shuttle service is available to the cruise terminals. A local area shuttle is also available to take guests downtown and to nearby attractions. The 211 rooms offer king or queen beds, microwaves, refrigerators, iPod stations, and 42-inch plasma televisions with premium cable channels. Some rooms also include wet bars, Jacuzzi tubs, and sofa sleepers. Other amenities include a seasonal outdoor pool on the rooftop, hot tub, fitness center, concierge, gift shop, conference rooms, and business center. Guest laundry facilities are available at no charge, and dry-cleaning services are also offered. Jimmy's on First is a casual, on-site restaurant and bar. Covered secure valet parking is available for $20/day.

SIXTH AVENUE INN $$
2000 6th Ave.
(206) 518-2677
www.sixthavenueinn.com

Just down the street from the Space Needle, this basic and comfortable hotel offers reasonable rates along with amenities such as a fitness center, valet laundry, meeting facilities, business center, on-site restaurant, and room service. The 167 rooms all include a microwave and refrigerator, premium cable channels, and choice of king, queen, or double beds. Some larger rooms and suites offer full kitchens, dining rooms, and sofa beds. Smoking rooms should be available; inquire for current policies. Guest parking is only $15/night, a steal in downtown Seattle.

SORRENTO HOTEL $$$$
900 Madison St.
(206) 622-6400
www.hotelsorrento.com

Seattle's first and oldest boutique hotel, the Sorrento has been a landmark historic hotel since it opened in 1909, just before the world exposition that year. It has been owned and operated by the Malone family since 1983 and was named one of *Cónde Nast Traveler*'s top 25 hotels. The magnificent Italian mission-style architecture creates a classic setting for the quiet hospitality that envelops guests. The hotel lobby and adjacent Fireside Room feature original mahogany wood panels and Rockwood fireplace, and jazz music or afternoon teas are often found there. The 76 exquisite rooms and suites feature fine Egyptian linens, Italian marble bathrooms, DirectTV with movie channels, and CD stereos. Suites include living areas, dining tables, wet bar, and JVC sound system. The Sorrento offers complimentary town-car service to nearby attractions, and valet parking is also available. Other services include a full-time concierge, same-day laundry, 24-hour Nautilus fitness center, complimentary shoe shine, business center, meeting facilities, and on-site massage therapy and Pilates studio. The hotel is pet-friendly, with select rooms for pet accommodation along with beds, treats, and bowls ($60 fee applies). The hotel even offers pet concierge services for walking, grooming, and day care. The Sorrento offers a host of entertainment, from weekly music to Night School—demonstrations and discussions from leading cultural institutions on topics ranging from books to cocktails. The Hunt Club restaurant offers classic fare from fresh, local ingredients.

W SEATTLE $$$$
1112 4th Ave.
(206) 264-6103, (877) 946-8357
www.whotels.com/seattle
This luxury 26-story urban hotel is a member of the distinctive W Hotels family. Its 415 stylish rooms and nine suites feature a king or two double W signature beds, the W Pillow menu that allows you to order your choice of pillow styles, 32-inch plasma televisions, CD and DVD players, and iPod docks. The WOW suites include designer living rooms, Bose surround-sound systems, Jacuzzi tubs, and loft-style bedrooms. The award-winning Earth & Ocean Restaurant is located at the W, as well as the flirty W Bar, named best hotel bar by *Seattle Weekly*. State-of-the-art fitness center SWEAT, the WIRED business center, and in-room spa services are always available. Wi-Fi is provided at $14.95/day. The W is a pet-friendly hotel, offering pet amenities, beds, litter boxes, and bowls for feline and canine guests, as well as pet-sitting, grooming, and walking services. A $25/day additional charge plus nonrefundable $100 fee applies to pet stays. The signature W "Whatever/Whenever" service goes beyond typical concierge facilities to assist guests with a variety of personal and business needs, including dry cleaning and valet parking.

WARWICK SEATTLE HOTEL $$$
401 Lenora St.
(206) 777-1982, (800) 203-3232
www.warwickwa.com
The Warwick Seattle is elegant and distinctive, in the midst of downtown yet offering European style. The 230 king or double rooms feature floor-to-ceiling glass sliding doors that open onto Juliet balconies with magnificent Space Needle or skyline views, minifridge, and movie and game system. There are also four suites. Fifteen smoking rooms are available on the ninth floor. On-site amenities include an indoor heated swimming pool, sauna, fitness room, business center, valet or self-parking for $27/day, and Wi-Fi for $11/day. The Brasserie Margaux combines Northwest cuisine with a French accent and offers a nightly prix-fixe menu for $18–$22, as well as an adjoining bar with tapas and drinks.

WESTIN SEATTLE $$$$
1900 5th Ave.
(206) 728-1000, (866) 716-8126
www.westinseattle.com

The twin cylindrical towers of the Westin are a downtown Seattle landmark. The Westin is located right next to the convention center and is one of the largest hotels in the city, with 891 rooms and suites that feature panoramic views of Puget Sound, the Space Needle, the Cascade Mountains, and the city skyline. The Westin's signature Heavenly Bed and Heavenly Bath are luxurious amenities; rooms offer a king or two double beds, as well as an assortment of king with sofa bed rooms. All rooms have iPod docking stations. Wi-Fi is available for a fee, as is garage parking. Other amenities include a fitness room, Jacuzzi, indoor pool, 24-hour room service, business center, in-room spa services, and the Coldwater Bar and Grill, as well as a lobby bar and cafe. The Westin Kids Club caters to traveling families, including those with infants, and the hotel accepts small pets. The Westin also offers 22 meeting rooms totaling 39,000 square feet of space, and all corporate amenities.

North Seattle

COMFORT INN & SUITES $$
13700 Aurora Ave. North
(206) 361-3700, (877) 424-6423
www.comfortinn.com/
  hotel-seattle-washington-WA217

Basic hotel located less than 5 miles from the University of Washington, Shoreline Community College, and Northgate Mall. Rooms come with king, queen, or double beds and premium cable channels; some rooms include a sofa or sofa bed, microwave, and refrigerator. Amenities include a fitness center, indoor hot tub, sauna, laundry facilities, and free deluxe continental breakfast. Small extra touches include things such as a popcorn machine, computer station for guests, and DVD rentals. Comfort Inn is a pet-friendly hotel and will accept up to two pets of 35 pounds or less, for a $15/night fee. Smoking rooms are also available, and there is on-site indoor parking.

DAYS INN SEATTLE MIDTOWN $
9100 Aurora Ave. North
(206) 524-3600, (800) 445-9297
www.daysinnseattle.com

Located just north of Green Lake, this Days Inn is near the University District and has fairly easy access to downtown via I-5. All guest rooms are equipped with one or two queen beds, a refrigerator, and microwave. Smoking rooms are available. Free parking and continental breakfast are included, and Thurs through Sat afternoon they offer fresh-baked cookies in the lobby.

ECONO LODGE NORTH $
14817 Aurora Ave. North
(206) 367-7880, (877) 424-6423
www.econolodge.com/
  hotel-seattle-washington-WA162

Located in far North Seattle close to the community of Shoreline, this clean and basic hotel offers 52 guest rooms with refrigerators and king, queen, or double beds. Some rooms also come with microwaves, coffeemakers, and whirlpool bathtubs. Smoking rooms are available. On-site amenities include use of business services, laundry facilities, free outdoor parking and free continental breakfast.

EXTENDED STAY AMERICA—SEATTLE
  NORTHGATE $
13300 Stone Ave. North
(206) 365-8100, (800) 804-3724
www.hotels.extendedstayamerica.com

This all-suite hotel offers rooms with queen, king, or two double beds. All rooms have fully equipped kitchens with cooking and eating utensils, refrigerator, microwave, and stovetop. They also feature plenty of work space with a computer dataport, personalized voice mail, and Wi-Fi for a onetime $4.99 fee per stay. Smoking and non-smoking rooms available. Pets are accepted with a $25 nonrefundable daily fee. It should be noted that because these are geared toward longer-term apartment stays, daily housekeeping is not included. Full cleaning and partial "refresher" services are available at a paid rate.

HOTEL DECA $$$–$$$$
4507 Brooklyn Ave. NE
(206) 634-2000, (800) 899-0251
www.hoteldeca.com

Originally opened in 1931, Hotel Deca remains a groovy art deco boutique hotel that is a vibrant oasis in the University District. The 158 stylish rooms and suites continue the Gilded Age, 1930s heritage, with a $2 million renovation in 2007 providing a fresh, modern spin. Each room has new furnishings, either a king or two queen beds, microwave, refrigerator, premium television channels, DVD player, and iPod docking stations. The penthouse suites have won awards for their design, and the specialty suites include gas fireplaces and expansive outdoor decks. The lobby features a recessed wine bar, and the Grand Ballroom is incredible, with a coffered ceiling and hand-blown glass chandeliers. The District Lounge on the first level is an intimate neighborhood restaurant, with a globally inspired menu and live jazz performances Wed through Sat. Meeting and event spaces are available, and exercise facilities are on-site.

HOTEL NEXUS $$$
2140 N. Northgate Way
(206) 365-0700, (800) 435-0750
www.hotelnexusseattle.com

This fun retro, yet completely modern hotel is located in the lively University District. The 169 stylish rooms include 12 two-room apartment suites and six spa studios with amazing in-room Japanese hydrotherapy soaking tubs. Every room includes a refrigerator and microwave, HBO and Nintendo on the television systems, and colorful artwork of Seattle images. Suites also come with a second television and DVD player. The hotel offers complimentary shuttle services, an outdoor pool with spa, business center, meeting rooms, and the Saffron Bar and Grill, which features unique Indian and Mediterranean cuisine. A complimentary hot breakfast is also served each morning. Parking for guests is free of charge, and Hotel Nexus welcomes pets with an additional fee. The Hotel Nexus is also a Certified Green Hotel.

MARCO POLO MOTEL $
4114 Aurora Ave. North
(206) 633-4090
www.marcopolomotel.net

This basic budget motel is five minutes north of downtown, with easy access to UW. It is a clean, bright facility with well-lit parking that is free for guests. The Marco Polo has a reputation as the only reputable place to stay within a couple-mile radius and is a great low-cost option to more expensive locations. The 37 guest rooms include one or two queen beds, premium cable television, refrigerators, and microwaves. Suites are available with one queen bed and separate living room, and a few rooms have three twin beds or a queen and two twins. Two rooms are available for smoking guests. The motel is not officially wheelchair accessible, but they have made modifications and will attempt to accommodate all guests; please inquire about any special needs. On-site amenities include a guest computer in the lobby (Wi-Fi throughout), coin-operated laundry facilities, and complimentary muffins in the morning. One unique, infamous claim to fame of the Marco Polo is being one of the last places that Kurt Cobain stayed during his short but eventful life.

SILVER CLOUD INN $$$
5036 25th Ave. NE
(206) 526-5200, (800) 205-6940
www.silvercloud.com

Located 1 mile from the UW campus and 2 blocks from the large, upscale University Village shopping center, the Silver Cloud's 179 rooms offer king or queen beds, microwaves, refrigerators, and 42-inch plasma televisions with premium cable channels. Some rooms also include wet bars and sofa sleepers. Other amenities include an indoor pool, hot tub, newly expanded fitness and business centers, concierge services, and conference rooms. Guest laundry facilities are available at no charge, and dry-cleaning services are also offered. Complimentary daily breakfast is available for guests, as well as a wine and cheese reception every Tues evening. On-site parking is free, and shuttles are available for the local area.

TRAVELODGE SEATTLE
UNIVERSITY $–$$
4725 25th Ave. NE
(206) 525-4612, (800) 578-7878
www.travelodgeseattleuniversity.com

This cross between a hotel and apartment building offers daily and long-term rates, and is perfect for students or their visiting parents

with a location 2 blocks from the University of Washington. The 151 units include rooms with double, queen, or king beds, and one- and two-bedroom apartment-style units. The apartments offer full kitchens with utensils, separate dining and living areas, extra closet space and balconies. On-site amenities include free continental breakfast, outdoor swimming pool (open May through Sept), and year-round Jacuzzi. On-site parking is available and free.

UNIVERSITY INN $$–$$$
4140 Roosevelt Way NE
(206) 632-5055, (800) 733-3855
www.universityinnseattle.com

This small neighborhood hotel is moderately priced and located 4 blocks from the University of Washington. Local artists are showcased in the lobby. The 102 family-friendly, comfortable rooms have king or queen beds. Premier and deluxe rooms feature a microwave and refrigerator; premier rooms also come with a sleeper sofa and a game table/chairs. There are a limited number of dog-friendly rooms that will accommodate a maximum of two dogs up to 75 pounds each, for a $20/night additional fee. Hotel amenities include complimentary breakfast and afternoon snacks, computer station in the lobby for guest use, free parking and shuttle services to nearby locations, free laundry facilities, access to the exercise room at Watertown Hotel 1 block away, and a seasonal outdoor pool.

UNIVERSITY MOTEL SUITES $–$$
4731 12th Ave. NE
(206) 522-4724, (800) 522-4720
www.university-hotel.com

This small, simple student-oriented hotel's slogan is a suite for the price of a room. Each of the 21 suites is 650 square feet and offers a separate living room, dining area, lots of closet space, cable with HBO, and complete kitchen facilities. Rooms come with a choice of one- to three-bed configurations. Laundry facilities and a free underground parking garage are on-site. The location is in a quiet neighborhood 5 blocks from UW, near the I-5 freeway.

WATERTOWN HOTEL $$$
4242 Roosevelt Way NE
(206) 826-4242, (866) 944-4242
www.watertownseattle.com

This unique urban hotel with a nautical theme is 4 blocks from UW, with family-friendly accommodations as well as romantic spa suites and business-oriented facilities. The 100 rooms and 20 studio suites offer king or queen beds, premium cable channels, microwave, and refrigerator; the spa suites also include a Jacuzzi tub. Hotel amenities include complimentary hot breakfast, free laundry facilities, free secure underground parking and shuttle services, a fitness center, as well as a business center and small-group meeting spaces. There is a very nice courtyard that is delightful on nice days, a general store, and a computer station in the lobby for guest use. The complimentary loaner bicycles are a very nice touch.

South Seattle

BEST WESTERN AIRPORT EXECUTEL $$
20717 International Blvd.
(206) 878-3300, (800) 648-3311
www.apexecutel.com

With extremely convenient access to Sea-Tac Airport, this Best Western with 140 rooms is a good choice for comfort and nice amenities less than 2 miles from the airport. Complimentary airport shuttle and Park-and-Fly

packages add to the convenience; on-site parking is free during your stay. Amenities include 70 free cable channels, indoor swimming pool, hot tub, fitness center, and daily complimentary breakfast. The hotel is also very business-friendly, with a business center and meeting spaces that will accommodate up to 60 people.

CEDARBROOK LODGE $$$
18525 36th Ave. South
(206) 901-9268, (877) 515-2176
www.cedarbrooklodge.com

This distinctive retreat in South Seattle is less than five minutes from Sea-Tac Airport and offers complimentary shuttle service. The lodge's location on 18 quiet, wooded acres allows guests to enjoy the Pacific Northwest beauty yet be only minutes from the city center. Contemporary event spaces and original works of art are found throughout Cedarbook. The Copperleaf Restaurant offers fresh farm-to-table regional cuisine from local farmers, and the great room of the lodge has a fabulous indoor fireplace. A fully equipped fitness center and billiards room are available for all guests, and the 110 rooms and one- or two-bedroom suites offer queen beds with luxurious linens, oversize soaking tubs, and gorgeous views through expansive windows.

CLARION HOTEL
SEA-TAC AIRPORT $$
3000 S. 176th St.
(206) 242-0200, (800) CLARION
www.clarionseattle.com

The Clarion is a full-service hotel located right at the airport, with free 24-hour shuttle service. On-site amenities include an indoor heated pool and Jacuzzi, restaurant and lounge, exercise room, and laundry rooms.

Each of the 214 rooms comes with cable television including HBO, wired and wireless Internet access, and work space; premium rooms have microwaves and refrigerators. Meeting rooms are also available for groups of 5 to 180, and the Triple 777 Restaurant and Lounge provide nice places to dine and relax.

DAYS INN SEA-TAC AIRPORT $-$$
19015 International Blvd. South
(206) 244-3600, (800) 329-7466
www.daysinn.com/hotel/04855
This basic but comfortable hotel is only 3 blocks south of the airport, with complimentary 24-hour shuttle service. Other amenities include free continental breakfast, business center, fitness center, and private Jacuzzi rooms. There are 86 total rooms, including family rooms with two queen beds and kitchenette. Smoking rooms are available.

DOUBLETREE GUEST SUITES
SEATTLE AIRPORT
SOUTHCENTER $$-$$$
16500 Southcenter Pkwy.
(206) 575-8220, (800) 222-TREE
www.seattle.doubletree.com
Located 3 miles from Sea-Tac Airport, this renovated, all-suite Doubletree Hotel offers 219 two-room suites with large work desks, televisions in both rooms, and sofa sleepers. Complimentary airport shuttles and free parking are available. This hotel caters to business travelers, offering a state-of-the-art conference center, 11,000 square feet of meeting and ballroom space, accommodations for up to 600 people for events, and a well-equipped business center. For relaxation and enjoyment, take advantage of the indoor pool and whirlpool, exercise room, and racquetball court, and dine in the NW

Landing Restaurant, serving regional favorites. Smoking rooms and suites are available.

DOUBLETREE HOTEL
SEATTLE AIRPORT $$-$$$
18740 International Blvd.
(206) 246-8600, (800) 222-TREE
www.seattleairport.doubletree.com
Another Doubletree Hotel near the airport, this one offers more standard hotel rooms in comparison with the Doubletree Guest Suites and is situated in a resortlike setting. The 850 rooms feature the Sweet Dreams plush-top beds that come with five jumbo hypoallergenic pillows (your choice of king or queen), complimentary HBO and other premium cable channels, nice work desks, and remote printing services. Suites with separate living areas are available. It is also geared toward business travelers, with 34,000 square feet of flexible meeting space. The outdoor pool and whirlpool are both heated year-round and the renovated fitness room features top equipment. A unique amenity is the Golf Club, a state-of-the-art simulator where you can play more than 50 of the world's top courses in a realistic environment. This hotel also offers a free shuttle to the airport, as well as the nearby Southcenter Mall. Parking here is available at $16/day, or $20 for valet parking. Pets are also allowed, up to 75 pounds with a $50 nonrefundable fee. Some smoking rooms are available.

EMBASSY SUITES SEATTLE-TACOMA
INTERNATIONAL AIRPORT $$$
15920 West Valley Hwy.
(425) 227-8844, (800) EMBASSY
www.seattletacoma.embassysuites.com
The 238 spacious two-room suites here offer a king or two double beds and come with refrigerators and microwaves in each

suite, as well as a sleeper sofa, two televisions, activity table, and MP3 port. The hotel offers complimentary breakfast and evening reception every day, as well as airport and local transportation. On-site amenities include an indoor pool, whirlpool, fitness center, business center, and restaurant. Parking is available for $8/day, and pets up to 75 pounds are allowed, with a $75 nonrefundable fee. Smoking rooms are available.

FAIRFIELD INN BY MARRIOTT
SEATTLE SEA-TAC AIRPORT $$
19631 International Blvd.
(206) 592-8542
www.marriott/seata

This hotel is 1 mile south of the airport, with complimentary shuttle service. Other amenities include a complimentary continental breakfast, indoor pool and whirlpool, exercise room, and free on-site parking. The 146 guest rooms all come with microwave and minifridge.

GEORGETOWN INN $
6100 Corson Ave. South
(206) 762-2233
www.georgetowninnseattle.com

The Georgetown Inn is very much a throwback to the old roadside motels of the mid-twentieth century. Since remodeling and opening its doors in 1988, the inn has been a favorite for budget travelers. It is clean and dependable, but it is a budget accommodation, and expectations should be along those lines. Some travelers and reviewers seem to feel that it is overpriced for such facilities, but it is often a temporary home base for extended-stay guests. The location provides about a 5- to 10-minute drive to either downtown or the airport, and on-site parking is free. The 52 rooms offer

refrigerators, queen or king beds, and free breakfast. Some units also include Jacuzzi tubs and kitchenettes. Amenities include a fitness center, sauna, and free laundry facility.

HAMPTON INN SEATTLE AIRPORT $$
19445 International Blvd.
(206) 878-1700, (800) HAMPTON
www.hampton-inn.com

Located 8 blocks from the airport, the Hampton Inn offers 131 rooms with a king or two double beds, refrigerators, and microwaves. On-site parking is free, as is breakfast—the hotel will even provide a Hampton's On the Run breakfast bag to go if you're pressed for time. Meeting rooms and valet laundry services are available for a nominal fee, and the property has a pool and fitness room. Some smoking rooms are available.

HILTON SEATTLE AIRPORT &
CONFERENCE CENTER $$–$$$
17620 International Blvd.
(206) 433-4800, (800) HILTONS
www.seattleairport.hilton.com

This Hilton location was rated one of the chain's top-performing hotels for delivering outstanding customer service. One of the best-located airport hotels, it is right across from Sea-Tac yet is not a typical airport hotel, offering a notch above the usual decor, service, and amenities to be a bit more luxurious than most. The 396 guest rooms and suites offer complimentary HBO and other premium channels, video games, remote printing, featherbed with down comforter and pillows, and spacious work area. Amenities include an outdoor pool, whirlpool, renovated fitness room, business center, laundry service, and 40,000 square feet of meeting space. Spencer's for Steaks and Chops is the on-site restaurant that serves breakfast, lunch, and dinner. Complimentary shuttle service to the airport is offered 24 hours, and to the Link light rail station upon request. Valet parking is available for $26/night, and self-parking for $20. Pets up to 75 pounds are allowed, with a $50 nonrefundable fee. This hotel also embraces the LGBT community, offering a portal site specifically for gay travelers to the area.

HOLIDAY INN EXPRESS HOTEL & SUITES SEATTLE AIRPORT $$–$$$
19621 International Blvd.
(206) 824-3200, (877) 865-6578
www.hiexpress.com/seattleairport
The 171 rooms and suites at this airport hotel all offer microwaves and refrigerators, and come with a king or two double beds. The suites also have full kitchens. A complimentary hot breakfast is provided for all guests. Free airport shuttle and on-site parking are also available, and there is a fitness center and business services including two meeting rooms. Pets are allowed with a $125 deposit ($50 is nonrefundable). This hotel does provide a few smoking rooms.

SEATTLE AIRPORT MARRIOTT $$–$$$
3201 S. 176th St.
(206) 241-2000, (800) 314-0925
www.seattleairportmarriott.com
The Marriott offers a larger, more upscale alternative to the plethora of generic hotels clustered around Sea-Tac Airport. The lobby features a dramatic two-story wood-beamed atrium and welcoming stone fireplace. The 459 newly renovated guest rooms offer luxurious bedding in king or two double bed arrangements, and five suites are available. On-site amenities include a pretty indoor atrium pool, 24-hour fitness center, meeting

rooms, and laundry service. Internet access is available for $12.95/day. The Aquaterra Restaurant is located inside the Marriott, and there is also a lounge in the atrium and a coffee bar offering Starbucks. Parking is available for $18/day, or valet parking for $22.

SLEEP INN SEA-TAC AIRPORT $
20406 International Blvd.
(206) 878-3600, (877) 424-6423
www.choicehotels.com/ires/hotel/wa090
Located less than 2 miles from the airport, this hotel provides free airport transportation 24 hours a day. The 105 guest rooms with king, queen, or double beds include refrigerators, microwaves, and HBO. Smoking rooms are available. Some also have sofa beds. An IHOP restaurant is located on the premises, and free continental breakfast is available daily. Other on-site amenities include an exercise room, laundry facilities, meeting rooms, and access to business services. Free parking is offered to guests during their stay.

i For a selection of green hotels in Seattle, check out www.istay green.org, which lists accommodations that implement environmentally sustainable business practices, along with user ratings and reviews.

BED-AND-BREAKFAST INNS

All bed-and-breakfast accommodations include free on-site parking and Wi-Fi unless otherwise noted. Guest rooms or common areas may not be wheelchair accessible, so unless otherwise noted please check with each property. They are also all nonsmoking facilities. The included breakfast varies greatly between simple continental and full, hot, sit-down meal—the type of breakfast is mentioned for each inn. Bed-and-breakfasts also often have two-night minimum stays and less flexible cancellation policies; be sure to check with each innkeeper. Lastly, many B&Bs do not accept children, or children under a certain age.

Downtown/Central

BACON MANSION $$$
959 Broadway East
(206) 329-1864, (800) 240-1864
www.baconmansion.com

Located within two blocks of the main Broadway shopping and entertainment district of Capitol Hill, the Bacon Mansion is one of Seattle's historic mansions. The classic Edwardian-style Tudor was built in 1909 and retains the original Bacon family crest, as well as an original chandelier with 3,000 crystals, marble fireplaces, glass pocket doors, woodwork, and a treasured library. Eight thousand square feet of living space is spread across four levels, and the outside patio leads to the Carriage House Suite, one of the 11 guest rooms on offer. The Carriage House has a queen bed, sleeper sofa, dining area, refrigerator, microwave, and private bath. Above is the Carriage Loft, a beautiful queen room with private bath. The other rooms are a mix of cozy hideaways and suites, and all have queen beds and cable television. Most include a private bath although a few rooms have shared bathrooms. Spacious common areas and patio are available for guests, and an expanded continental breakfast buffet is included. Dogs are accepted in the Carriage House rooms and the Emerald Room. One guest room is wheelchair accessible.

BED & BREAKFAST ON
BROADWAY $$$
722 Broadway East
(206) 329-8933
www.bbonbroadway.com

This B&B offers four comfortable, spacious rooms in a residential neighborhood, all with a private bath. The cozy Capitol Hill inn is noted for the owners' delightful collection of fine art and antiques, which fill the beautiful home. Music enthusiasts will appreciate the Steinway grand piano, which they may play. Guests may take the complimentary continental breakfast in the dining room or garden deck.

BED & BREAKFAST ON
CAPITOL HILL $–$$
739 Broadway East
(206) 325-5300
www.bbcapitolhill.com

This inn is located in the Harvard-Belmont Historical District in the Capitol Hill neighborhood. Built in 1903, it is a comfortable, midsize home that is characteristic of turn-of-the-twentieth-century Seattle architecture. The atmosphere is quiet and friendly, and each of the three guest rooms features a double bed with down comforters and pillows, and cable television. The Rose Room has a sitting area and private bath, while the Hawthorne and Laurel Rooms share a bath. A continental breakfast is included each day between 6 and 10:30 a.m. A house dog, Madeleine, and cat, Grace, are in residence. The B&B is not wheelchair accessible.

CORNER HOUSE $
102 18th Ave. East
(206) 323-6039
www.thecornerhousebandb.com

This small inn on Capitol Hill offers quiet comfort and very reasonable rates. The two queen guest rooms have a warm, simple decor. The East Room offers a private bathroom en suite, while the West Room has a private bathroom that is located across the hall. There are no televisions or phones in the rooms, although Wi-Fi is provided. The hosts live on-site and treat visitors like personal guests; you are welcome to use the fridge or microwave. There is also a resident cat named Spot, who is not allowed in the guest rooms. Generous breakfasts are included, and the garden is nice. The Corner House is not wheelchair accessible.

11TH AVENUE INN $$
121 11th Ave. East
(206) 720-7161
www.11thavenueinn.com

This charming yellow 1906 house on a tree-lined street in Capitol Hill is an eight-room inn in a quiet residential area. The rooms are comfortable and lovely, with queen beds and TV with cable and DVD. Four of the rooms also have a second, twin-size daybed. There are no phones in the rooms, although a phone is available for guests, as well as a computer. Most have private baths, although two rooms share a bath. Walking the neighborhood is a great way to spend some time, as surrounding streets abound with incredible mansions. The 10-acre Cal Anderson Park is a half-block away, and a 10-minute walk gets you to the 45-acre Volunteer Park and Asian Art Museum. Rates include full sit-down breakfast and parking. The 11th Avenue Inn does not have any wheelchair accessible accommodations.

FOXGLOVE GUESTHOUSE $$
117 18th Ave. East
(206) 328-4173
www.foxgloveguesthouse.com

Foxglove offers an intimate bed-and-breakfast inn, located in a lovingly restored 1905 "Seattle Box." This term refers to authentic arts and crafts homes of the period.

Foxglove is filled with furniture from the era, American art pottery, and Northwest Native American art. Located on a residential street within walking distance of Volunteer Park and local shops and restaurants, the inn offers three guest rooms with double or queen beds, private bathrooms, refrigerators, cable television, and telephone with voice mail. The living room is very cozy, with a fireplace and wood-beam ceilings. Foxglove also has beautiful gardens, and a continental breakfast is included.

GASLIGHT INN $$
1727 15th Ave.
(206) 325-3654
www.gaslight-inn.com

This very small, eclectic, old-fashioned inn is a great find in the Capitol Hill neighborhood, in a gorgeous arts and crafts–style house. The eight guest rooms feature unique touches such as peeled-log furniture, Navajo fabrics, antique carved beds, and gas fireplaces. Most rooms come with a private bath, but two share a bath. Each room has a double or queen-size bed, refrigerator, and television, but no telephone. Some also have decks or fireplaces. The large common room is rich with oak wainscoting and high ceilings, and custom paint finishes decorate the walls gorgeously throughout the inn. One of the treasures of the Gaslight is the exquisite artwork collection that fills it, including paintings, sculpture, glass art, and antique Native American artifacts. The heated pool is a rarity among B&Bs, and the Gaslight also boasts a charming backyard. Continental breakfast is included, and laundry facilities are available.

HALCYON SUITE DU JOUR $$
1125 9th Ave. West
(206) 282-7841

Offering only one accommodation, a charming European-style suite, the Halcyon Suite is located in the Queen Anne district just up the hill from downtown Seattle. Unlike most B&Bs, this is a casual, Northwest contemporary style. The guest room enjoys a private entrance via a covered balcony, surrounded by lush landscaping. A queen bed with down duvet, sea grass carpeting and slate floors, flat-panel satellite television, DSL Internet service, DVD, refrigerator, microwave, and private phone line provide all the amenities and comforts. The covered balcony also has a bistro table and chairs for enjoyable mornings or evenings over the Elliott Bay view. Continental breakfast is included.

INN OF TWIN GABLES $$$
3258 14th Ave. West
(206) 284-3979, (866) INN-3979
www.innoftwingables.com
Situated in the historic, highly desirable Queen Anne neighborhood just north of downtown, this classic Craftsman house features original woodwork, box-beamed ceilings, fir floors, and period antique furnishings. A sunny, enclosed front porch filled with plants makes a nice sitting area. Three comfortable upstairs guest rooms all include private baths, ceiling fans, and king, queen, or twin beds. Two of the rooms can also connect to become a suite. Downstairs is the Garden Suite, a two-bedroom apartment offering a queen bedroom and full bedroom that sleep up to four guests, and includes a separate living/dining area and fully equipped kitchen. The Garden Suite has a separate entrance and side patio, and is also available on a weekly or monthly basis. Children of all ages as well as pets are accepted in the Garden Suite, which is also semi-wheelchair accessible, with just

a couple of steps and an accessible tub/shower. A substantial gourmet breakfast is served each morning, incorporating fresh herbs from the garden, and special requests can be made. A courtesy phone and mini-fridge are available for guest use, and your hosts offer Seattle Super Saver coupons as well as other discounts to local attractions.

MILDRED'S BED & BREAKFAST $$
1202 15th Ave. East
(206) 325-6072, (800) 327-9692
www.mildredsbnb.com
Mildred's is situated in a large, double-turreted 1890 Victorian home, maintained in original style with beautiful natural wood in the entry. Red carpets, a grand piano, and a fireplace welcome you into the common area, where homemade cookies, coffee and tea, and a reading library can be found at all times. The wraparound front porch is charming. Four guest rooms all feature queen beds, private baths, televisions with VCR, writing desks, and comfortable seating. A full breakfast is served daily, and the host will deliver coffee and juice to your room a half-hour before breakfast. Volunteer Park is across the street, and Mildred's yard has a small putting green for guest enjoyment.

MUSICAL HOUSE ON HARVARD $$
2612 Harvard Ave. East
(206) 650-7622
www.musicalhousebandb.com
Located with Capitol Hill's Roanoke Park Historic District, the Musical House is a 1909 Spanish mission-style home. The four large guest rooms include down comforters and pillows, televisions with cable, and DVD players. They also feature a lot of natural light with seven windows each, and long window seats. There are two queen rooms, one

king, and one room with two twin beds. Three rooms have private baths, and the remaining two share a bath. The grand living room has a fireplace and inlaid wood floors, and original windows are found throughout the house with their artistic beveled-crystal, tulip leaded-glass design. An expansive front porch with swing, or the back porch with Adirondack chairs, makes a nice spot for relaxing. One off-street parking space per room with 24/7 video security is provided. A computer station is available for guest use, although Wi-Fi is operated throughout the house. A nice, fresh breakfast is included, and full board with all meals can be arranged in true European style. No wheelchair accessibility. Musical House accepts pets and will even provide them breakfast as well! If you forgot yours, the hosts will offer you their loaner cat or dog to pet at no extra charge.

PACIFIC RESERVATION SERVICE $–$$$$
(206) 439-7677, (800) 684-2932
www.seattlebedandbreakfast.com

This rental management company features more than 225 lodging establishments in the Pacific Northwest, including more than 90 in Seattle. Properties include everything from single rooms to condominiums and entire houses, which can be rented on a daily, weekly, or monthly basis. Visit the Web site to browse listings and inquire about specific rental units.

PENSIONE NICHOLS $$–$$$
1923 1st Ave.
(206) 441-7125
www.pensionenichols.com

This is the only B&B in downtown Seattle, with a delightful location right in Pike Place Market. The 10-room European-style inn is celebrating its 20th year, and it has been awarded best B&B by Seattle Citysearch and AAA's *Via Magazine*. It was also named a "Place of a Lifetime" by *National Geographic Traveler*. Pensione Nichols is situated on the second and third floors of a century-old building in the historic Smith Block, and features eclectic antiques from England throughout. Guests enjoy stunning water and mountain vistas, and several rooms have great city views. Accommodations consist of 10 cozy guest rooms that share four bathrooms, as well as two spacious 900-square-foot suites, each with a private bath and full kitchen. There are also inviting common rooms for reading or entertaining. Continental breakfast is included, and parking options include several secured parking garages that are very nearby (though not cheap). Pets are accepted with a onetime $15 fee; in fact, the Pensione's own "official greeter," a King Charles spaniel named Theo, may wag a hello as you arrive.

SALISBURY HOUSE $$$
750 16th Ave. East
(206) 328-8682
www.salisburyhouse.com

This stately 1904 house near Volunteer Park in Capitol Hill is on a quiet residential street and exudes warmth and charm. Once the home of prominent Seattle families, the house was carefully restored to maintain the historical integrity. Five guest rooms each have a private bath. Four rooms are each situated on a corner of the second floor, sharing a wonderful sunporch filled with plants, wicker furniture, a refrigerator, and coffee and tea. The spacious 640-square-foot Salisbury Suite is on the ground floor. Each room features a queen bed with down comforter and crisp white linens, and telephone with voice mail. Some have showers and others have tubs. Only the suite has a television, and also has a king bed, sleeper sofa, whirlpool bath, refrigerator, and coffeemaker. Common areas include a well-stocked library with cozy fireplace and sunny dining room. A guest computer is also available (Wi-Fi provided throughout the inn). A full breakfast is included and can be made to go by guest request. The Salisbury House has been featured in many travel publications including *Fodor's*, *Frommer's*, and *National Geographic Traveler*.

SEATTLE GUEST HOME $$
1808 E. Denny Way
(206) 412-7378
www.seattleguesthome.com

Ten blocks from downtown Seattle, this inn provides a quiet oasis in Capitol Hill. The 10 guest rooms include twin, double, or queen beds, desk with chair, cable television, and iPod docking station. Only one room offers a private bath; the rest are shared-bath arrangements. Common areas include balconies and sitting areas. Guests are also welcome to use the gourmet kitchen, computer (Wi-Fi is included), bicycles, and laundry facilities. The local All Star Fitness can be used for $12 per visit. Nightly, weekly, and monthly rates are available. One-night reservations are usually accepted for an additional $10 to the rate, and pet-friendly rooms are available.

SEATTLE HILL HOUSE $$
1113 E. John St.
(206) 323-4455, (866) 417-4455
www.seattlehillhouse.com

This unique setting offers twin houses that sit side by side in Seattle's Capitol Hill neighborhood. The homes were built by two brothers in 1903 and are filled with antiques,

beveled windows, hardwood floors, and a mix of Asian and traditional artwork. The welcoming atmosphere offers walks down tree-lined streets or to nearby Volunteer Park. There are eight guest rooms total in the two buildings, offering an assortment of king, queen, or full-size beds. Six rooms have private baths, and the two economy rooms share a bath. Various rooms feature amenities such as sitting rooms, sleeper sofa, private decks, flat-screen televisions, and refrigerators. A large gourmet breakfast is included each morning from the inn's five-star chef, with delectable dishes such as eggs Benedict and bread pudding; they are happy to accommodate special requests. There is a guest computer station for use, although Wi-Fi is provided throughout the properties. Common areas include the dining room, front rooms, and a large back porch overlooking a small garden.

SHAFER BAILLIE MANSION $$$
907 14th Ave. East
(206) 322-4654, (800) 985-4654
www.sbmansion.com

This Capitol Hill mansion is a magnificent 14,000-square-foot Tudor revival home, filled with the history and atmosphere of a bygone era. This is the largest of the majestic homes on 14th Avenue, known as Seattle's "Millionaires' Row." The opulent entry hall and staircase feature ornately carved woodwork; the library, airy sunroom, and grand salon with baby grand piano are equally exquisite. A less formal arts and crafts–style hall on the lower level is great for congregating or relaxing. Eight guest rooms and suites all feature private baths, king or queen beds with pillowtop mattresses and luxury linens, rich oriental rugs, 32- to 50-inch flat-panel televisions with cable, DVD/CD players, and telephones with voice mail. Some rooms also have sofa sleepers or trundle beds, or unique amenities such as a 450-jet horizontal-arm shower, original bathtubs, and leaded casement or stained-glass windows in what used to be ballrooms. A guest microwave and refrigerator are available, as well as a computer and printer for guest use (though wired and Wi-Fi are available throughout the property). Weddings are quite popular here, and the house can be rented for a variety of events. From the Shafer Baillie Mansion you can walk to Volunteer Park a block away, as well as the restaurants and shops on Broadway. The expanded continental breakfast is quite nice and is served over extended hours to accommodate both business and leisure travelers. There is no wheelchair accessibility.

WALL STREET INN $$–$$$
2507 1st Ave.
(206) 448-0125, (800) 624-1117
www.autopenhosting.org/wallstreetinn

This comfortable inn is in Belltown, a terrific location in the heart of the entertainment district and happening heart of downtown. It offers the comforts of a bed-and-breakfast, with the amenities of a larger hotel. The historic building was originally the Sailors of the Pacific Union, where traveling marines lodged between voyages. The owners carefully renovated the site, adding plush amenities and an outdoor patio. Rooms include private baths, cable television, and state-of-the-art telephone systems. Five rooms also have fully equipped kitchenettes. Continental breakfast is included, and the comfortable lobby living room with fireplace makes for a great place to relax. There is also an outdoor terrace with adjoining lounge.

North Seattle

ADMIRAL ARMS $$$
4761 21st Ave. NE
(206) 528-7800
www.admiralbedandbreakfast.com

This restored Victorian home is located a three-minute walk from UW, with beautiful English rose gardens and a peaceful old-world charm. The five tastefully decorated guest rooms with queen beds all have private bathrooms and sitting areas. For more space or larger parties, request the three-room suite, offering two separate bedrooms and a common area. Off-street parking is available, and hot breakfast is included. The relaxing front porch lets you take in the garden, and many park trails are available nearby.

CHAMBERED NAUTILUS
BED & BREAKFAST INN $$$
5005 22nd Ave. NE
(206) 522-2536, (800) 545-8459
www.chamberednautilus.com

Perched on a peaceful hill in the University District, this elegant inn offers a quiet urban oasis within walking distance of the University of Washington. While the 1915 Georgian colonial home is very charming, it is also equipped for the business traveler and features modern amenities. The 10 guest rooms include 6 in the main house and 4 University Suites just across the garden. All rooms have private baths, telephones, flat-screen televisions, CD players, iPod docking stations, and well-stocked bookshelves. The suites offer more space and full kitchen facilities, and are perfect for families or longer-term travelers. The one- and two-bedroom suites are also pet-friendly, with a $20/night additional fee that comes with a Pampered Pooch Basket. Many rooms feature antiques, fireplaces, and private porches. The grounds are beautiful, with exquisite gardens; Ravenna Park is accessible at the end of the street. The Chambered Nautilus also offers a fully equipped business center, and the gourmet breakfasts are absolutely amazing.

CHELSEA STATION INN $$$
4915 Linden Ave. North
(206) 547-6077
www.chelseastationinn.com

Situated at the south entrance to the Woodland Park Zoo and a short walk to Green Lake, the romantic Chelsea Station offers four large, elegant suite accommodations that are more like luxury apartments. Each 900-square-foot suite features a spacious living room, dining room, kitchenette, sumptuous queen master suite with bathroom, and separate powder room. These are grand quarters for someone who wants space and privacy, and they can accommodate up to four guests. Each suite is surprising in its size and elegance; the living room sofas are queen-size sleepers, and the master baths feature double showers. Other amenities include flat-screen televisions with cable, microwave, refrigerator stocked with snacks, iPod docking station, and telephone. A full, hot breakfast is delivered to your room each morning. There is also a lovely patio with a chiminea fireplace, plants, seating areas, and a hot tub. The Chelsea Station is not wheelchair accessible.

COLLEGE INN GUEST HOUSE $
4000 University Way NE
(206) 633-4441
www.collegeinnseattle.com

College Inn, just across the street from UW, provides old-fashioned, European-style accommodations in a historic complex that offers many amenities and extremely reasonable rates. The building opened in 1909 for the Alaska-Yukon Exposition, and the historic landmark continues to offer old-world charm and hospitality. On the first floor you will find the Banana Leaf Café, the College Inn Pub, Easy Shoppe convenience store, and Bean and Bagel coffee and lunch stand. On the floors above are 27 guest rooms that range from small twin accommodations to rooms with two queen beds. Each room has an eclectic decor, telephone, and its own en suite sink and mirror; baths are shared, separated into men's and women's bathrooms. Many rooms have views of Lake Union or downtown Seattle. A generous continental breakfast is served each morning in the fourth-floor lounge, which also provides a nice place to read or socialize at other times. There is no Wi-Fi throughout the property, but a high-speed Internet room with computer is available to guests. Limited free parking is also available on local surrounding streets; several pay parking garages are also available. Long-term stay discounts are available.

GREENLAKE GUEST HOUSE $$$
7630 E. Green Lake Dr. North
(206) 729-8700, (866) 355-8700
www.greenlakeguesthouse.com

This 1920 Craftsman house is across the street from the popular, beautiful Green Lake in a pretty residential neighborhood of North Seattle. The urban lake has extensive parks, 3 miles of bike and running paths, boat rentals, and other enjoyable recreational activities along its shores. Greenlake Guest House offers four elegant rooms with king, queen, or two twin beds, private baths with heated floors, luxury Provence Sante bath products, televisions with cable, DVD players, ceiling fans, and phones. Some also have jetted tubs or gas fireplaces. The inn serves an incredible gourmet breakfast each morning and offers beverages and fresh-baked cookies throughout the day. A guest computer is available for use (Wi-Fi is also throughout the house), and an extensive DVD movie collection of Academy Award winners is at guests' disposal. A two-night minimum is usually required; three nights during high season.

PROSPERITY HOUSE B&B $$
7842 Lake City Way NE
(206) 922-3391
www.innharmonyguesthouse.com/
    prosperity.html

This charming, restored 1925 home offers two guest suites, although the entire three-bedroom, two-bath house can also be rented. The Retreat Suite occupies the entire top floor, with a king bed, TV and DVD player, two-person whirlpool tub in the private bath, and separate shower. The Celebration Suite on the first floor is a two-bedroom suite, with one queen bedroom and one full-size bedroom. Also featured are ceiling fans, TV with cable, soaking tub and shower in the private bath, and large windows. This is a great option for traveling families. The mostly organic continental breakfast is included, and the hosts use 80 percent organic and nontoxic cleaning products. Beverages and snacks are available 24 hours a day, and guests are welcome to use the kitchen. Parking for one car per room is available.

South Seattle

CHITTENDEN HOUSE $$
5649 47th Ave. SW
(206) 935-0407
www.chittendenhouse.com

Located in the heart of West Seattle, near Alki Beach and minutes from downtown, Chittenden House provides an oasis of serenity in the city. The 1926 Craftsman home is now a European-style bed-and-breakfast, with friendly and attentive service. From the back deck you can enjoy views of Puget Sound, and the beautiful gardens make for a wonderful place to relax. Three romantic guest rooms all feature private baths, featherbed toppers, and ceiling fans. The Evergreen Suite offers one bedroom with a queen four-poster bed, a second bedroom with double bed, separate living room with gas fireplace, and full kitchen. A television and DVD player are also provided, and the suite has a private entrance. The Castle Room offers two twin beds and an English slipper tub in the bathroom. The Jungle Room has a queen four-poster bed and claw-foot tub. Full breakfast is included.

GUEST HOUSE BED &
BREAKFAST $$–$$$
1121 SW 160th
(206) 439-7576, (866) 439-7576
www.guesthousebnb.com

The Guest House is an inviting two-bedroom suite that can accommodate up to four people, conveniently located near Sea-Tac Airport. Here you receive personal attention and pampering, as you are the only guest. The suite includes a living room with fireplace, cable television, DVD and CD player, and two queen bedrooms. Nice touches such as fresh-cut flowers and local handmade soaps add to the experience. The furnishings are comfortable and tasteful, and the Guest House provides a nice home away from home. Coffee, tea, and fresh-baked cookies are always available, and the superb hot breakfast that is included can be sit-down or to go. French doors open up onto beautiful gardens with a deck and relaxing hot tub to end the day.

MARINE VIEW B&B $$
16923 32nd Ave. SW
(206) 241-0796
www.marineviewbb.com
This is a private cottage with a queen bed, private bath, large landscaped patio with a view, and private hot tub. The interior features knotty-pine walls, and the outside gardens are really lush and lovely.

OLYMPIC VIEW BED AND
BREAKFAST COTTAGE $$$
2705 SW 164th Place
(206) 200-8801
www.olympicviewbb.com
This charming and private B&B is nestled on a quiet hillside, with incredible Puget Sound and Olympic Mountain views, surrounded by evergreens. The single cottage accommodation offers complete privacy to enjoy this Northwest retreat with magnificent sunsets. The cottage includes a king-size pillowtop bed, fully furnished kitchen, dining area, separate living room with cable television, DVD and CD players, and bathroom. There is also a private phone and Wi-Fi, as well as a laundry room. Hardwood floors and interesting seafaring photographs lend a nice feel. The cottage opens up to a deck with Jacuzzi hot tub and gas barbecue grill, surrounded by lush landscaping. Bocce ball and horseshoes are available for playing on the lawn, and the waterfall koi pond is soothing. You can walk 1 block to Three Tree Point Beach, and historic Indian trails are a five-minute walk away.

SOUNDVIEW COTTAGE $$$
17600 Sylvester Rd. SW
(206) 244-5209, (888) 244-5209
www.soundviewcottage.com
Soundview is the nearest B&B to the Seattle airport, yet is quiet and secluded. It offers one private cottage off the beaten path, perfect for a personal retreat or romantic hideaway. The location offers dramatic views, and eagles are often spotted in the surrounding treetops, which you can enjoy from the private deck and hot tub. The cottage includes a living room with sleeper sofa, woodstove, cable television, and DVD/CD player; sunny dining area; and master bedroom with king bed. Breakfast is provided in the cottage for guests to enjoy at their leisure in the full kitchen, which includes a microwave and dishwasher. Soundview can also be rented by the week or the month.

THREE TREE POINT
BED & BREAKFAST $$$
17026 33rd Ave. SW
(206) 669-7646, (888) 369-7696
www.3treepointbnb.com
Located on a quiet hillside overlooking Puget Sound, this South Seattle inn has spectacular panoramic mountain and water views. Fifteen minutes from downtown and 10 minutes from the airport, Three Tree Point is situated on the shoreline and offers a peaceful setting with two private guest accommodations. The suite is decorated in soothing blues and white, and includes a living room, kitchen, dining area, bedroom with queen-size bed, and large bathroom. The bedroom opens onto a patio with views of the water, and an umbrella table and chairs. The cottage is decorated with warm earth tones, featuring overstuffed chairs in front of the living room river-rock fireplace, full kitchen, private patio with umbrella and chiminea fireplace, a bedroom with a beautiful copper-river design queen bed, and large bathroom. Both suites have televisions with

cable, CD stereo, DVD player with a movie library, computer and Wi-Fi, private phone with voice mail, and a laundry room with washer and dryer. Hand-pressed Ralph Lauren bedding and down comforters encourage a restful night's sleep, and the kitchens are complete and fully stocked, including a prearranged breakfast left for you to enjoy on your own. The handmade olive oil soaps in the bathrooms are a nice touch.

VILLA HEIDELBERG $$$
4845 45th Ave. SW
(206) 938-3658, (800) 671-2942
www.villaheidelberg.com

This charming B&B is located in the fun Alki neighborhood of West Seattle, only 10 minutes to downtown by car or water taxi. Villa Heidelberg has an old-world charm and relaxing environment, with a great wraparound porch from which you can sit and take in the fantastic sunsets. Built as a family home in 1909, the Craftsman-style house retains the original gas and electric light fixtures, beamed ceilings, leaded-glass windows, and open staircase. The living room features a Klinker brick fireplace and a piano that's ready for anyone to play. An assortment of games and books is also available. The six guest rooms offer mostly king beds—one room has a queen and one has two twins. Two rooms have private baths, and the others share two bathrooms. Some rooms have fireplaces, original crystal chandeliers, or claw-foot tubs. There is a shared portable guest phone and a refrigerator. A full, hot breakfast is served every day, and the hosts are happy to accommodate special diets or requests. Ten minutes away is Alki Beach, the spot where the first Seattle settlers landed, today a fun boardwalk of beach, shops, and restaurants.

WILDWOOD BED & BREAKFAST $$
4518 SW Wildwood Place
(206) 819-9075, (800) 840-8410
www.wildwoodseattle.com

This large, historic 1923 home is reminiscent of an English Cotswold country cottage, filled with nooks and crannies. The gardens are magical, with perennial gardens and quiet sitting areas. Brick courtyards and covered porches are also peaceful spots to relax. Six guest accommodations are available, with king, double, or twin beds. The four standard rooms offer shared baths, with televisions in all rooms. The Victorian Suite is a third-floor retreat with private bath, telephone, and sitting room, accommodating up to four guests. The Keith Cottage is its own little home, located 3 miles away. The cottage offers a private one-bedroom accommodation, with king bed and sleeper sofa. Wi-Fi is available here, too. A sumptuous breakfast is included daily.

HOSTELS
Downtown/Central

CITY HOSTEL SEATTLE $
2327 2nd Ave.
(206) 706-3255, (877) 8-HOSTEL
www.hostelseattle.com

This cool place is the only art hostel of its kind in the United States. Located in a great spot between the Space Needle and Pike Place Market, all of the rooms here have been painted by local artists and the place is filled with amazing murals. City Hostel also supports the local arts with exhibits, poetry readings, live music, and indie films shown in the 20-seat movie theater on-site. You can even buy the affordable, original artwork on exhibit. Room types range from four- to six-bed dorm rooms with shared hall baths, four-bed dorms with private baths en suite, family rooms with four beds, and private rooms with shared or en suite bathrooms. The bathrooms here are clean and nice. Included amenities are free all-you-can-eat breakfasts, free regular dinners in the spring and summer, Wi-Fi, hot tub, DVD and book library, board games, and fishing-pole loaners. Common areas include the theater, Moroccan lounge, computer room with webcams, outdoor garden, and three full kitchens for guest use. City Hostel hosts a lot of parties and communal events, as well as trips to local attractions and museums, making for an atmosphere that can be as social or private as you like. At the time this book was going to publication, the hostel had plans to install a rooftop deck. They also offer a work trade program, so if you're willing to put in some hard work, you could trade for accommodations.

GREEN TORTOISE HOSTEL $
105 Pike St.
(206) 340-1222
www.greentortoise.net

There is a reason the Green Tortoise remains perennially popular, and somewhat famous, among budget travelers. Its can't-be-beat location right across from Pike Place Market is incredible, it's a fun and lively place with newly built quarters, and the rates are very reasonable. The Web site states that the Green Tortoise is created around a social communal experience and the tradition that gratifying travel experiences are built on beautiful places, great food, and sociable people. Accommodations include a queen-size dorm room for two people (which can be shared or booked as a private room), and four- to eight-bed dorm rooms. The bathrooms are remodeled and very

nice, particularly for a hostel, and include state-of-the-art radiant heated floors. Each bathroom is private with its own entrance from the hallway, meaning that even though you are sharing the bathrooms with others, when you are using it you have complete privacy—they are not communal. All bunks include privacy drapes, reading light, fan, and outlets. The hostel's amenities include free Wi-Fi and Internet terminals available for guest use, free full breakfast every day from 6 to 9:30 a.m., and free dinner three times a week. The hostel also hosts a lot of parties and fun events for its guests. Green Tortoise also has its own Adventure Travel company, which can help guests book activities and vacations in Seattle and all over North and Central America. This is definitely Seattle's premier hostel for travelers who don't want to spend much but want to be right in the middle of town and socialize with others.

HOSTELLING INTERNATIONAL SEATTLE AT THE AMERICAN HOTEL $
520 S. King St.
(206) 622-5443
www.hiusa.org/seattle

HI is one of the most well-known international names in hostelling, representing hundreds of hostels worldwide. The Seattle hostel opened in 2009, in a convenient location in the International District just 1 block from the King Street station Amtrak and light rail stop. The newly renovated facility offers 320 beds, including 15 private one-bed rooms and an assortment of two- to six-bed dorms, with family rooms available. Breakfast is included, and like most hostels the HI provides a wide assortment of outings, tours, and on-premises events for its guests. Other amenities include a game room, laundry facilities, Internet access, television room, and self-catering kitchen. On-site parking is not available, only metered street parking or local paid garages. HI also has a volunteer program, where you can trade work at the hostel for accommodations.

South Seattle

SEATTLE HOSTEL SERVICES   **$**
(206) 380-5500
www.seattle-hostel.com
This small property offers one of the absolute most economical nightly rates possible, as low as $15 in a six-person dorm. It serves as both a low-cost hostel option for travelers, as well as hospice facilities for special-needs individuals. The building is very new, and very nice, with hardwood floors and a beautiful kitchen that has stainless-steel appliances and granite countertops. There are separate men's and women's dorms with shared bathrooms, and the building facilities include the kitchen, laundry room, and computer stations. Private rooms and guest cottages are also available, as well as weekly rental rates. Wi-Fi, public telephones, cable televisions, and parking are available. The hostel can also arrange for pickup service from the airport or train or bus stations. Its staff arrange city tours and day trips for guests, and small pets are okay. Seattle Hostel bans all alcohol and drugs on the premises. The location is off I-5 in South Seattle, just by the Boeing Field/King County airport; the exact address is not given publicly due to privacy concerns for hospice guests. Please inquire personally.

VACATION RENTALS

GO NORTHWEST   **$$-$$$$**
(206) 715-1704
www.gonorthwest.com

This online travel guide has a section dedicated to individual property ads for vacation rentals. The selection isn't huge, and many of the permanent, managed rentals are already listed in this book. However, the inventory can vary, as individual property owners may add listings, so it's worth checking into.

GREENLAKE 85TH STREET
  GUEST HOUSE   **$$$**
85th Street
(206) 229-8853
www.seattlebandb.com
This private home is available for rent by the month and can accommodate up to eight guests. The home offers one queen bed, one double bed, two twin beds, and a sleeper sofa. There is a full kitchen, decorative, nonworking fireplace, telephone, one full bathroom, and a half-bath. Parking is available on-site. No Internet service, and no wheelchair accessibility. There is generally a 30-day minimum, but the staff may be flexible depending on availability.

HARMONY HOUSE   **$$$**
7842 Lake City Way NE
(206) 922-3391
www.innharmonyguesthouse.com
This three-bedroom, one-bath house functions as both a bed-and-breakfast, renting individual rooms, and a vacation rental. The entire home can be rented on a short- or long-term basis. This charming home has an old-world style, with queen beds, full kitchen on the main floor and kitchenette on the top floor, on-site parking, Wi-Fi, television, and telephone. The home is not wheelchair accessible.

HOME AWAY $$-$$$$
(800) 876-4319
www.homeaway.com/vacation-rentals/
  washington/seattle/r6079

This nationwide vacation rental listing site offers hundreds of properties in Seattle, from small apartments to large family homes. Each is individually listed by the owner with Home Away, and you can check availability and rates, and inquire about any property online.

HOUSEBOAT VACATION RENTAL $$$$
Lake Union—Hamlin Pier
(206) 940-1180
www.duckin.com/listings/rntl.php

Realtor Joyce Miner lists and offers this Lake Union houseboat as a longer-term vacation rental. If you are interested in a truly unique Seattle stay and want to experience living on the water, this is highly recommended (although not cheap). The fully furnished floating home offers two bedrooms and two baths, and can sleep up to six guests. It is amazingly spacious and beautifully decorated, with the second sleeping area on the upper level. There is a great deck for watching the lake and surrounding floating-home community, and a kayak is available for use. The fully stocked gourmet kitchen Downtown Seattle is only five minutes away. No pets or smoking, and no wheelchair accessibility.

OLX VACATION RENTALS $-$$$$
http://seattle.olx.com/
  vacation-rentals-cat-388

OLX is a free classified-ad Web site for Seattle, similar to Craigslist. The section for vacation rentals offers numerous choices posted by individual owners or agents, and can be a good place to find short- or long-term vacation properties.

PACIFIC RESERVATION
  SERVICE $-$$$$
(206) 439-7677, (800) 684-2932
www.seattlebedandbreakfast.com

This rental management company features more than 225 lodging establishments in the Pacific Northwest, including more than 90 in Seattle. Properties include everything from single rooms to condominiums and entire houses, which can be rented on a daily, weekly, or monthly basis. Visit the Web site to browse listings and inquire about specific rental units.

SEA TO SKY RENTALS $$-$$$$
4231 6th Ave. NW
(206) 632-4210
www.seatoskyrentals.com

Sea to Sky Rentals provides an inventory of vacation homes, apartments, and condos throughout numerous Seattle neighborhoods. These rentals are available by the night, week, or month, starting at around $85/night. Each rental that Sea to Sky represents is completely furnished with all linens and fully equipped kitchens, and the company provides a supply of Tully's coffee for your first morning and the *Best Places Seattle* book of area attractions. It also offers free movie rentals and children's accoutrements such as cribs, strollers, and booster seats.

SEATTLE DUCK HOUSE $$$$
13218 Bitter Place North
(888) 636-2305
www.seattleduckhouse.com

This remodeled three-bedroom, two-bath home is called the Duck House because of its location with 80 feet of private waterfront on a serene, duck-filled lake. A brand-new deck and dock have been added, and the site is surrounded by evergreens. You can take the home's canoe into the lake, fish, walk to the large park, or use its free playground and tennis courts. Located 9 miles from downtown Seattle, the fully stocked home is extremely child- and pet-friendly. It is even already furnished with a crib, high chair, and toys if you need them. There is a king bed, queen bed, and full bed, along with a living room, full kitchen, laundry room, and parking spaces. Other amenities include three televisions with cable and DVD players, stereo system, Wi-Fi, books and movies, games, and free boat usage. There is no smoking. A minimum stay of three or four nights, depending on the season, is required.

SEATTLE TIMES $-$$$$
http://vacationrentals.seattletimes.com/
   vacation-rentals/united-states+
   washington+seattle+3+1854

Seattle's daily newspaper offers a section for vacation rentals that is available online as well as in the printed paper. These ads run a wide range of apartments, hotels, condos, and houses that are available by the night, week, or month. Obviously, the selection changes daily.

SEATTLE VACATION RENTALS $$-$$$
(206) 898-3218
www.seattlecitysuites.com

This vacation rental agency offers a choice of stylish condominiums, all of which are located in the central part of Seattle and offer secured building entrances, secured covered parking, fully equipped kitchens, Wi-Fi, and many other personal touches. They are primarily one-bedroom, one-bath units that sleep four, with queen beds and additional Aerobed. Other amenities include indoor pools, hot tub, sauna, fitness center, laundry facilities, and rooftop patios.

However, the company may have different properties and listings at different times, so check availability online or call. Offered for nightly, weekly, or monthly stays.

SERENITY HOUSE $$$
7842 Lake City Way NE
(206) 922-3391
www.innharmonyguesthouse.com

This beautiful four-bedroom home is full of old-world charm but with a modern design. Hardwood floors, marble woodburning fireplace, and a stunning kitchen with granite countertops are some of the nice features. One bedroom has a king bed, one has a queen bed, and the remaining two bedrooms offer double beds. There is a full bathroom and a half-bath. Televisions, DVD player, Wi-Fi, and fully equipped kitchen complete the amenities. On-site parking and washer/dryer are available (requires coins). Individual rooms or the entire home can be rented on a short- or long-term basis.

CAMPGROUNDS AND RV PARKS

SEATTLE TACOMA KOA $
5801 S. 212th
Kent, WA
(253) 872-8652, (800) 562-1892
www.seattlekoa.com

The Seattle KOA is located 20 minutes from downtown, adjacent to the Green River in the Seattle suburb of Kent. The campground offers deluxe RV sites with 30/50 amp service, as well as shaded tent sites. Amenities include hot showers, Wi-Fi, laundry room, playground, dog walk area, horseshoes, fishing, a bird sanctuary, jogging and bike paths, and bike rentals. They also have a seasonal outdoor pool and offer specialty coffee and pancake breakfasts. KOA offers guided city tours from the campground.

TRAILER INNS RV PARK $
15531 SE 37th
Bellevue, WA
(425) 747-9181, (800) 659-4684
www.trailerinnsrv.com

Located in the nearby suburb of Bellevue, this RV park offers 100 percent full hookups with 15/30/50 amp service, large super sites that are up to 67 feet long, phone hookups, and free cable TV and Wi-Fi. The park includes a playground, clubhouse, and game room, as well as indoor heated swimming pool, sauna, and indoor hot tub. Laundry facilities are available, and pets are welcome.

RESTAURANTS

The dining scene in Seattle is eclectic, to say the least. From the strong influences of Asian and Scandinavian cuisines, along with the Pacific Northwest's bounty of some of the best seafood in the country, come a plethora of highly inventive, extremely fresh, and often ethnically fused culinary experiences from which to choose. Many of America's most talented and talked-about chefs are here, giving the restaurant landscape a definite excitement.

Eating out in Seattle can be pricey, without a doubt. When I first arrived I was shocked at restaurant prices, which are closer to San Francisco figures than other western cities. Part of this comes from the higher grocery costs and prepared-food tax. At the same time, I've rarely had a bad meal—even a mediocre one, for that matter—in this city. Seattle is the place to splurge on food, and there are many fine dining icons that will give you the gourmand treat of a lifetime. That said, the city was literally built on inventiveness, and the combination of its youthful vibe and down-to-earth attitude has also produced plenty of amazing choices for eating on the cheap. Oh, and have I mentioned that Seattle has a great street-food scene that is very hipster and "in the know"? Maverick chefs have come together here to build their own creative, authentic, purist food experiences at modest prices.

OVERVIEW

The regional specialty, Pacific Northwest cuisine, incorporates coastal flavors with local ingredients and a fresh simplicity in the execution. Catch-of-the-day menu specials take advantage of the abundance from the waters of Puget Sound, the Pacific Ocean, and up in British Columbia and Alaska; while the area's rich volcanic and forest soils provide robust flavors in earth-bound ingredients. Some of the common foods to be found in Pacific Northwest dishes include salmon, Dungeness crab, shellfish, mushrooms, Yukon Gold potatoes, sweet onions, and herbs. Local organic foods and farm-to-table cooking are highly popular and prized in the Seattle area, and much Pacific

Northwest cuisine will have a Pacific Rim influence.

The terrific vineyards in Washington contribute a wonderful wine partnership to the food. Riesling, Chardonnay, Cabernet Sauvignon, Merlot, and Syrah are common varietals to the area, from the second-largest wine-producing region in the country. Walla Walla, the Columbia Valley, Woodinville, and the Yakima Valley are home to dozens of vineyards, and a large selection of Washington wines is offered at most restaurants to complement the regional dining. And don't forget about beer—the Pacific Northwest started the craft brewing craze in the 1980s, and many fine microbreweries and pubs are found throughout Seattle.

The Asian influx to the area over the years has also resulted in a high concentration of Thai, Cantonese, Sichuan, Korean, Japanese, and Vietnamese food, as well as the previously mentioned prevalence of fusion cuisine. And as with any large city, you will also find just about any type of food available in Seattle.

Price Code

The following price code represents the average price of two dinner entrees, excluding drinks, appetizers, dessert, tax, and tip. Lunch and breakfast are generally 20–40 percent less expensive.

$	Less than $20
$$	$20 to $40
$$$	$41 to $60
$$$$	More than $60

This chapter is organized by type of cuisine, with the area of town noted after the address. We have included a quick index before the main listings for added convenience. All restaurants accept major credit cards unless otherwise noted. Washington law prohibits smoking inside any public building or business or within 25 feet of its front door, and all restaurants are completely nonsmoking. All restaurants comply with the Americans with Disabilities Act, unless any obstructions or other entry difficulties are noted.

Trophy Cupcakes, Pastry/ Dessert Shops, $, p. 97

Txori, Spanish/Tapas, $$, p. 100

Veraci Pizza, Pizza, $$, p. 98

Victrola, Coffeehouses , p. 89

Wedgwood Ale House & Café, Brewpubs, $$, p. 86

Wild Ginger, Pacific Rim/ Asian Fusion, $$$, p. 96

Willie's Taste of Soul, Barbecue, $$, p. 85

Zeitgeist Art & Coffee, Coffeehouses , p. 89

AMERICAN/PACIFIC NORTHWEST REGIONAL

AVILA $$$
1711 N. 45th St. (North)
(206) 545-7375
www.avilaseattle.com

This Wallingford restaurant is perfect for the adventurous gourmand who is eager to try something off-the-charts new. Cavalier chef Alex Pitts and his staff create dishes such as bone marrow beignets and braised cockscombs, made from the red crown that tops roosters and turkeys, braised in red wine and served over risotto. This inventiveness is often as showstopping as it is dining worthy, as when a leg of lamb is wrapped in hay and set afire, perfectly visible by diners through the open kitchen. This bold restaurant would be perfectly at home in New York and has received quite the buzz in Seattle.

THE CORSON BUILDING $$$$
5609 Corson Ave. South (South)
(206) 762-3330
www.thecorsonbuilding.com

From an unlikely spot in industrial Georgetown, under the shadow of I-5 in South Seattle, The Corson Building is truly unique in the city. Billing itself as a home, a restaurant, and a community, celebrity chef Matthew Dillon (of Sitka & Spruce) opened this location almost as a social experiment, directly connecting food with its cultural and communal roots. Dillon wants his patrons to share one of the few human experiences we all have in common—that of eating. Strangers sit down with one another at candlelit group tables to partake of the menu of the day, which changes on both Dillon's whim as well as available ingredients from The Corson Building's own garden and local farmers. The organic processes that form the backbone of The Corson Building include relationships with winemakers, fishermen, artists, and the local community. Dillon also offers cooking and wine workshops, private events, and special fund-raisers here.

DAHLIA LOUNGE $$$
2001 4th Ave. (Central)
(206) 682-4142
www.tomdouglas.com/dahlia

Don't let the name fool you—Dahlia is a full restaurant with a sophisticated lounge ambience. Part of the Tom Douglas empire, Dahlia was one of the early restaurants to embrace the sustainable-food movement. With a distinct Asian and seafood bent, the Sea Bar starts you off with appetizers from the ocean, and entree items such as pan-seared shrimp pot stickers, lemon-scallion Dungeness crab cakes, and five-spice Peking duck populate the menu. Don't miss the Dahlia Bakery next door.

i To request a free coupon book that will give you some great savings on restaurants, attractions, and shopping, go to www.seattlesupersaver.com.

HERBFARM $$$$
14590 NE 145th St., Woodinville (North)
(425) 485-5300
www.herbfarm.com

Although virtually all the listings in this book concentrate specifically on Seattle proper, Herbfarm is too special to leave out when you are talking about restaurants. This Pacific Northwest icon regularly tops the lists of best restaurants in the United States and even globally—as well as the most-expensive lists. Ahead of its time, Herbfarm was one of the first restaurants in the country to focus solely on preparing regional food that was locally sourced. The nine-course dinners, infused with local herbs and lovingly paired with wine, leave diners stunned. Menus are themed with the season, often changing as frequently as every few weeks or even days. The dining room is a treat for the eyes, designed with objects collected from around the world and centered on the century-old fireplace, created with two tons of whimsical tiles saved from an Atlantic seaboard mansion. There is a single seating nightly, with an optional predinner Wine Cellar Open House and outdoor hosted garden tour. Herbfarm is about a twenty-minute drive north from downtown Seattle, and dining here is an orchestrated event to be absorbed and treasured.

LARK $$$
926 12th Ave. (Central)
(206) 323-5275
www.larkseattle.com

This rustic Capitol Hill restaurant enjoys a unique location in a former woodworking shop, with an exposed-beam ceiling softened by creamy walls and sheer curtains. The menu is a wide variety of small plates, none over $20, providing an affordable dining option and opportunity to try and share plenty. The yellowtail carpaccio is particularly sublime. Dishes offer a range of cheese, charcuterie, vegetables, fish, and meats in an ever-changing selection that culls from the best of the current season. Lark works with local farmers and artisans for ingredients to create a blend of adventurous yet simple menu selections. Special dinners are sometimes offered, such as a recent Argentina Dinner. Try not to miss dessert; everything on offer is sublime.

LICOROUS $$
928 12th Ave. (Central)
(206) 325-6947
www.licorous.com

This is Lark's little sister, located just next door. Licorous has more of a lounge feel to it, yet also offers small plates that are served until midnight. Licorous makes for an ideal spot to enjoy a cocktail and appetizer while awaiting a table at Lark, an after-show late dinner, or a full meal anytime. The seating consists of a bar and comfy sofas scattered throughout the cozy setting.

MATT'S IN THE MARKET $$
94 Pike St. (Central)
(206) 467-7909
www.mattsinthemarket.com

Enjoying an excellent location right in Pike Place Market, Matt's was a simple lunch counter at one point, popular for upscale sandwiches. Matt's in the Market has since expanded, offering a great selection of original American and Northwest cuisine such as mussels with absinthe and tarragon, Penn Cove clams with homemade chorizo, and grilled octopus. The top-notch soups and sandwiches are still available, and the seafood-based menu is sourced from the market itself.

MISTRAL KITCHEN $$$

2020 Westlake Ave.
(206) 623-1922
www.mistral-kitchen.com

Elegant and artistic are the key words here, from the creation on the plate in front of you to the sculptural interior design from award-winning architect Tom Kundig. Mistral caters to a well-heeled crowd and receives kudos in the local media for its $200-per-person private Chef's Table. Dishes include seared medallions of lamb, hamachi crudo, striped bass, and rabbit loin with seared foie gras, but the menu changes daily. Don't miss the dessert creations by the city's top pastry chef, Neil Robertson. Mixologist Andrew Bohrer whips up some incredible cocktails.

94 STEWART $$$

94 Stewart St. (Central)
(206) 441-5505
www.94stewart.com

A Pacific Northwest bistro located at the top of Pike Place Market, 94 Stewart is a Seattle classic. Fresh, wild, and organic are the foundation for menu ingredients here, and an extensive cheese and wine selection adds to the dining experience. There are also plenty of local microbrews and a fun cocktail list on the menu. 94 Stewart is highly obsessed with the guest experience, to the extent that its Web site implores diners to let the restaurant know if they are not thoroughly satisfied. It also boasts a rarity—a female chef/owner, Celinda Norton. Though 94 Stewart takes its cuisine seriously, it doesn't take the experience seriously—it's a laid-back, kid-friendly place with crayons and paper on every table.

PALACE KITCHEN $$

2030 5th Ave. (Central)
(206) 448-2001
www.tomdouglas.com/palace

This is down-home comfort food with a Northwest and German flair to it. The all-over-the-place menu includes items such as steak, chicken, pork, and trout, as well as spaetzle gratin with aged Gruyère and their house-made bratwurst. The appetizer menu lists some pretty original offerings: goat cheese and lavender fondue, braised octopus, and wood-grilled beef tongue.

SITKA & SPRUCE $$

1531 Melrose Ave. (Central)
(206) 324-0662
www.sitkaandspruce.com

Chef Matthew Dillon is one of Seattle's best-loved and most inventive. Originally located in Eastlake, Sitka & Spruce closed that location in Dec 2009 to open the new restaurant between Pike and Pine in spring 2010. The new site is a bit larger in size, though not by much, adding a handful of seats to the often standing-room-only crowd amid half a dozen tables. Reservations are not accepted except for one reservation per evening, between 7:30 and 8 at the communal table. Otherwise it is first-come, first-served; the chalkboard at the bar boasts, "Food worth standing up for." Sitka & Spruce is known for extremely fresh, regional dishes such as Stellar Bay oysters, mushrooms, leeks, octopus, and quail. A nice touch is that most dishes can be ordered in full or half portions, making it easier to eat on a budget or to try and share a variety of things. Check out Dillon's other offering, The Corson Building.

SPRING HILL $$$

4437 California Ave. SW (South)

(206) 935-1075

www.springhillnorthwest.com

This critics' darling is a cross between a fine dining restaurant and cozy neighborhood bistro. Spring Hill serves everything from veal sweetbreads and mulling spiced duck to burgers—but what burgers they are! Made with twice-ground organic chuck beef, grilled over applewood and topped with house-cured bacon, Beecher's flagship cheese, and a special sauce, this is no ordinary hamburger. Spring Hill shines with its seafood, from smoked shrimp served over grits to a cedar-basted arctic char with capers, salmon roe, and béarnaise sauce. Chef/co-owner Mark Fuller is committed to utilizing local ingredients from Northwest farmers and fishermen.

STUMBLING GOAT
BAR & BISTRO $$$

6722 Greenwood Ave. North (North)

(888) 573-6206

www.stumblinggoatbistro.com

This cozy, quaint restaurant is filled with rich reds and vintage lamps, giving it a warm yet funky vibe. The Stumbling Goat features seasonal, organic, locally grown ingredients in small plates, entrees, and desserts. The rainbow trout and butternut squash ravioli are both exquisite, as is the bread pudding. The unusual name comes with a funny story; the original name was to be Drunken Boat, the title of a poem by Arthur Rimbaud. However, the state liquor control would not allow the use of the word "drunken," due to a very outdated Prohibition statute. With less than two days to the restaurant's opening, over a bottle of wine the rhyming Stumbling Goat was arrived at in its place. This is an excellent place to spend a special occasion and is one of this writer's favorite restaurants in Seattle.

TILTH $$$

1411 N. 45th St. (North)

(206) 633-0801

www.tilthrestaurant.com

Tilth gets a lot of buzz and is a great place to get a feel for the Seattle mind-set. Situated in a two-story Craftsman house in the charming Wallingford neighborhood, Tilth serves all-organic fare that is fresh and subtle. Gourmet salads are a specialty here, along with light dishes such as house-cured prosciutto and sockeye salmon, or heartier offerings like beef tongue ragu. Chef-owner Maria Hines, a James Beard Award winner for Best Chef of the Northwest, likes to create dishes from seemingly disparate items, such as a baked apple stuffed with fresh Dungeness crab and topped with crème fraîche. Everything is certified organic or wild, and sourced from the local farmers whom Hines passionately supports.

BARBECUE

ROY'S BBQ $

4903½ Rainier Ave. South (South)

(206) 723-7697

www.royscolumbiacity.com

Seattle magazine rates Roy's Georgia Gold pulled pork as the best pork sandwich in the city. It comes with slaw and a distinctly different, Asian-inspired mustard barbecue sauce, and this joint also does a few other things differently on the menu. While there is always your standard beef brisket, pulled chicken, and potato salad, Roy's also offers a meatloaf sandwich, fish tacos, smoked oyster po'boy, and andouille red beans and rice (as well as a vegetarian version). All of the meats are hickory smoked, and while small, the restaurant itself is fun, with turquoise walls cluttered with all manner of framed photos and memorabilia.

SMOKIN' PETE'S BBQ $$
1918 NW 65th St. (North)
(206) 783-0454
www.smokinpetesbbq.com
The hickory- and cherrywood-smoked brisket at this Ballard restaurant is all-natural beef from Painted Hills Farms that has been smoked for 14 hours. Smokin' Pete's also serves pork, chicken, sausage, and catfish and is vegetarian-friendly—unusual for meat-heavy barbecue cuisine. The sides are pure Southern comfort food, from collard greens and dirty rice to blackened broccoli and mac-n-cheese.

WILLIE'S TASTE OF SOUL $$
3427 Rainier Ave. South (South)
(206) 722-3229
www.williestasteofsoul.com
Anyone who loves barbecue knows that there are many styles completely different from one another, from sweet molasses-based Kansas City BBQ to the spicy Texas variety. Willie's boasts Louisiana-style cooking, with ribs, brisket, chicken, and sausage along with a variety of side dishes. The succulent meats are all slow-smoked on-site, and the service prides itself on having a hospitable southern style. The sweet potato pie dessert is simply heavenly; if you've never tried this before, one taste of Willie's and you will be sold.

BREWPUBS

Special note about brewpubs: Pubs offer both beer and food, usually a fairly extensive, high-quality menu. They could be categorized under both Restaurants and Nightlife. However, some pubs are family-friendly whereas others are strictly over 21, no minors allowed. For the purposes of this book, I have used this as a guideline to make the distinction. Family-friendly brewpubs that are more restaurant-centric are found in this section. Over-21-only pubs, typically open until 2 a.m. and more bar-centric, are listed in the Nightlife section.

ELLIOTT BAY BREWERY PUB $$
4720 California Ave. SW (South)
(206) 932-8695
www.elliottbaybrewing.com
Besides its half-dozen year-round beers, Elliott Bay offers a variety of seasonals made with only 100 percent organic barley and a number of other imported and domestic selections as well. The brewery boasts some of the highest quality pub food, with items from hummus and crab cakes to gourmet burgers, all made from scratch. And if you're interested in organic eating and drinking, 12 of Elliott Bay's house-brewed beers have been awarded organic certification by the Washington Department of Agriculture. The brewpub also practices sustainability, receiving 60 percent of its electricity from wind power sources and recycling all its food waste. No hard liquor is served, only beer and wine.

HOPVINE PUB $$
507 15th Ave. East (Central)
(206) 328-3120
www.3pubs.com
Hopvine is one of, you guessed it, three pubs in the 3 Pubs family. Its mission is to introduce you to some of the best beers in the world—meaning, to the owners, beer brewed in their own backyard. Hopvine is in the Capitol Hill neighborhood, while Latona Pub is in Green Lake and Fiddler's Inn is farther north. All three pubs are neighborhood-type places, with basic pub food and lots of

events usually going on. A fun, casual place to hang out and drink good beer.

PIKE BREWING COMPANY $$
1415 1st Ave. (Central)
(206) 622-6044
www.pikebrewing.com

Charles Finkel started this pub in 1989, housed in a former bordello in Pike Place Market. The pub still has "Naughty Nellie" rooms for private parties, and you can watch the brewers at work as you savor their end product at this unique, multilevel brewery. The food is local, sustainable, and seasonal, with offerings such as bratwurst, smoked salmon, and farmhouse artisan cheeses. Brewery tours are available, or take a stroll through the museum. Michael Jackson—the beer critic, not the late pop star—has called Pike Brewing "a shrine to beer."

PYRAMID ALEHOUSE BREWERY & RESTAURANT $$
1201 1st Ave. South (Central)
(206) 682-3377
www.pyramidbrew.com

The original pub location of Pyramid Breweries, this alehouse serves Pyramid year-round drafts as well as rotating seasonals and is a great place for friends or families to gather. Its location right across the street from Safeco Field and down the street from Qwest Field make it the ideal spot to gather before or after a game. Can't decide on a beer? Try one of the sampler trays. The pub also has a full menu of American and Northwest fare.

WEDGWOOD ALE HOUSE & CAFÉ $$
8515 35th Ave. NE (North)
(206) 527-2676
www.wedgwoodalehouse.com

Wedgwood is very family-friendly, with a separate cafe seating area just for families

and a kids' menu, coloring books, and crayons. For the adults, they offer 18 draft taps that are constantly rotating with small, hard-to-find brewery creations. A full bar also is available for any cocktail you wish to order. Like many good pubs, Wedgwood is known for its burgers, using highly seasoned patties with fresh garlic. Veggie burgers are also on the menu, as are Philly steak sandwiches, buffalo-style chicken wings, and an assortment of house-made soups daily. Dogs are welcome on the outdoor seating patio.

CAJUN

SAZERAC $$$
1101 4th Ave. (Central)
(206) 624-7755
www.sazeracrestaurant.com

Sazerac promises "serious fun and damn good food." This hopping restaurant in Hotel Monaco is a lively gathering place with a unique menu that adds the flavors and styles of the Northwest into traditional southern Cajun recipes. Flash-fried catfish with jalapeño meunière sauce and a rooster, crawfish, and andouille gumbo are two of the more unusual finds on the menu, and the restaurant always has an excellent selection of charcuterie and cheeses. Sazerac also has multicourse tasting lunches and dinners, as well as cooking and bartending classes for a fun option. Don't miss the bar; the name Sazerac comes from a very old cocktail, and the mixology on hand here is truly inventive.

CHINESE

CHEF LIAO $
6012 Phinney Ave. North (North)
(206) 789-6441
www.chefliao.com

This is the place to come if you want pot stickers. The traditional Chinese dish is so ubiquitous and deceptively simple that many places churn out rubbery, tasteless versions. At Chef Liao they are delivered perfectly crispy on the outside, while tender and flavorful on the inside. The Yummy Yam Fish, whitefish stir-fried with sliced sweet potato, is also popular. Along with noodle soups, chow mein dishes, and a decent vegetarian selection, Chef Liao also offers Vietnamese, Thai, and Japanese dishes.

HING LOON $$
628 S. Weller St. (Central)
(206) 682-2828
This authentic Cantonese-style restaurant in the International District offers traditional, country-style dishes such as hot pots, chicken in black bean sauce, salt and pepper pork, and noodle bowls. The fried bread appetizer is very popular, served with a dish of sweet condensed milk for dipping.

HONEY COURT $
516 Maynard Ave. South (Central)
(206) 292-8828
Using high-quality, fresh ingredients, this simple spot with friendly service is the place to go for good Chinese food at a good price. Specialties include a steamed whole tilapia, sautéed squid with broccoli, shredded squab, and honey-walnut prawns. Honey Court also serves dim sum, a popular lunch option.

JACK'S TAPAS CAFE $$
5211 University Way NE (North)
(206) 523-6855
www.jackstapas.com
While tapas is generally Spanish small plate dishes, Jack's unabashedly calls its delicious northern Chinese home cooking by the name. Jack's serves small dishes made for sharing of

dim sum, noodles, sesame bread, and pickled vegetables. Unusual finds such as leek calzones can be found, and there are great vegetarian dishes that are not just afterthoughts.

SEA GARDEN $$
509 7th Ave. South (Central)
(206) 623-2100
Seemingly always busy, Sea Garden is a popular International District spot serving delightfully named dishes such as Eight Treasure casserole and Double Pleasure whole flounder. Items that consistently get the most raves from diners are the salt and pepper pork chops, crab in black bean sauce, congee, and the salt and pepper squid. You can choose your seafood from the tanks if you wish. The dining room is nice and roomy, service is generally very good, and a full bar is available.

COFFEEHOUSES

If there are two things that most non-Seattleites think of when you mention the city, it is the rain and coffee. Is that a coincidence? Did Seattle's coffeehouse culture spring up as a way to stay warm and dry inside during the dreary winters, sharing a cup of joe in the communal fashion that is so popular here?

Perhaps, but whatever its greatest influences, the city is synonymous with coffee. And how can it not be? It's home to the most well-known coffee icon in the world, Starbucks. With more than 16,000 stores worldwide—and nearly 1 in 3 of those outside the United States—you could plop down someone from Bulgaria, Tel Aviv, Uruguay, or Beijing in the middle of Seattle and they would instantly recognize the round green-and-white Starbucks logo.

The original store that opened in 1971 is still there, a narrow storefront in Pike Place Market that looks nothing like most of the other, more polished Starbucks. There is almost always a long line at the counter and a congestion of people on the sidewalk out front—mostly tourists wanting to see and experience the first location of the holy grail.

But according to most Seattle residents, Starbucks is not the soul of coffee culture here. The town is literally inundated with coffeehouses; at some intersections there is a different one on each corner. The city's java aficionados each have their personal favorites, and many seem to regard Starbucks with disdain, a place for the uninitiated masses. Some of the most popular cafes are lacking in customer service, as if the more unpleasant the barista, the better the brew. Regulars seem to enjoy the surliness, comparing notes and blogging with glee about the worst attitudes.

Unkempt hipsters sprawl on vintage couches and at mismatched tables for hours on weekdays, hunched over their Kerouac novels and causing one to wonder what sort of jobs they have or just what they do all day. Young mothers meet, their strollers in tow, while other patrons click away on their MacBooks industriously. Often people sit in cleared corners reading poetry or plucking an acoustic guitar. Coffeehouses truly do seem to be where all of Seattle congregates as if by unspoken agreement.

Here are some of Seattleites' most beloved coffeehouses, compiled through a highly scientific study. OK, I asked around my friends, but trust me—they are all very cool people and you can't go wrong at any of these spots.

BAUHAUS BOOKS & COFFEE
301 E. Pine St. (Capitol Hill)
(206) 625-1600
www.bauhauscoffee.net

Although this place can be at times tragically hip, it is still one of my favorite spots in Seattle. As the name implies, it's very literary, with a vintage library and the feel of a place that Dylan Thomas or William Burroughs would have hung out. Its corner location with big windows all around offers a view of the pedestrian-heavy surrounding neighborhood, with the Space Needle as a backdrop. It's definitely a community spot, with exhibits of local artists' works and a movie screening on the first Thurs of each month. In addition to serving excellent coffee drinks, Bauhaus also has a great selection of teas and scrumptious scones and croissants.

EL DIABLO COFFEE COMPANY
1811 Queen Anne Ave. North #101
  (Queen Anne)
(206) 285-0693
www.eldiablocoffee.com

This is Seattle's only Latin-style coffeehouse. They do not do extra-tall non-fat mocchiatos or raspberry cappuccinos. What they do, and very well, are traditional Latin coffee drinks made with the finest beans that are custom blended just for El Diablo and roasted Cuban-style, at a higher temperature for a deep brew without any burnt flavor. According to the El Diablo Web site, you will go to hell if you drink other coffee. Try the Cubano, with two shots of espresso and a lovely caramelized sugar, or the Cortadito, topped with steamed milk and foam. Even if you're not a coffee drinker, El Diablo can be addictive—I dare you not to get hooked after just one Batido, a Cuban shake made with fresh fruit and milk. The atmosphere is just as good, with hand-painted murals and Brazilian or Cuban music filling the air.

VICTROLA
411 15th Ave. East (Capitol Hill)
(206) 462-6259
www.victrolacoffee.com
Victrola calls itself the "living room of Capitol Hill," and it just may be. Local neighbors frequent the place regularly; within a few weeks of opening, one couple had even written their wedding vows on a couch here. Victrola is very engaged in the life of the community, with art openings, rockabilly shows, live radio broadcasts, and movie nights. I heard there was an insect safari here once, though I'm not entirely certain what that means. Suffice it to say, Victrola is an endearing blend of quirky and reliable. They serve beautifully made drinks, artisan pastries, and yummy sandwiches. And they are passionate about quality coffee, researching every farmer, bean, and roast thoroughly before serving them. Check out the two other locations as well, at 310 E. Pike St., a little closer to downtown, and at 3215 Beacon Ave. South, in the Beacon Hill neighborhood of South Seattle.

ZEITGEIST ART & COFFEE
171 S. Jackson St. (Pioneer Square)
(206) 583-0497
www.zeitgeistcoffee.com
Zeitgeist is just as committed to the local arts community as it is top-notch coffee. The raw-brick walls are used to showcase the works of emerging and established artists, constantly pushing the envelope of what is considered art. They don't focus only on textile arts either; their Independent Cinema provides a forum for new media and independent films, shown regularly on their huge motorized screen. As far as the coffee, at Zeitgeist it tends to be stronger and simpler, minus the sky-high foam; it may come as no surprise that the place has a large European customer base.

Don't miss the First Thursday Art Walk in Pioneer Square, of which Zeitgeist is a big part, along with area galleries.

Still not sure? Take the two-hour Coffee Crawl tour, offered Fri and Sat by Seattle By Foot (http://seattlebyfoot.com).

CONTINENTAL

PAIR $$$
5501 30th Ave. NE (North)
(206) 526-7655
www.pairseattle.com
Pair is a sweet restaurant with a warm ambience that makes you feel part of the neighborhood. The European-inspired fare is created with ingredients from local farms, and the menu changes seasonally. Inspiring the name, Pair is known for its beautifully paired wine list. Chef-owner Felix Penn lives upstairs with his wife, Sarah. The small plate menu includes dishes such as braised rabbit, cinnamon roasted lamb, duck confit, and an excellent selection of cheeses and salads. A specialty of the house is the natural beef brisket, served with scallions and a horseradish crème fraîche.

ROVER'S $$$$
2808 E. Madison (Central)
(206) 325-7442
www.thechefinthehat.com/rovers
French chef and owner Thierry Rautureau visited Seattle and Rover's in 1987 and discovered that the restaurant was for sale. He promptly bought it, moved to Seattle, and began serving his unique menu of locally sourced Pacific Northwest food, prepared with traditional French techniques and accents. Rautureau, known as the Chef in the Hat for his ever-present fedora, is a James Beard Award winner who trained in his home country. He is passionate about using local ingredients that are sustainable,

organic, and seasonal, changing the menu daily to accommodate this supply. To complement the incredible food, Rover's offers a wine list that reads like *War and Peace*, with more than 500 labels from both classic wine regions and lesser-known gems.

TILIKUM PLACE CAFE $$
407 Cedar St. (Central)
(206) 282-4830
www.tilikumplacecafe.com

This European bistro in Belltown is a favorite spot for brunch, serving delectable house-made pastries, Dutch baby pancakes with apples, and the signature baked beans with toast and fried eggs. But Tilikum also serves a great lunch and dinner, offering an assortment of meat and seafood dishes as well as an always-inspired cheese and charcuterie board, which no self-respecting European bistro would be without. The light streaming through the wall of windows makes this one of the lightest, cheeriest places to dine in Seattle. Don't miss the homemade desserts.

DELI/SANDWICHES

DELICATUS $
103 1st Ave. South (Central)
(206) 623-3780
www.delicatusseattle.com

Built in the style of a traditional European delicatessen while incorporating Northwest resources, Delicatus is a sustainable, cross-cultural success story. It was founded in Pioneer Square on the simple premise that people in Seattle deserve a better sandwich, with ingredients that are purchased directly from local farmers and artisans. The daily menu ranges from classic pastrami and corned beef to house-cured salmon lox and duck confit. Table service, takeout, and catering are available.

I LOVE NEW YORK DELI $
93 Pike St. (Central)
(206) 381-3354
www.ilovenewyorkdeli.net

This authentic New York–style deli in the Pike Place Market hearth-bakes its bread daily, including four types of rye. This fresh-baked bread ensures some of the best sandwiches around, stacked high with a variety of sliced hot and cold meats. Just try to finish one—they're huge. The menu is also loaded with comfort food like chicken soup and matzo balls, as well as New York staples such as bagels, lox, knishes, chopped chicken liver made from an old family recipe, and kosher frankfurters from Brooklyn. A second location in the University District is located at 5200 Roosevelt Way NE.

TAKE 5 URBAN MARKET $
6757 Eighth Ave. NW (North)
(206) 420-8104
www.take5urbanmarket.com

A full-time chef's team on-site provides a wide selection of fresh foods each day, to take away or eat at the counters: hot and cold sandwiches, salads, and soups, as well as daily dinner specials and desserts. Take 5 is also, as the name says, a small market where you can buy dairy products, beer and wine, bread, fruits and vegetables, and other groceries. It's a little like a clean, light-filled New York bodega.

DINNER THEATER/ ENTERTAINMENT

PINK DOOR $$
1919 Post Alley (Central)
(206) 443-3241
www.thepinkdoor.net

A visit to the Pink Door promises to be one of the most fun evenings you will have. Part cabaret and part restaurant, the place has the look of an old-fashioned bordello and lets its guests escape the ordinary. Don't let the entertainment and environment make you suspect the food is an afterthought or in any way ordinary, however. The Pink Door's homespun Italian-American cuisine is delicious, made with fresh organic ingredients and uncomplicated recipes. Dishes from light to hearty include no-hormone steak, wild salmon, risottos, and pastas. While you eat, a trapeze artist may be swinging above your head; after the delectable dessert, move to the back room for a funny and raunchy burlesque show in the cabaret. The Pink Door also has one of the best outdoor decks in Seattle. Located in an alley in Pike Place Market, there is no sign, but look for—you guessed it—a pink metal door.

TEATRO ZINZANNI $$$$
222 Mercer St. (Central)
(206) 802-0015
http://dreams.zinzanni.org

"Love, Chaos & Dinner" is the slogan of Teatro ZinZanni, and it provides three hours of dining and entertainment like no other. A five-course feast is served during a whirlwind of cirque, vaudeville, and cabaret as provided by the energetic performers in constantly revolving productions. The result is something that's part circus and part dinner theater that is sometimes interactive with the audience; during intermission on my visit, several of the cast members stopped by the table to share a one-liner. Many of the customers also get into the spirit of the act by dressing up in flamboyant costumes, and accoutrements such as hats, tiaras, masks, and boas are available in the lobby. The food can range from very good to hit-or-miss, with menus designed by celebrated chef Tom Douglas. All in all, a very fun night.

FRENCH

BASTILLE CAFÉ & BAR $$
5307 Ballard Ave. NW (North)
(206) 453-5014
www.bastilleseattle.com

Bastille is dramatic, resplendent, bombastic—a visual feast for the eyes. Against a black and white canvas rises a clock that once adorned a Paris metro station, French flea market light fixtures, 19th-century cathedral sconces, black ironwork, and a 45-foot zinc bar. The back bar once graced a Seattle mansion, and pendants salvaged from a local school line the walls. The space has been reinvented in what was once the Obermaier Machine Works, up to the rooftop garden where lettuce and herbs are grown for the kitchen. The result is a special place to enjoy *plats du jour* such as boneless quail, fricassée de poulet, and braised lamb shank.

CAFÉ CAMPAGNE $$
1600 Post Alley (Central)
(206) 728-2233
www.campagnerestaurant.com

This casual, inexpensive bistro is a bohemian alternative to its big sister, Campagne Restaurant, and is truly a little slice of the cafe culture of Paris. It's casual yet romantic, with an excellent wine list and terrific weekend brunch. Try the poached eggs *en meurette*, with bacon and champignons in a red wine and foie gras sauce. Typical French bistro fare populates the dinner and lunch menus, from croque monsieur and burger d'agneau (lamb), to a cassoulet stew with lamb and duck. House-made sausage and salmon gravlax are special, and the cafe offers prix-fixe meals that are an excellent value. For a more sophisticated evening, visit Campagne Restaurant upstairs.

CHEZ SHEA $$$
94 Pike St. (Central)
(206) 467-9990
www.chezshea.com

Another romantic French option in the Pike Place Market, Chez Shea is perched atop the market with arched windows overlooking the views, and candlelit tables. The contemporary French recipes are made with Northwest ingredients such as Alaskan sablefish and Hudson Valley foie gras, resulting in dishes like the roasted squab and pan-seared fish. As popular as the restaurant is Shea's Lounge, where guests may order small plates a la carte or choose the three-course prix-fixe menu, which is a great value ($25 at the time of this writing).

GERMAN

FEIERABEND $$
422 Yale Ave. North (Central)
(206) 340-2528
www.feierabendseattle.com

You'll feel like you have been transported to a biergarten on the Rhine. This lively neighborhood tavern serves 18 imported German brews on tap, served in the appropriate glass for each style of beer—a distinction that beer purists will appreciate. Hearty plates of weiner schnitzel and bratwurst and sauerkraut, as well as dreamily soft Bavarian pretzels, are on the menu, but there are also some surprising items like deep-fried pickles and a stuffed portobello mushroom. Feierabend is for those 21 and older; no minors allowed.

INDIAN

INDIA BISTRO $$
2301 Market St. (North)
(206) 783-5080
www.seattleindiabistro.com

Situated on a busy corner in Ballard, this cozy spot is rich in hearty, sauce-based northern Indian dishes such as masalas, curries, and vindaloos. A full tandoori menu is also available and ingredients that make up the dishes include chicken, lamb, seafood, and full vegetarian options. A second location in North Seattle is located at 6417 Roosevelt Way NE.

TASTE OF INDIA $$
5517 Roosevelt Way NE (North)
(206) 528-1575
www.tasteofindiaseattle.com

This Zagat-rated restaurant is consistent and popular, with a wide variety of Indian and Mediterranean dishes including a *mazza* plate with hummus, tabbouleh and dolmades, tikka, and tandoor plates. There are plenty of vegetarian options as well; try the madras chili masala with crisp-cooked squash and peppers. Taste of India may well have the largest menu of naan breads of any Indian restaurant I have ever seen, with varieties such as spinach, mint, and cherries.

ITALIAN

ANCHOVIES & OLIVES $$$
1550 15th Ave. (Central)
(206) 838-8080
www.anchoviesandolives.com

It's hard to know whether to classify this new favorite as an Italian or a seafood restaurant. It's a beautiful fusion of both, presenting fresh, local seafood in all its forms, prepared with a traditional Italian sensibility. *Seattle* magazine says that the cold crudo starters can "stop you in your tracks," and the wine list is filled with offbeat selections from Italy. The menu changes daily and can include delicate fried clams, succulent cuttlefish in a Parmesan broth, sea scallops over squid-ink risotto, and duck gnocchi.

ASSAGGIO $$$

2010 4th Ave. (Central)
(206) 441-1399
www.assaggioseattle.com

The atmosphere at Assaggio is welcoming, with warm lighting and Michelangelo-inspired art adorning the walls. The carefully composed menu of robust central and northern Italian cuisine includes gourmet pastas and pizzas with flavorful sauces, and a nearly endless wine list stocked from chef Mauro Golmarvi's trips back to Italy. Golmarvi is self-taught, inspired by his mother to begin his career in Rome. He starts each day shopping for the freshest seafood at Pike Place Market and can often be seen roaming among the tables and customers at Assaggio. His goal is to remove salt and pepper from tables entirely, so that diners can experience the food's flavor as it is in the old country.

HOW TO COOK A WOLF $$$

2208 Queen Anne Ave. North (Central)
(206) 838-8090
www.howtocookawolf.com

With a name you can't forget (derived from a book title), this small restaurant generated a huge buzz when it first opened and is still talked about. The warm wood interior provides a nice setting for the small plates menu featuring seafood-heavy dishes with an Italian flair and simple, flavorful preparation. The house-made pastas are particularly beloved by regulars, but every dish here is sublime. Consider the mussels in a rich broth with pearls of fregola pasta, or the caramelized cauliflower *agnolotti*.

SPINASSE $$$

1531 14th Ave. East (Central)
(206) 251-7673
www.spinasse.com

This Capitol Hill restaurant serves traditional cuisine of the Piedmont region in northern Italy. The simple, refined dishes are created using authentic Piedmontese techniques, handmade pastas, and seasonally inspired ingredients, and chef Jason Stratton incorporates products from local farmers and artisans. The pastas may be stuffed with rabbit, squash, or pork, and other dishes include venison stewed with red wine and currants and cold poached veal with house-cured tuna. For the ultimate dining experience, reserve the Chef's Table on Fri or Sat night to enjoy a fabulous 10-course serving, with a bird's-eye view into the kitchen, for $100 per person.

JAPANESE/SUSHI

BOOM NOODLE $$

1121 E. Pike St. (Central)
(206) 701-9130
www.boomnoodle.com

A popular term in Japan is "my boom," which means something the person is obsessed with. Boom Noodle was opened with the goal of creating a following for those obsessed with its incredible noodles, and the owners are obsessed with Japanese culture in general. Boom dishes are authentically Japanese or inspired by trends in Japanese cooking, and in addition to the noodles include soups, wok creations, dumplings, sashimi, sake-marinated flatiron steak, and a variety of salads. Try the Okonomiyaki, a shredded pork and cabbage pancake.

KISAKU SUSHI $$

2101 N. 55th St. (North)
(206) 545-9050
www.kisaku.com

Reliably fresh and memorable, Kisaku is a sushi purist. The menu changes with seasonal ingredients, and the cooked dishes are every bit as good as the sushi. The place has a comfortable neighborhood feel and is refreshingly free of the pretentious decor and vibe that seem to accompany most sushi restaurants these days.

MASHIKO $$
4725 California Ave. SW (South)
(206) 935-4339
www.sushiwhore.com

Yes, go ahead and notice the Web site address and have a chuckle. Mashiko does indeed take its sushi so seriously that they assume everyone who experiences it will do just about anything for it. Mashiko presents a fun, irreverent environment, with a sushi bar webcam you can watch online and sushi-making classes taught by chef/owner Hajime Sato himself. Sato is very dedicated to sustainability, heavily featuring local fish such as salmon, catfish, and Dungeness crab while eschewing endangered unagi and hamachi to create Seattle's first fully sustainable sushi bar. Sato adores Alaskan mackerel and prepares it just about every way possible. On a funny side note, Mashiko also prides itself on having the best toilets in Seattle—technological marvels with heated seats and electronic bidets.

SHIRO'S $$$
2401 2nd Ave. (Central)
(206) 443-9844
www.shiros.com

These are perhaps the most famous sushi restaurant and chef in Seattle. Master chef Shiro Kashiba is a two-time James Beard nominee and has been profiled everywhere from the *New York Times* to *Bon Appetit*. Born in Kyoto, Shiro opened Nikko sushi restaurant in Seattle in 1967, selling it to Westin Hotels 20 years later. In 1994 he opened Shiro's in Belltown, blending classical Japanese sushi techniques with Northwest ingredients. Today Shiro is semiretired and can be found behind the sushi bar only a few nights a week, but you can still get his legendary rolls and sashimi.

KOREAN

KAYA BBQ AND GRILL $$
20109 Aurora Ave. North (North)
(206) 546-2848
www.kayaseattle.com

While Korean barbecue may not be terribly rare or original, Kaya brings a whole new experience to the table, literally. Each booth in the restaurant comes with its own gas grill and vent, and customers cook their own food right at their tables. Order short ribs, bulgogi beef, pork belly, or shrimp, and keep in mind that the portions are very large and easy to share. Yet despite the do-it-yourself ritual, service is extremely attentive and the food presentation is delightful. And they will cook the food for you if you prefer, or if you are dining solo.

MEXICAN/LATIN AMERICAN

EL PUERCO LLORON $
1501 Western Ave. (Central)
(206) 624-0541
www.elpuercolloron.com

This cheerful, casual taqueria hidden away in the Pike Place Market area serves vibrantly seasoned meats on fresh, soft tortillas, all at more than reasonable prices. The taquitos and carnitas that are so tender the meat falls apart are also good bets. House-made limeade *horchata* provides a not-too-sweet ending.

EL QUETZAL $
3209 Beacon Ave. South (South)
(206) 329-2970
www.elquetzalseattle.com

This Beacon Hill establishment gets top ratings for its friendliness; the Monteil family that owns and runs El Quetzal makes all their guests feel like they have just arrived for a huge family dinner. The portions are extremely generous and perfect for sharing. Popular specialties include the *tortas*, huge Mexican sandwiches stuffed with steak or even cactus, *chilaquiles*, and the huaraches corn cakes with black beans, meat, and eggs. Inventiveness is on display as well; take, for instance, the *pombazo*, a bun filled with sausage and mashed potatoes and then doused in salsa.

LA CARTA DE OAXACA $$
5431 Ballard Ave. NW (North)
(206) 782-8722
www.lacartadeoaxaca.com

This small, authentic restaurant is tucked subtly in among Ballard's trendy bars and boutiques. Oaxacan dishes such as *tasajo, molotes,* empanadas, and lamb *birria* are served here, along with bowls of posole, a thick and hearty pork stew. Familiar standbys are also available, including tamales, chile rellenos, and several varieties of tacos. The house specialty is Mole Negro Oaxaca, a rich black chile/chocolate mole sauce served with chicken or pork and La Carta's fresh homemade tortillas. In fact, you can watch the tortillas being made in front of your eyes at the counter.

MIDDLE EASTERN/ MEDITERRANEAN

BRASA $$$
2107 3rd Ave. (Central)
(206) 728-4220
www.brasa.com

The attention to detail at this Belltown restaurant is what makes it special. Executive chefs Tamara Murphy and Juli Guillemette are committed to using local, organic meats and produce, and the freshness shows in the quality of the dishes. A signature dish is the clams with chorizo, chickpeas, croutons, and Spanish pimentos, but most of the menu is a carnivore's dream. The happy hour is popular and lively.

KABUL $$
2301 N. 45th St. (North)
(206) 545-9000
www.kabulrestaurant.com

Serving cuisine from Afghanistan's capital, where the trade crossroads between India and Central Asia influenced the culture and food, Kabul is a charming Wallingford cafe. Owner Wali Khairzada is the son of Afghan bankers, and he serves expected classics such as kebabs and palaw, as well as dishes such as fresh pasta filled with scallions, leeks, and cilantro and sautéed eggplant topped with seasoned ground beef. The vegetarian options are varied and plentiful.

LOLA $$
2000 4th Ave. (Central)
(206) 441-1430
www.tomdouglas.com/lola

Tom Douglas's Greek-inspired *taverna* serves modern Mediterranean food with a North African riff. A selection of kebabs and *tagines* is on the menu, along with several *meze* plates as starters and a fish of the day. Try the Lola Sampler, which gives a great variety of kebab, olives, dolmades, hummus, and pita. Lola offers a late-night menu and breakfast as well as lunch and dinner; *Seattle Metropolitan Magazine* called it the best breakfast in town.

MARRAKESH $$$

2334 2nd Ave. (Central)
(206) 956-0500
www.marrakeshseattle.com

This place is as much an experience for all the senses as it is a restaurant. It's a great place for groups or parties, where you can sit around a large, low table on floor pillows and share the large platters of kebabs, *tagines*, and couscous dishes. They will even cook a whole lamb for you, with three days' notice, for parties of eight or more. As may be expected with a place like this, they have belly dancers; in fact, everything is a performance here, even down to the tea service poured in the traditional style, from about 2 feet above the glasses. The entire restaurant is sensory overload for the eyes, with intricate tile mosaics, sumptuous textiles, stained glass windows, fountains, and gorgeous Moroccan lanterns.

PACIFIC RIM/ASIAN FUSION

JOULE $$$

1913 N. 45th St. (North)
(206) 632-1913
www.joulerestaurant.com

In the charming neighborhood of Wallingford lies this gem of a restaurant. Joule embodies the uniquely Seattle American/Asian fusion cuisine. One half of the husband-and-wife team that owns the restaurant is Rachel Yang, who expresses her Korean roots in the food, along with a style that is long on French technique. Yang and her husband, Sief Chirchi, did much of their culinary training in New York, and the dishes they serve up are as varied as shiitake lasagna, whole mackerel, Chinese sausage, and Kasu brined pork chops. Some Chirchi Egyptian spices are even thrown into most dishes. A specialty is the kimchee— small side dishes of homemade pickled cucumbers, shitake mushrooms, and even beef tongue—that are a staple of Korean restaurants.

POPPY $$

622 Broadway Ave. East (Central)
(206) 324-1108
www.poppyseattle.com

In a brightly colored, very mod space, Poppy serves up prix-fixe *thali* plates from a constantly changing menu. *Thalis* are Indian trays of an assortment of dishes, and Poppy's *thali* offerings are about as inventive as they come. The owner, Jerry Traunfeld, used to be the executive chef at the celebrated Herbfarm restaurant. Some of the dishes that may be found in Poppy's seven- or nine-item *thali* plates are braised pork belly, tandoori chicken wrapped in naan, chickpea-coated fried eggplant, or ricotta dumplings with stinging nettle sauce. Full vegetarian options are always available, and items can also be ordered a la carte.

WILD GINGER $$$

1401 3rd Ave. (Central)
(206) 623-4450
www.wildginger.net

One of the best-known and celebrated restaurants in Seattle, indeed in the country, Wild Ginger was inspired by a trip that owners Rick and Ann Yoder took to Southeast Asia more than twenty years ago. Bringing back their experiences with the food and culture to open the restaurant, the Yoders created what became a pillar of pan-Asian fusion dining in the Northwest. The chef staff is a melting pot itself, and the menu features everything from Malaysian seafood *laksa* to Bangkok Boar. Satay is featured heavily here, and there is even a satay bar. Zagat included Wild Ginger in its Best Restaurants of the World list.

Surprisingly, then, most of the dishes are affordable, and although you can spend a bundle here with wine and the delectable desserts, Wild Ginger is far from one of the most expensive restaurants in town. Tip: The Triple Door, a live music and event venue next door, serves a full menu from Wild Ginger in its plush supper-club environment.

PASTRY/DESSERT SHOPS

CUPCAKE ROYALE $
1111 E. Pike St. (Central)
(206) 328-6544
www.cupcakeroyale.com

Offering four locations in Capitol Hill, Ballard, Madrona, and West Seattle, Cupcake Royale makes their own buttercream frosting using organic sugar, local milk, and free-range eggs. The cupcake batter is made with specially milled Shepherd's Grain flour sourced from east Washington farmers. Regular daily flavors are chocolate and vanilla with a variety of frostings, as well as a Cupcake of the Month flavor, such as Irish Whiskey Maple and Huckleberry. They also take special orders and deliver.

LE PANIER VERY FRENCH BAKERY $
1902 Pike Place (Central)
(206) 441-3669
www.lepanier.com

Yes, it is très French, considering Le Panier was opened in 1983 by a Frenchman who missed his daily baguette. This charming little shop feels as if you've stepped from the Pike Place Market into a Parisian bakery when you enter the doors. The delicate sweet specialties include pistachio and orange pastries, a variety of tarts, meringues, croissants, and absolutely divine *pain au chocolate*. You can also pick up baguettes and other loaves of bread, as well as sandwiches.

MOLLY MOON'S $
917 E. Pine St. (Central)
(206) 708-7947
www.mollymoonicecream.com

This is Seattle's favorite ice cream shop, with locations in Capitol Hill and Wallingford. Owner Molly Moon Neitzel calls it a neighborhood hangout where families, kids, hipsters, and ice cream addicts can congregate. The dairy is provided from hormone-free Washington cows, and seasonal fruits and herbs are used in the recipes, resulting in unusual flavors such as lavender, cantaloupe, and maple bacon. The ice cream can also be found on the menu of many local restaurants, and vegan options are always available.

TROPHY CUPCAKES $
1815 N. 45th St., Suite 209 (North)
(206) 632-7020
www.trophycupcakes.com

This charming little shop does nothing but cupcakes, offering 12 flavors every day including some highly unusual ones, such as Chocolate Guinness Stout, Chai Cardamom, and Snowball. There is also a shop in University Village, at 2612 NE Village Lane.

PIZZA

DELANCEY $$
1415 NW 70th St. (North)
(206) 838-1960
www.delanceyseattle.com

Before opening Delancey, chef Brandon Pettit traveled all over the USA on a quest to develop the perfect pizza crust. According to most locals and food reviewers, he succeeded. At his rather spare Ballard restaurant, the brick-oven pizza achieves the perfect balance of soft and crunchy, topped with ingredients such as Basque Padron peppers, crimini mushrooms, Leporati prosciutto, house-made pork fennel sausage, and fresh or aged mozzarella. A rather limited choice of wine and beer is also available. Note: At the time of this writing, Delancey is open only for dinner, starting at 5 p.m.

PIECORA'S NEW YORK PIZZA $$
1401 E. Madison St. (Central)
(206) 322-9411
www.piecoras.com

Piecora's is a family-owned and -run pizzeria with the old, hipster-free Capitol Hill vibe— it's been here for more than 25 years. As the name implies, this is Brooklyn-style pizza, with hand-tossed dough and slices that you fold in half to eat properly. Whole and half pizzas are available, as well as calzones, subs, pasta, and salads.

SERIOUS PIE $$
316 Virginia St. (Central)
(206) 838-7388
www.tomdouglas.com

This is my favorite pizzeria in Seattle. It's cramped and there's precious little room to wait, but a spot always seems to open up fast at the long communal tables. You can look right over the counter into the big applewood ovens, to see your pie being prepared and cooked. The crusts are perfectly blistered and crunchy, and they're topped with local artisan cheeses. As far as toppings go, the old stand-bys are here, as well as regional additions like Yukon Gold potatoes, delicata squash, yellow-foot mushrooms, and Penn Cove clams. Each pizza pie is just about enough for one person, so why not order two and share?

VERACI PIZZA $$
500 NW Market St. (North)
(206) 525-1813
www.veracipizza.com

Veraci started out as a traveling pizzeria that was a staple of the Ballard farmers' market. Now, it has established a permanent restaurant serving wood-fired pizza by the slice or the pie, on its signature ultrathin artisan crust. Toppings and menus change with the season and continue to offer the best of what's fresh at the market. You can still find Veraci at the Ballard and Fremont markets year-round as well.

SEAFOOD

CHANDLER'S CRABHOUSE $$$
901 Fairview Ave. North (Central)
(206) 223-2722
www.schwartzbros.com/chandlers.cfm

As the name suggests, Chandler's specializes in crab. A lot of it. In fact, Chandler's Crabhouse serves more crab than any other restaurant in the entire Northwest. Numerous fresh daily selections are available, from Washington Red King and Alaskan Dungeness to Gulf Coast soft-shell, and chef Kevin Rohr makes frequent changes to the menu to reflect the freshest crab on hand. In addition to the ever-present crab dishes, full seafood choices are available including calamari, tuna, lobster, prawns, salmon, and oysters; there is also a very nice selection of meat, from Colorado lamb riblettes to kimchee beef.

ETTA'S SEAFOOD $$$
2020 Western Ave. (Central)
(206) 443-6000
www.tomdouglas.com

People-watch along Pike Place Market and the waterfront through huge plate-glass windows, as you enjoy Tom Douglas's take on seasonal, market-inspired seafood. From classic fish-and-chips to Dungeness crab cakes, lobster, pit-smoked salmon, and a tuna sashimi salad, the dishes are all fresh and superb. The weekend brunch is definitely worth a visit, and you can stroll through the market to work off all those extra calories afterward.

IVAR'S $$
1001 Alaskan Way, Pier 54 (Central)
(206) 587-6500
www.ivars.net

Ivar's is one of the true Seattle classic experiences, and no visit would be complete without a stop at one of several locations around the area; Pier 54 is the original, a tradition since 1938. Ivar Haglund was a colorful local character who remains beloved since his death in 1985 (see Eccentric Seattle Residents on p. 29). The waterfront Acres of Clams location still showcases Ivar's original recipes, and many consider the clam chowder here the best in the city (myself included). Besides the chowder, Ivar's offers fresh steamed clams, traditional fish-and-chips, jumbo prawns, salmon, and halibut.

SALTY'S ON ALKI BEACH $$$
1936 Harbor Ave. SW (South)
(206) 937-1600
www.saltys.com

The food is good at Salty's, but the waterfront view is even better. The vantage point across the bay in West Seattle offers the best, most breathtaking vistas of the city, as made famous in the opening of the *Frasier* television series. The seafood dishes are decidedly influenced with Pacific Northwest flair, using ingredients such as chèvre cheese in the shellfish stuffing and fresh, local herbs in just about everything. The coconut prawns and blackened salmon are favorites, and of course the menu abounds with a large variety of fish and shellfish, as well as steaks. The

in-house pastry kitchen turns out incredible desserts from scratch. Salty's is crowded almost all day on the weekends, from the popular brunch right through the evening, but the restaurant is large and accommodating. If you're in Seattle over the winter holidays, it makes a fun time to visit—Salty's really goes overboard with the lights and decoration, and it's really quite special.

STEELHEAD DINER $$
95 Pine St. (Central)
(206) 625-0129
www.steelheaddiner.com

Just around the corner from Pike Place Market, Steelhead feels as close to the water as it is, with the hand-tied fishing lures and large color photographs of fishermen lining the walls. New Orleans native Kevin Davis is the chef and owner, and turns out chicken and andouille sausage gumbo, along with dependable crab cakes and seafood chowders. Steelhead aims to be a diner without pretension, where locals hang out and bring their out-of-town visitors. The views are great, overlooking the market, Elliott Bay, and the Olympic Mountains.

SPANISH/TAPAS

HARVEST VINE $$
2701 E. Madison (Central)
(206) 320-9771
www.harvestvine.com

Serving a menu straight out of Basque country, Harvest Vine presents dishes such as venison leg poached in coffee oil, whole salt-crusted daurade fish, pan-seared tuna belly with saffron rice, and seared foie gras with caramelized pumpkin. Authenticity is of utmost importance, as genuine Basque ingredients are imported from Spain and underappreciated finds such as oil-slicked sardines are prized. Chef Joseba even shares recipes on the Web site.

OCHO $$

2325 NW Market St. (North)
(206) 784-0699
www.ochoballard.com

This lovely little tapas bar has a nice wine selection, but its real drink specialties are the signature cocktails. The food is simple and rustic, from *albondigas* (lamb meatballs in a brandy sauce), *chorizo con huevo,* and *gambas al ajillo* (spicy garlic prawns). The dates stuffed with blue cheese seem to get raves from everyone. The *pan con chocolate* also wins raves—a chocolate dessert toast that is at once sweet, salty, and spicy.

TANGO $$$

1100 Pike St. (Central)
(206) 583-0392
www.tangorestaurant.com

The Latin-inspired small plates and cocktails at Tango are served in a sophisticated, warm environment filled with local artwork. Dishes from Spain and Portugal and down into North Africa are served, and the paellas are authentic and plentiful. Accompanying the food is a well-rounded wine list and a wide assortment of high-quality tequilas and rums from the charming bar lounge. Every Mon evening, bottles of wine are half price. If you skip the El Diablo decadent chocolate cake, you are really doing yourself a disservice.

TXORI $$

2207 2nd Ave. (Central)
(206) 204-9771
www.txoribar.com

The same team that opened the wildly popular Harvest Vine is behind Txori. It's in a very New York–looking space, long and narrow with shelves that stretch to the ceiling, all stocked with wine or jars and cans of food. Txori serves tapas from the Basque region of Spain, and the owner comes from San Sebastian—probably the reason that the food is so authentic and wins rave reviews just about everywhere. *Pintxos,* as the San Sebastian tapas are known, are served here. From chunks of slow-braised pork caramelized to a crisp and served on a slice of tomato-soaked baguette, to octopus tentacle, to piquillo peppers stuffed with sausage and then fried, everything at Txori is both authentic and delectable.

> **i** A great way to see and eat your way through Seattle is on one of several fun, delicious guided walking tours. Companies such as Seattle Bites Food Tours, Savory Seattle, and Seattle By Foot offer great culinary adventures through the city. Check out the tour listings in our Attractions section for more details.

STEAK HOUSES

EL GAUCHO $$$$

2505 1st Ave. (Central)
(206) 728-1337
www.elgaucho.com

Chances are, if you stay in Seattle long, you will hear tales of El Gaucho, a legacy in the Northwest. Miles away from the traditional steak house, El Gaucho is part speakeasy and part midcentury throwback. The tableside salad-tossing and steak-carving service is totally retro, as is the live pianist playing in the background. The famous steaks are certified prime Angus beef, dry-aged to a juicy tenderness. More exotic steaks are also on the menu, including ostrich and venison. For those not into red meats, El Gaucho offers fresh fish and lobster, a healthy list of sides and salads, and a divine wild mushroom risotto. The wine list is heady and covers a wide price range; however, you can bring your own bottle for a $30 corkage fee. El Gaucho should be visited for more than a meal; it's a night to remember, and perfect for those special occasions. Check out the Pampas Room next door, for cabaret and burlesque entertainment.

METROPOLITAN GRILL $$$$
820 2nd Ave. (Central)
(206) 624-3287
www.themetropolitangrill.com

Where El Gaucho is unconventional, Metropolitan exudes everything that comes to mind when you think about a steak house. The decor is classic, with mahogany and brass fixtures and walls filled with framed photographs of the celebrities who have patronized Metropolitan. They even have a glass display filled with red hunks of meat at the front entrance. The thick porterhouses combined with an icy martini are timeless. Japanese Wagyu beef and plenty of seafood are also on the menu. The black marble bar is always packed, partly because of the boys'-club feel that is warm and welcoming to both genders, and also because Metropolitan offers one of the best happy hours in town.

STREET FOOD

Special note about street food: For enterprises located in a constant spot keeping regular hours, this is noted in their listings. Other street food entrepreneurs operate on a rolling schedule of sites; if a location is not specified, check their Web site for where to find them. Many also post Twitter or mobile

schedules that you can check or subscribe to. But hey, chasing down awesome street food around town is a very Seattle thing to do!

DANTE'S INFERNO DOGS $
5219 Ballard Ave. NW (North)
(206) 283-3647
www.dantesinfernodogs.com

From one hot dog cart that Dante Rivera ran with his dog, Josie, for five years, Dante's now boasts five units that roam all around the city. But these are not your ordinary hot dogs. The Mexican chipotle veggie dog, chicken andouille sausage dog, and apple sage will set your idea of hot dogs on its head. A bricks-and-mortar window was recently established in Ballard as a permanent location. For other locations and hours around the city, see the Web site; Dante's Inferno Dogs can be found in University Village, Bellevue, and West Seattle every day. And yes—Dante is his real name.

EL CAMION $
11728 Aurora Ave. North (North)
2918 1st Ave. South (South)
(206) 367-2777
www.elcamionseattle.com

Two locations of El Camion serve up authentic Mexican food in some of the most pristine, spotless mobile kitchens you will ever see. From simple favorites like tacos and burritos, to mouth-watering carne asada, carnitas, tamales, and *mulitas*, El Camion has an extensive menu that is sure to please everyone. Condiments include salsa in four levels of hotness, from mild to smoking, and a big jar of pickled vegetables on the counter from which you help yourself. Both locations are generally open from 8 a.m. to 10 p.m. every day.

HALLAVA FALAFEL $
5825 Airport Way South (South)
www.myspace.com/hallava

Take a traditional falafel, cooked to a crispy golden perfection, wrap it in a soft grilled pita, and top it with your choice from an amazing list of condiments. Beet salad, sautéed peppers, tomato zucchini spread, spinach, salted cucumbers, and tahini are all on the list. Oh, and traditional tzatziki sauce, too. *Gourmet* magazine reported that "every bite is an adventure." Look for the big yellow truck.

KAOSAMAI $
1010 Valley St. (Central)
3 W. Nickerson St. (North)
(206) 288-3534
www.kaosamai.com

This brightly colored truck at South Lake Union serves the street version of the Thai food found at its bricks-and-mortar restaurant in Fremont. Go with a standby favorite like pad thai, or try the pad kee mao, drunken noodles with chicken, vegetables, and plenty of chiles. The two mobile locations are open Mon through Fri from 11 a.m. until 2:30 p.m. They also bring catering onsite via the mobile restaurants.

MARINATION MOBILE $
www.marinationmobile.com

Calling itself "Seattle's sauciest food truck," Marination won the best food cart in the country on *Good Morning America* in 2009. The cart specializes in Hawaiian and Korean food, marinated in their own signature sauce and mostly served in tortillas, but sometimes on buns. The pulled-pork sliders win raves from everyone who tries them, and there are great vegetarian options as well. Marination also serves unexpectedly inventive items like

the miso ginger chicken and what they call Spam sushi—a grilled slice of Spam, making love to a ball of rice and wrapped in a seaweed blanket. Seriously, I know how it sounds, but you have to try it. You'll never badmouth Spam again.

MAXIMUS/MINIMUS $
Southeast corner of 2nd and Pike
   (Central)
(206) 601-5510
www.maximus-minimus.com

Calling itself SomePig and its tweets Tw'Oinks, this crazy-looking metal food trailer has been customized to resemble a giant silver pig. This food destination is all about making the most delectable pulled pork sandwiches possible, which come either hot and spicy or tangy and sweet. You can add Beecher's Flagship cheese for less than a dollar, and a veg version is also available. The slaw makes a nice addition. Maximus/Minimus is usually found at 2nd and Pike downtown from 11 a.m. to 3 p.m., but it sometimes adds other locations and also provides mobile catering services.

SKILLET $
www.skilletstreetfood.com

Josh Henderson and his wife, Kelli, buy old Airstream trailers and outfit them with full commercial kitchens. Then Josh and his staff roam the streets of Seattle to serve impeccably executed, locally sourced bistro food. Josh graduated from the Culinary Institute of America in New York but felt that the upscale mobile food market in Seattle was underserved, and made it his mission to fill that niche. Skillet's specialty is bacon jam, which is bacon rendered with spices and onions, simmered for six hours, and then pureed. It's great served over the grass-fed beef burger; other menu items include a mushroom-pesto linguine, duck tacos, and Canadian *poutine* (crispy fries with gravy and cheese). Skillet moves all over the city and can be found on its Web site and Twitter/Facebook feeds.

TACOS EL ASADERO $
3517 Rainier Ave. South
7300 Martin Luther King Jr. Way South
(206) 722-9977

Known as the "taco buses," these two converted school buses serve what are regularly called the best tacos in Seattle. Traditional, old-school Mexican tacos are served in *mulitas* (a crispy tortilla sandwich) with avocado, cheese, and salsa. You can eat them right inside the bus, where a television is usually playing Spanish-language soap operas. Beef and chicken tacos as well as tamales and quesadillas are on the menu, and be aware that portions are large.

THAI

KAOSAMAI $$
404 N. 36th St. (North)
(206) 925-9979
www.kaosamai.com

In case you are wondering how to say the name of this restaurant, it's pronounced "gow sa mai," which means the ninth dynasty of the royal family. This coral-colored house in the lively Fremont neighborhood just underwent a remodel and serves very traditional Thai food, such as noodles and curries, as well as some specialty dishes like Swimming Rama (chicken or tofu served on spinach with peanut sauce) and Pla Sam Rose (a whole trout deep-fried, then smothered in sweet and sour sauce with fresh mango). When the weather is lovely, dine al fresco on the 1,000-square-foot sun deck.

MAY RESTAURANT AND LOUNGE $$
1612 N. 45th St. (North)
(206) 675-0037
www.mayrestaurant.com

I really like the Wallingford neighborhood, and I really like May. Housed in a two-story pagoda-style teak building with bright blue doors, the restaurant is upstairs while a lounge is on the ground floor. The interior is filled with so many gorgeous antique doors, statues, and other objects that it is a feast for the eyes. The entire ambience is warm and sophisticated, and the service is impeccable yet almost invisible. The same drama mixed with quality infuses the food—consider the pad thai, perhaps the most pedestrian of all Thai dishes in America. At May's, it is served in the traditional way, wrapped in a banana leaf and presented with a flourish. Other top dishes include seafood sautéed in basil sauce and the Gai Yang grilled chicken. Due to the full bar and lounge downstairs, cocktails are top-notch and inventive; check out the romantic lounge on a Thurs or Fri night, when they feature live jazz.

ORRAPIN THAI $
10 Boston St. (Central)
(206) 283-7118
www.orrapin.com

This Queen Anne restaurant is consistently reliable, with a neighborhood feel. The strongest dishes are the brothy noodles and the curries, which are spicier (as opposed to overly sweet) than many Thai restaurants. It's a pretty and elegant space, and all dishes are prepared with fresh ingredients.

VEGAN/VEGETARIAN

CAFE FLORA $$
2901 E. Madison St. (Central)
(206) 325-9100
www.cafeflora.com

This light-filled restaurant with a stylish, minimalist decor consistently wins "Best of" readers' polls among Seattle Web sites and magazines. It used to be an old Laundromat, until three friends decided to gut it in 1991 and open a community-based restaurant serving creative vegetarian cuisine. Cafe Flora is dedicated to using sustainable produce and environmentally friendly design and practices. Specialties are the spicy Oaxaca tacos and the portobello mushroom Wellington. For extra serenity, request a table in the tranquil indoor patio garden with its bubbling fountain.

CHACO CANYON ORGANIC CAFE $$
4757 12th Ave. NE (North)
(206) 522-6966
www.chacocanyoncafe.com
A favorite not just for vegans and vegetarians, Chaco is the destination for raw-food and healthy-eating aficionados. One of the few restaurants in the nation that can say it is more than 90 percent certified organic year-round, this Southwestern-style cafe features a daily raw-foods menu, as well as vegan sandwiches and soups, rice and quinoa bowls, baked goods, smoothies, and fair trade tea and espresso. Organic wine, sake, and beer are also served. Chaco is committed to sustainable practices not only with its food, but throughout all business decisions and the staff.

HILLSIDE QUICKIE VEGAN SANDWICH $
4106 Brooklyn Ave. NE (North)
(206) 632-3037
www.hillsidequickie.com
Hillside is always crowded at lunchtime, a popular spot with students and faculty in the University District. A variety of sandwiches,

burgers, soups, and sides are on the menu, including the Crazy Jamaican Burger with jerk seasoning and the fire-roasted yam on focaccia. For more extensive fare, check out their sister restaurant, Sage Cafe, below.

PIZZA PI $
5500 University Way NE (North)
(206) 343-1415
www.pizza-pi.net
This 100 percent vegan pizza joint uses the freshest ingredients and no animal products in anything, and offers a gluten-free dough choice. Along with veggie topping favorites, there are also meatless "meats," such as pepperoni and sausage. Salads, calzones, sandwiches, and desserts are also on the menu.

SAGE CAFE $
324 15th Ave. East (Central)
(206) 325-6429
www.hillsidequickie.com
Sage offers many of the same types of burgers and sandwiches that Hillside does, but extends the offerings with a wide range of pizza by the slice, with toppings such as heirloom tomato, roasted squash, Thai red curry, and enchilada. The burger menu is also expanded, with gourmet burgers like the Portabella and the Mahalo.

VIETNAMESE

GREEN LEAF $
418 8th Ave. South (Central)
(206) 340-1388
www.greenleaftaste.com
This small, sweet restaurant is a perennial favorite of Seattleites for fresh dishes heavily flavored with cilantro, mint, and lime. The noodle bowls with grilled pork, crab soup, and mint shrimp rolls are always good, but the beef noodle pho soup, scented with

anise, gets raves. Green Leaf is family owned and operated, and highly focused on customer service.

MONSOON $$$
615 19th Ave. East (Central)
(206) 325-2111
www.monsoonseattle.com
Sibling chefs Eric and Sophie Banh, natives of Saigon, bring their traditional Vietnamese cuisine to this Capitol Hill restaurant and marry it with Pacific Northwest innovation. Their signature crispy drunken chicken is constantly lauded, and other dishes are equally innovative. Try the caramelized catfish claypot, or the Carlton Farm flank steak that is wrapped in *la lot* leaves and then grilled. Not only is the food local and fresh, but it also arrives looking so beautiful that you're almost loath to dig into it. Monsoon boasts an extensive wine list

TAMARIND TREE $
1036 S. Jackson St. (Central)
(206) 860-1404
www.tamarindtreerestaurant.com
This provincial Vietnamese restaurant is a little quirky, a hidden gem in a rather unremarkable strip mall in the International District. The fresh rolls are highly recommended, from the crunchy tofu to the cilantro spring rolls. The aromatic Thang Long yellowfish is tender and one of the most popular dishes, but the menu is plentiful with traditional soups, satay, seafood, beef, noodles, and specialty dishes such as the scallop, pork, and mushroom crepes. The decor and ambience are very stylish, with artistic lighting and an inventive cocktail list that will make you feel as if you're in 1930s Saigon. Don't skip the roasted coconut ice cream.

NIGHTLIFE

As you may have deduced by now, Seattle is an eclectic city that is home to preppy techies, tattooed hipsters, creative musicians, granola hippies, young families, outdoor adventurers, health nuts, urban sophisticates, and everyone in between. The nightlife scene in the city certainly reflects this; you could watch a world-class opera, catch a movie at a theater that used to be a school, dance the night away at a trendy club, watch a drag show at a gay bar, throw back a few of the Northwest's famous craft beers at an old-fashioned pub, or hear a great band at a hole-in-the-wall club for a few bucks—you can even do several of these in the same night and neighborhood!

A FEW BASICS . . .

Before we get started on the details, let's cover a few basics to ensure a safe and fun night out. First of all, please don't drink and drive. In Washington state, drivers are cited for DUI if the breath or blood test returns an amount of alcohol in the blood of .08 or higher (.02 or higher for minors under 21). If a suspected driver refuses to take a test for blood alcohol levels, his or her license will be revoked. Under Washington's Implied Consent law, simply operating a motor vehicle automatically gives consent to have your breath or blood tested if a law enforcement officer suspects you of driving under the influence.

If you don't have a designated driver, taxis are plentiful in Seattle even if they aren't constantly plying the streets. Any bartender or club manager would be happy to call a cab for patrons. Also, don't equate drunk driving with the evening; a March 2010 report by the Washington State Patrol showed a concerning increase in daytime DUI arrests, and officers are alert for this accordingly.

i Anna's Ride Home is a great program that provides an alternative to getting behind the wheel if you've been drinking. It's a free cab voucher program sponsored by 32 bars in the Seattle area and has kept more than 4,000 intoxicated drivers off the road since it began in 2003. For more information and a list of participating establishments, go to www.annasride home.com.

The legal drinking age in Washington is 21, and many establishments that have both a restaurant and a bar or lounge will not allow minors in the bar area. The state also has some of the strictest open-container laws in full federal compliance, meaning that there must be no possession or consumption of any alcoholic beverages by any passenger or driver, anywhere in a motor vehicle. There are additional penalties for trying to disguise an open container of alcohol.

Washington state liquor laws require bars to stop serving alcohol at 2 a.m.; therefore, most places have "last call" at 1:30 a.m.

The state liquor board operates differently from those of a lot of states, and there are some quirks to be aware of. Mainly, the state operates all liquor stores—there are no privately owned liquor stores (although there are a few contract stores here and there). While grocery stores, markets, and specialty stores do sell beer and wine, to buy hard liquor you will have to go to a government store run by the Washington State Liquor Control Board. Also, the state stores are not open on Sunday, although a few of the contract stores are. To find a liquor store, visit the Control Board's Web site at http://liq.wa.gov/services/storesearch.asp.

Seattle law requires all bars serving hard liquor to also serve food, resulting in some great lounges-cum-restaurants with often excellent menus. All bars serve at least small plates, and even the most dive hole-in-the-wall spots will have basic pub grub available—good to know if you're drinking the night away on an empty stomach. The only establishments not required to serve food are those with a tavern license, which can sell only beer and wine.

Lastly, as mentioned previously, Seattle has a smoking ban that prohibits smoking inside any public building or business or within 25 feet of its front door. All nightlife spots are, therefore, smoke-free (although some of the older, historic venues were so thoroughly steeped in smoke for so many years that a smell still permeates). There is a $100 fine if you are caught smoking in a banned area, which includes all bars, lounges, music venues, and nightclubs.

A Quick Note: I found many venues in this chapter a bit challenging to classify. Is a spot that has a live DJ with dancing two nights a week a bar, or a dance club? While there can certainly be some crossover with the definitions of different nightspots, I have tried to organize them by their primary persona. Therefore, only clubs that are primarily for dancing, and where that occurs on most every night they're open, go under the Dance Club section.

BARS AND COCKTAIL LOUNGES

CAPITOL CLUB
414 E. Pine St. (Central)
(206) 325-2149
www.thecapitolclub.net
The rich, warm reds of the Moroccan-inspired decor in this Capitol Hill lounge are immediately inviting. The upstairs bar is the place to be for serious drinking and socializing, and if you get there early enough for sunset, the outdoor deck provides a spectacular view. A nice mix of entertainment is offered at Capitol Club, from live flamenco or belly dancing to acoustic guitar performances and trivia nights. Thurs through Sat nights always have a DJ, and there is no cover from 10 p.m. on. The food is also good, with service until midnight.

CHAPEL
1600 Melrose Ave. (Central)
(206) 447-4180
www.chapelseattle.com
This intimate bar is situated in a 1920s building that was once a place for spirits of a different sort—it used to be a mortuary. Bruce Lee was laid out here before his burial in a nearby Capitol Hill cemetery. Now the space is stylish and warm, serving a full menu until 10 p.m. and a sophisticated bar menu during all open hours. The VIP balcony lounge is available for private gatherings, and various performers entertain, such as popular local DJs and hip-hop acts. The Chapel's happy hours are cleverly named Communion and Midnight Mass.

FEEDBACK LOUNGE
6451 California Ave. SW (South)
(206) 453-3259
www.feedbacklounge.net

This cool, retro Alki Beach joint has been around only since 2009 but has already made a splash in West Seattle. It's a full-service cocktail lounge with an excellent food menu and great music theme; check out the extensive collection of music memorabilia that decorates the Feedback, and don't miss the vintage guitars on display in the Whammy Bar. The Sunndeck is a 40-foot outdoor lounge where patrons are allowed to smoke. Co-owner and bartender Matt Johnson features special Sunday Market Cocktails; each Sunday he goes to the West Seattle farmers' market, picks two ingredients, and invents that day's drink out of them.

GREY GALLERY AND LOUNGE
1512 11th Ave. (Central)
(206) 325-5209
www.greygalleryandlounge.com

This fantastic Capitol Hill space features the painting, sculpture, installation, video, and performance art of local emerging artists in a unique and compelling atmosphere. Owner and artist Erik Guttridge struggled for years to get an art gallery on its feet, until he found the secret ingredient: booze. Along with the fantastic exhibited work at any given time, Grey also features lectures, theater performances, silk-screening parties, and many other events. The bar is impressively stocked and there is a nice food menu as well. Grey definitely reaches the goal that Guttridge had in mind, that of a melting pot of culture for the community.

HAZLEWOOD
2311 NW Market St. (North)
(206) 783-0478
www.myspace.com/hazlewoodbar

Some of the most surprising, even outrageous alcoholic concoctions can be found at this small Ballard lounge. Case in point: the Blackbird, made with pomegranate liqueur, crème de cassis, and squid ink. Seriously. The Hazlewood may be one of the best cocktails in the city—Bushmills Irish whiskey, honey peppermint tea, and a splash of amaretto. Did I mention that it's served with a Theo chocolate truffle and a Nat Sherman clove cigarette? Great for aromatherapy even if you don't smoke (and the cigarettes are not allowed to be smoked inside). Downstairs is standing room only, and the upstairs loft is filled with plush sofas and a nice collection of artwork adorning the walls.

JUJU
2224 2nd Ave. (Central)
(206) 728-4053
www.jujulive.com

This is the second incarnation of Juju, which moved from 10th Avenue in 2009. And they still don't require a cover charge. Blown-glass flames above the bar are a wicked touch to the serious drinks served here. The music is a revolving set of live local bands and DJs, who play mostly alternative, indie, and punk sounds. Some fun spots of kitsch include the miniature koi pond and old-fashioned photo booth (even more fun after you've tossed back a few). The front patio area is smoker-friendly, and the garden patio out back is heated by lamps, making it accessible year-round.

MONKEY PUB
5305 Roosevelt Way NE (North)
(206) 523-6457
www.myspace.com/monkeypub

This University District spot is a revolt against trendy, hipster lounges. Monkey Pub is a bar that's all about going back to the basics, from the jukebox with a great indie playlist to the pool and pinball tables. The scene is ultra laid-back and casual, with even the occasional live local band. Beer and simple, traditional mixed drinks are the beverages of choice here; although the bartender would certainly make an appletini, be prepared for the derisive looks. Best to stick with a vodka tonic or Bear Creek Porter.

REDWOOD
514 E. Howell St. (Central)
(206) 329-1952
www.redwoodseattle.com
Like Monkey Pub, this is not a martini bar and the bartenders will make sure you know it. Order a beer from one of several on tap or a "real drink" made with Old Crow whiskey, then partake of the plentiful peanuts whose shells cover the floor in true dive bar fashion. Unlike Monkey Pub, plenty of skinny jeans and carefully messy beards are to be found here. Mat Brooke of indie darlings Band of Horses and currently, Grand Archives, opened Redwood in 2006, giving it definite musician cred. The place has a tongue-in-cheek kitsch lodge decor, from the spray-painted mural of a bear to the bar featuring rows of bullet casings. The jukebox is well-stocked with classic and modern rock, and the kitchen serves southern comfort food with a variety of vegetarian choices.

SAINT
1416 E. Olive Way (Central)
(206) 323-9922
www.thesaintsocialclub.com
The Saint is primarily a tequila bar—in fact, it calls itself "tequila salvation." The teal matador-themed watering hole elevates tequila to the elegant status of a martini,

with 85 top-notch agaves going into drinks along with fresh-squeezed juices and their own house-made syrups and infusions. The El Santo is the most popular drink, a made-from-scratch margarita that will ruin mixes forever for all who taste it. But this is the place to try a tequila cocktail besides a margarita—how about the Angelflower, with fresh mint, blue agave syrup, and cucumber; or the Campanilla, which they warn is not for the faint of heart, made with house-ground Arbol pepper, lime, and sugar. The Saint also serves tequila flights, and a few other drinks made with gin, bourbon, and rum are available. A full brunch and dinner menu of Mexican classics complete the offerings.

TAVERN LAW
1406 12th Ave. (Central)
(206) 322-9734
www.tavernlaw.com
Tavern Law celebrates the Prohibition-era speakeasy, with its low-lighted ambience and hidden rooms. Named after the 1832 Pioneer Inn and Tavern Law that legalized drinking in Seattle saloons, this cozy Capitol Hill spot clearly enjoys the pleasure of a well-crafted cocktail. The drink menu is large; *Gourmet* magazine called it "encyclopedic," and it sits on the long, curving bar awaiting your perusal. The drinks are classic, using traditional techniques such as fresh-squeezed juices and house-made syrups. The menu is full of dishes inspired by local farm ingredients.

VESSEL
1312 5th Ave. (Central)
(206) 652-0521
www.vesselseattle.com

Vessel's tagline is modern nightlife with timeless style, and that's what they strive to deliver. Housed in the historic 1926 Skinner Building, Vessel is not dank or pitch-dark like many Seattle bars. The clean lines with white walls and subtle amber lighting provide a soothing and elegant environment in which to socialize over great cocktails. Wines are carefully chosen, and the beer list is award-winning. A specialty cocktail menu offers refreshing spins on old classics, and a small plate menu is exceptionally good—try the lamb ragu. Vessel is a classic cocktail bar, without too much attitude or hipster cred that can be so annoying.

W BAR

1112 4th Ave. (Central)
(206) 264-6000
www.starwoodhotels.com
The bar at the W Hotel provides a sexy lounge scene ripped from the pages of a fashion magazine. You wouldn't know you were in Seattle here; it could be New York or Dallas or London. Dark wood and velvet drapes create an intimate atmosphere where stylish patrons of all ages gather elegantly; you won't see much flannel here. The W Bar is a popular place for before-dinner and after-show martinis or wine from a menu heavy with Washington and Oregon selections. A great globally inspired menu promises you won't leave hungry.

ZIG ZAG CAFÉ

1501 Western Ave., Suite 202 (Central)
(206) 625-1146
www.zigzagseattle.com
This charming, classic cocktail bar at the top of the hill that rises from Pike Place Market has one of Seattle's most famed bartenders. Murray Stenson, known in these parts as "Mur the Blur," is often called one of the

best bartenders in the country, and he alone makes Zig Zag worth coming to. His cocktail list is award-winning, featuring a number of hard-to-find spirits and drinks with interesting histories. Try Satan's Soulpatch, a bourbon concoction, or the Drink Without a Name, a glowing green libation made with vodka. A full-service restaurant churns out high-quality fare, mostly sourced from the market down the street. The specialty of the house is the flatbread pizza, but there is also a nice seafood selection and interesting Martini Steak rubbed with juniper and served with vermouth-pickled onions.

BILLIARDS AND BOWLING

BALLROOM

456 N. 36th St. (North)
(206) 634-2575
www.ballroomfremont.com
Fremont's pool hall and lounge offers six regulation-size billiards tables, big-screen HDTVs, and an outdoor bar and fire pit. Besides the pool-playing that dominates here, DJs also spin some good music, and trivia nights are popular. A full selection of beer, wine, and mixed drinks is available from three bars, and the in-house pizza oven churns out hand-tossed, New York–style 28-inch pizza pies until 1 a.m.

GARAGE

1130 Broadway Ave. (Central)
(206) 322-2296
www.garagebilliards.com
Deriving its name from the auto repair shop that was once housed in the 1928 building, Garage is very much a throwback to the '70s, with its multipurpose bowling alley, billiards rooms, and bar space. Although it's popular with local college students and hipsters, it also draws very serious pool players and often

features tournaments. The bowling alley portion is one of a kind, three stories high and the first to open within Seattle city limits. The recreation provides plenty of fun for your night out, but there are also plentiful lounging rooms with minimalist 1950s decor, full of Eames and Saarnin furniture. You can also catch reminders of the auto garage legacy in the chrome accents and high-gloss automotive paint. The restaurant serves a menu that is largely Italian and Mediterranean, with items such as hummus and antipasto. The crowd tends to be on the younger side, and Garage is frequented by aspiring musicians—not surprising when you learn that Pearl Jam's Mike McCready is one of the partners.

TEMPLE BILLIARDS
126 S. Jackson St. (Central)
(206) 682-3242
www.templebilliards.com
Temple has a decidedly old-fashioned billiards hall feel, with pizzas and sandwiches in addition to a full bar. Revolving DJs and a basement karaoke lounge provide diversions when a break from playing pool is needed.

BREWPUBS

Special note about brewpubs: Pubs offer both beer and food, usually a fairly extensive, high-quality menu. They could be categorized under both Restaurants and Nightlife. However, some pubs are family-friendly whereas others are strictly over 21, no minors allowed. For the purposes of this book, I have used this as a guideline to make the distinction. All of the pubs in this section are 21-and-up-only places that are more bar-centric and usually are open until 2 a.m. Family-friendly, restaurant-based brewpubs are found in the Restaurants section.

BROUWER'S CAFÉ
400 N. 35th St. (North)
(206) 267-2437
www.brouwerscafe.com
The big draw here is the amazing selection of 300-plus beers from around the world, including more than 60 on draft and more than 60 scotches. The food is classic, hearty pub food; try the Hunters Plate, juicy house-made sausage partnered with sauerkraut and a beer-mustard reduction. Salads, light seafood plates, and even falafels are served as well. Brouwer's also has blending classes and cask fests, as well as special brewmaster dinners with food and beer pairings.

ELYSIAN BREWING COMPANY
1221 E. Pike St. (Central)
(206) 860-1920
www.elysianbrewing.com
Elysian likes to claim that its brewpub began in the 17th century, when the owner's ancestors began smuggling hops and brewing equipment onto ships headed for the New World. Of course, Elysian assumes you are in on the joke, because that's just the kind of place it is. Since its start in 1996, Elysian has brewed more than 60 different beers and always serves six standard brews and a variety of changing seasonals. The full-service restaurant features a wide variety of typical pub grub, and often a beer festival or live music is going on. The original location is in Capitol Hill, with additional brewpubs across from Qwest Field and in Greenlake.

HILLTOP ALE HOUSE
2129 Queen Anne Ave. North (Central)
(206) 285-3877
www.seattlealehouses.com
The driving mission of Hilltop was to offer adults an upscale place to get a high-quality

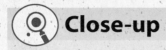

Close-up

The Pacific Northwest Microbrew Craze

"Beer is proof that God loves us and wants us to be happy," Benjamin Franklin famously remarked. It's a philosophy that the Pacific Northwest heartily embraces, judging by the recent craft-beer craze and sheer number of small brewpubs in the region.

America's love affair with beer existed long before Franklin, as colonists brought shipments of the beverage from England. The first help-wanted ad ever placed in the fledgling country was one looking for a brewer, in 1609; in 1612 Adrian Block and Hans Christiansen established the first known brewery in the New World, at the southern tip of what is now Manhattan. The adoration continued until the fateful hand of Prohibition intervened; after its repeal in 1933, brewing continued, but the small brewery fell by the wayside in drastic numbers over the next five decades, in favor of huge brewing giants such as Coors and Anheuser-Busch.

Enter Bert Grant, a colorful Scotsman who resettled in Washington state and opened the first brewpub in the modern United States, in Yakima in 1982, reviving the American tavern. It was the start of a new wave of craft microbrew pioneers. A microbrewery, by definition, is a small brewery that produces less than 15,000 barrels of beer annually and is typically focused much more on quality, variety, and local ingredients than corporate breweries.

Seattle and Portland led the way, from the 1980s on, in what has turned into a full-fledged craft brewery craze. The **McMenamin brothers** operate an ale empire of more than 50 pubs throughout Oregon and Washington, including locations in Queen Anne, Fremont, and Capitol Hill. **Pyramid Breweries** also has pubs in Washington, Oregon and California, but the Seattle Alehouse across the street from Safeco Field is the original location. The Great American Beer Festival dubbed the brewery innovators in the fruit beer category, for the unique Audacious Apricot Ale.

---

selection of imported and local microbrew beers in a traditional English pub environment, while also offering a gourmet menu. Hilltop has great food, far surpassing that of most bars. Try the asparagus ravioli with Dungeness crab, New Orleans–style gumbo, or the Bangkok Chicken Salad. More traditional pub fare is also available, such as pulled pork sandwiches, burgers, and a variety of soups and sandwiches, and specials change out every Wed. Two other locations worth checking out are the 74th Street Ale House at 7401 Greenwood Ave. North, and the Columbia City Ale House at 4914 Rainier Ave. South.

JOLLY ROGER TAPROOM
1514 NW Leary Way (North)
(206) 782-6181
www.maritimebrewery.ypguides.net
The taproom at Maritime Pacific Brewing Company, Jolly Roger is an intimate pub with a nautical theme. The selection of hand-crafted ales and lagers served on 14 taps are all fresh brewed right next door at Maritime, along with a selection of wines and nonalcoholic beverages. The menu runs the gamut from classic pub food to innovative dishes, most of which include one of the Maritime brews as an ingredient.

One of Washington's most popular brewpubs is **Elliott Bay Brewing Company,** with locations in West Seattle and Burien. Elliott Bay was the first brewery in King County to make organic beer, with 12 beers certified organic by the USDA and using 100 percent organic barley since 2005. Elliott Bay is a place where families abound, often outnumbering couples even on a weekend night in an atmosphere reminiscent of European pubs that have always been community watering holes where families socialize. The brewpub courts families, in fact, with its closing hours set at midnight and lack of hard alcohol (most pubs in Seattle are 21 and over only).

A few miles away, in the historic Pike Place Market, a different sort of brewer emerged. Charles Finkel and his wife, Rose Ann, operated an importing company in the 1970s to satisfy their own thirst for authentic, quality beers. The couple was frustrated by the lack of great American beers, and Finkel became the first modern contract brewer in the country, creating and exporting his own labeled beer out of existing breweries.

Finkel greatly influenced craft brewers to follow by introducing them, and the American public, to the glories of how good a beer could be. Finally, in 1989, the Finkels opened the **Pike Place Brewery** in a former bawdy house, to create world-class ale in the traditional European style. They even have the Seattle Microbrewery Museum downstairs—*Seattle* magazine calls it the "best place to learn about beer."

If you want to get in on Seattle's love for a good microbrewed beer, don't miss **Seattle Beer Week,** held each May; or the **International Beerfest** over Fourth of July weekend. For more info, check out the event Web sites www.seattlebeerweek.com and www.seattlebeerfest.com. The tour company Seattle By Foot also offers a great two-and-half-hour pub crawl on Fri and Sat nights, beginning at Pike Place Brewery. Check the Web site http://seattlebyfoot.com for more information.

McMENAMINS SIX ARMS
300 E. Pike St. (Central)
(206) 223-1698
www.mcmenamins.com

The Six Arms pub is named, improbably, after a six-armed Hindu goddess. Even the beer label has the image of the idol on it, and the odd juxtaposition fits right in with the funky Capitol Hill neighborhood where this pub is located. Filled with a long wooden bar, booths, an upstairs section with cafe tables, and a huge collection of chandeliers, Six Arms is among the large empire of brewpubs by the brothers McMenamin.

Handcrafted ales, a menu of classic pub fare, and daily specials are always on offer. Check out the McMenamins' other Seattle pubs; the British-style Dad Watsons in Fremont and the Queen Anne location near the Space Needle. Minors are allowed until 8 p.m.; after that, it's 21 and over only.

QUINN'S GASTROPUB
1001 E. Pike St. (Central)
(206) 325-7711
www.quinnspubseattle.com

Quinn's definitely meets the expectation that is implied by its name. This neighborhood spot is the perfect combination of pub bar and gastronomical experience. The 14 beers on tap are heavy on the Trappist-style ales, but the wine list is equally splendid, and there is even a sommelier on staff to make recommendations. The food is rich European fare such as pork pâté, fried frog legs, wild boar sloppy joes, and fish-and-chips. The environment is less that of a traditional pub and more a bistro cafe, with large plate-glass windows facing the Capitol Hill street outside.

BURLESQUE

CAN CAN
94 Pike St. (Central)
(206) 652-0832
www.thecancan.com
Seattle is one of those American cities in which the art of burlesque has been revived in a fairly big way. Tucked into a little Pike Place Market spot, the Can Can feels like a combination of burlesque, French Moulin Rouge, and 1920s speakeasy. In addition to the great burlesque and traditional cancan acts, the performances also generally feature comedy, acrobatic feats, and vaudeville. You can also include a three-course dinner with the show, but the food receives moderate, mixed reviews. They also feature Seattle's only absinthe bar, serving real absinthe (not the mixed or flavored liquor).

PINK DOOR
1919 Post Alley (Central)
(206) 443-3241
www.thepinkdoor.net
Part cabaret and part restaurant, the place has the look of an old-fashioned bordello and lets its guests escape the ordinary. Every night except Mon, the Pink Door provides entertainment including burlesque, but also

adding opera, magic, and even tarot. From a trapeze artist swinging from the 20-foot ceilings to a tap-dancing saxophone player, you're never sure which way to look in this cabaret. But naughty, feathered burlesque is the star of the show, with some of Seattle's best performers. Located in an alley in Pike Place Market, there is no sign, but look for—you guessed it—a pink metal door.

SINNER SAINT BURLESQUE AT CLUB NOC NOC
1516 2nd Ave. (Central)
(206) 223-1333
www.sinnersaintburlesque.com
Combining bawdy burlesque with truly talented song and dance numbers, this fun show also weaves in a streak of blue humor. The burlesque show is held every Thurs night at Club Noc Noc, as well as other area nightclubs and theaters (check the Web site for other show dates).

CINEMAS

AMC PACIFIC PLACE 11
600 Pine St. South (Central)
(206) 652-8908
**www.pacificplaceseattle.com/cinema/
index.aspx**
Right in the center of downtown Seattle, in the Pacific Place mall, is this 11-screen, state-of-the-art cinema featuring first-run movies. Each auditorium features cup holders at every seat, as well as special "love seats" with enough snuggling room for two. AMC has also partnered with other Pacific Place merchants to offer discounts when you present your same-day AMC movie ticket. Garage parking is available at the Pacific Place garage, from 6th or 7th Avenues, for $6 all evening after 5 p.m.

BIG PICTURE
2505 1st Ave. (Central)
(206) 256-0566
www.thebigpicture.net

This cinema was opened to try to combine a better moviegoing experience with more interesting meeting spaces. The result is a venue that offers corporate rentals, private parties, and private movie screenings, but they also have regularly scheduled public film showings. You can enjoy cocktails in the Big Picture lounge before your movie and then settle into the ultra-comfortable TempurPedic theater seats. You can even order your cocktails to be delivered right to your seat—it doesn't get much better than that. Only ages 21 and over are admitted.

CENTRAL CINEMA
1411 21st Ave. (Central)
(206) 686-MOVI
www.central-cinema.com

Although several local cinemas have restaurants on premises or attached, or serve cocktails, Central Cinema is Seattle's only dine-in movie house, where you can actually eat while you watch the movie. The theater has sofa seating and waiter service; you order at your seat, and your food and beverages come straight to you. It's like watching a first-run movie in your own living room, but with a huge screen and surround sound. Stone oven–baked pizza is the specialty, but salads, sandwiches, small plates, and even seared salmon are also on the menu. After the film, cozy up in Café Noir for dessert and coffee, located in the lobby. A couple of things worth mentioning are that if you buy your ticket at least one day in advance of the show, you get $2 off, and there are no service charges for tickets purchased online.

CINERAMA
2100 4th Ave. (Central)
(888) 262-4386
www.cinerama.com

Back when Microsoft cofounder Paul Allen was a kid in Seattle, he watched many films at the Cinerama, which opened in 1963. It was his memories of movies such as *2001: A Space Odyssey* shown on the unique three-panel Cinerama screen that motivated him to save the cinema in the 1990s, when it was nearly closed down. His rescue and multimillion-dollar renovation made him the owner of the last remaining Super Cinerama theater in the world. Technology was enhanced, but the original carpet, wallpaper, and gorgeous blue and green Italian mosaic tile work remain. Now you, too, can come and enjoy this one-of-a-kind movie experience. Cinerama shows first-run films as well as old favorites and cult classics, and is a don't-miss experience for cinema aficionados.

EGYPTIAN
805 E. Pine St. (Central)
(206) 781-5755
www.landmarktheatres.com/market/
   Seattle/EgyptianTheatre.htm

This classic cinema was built in 1915 as a Masonic temple; in the 1970s, the Masons used the auditorium as a wrestling arena to bring in extra money. By the 1980s they had vacated, and the facility became the home of the Seattle International Film Festival. The Egyptian continues to host the SIFF, as well as regular daily screenings of first-run, indie, foreign, documentary, and classic films. The Capitol Hill location means parking can be a challenge, particularly on weekend nights. Try the Community College Garage at Harvard and Pine; otherwise, you may end up walking a bit if you drive here.

GRAND ILLUSION CINEMA

1403 NE 50th St. (North)
(206) 523-3935
www.grandillusioncinema.org

In a city with a wealth of historic, independent movie houses, the Grand Illusion is possibly the most unique. It's the longest-running independent cinema in Seattle, opened in 1986 in a converted dentist's office. It quickly became known as a showcase for art-house, foreign, and revival films, and has always been passionately supported by a group of community volunteers. The Grand Illusion was threatened with closure in 1997, and the Northwest Film Forum swooped in to save it. Seeing a movie here is a true experience; the auditorium is small but exceedingly charming, with an intricate gold ceiling, custom upholstery on the chairs, and red velvet curtains. It tends to show a lot of films that you otherwise may not have ever heard of.

GUILD 45TH

2115 N. 45th St. (North)
(206) 781-5755
www.landmarktheatres.com/Market/
    Seattle/Guild45thTheatre.htm

This is one of Landmark's historic cinemas that was originally a theater. Built in 1919, the gorgeous building was the Paramount Theatre in the '20s and later began showing movies. The Guild still has a great art deco marquee. A second auditorium opened in the '80s, with a restaurant in between the two theaters. Both theaters have plush stadium seating, a wall-to-wall screen, and 70 mm/Dolby Digital sound capabilities. Francis Ford Coppola has conducted audience test screenings here many times.

HARVARD EXIT

807 E. Roy (Central)
(206) 781-5755
www.landmarktheatres.com/market/
    Seattle/HarvardExitTheatre.htm

This theater is located on a quaint, tree-lined street at the north end of Broadway, on Seattle's Capitol Hill. The building in which the Harvard Exit currently resides was originally constructed as a clubhouse for the Woman's Century Club in 1925. Today the theater offers Seattle's finest in independent film and foreign language cinema in a cozy atmosphere. Its large and glorious lobby retains a 1920s atmosphere, adorned with a fireplace, grand piano, and chandelier. A recent remodel adds a fully wheelchair accessible restroom on the main floor, expanded concession stand, and inside box office for those rainy Seattle nights. One of the very first "art" theaters in Seattle, the Harvard Exit set the standard for the exhibition of independent film and foreign language cinema. Annually, the Harvard Exit is one of the venues for the Seattle International Film Festival as well as the Lesbian and Gay Film Festival.

NEPTUNE

1303 NE 45th St. (North)
(206) 781-5755
www.landmarktheatres.com/Market/
    Seattle/NeptuneTheatre.htm

This University District cinema was built in 1921 and is one of the last single-screen movie theaters in Seattle. It was completely remodeled in 1994, keeping the nautical theme and upgrading to a top-notch sound system with Dolby and SDDS Digital. The concession stand was actually created by a local boat builder, and the auditorium is lined with heads of the sea god Neptune.

SEVEN GABLES
911 NE 50th St. (North)
(206) 781-5755
www.landmarktheatres.com/Market/
  Seattle/SevenGablesTheatre.htm
It would be easy to pass this cinema by and never even know it was a movie theater. Built in 1925 as an American Foreign Legion dance hall, it looks more like a looming residential home with its gabled roof. In 1976 it was converted into Landmark Theatres' first cinema and today offers a mix of independent and foreign films, with an occasional first-run Hollywood hit. Don't let the cozy home look be deceptive—the Seven Gables is outfitted with all modern features, including Dolby Digital surround sound and stadium seating.

COMEDY CLUBS

COMEDY UNDERGROUND
109 S. Washington St. (Central)
(206) 628-0303
www.comedyunderground.com
With a wide variety of performers and acts, Comedy Underground puts on a show at 8 every night, with a second 10:15 p.m. show on Fri and Sat. Shows on Sun through Thurs are all ages. A full kitchen is available during the show, serving appetizers, sandwiches, burgers, pizza, and a few other dishes. Open-mic nights and courses in stand-up comedy are also offered. The location can be a bit hard to find and the neighborhood slightly sketchy.

GIGGLES COMEDY CLUB
5220 Roosevelt Way NE (North)
(206) 526-5653
www.gigglescomedyclub.com
Located in the University District, Giggles is open to all ages and serves food as well as drinks from the full-service bar. Performers are national touring comedians as well as local talent, and shows are held on Fri and Sat at 7:30 p.m. Thurs and Sun are open-mic nights at 8:30. It's a basic place with no frills or gimmicks, just a focus on quality comedy shows. Note that Giggles is a cash-only establishment; an ATM machine is available on the premises.

LAFF HOLE AT CHOP SUEY
1325 E. Madison St. (Central)
(206) 324-8000
www.myspace.com/laffhole
This comedy club calls itself the "People's Republic of Komedy" and takes place on the first and third Wed of each month in the Asian-themed Chop Suey nightclub. Laff Hole is an alternative stand-up comedy act with virtually no holds barred, and you never know who may drop in. A couple of years ago, Robin Williams surprised patrons by showing up and laughing heartily at the show—then jumping on stage to perform his own manic, completely improv set.

UNEXPECTED PRODUCTIONS
1428 Post Alley (Central)
(206) 587-2414
www.unexpectedproductions.org
Seattle's longest-running improv comedy show is housed in the historic Market Theater in Pike Place Market. The production company has performed all over the world, and various shows run Sun through Wed nights. The shows allow all ages, and the company gives them a rating of PG-13. A concessions booth is outside the theater, and a full bar lounge is accessible for those 21 and over. Check out the rather disgusting but somehow intriguing exterior brick wall as you enter the theater, which is covered

in thousands of wads of used chewing gum deposited by countless former patrons.

DANCE CLUBS

ALIBI ROOM
85 Pike St., Suite 410 (Central)
(206) 623-3180
www.seattlealibi.com
This hip, stylish little spot is located under the Pike Place Market and serves a menu of old-fashioned, stiff drinks in a see-and-be-seen kind of atmosphere. On Fri and Sat nights a DJ plays eclectic music, and the dance floor is usually hopping. The Alibi Room is also a hub for Seattle's arts communities, and regular multimedia events and art exhibits are held.

BALTIC ROOM
1207 Pine St. (Central)
(206) 625-4444
www.thebalticroom.net
The Baltic Room is primarily a club for dancing, with a diverse mix of DJs and occasional live artists delivering cutting-edge music. The stylish decor is an homage to the decadent bars of New York and London, with a mix of gritty and elegant. The crowd tends toward a professional thirty-something mix of straight and gay. Just because the Baltic features a DJ most of the time, don't think it is only dance beats: This lounge can surprise you, with everything from slinky torch singers to world-beat drummers; on the second and fourth Sat each month is Bollywood Bhangra. Check out the loft mezzanine for a bird's-eye view of the action, with its gorgeous mohair booths.

SEE SOUND LOUNGE
115 Blanchard St. (Central)
(206) 374-3733
www.seesoundlounge.com

This Belltown designer lounge is almost always packed after 10 p.m., seemingly with all of Seattle's beautiful people. The bar front is huge windows that slide open, and the interior walls are covered with waterfalls and television screens running films of deep-sea life. Take a seat on a plush couch in front of a fish tank and sip on your delicious cocktail presented by another of Seattle's model set. There is a good rotating list of DJs from around the world; if your goal is conversation, See Sound can get very loud. The food is surprisingly good, with a European bistro-style menu; See Sound is a popular weekend brunch spot for locals.

GAY AND LESBIAN

CHANGES BAR & GRILL
2103 N. 45th St. (North)
(206) 545-8363
www.changesinwallingford.com
Changes provides a comfortable, friendly atmosphere with good service and reasonable prices. One of the longest-running gay bars in Seattle, it is located in the quaint Wallingford neighborhood and hosts a variety of daily specials and events. One of the most popular is the casual karaoke show three nights a week; pool tables, dartboards, and video games are also available. A decent beer selection and full bar are complemented with a menu featuring basics such as burgers and tacos. Even first-timers to Changes are treated like regulars.

ELITE
1520 E. Olive Way (Central)
(206) 860-0999
www.theeliteseattle.com
After closing its doors as the oldest gay bar on Capitol Hill, the Elite reopened in 2007 with its same motto of "Enter as strangers,

leave as friends." It's a friendly place with a pretty big roster of regulars, and a discernable lack of attitude or posturing. Pool tables, darts, a jukebox, and four large HDTVs give the Elite its living room feel.

i Seattle is extremely gay-friendly, and although Capitol Hill is the neighborhood that is sort of the "heart" of the LGBT community, the city is not at all segregated between gay and straight. There is a mixture of both practically everywhere, and while a few leather or cruise bars are for a specific clientele, for the most part you will find plenty of straight people at "gay" bars, and vice versa. "C'est la vie" is the motto here!

JULIA'S ON BROADWAY
300 E. Broadway (Central)
(206) 860-1818
www.juliasrestaurantseattle.com
Although Julia's is a full-service restaurant in Capitol Hill, its real draw is the drag show every Fri and Sat night that will keep you laughing the entire time. Tickets aren't inexpensive, and be aware that each drink ordered during the show will come with an additional service charge. As far as the food, it generally receives very mixed reviews, so my advice would be to eat first or stick to the basics.

LOBBY BAR
916 E. Pike St. (Central)
(206) 328-6703
www.thelobbyseattle.com
One of Seattle's newest LGBT bars, the lounge-style Lobby has a decidedly French cafe feel to its black-and-white color scheme. The setting is both cosmopolitan and relaxed, with specialty cocktails and a small plates menu. Various events and shows are held in the two-level Lobby Bar.

PURR COCKTAIL LOUNGE
1518 11th Ave. (Central)
(206) 325-3112
www.purrseattle.com
This Capitol Hill hangout is disproportionately filled with the pretty set, with a bartending crew that is generally very friendly and knowledgeable. It's a place where just about anyone would feel at home, no matter the sexual orientation—one Yelp reviewer even says he brings his mother. A fun aspect to Purr is the karaoke on Mon and Tues nights, which draws a mixed crowd and provides surefire entertainment. There's also a fairly extensive menu of Mexican-inspired dishes, if you come hungry.

R PLACE
619 E. Pine St. (Central)
(206) 322-8828
www.rplaceseattle.com
This three-level, hopping club is hard to classify—it's a dance spot with DJs and hip-hop music; it's also a drag show and has lots of male go-go dancers, with an amateur strip show on Thurs (appropriately called by its acronym, ASS). The decor is fun and eclectic, from photo booths to the fully decorated, upside-down Christmas tree hanging from the ceiling. One of the perennial favorites is the Lashes Cabaret show with Lady Chablis on Fri and Sat nights. R Place is doing something right, since it's been here for 25 years.

RE-BAR SEATTLE
1114 Howell St. (Central)
(206) 233-9873
www.rebarseattle.com

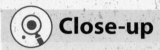 **Close-up**

Gay Pioneer Square: Coming Out from Underground Tour

If you really want a historic perspective on Seattle's LGBT community, check out this fun and interesting tour offered by the Seattle Architecture Foundation. Experience a time when more than the buildings had facades, as the tour delves into Pioneer Square's surprising past as the hotbed of LGBT life in the community. This historic area's once rowdy and run-down character gave cover to hidden outposts (frequently bars and taverns) where being gay was OK in contrast to the larger disapproving world of the early and mid-20th century. Learn how these safe havens for onetime outcasts developed into a community that eventually sought greater social and political recognition.

This tour lasts approximately 2 hours and begins in Pioneer Square on the corner of 3rd Avenue South and S. Washington Street at 10 a.m. Advance registration is strongly encouraged; walk-ups are limited to space available. Tour is $15 in advance, $20 on the day of tour. (206) 667-9184, www.seattlearchitecture.org/tour_gay pioneersquare.html.

This funky, inclusive, beloved Belltown nightclub has something different going on every night of the week. The sign at the entrance basically describes the clientele: "No minors, drunks, drugs, bigots, or loudmouths." Although Re-Bar caters to its loyal gay clientele, the patrons are a real mix of gay and straight, couples and groups. Local celebrity DJs pump the dance beats, and campy shows like Hedwig and the Angry Inch or Dina Martina perform in the fringe theater environment. It's even possible to see full frontal male nudity on occasion; truly, anything can happen at Re-Bar.

WILD ROSE
1021 E. Pike St. (Central)
(206) 324-9210
www.thewildrosebar.com
This is the most popular lesbian bar in Seattle, with a lot of events from karaoke and trivia nights to live bands and Fri wet T-shirt contests (possibly a reason for its popularity). Queer Spoken Word performances and numerous dance parties bring in a regular following. A full bar with good cocktails is offset by some very basic food that seems to come from a fairgrounds—corn dogs and tater tots. To be fair, the menu also includes pasta, pizza, burgers, tacos, and salads. One caveat is that people say, over and over, that the Wild Rose is not very welcoming to men, gay or straight.

LIVE MUSIC VENUES

CENTRAL SALOON
207 First Ave. S. #1 (Central)
(206) 622-0209
www.centralsaloon.com
Seattle's oldest bar (since 1892!) still knows how to party. It shows its age and stubbornly sticks to a dive bar mentality, with

sticky floors, bartenders with attitude, and truly frightening bathrooms. It's also a lot of fun and still very, very popular. The prices are good, with cheap tap beer and shots, making it one of the few places where you can avoid paying $8–$15 per drink. The music tends toward hard rock and metal, ranging from local acts to hilarious cover bands seven nights a week, and the crowd is mixed and tends to be more mellow than you may expect. All in all, a place where most bar crawlers will feel comfortable, and a slice of Seattle history at that—Nirvana, Soundgarden, and Alice in Chains have all played here.

CHA CHA LOUNGE
506 E. Pine St. (Central)
(206) 329-9978
www.chachalounge.com/seattle.html
The Cha Cha is a throwback, filled with retro kitsch and a sign on the door prohibiting attitude. Red light infuses the black velvet paintings that cover the walls, and it tends to draw the pierced punk and goth crowd. It was even written up in *Rolling Stone* magazine's 2008 Hot List. But don't think that it's not about the music here—acts like the Melvins and Modest Mouse have played. Bimbo's Cantina is upstairs if you get hungry, featuring burritos so huge you may need to work out to eat them. The cooks at Bimbo's are mostly musicians who also play the Cha Cha. Check out the ginormous vending machine that spits out all kinds of crap like *Yo! MTV Raps* cards, and don't forget to slide into the photo booth for a picture strip to tack up on the wall of shame.

CROCODILE CAFÉ
2200 2nd Ave. (Central)
(206) 441-7416
www.thecrocodile.com

The Crocodile was the epicenter of the grunge scene in the '90s and is still one of the best places in Seattle to catch indie and alternative music acts. From Nirvana and Pearl Jam to R.E.M. and Yoko Ono, the Croc has seen some of the biggest acts in the world. The place closed abruptly at the end of 2007, but after reconstruction and renovations, has thankfully reopened with an upgraded stage and serious sound system.

i For a weekly list of what's going on around town for live music and other nightlife, check out *Seattle Weekly*, the definitive source of information for music, movies, restaurants, and events around town (www.seattle weekly.com). The *Stranger* also provides great entertainment listings, as the free weekly alternative arts and culture newspaper (www.thestranger.com). You can pick them up at hundreds of street racks, restaurants, hotels, and stores.

DIMITROU'S JAZZ ALLEY
2033 6th Ave. (Central)
(206) 441-9729
www.jazzalley.com
Jazz Alley downtown is reminiscent of a classic 1940s supper club—plush seating, dim lighting and candles, excellent music, and innovative cocktails and food. The menu features Northwest cuisine with a Greek/Mediterranean flair, and service is generally very good. Table reservations are usually for those having a full dinner, but there is also a bar where you can just have drinks and listen to the music. A wide variety of musical styles and artists are found here, from legendary jazz musicians such as New Orleans' Preservation Hall Jazz Band to world music and indie singer-songwriters.

EL CORAZON

109 Eastlake Ave. East (Central)

(206) 262-0482

www.elcorazonseattle.com

This live rock venue tends toward hardcore, metal, experimental, and emo music, though occasionally you can find some more traditional and indie rock acts. The sound system is heavy-duty and state-of-the-art; your ears will come away blazing. The shows can sometimes get a little rough, as can the neighborhood, but the bar is fully staffed with security and it's easy to see why.

HIGHWAY 99

1414 Alaskan Way (Central)

(206) 382-2171

www.highway99blues.com

Highway 99 is a lively blues and rockabilly club housed in a historic 1909 brick building on the waterfront. The ambience is a combination of southern juke joint and Chicago blues bar, with a high-quality roster of musical performers. The interior is a clashing hodgepodge of blue velvet benches salvaged from the Masonic temple, blues memorabilia, and a fantastic 34-foot bar that was made from antique doors. Strings of lights give it a backyard, down-home feel, and the kitchen serves barbecue and Louisiana-style dishes. Besides blues and rockabilly, other featured music styles include honky-tonk, zydeco, and roots.

MOORE THEATRE

1932 2nd Ave. (Central)

(206) 682-1414

www.stgpresents.org/moore

Part of the Seattle Theatre Group, the Moore is a venerable institution in the city. Built in 1907, it's the oldest remaining theater in Seattle. Through the years it has seen operas and symphonies, stage plays and musicals, vaudeville acts, singers, and musicians. Just a few of the legends who have graced its stage include Sarah Bernhardt, Anna Pavlova, the Barrymores, Gypsy Rose Lee, Bob Dylan, Joan Armatrading, and Pearl Jam. Today you can see the biggest music acts in all genres, comedians, Cirque du Soleil, speaking engagements, and much more. The Moore does not have its own parking lot; you'll need to park in a garage or, better yet, take public transportation or a taxi.

NEUMOS

925 E. Pike St. (Central)

(206) 709-9442

http://neumos.com/neumos.php

The official name of this legendary Seattle music venue is Neumos Crystal Ball and Reading Room, but everyone just calls it Neumos. It has seen performances by the Shins, Bloc Party, the Raconteurs, Muse, and Seattle's own Band of Horses, to name just a few. Neumos features live music by national and local artists alike in several musical genres, including but not excluded to indie rock, hip-hop, punk rock, DJs, metal, singer-songwriters, country, and much more. There are three full-service bars and a nice mezzanine and balcony.

SHOWBOX AT THE MARKET

1426 1st Ave. (Central)

(206) 628-3151

www.showboxonline.com

This is one of the most storied of all live music venues in Seattle. Since its opening in 1939, the gorgeous art deco Showbox has survived from the Jazz Age to the era of grunge, welcoming performers as varied as Gypsy Rose Lee, Al Jolson, Muddy Waters, the Ramones, Iggy Pop, Blondie, Snoop Dogg, and the Dave Matthews Band. Its contribution to the Seattle music scene can't be underestimated, and today the Showbox still presents more than 200 shows each year. Don't miss the intimate Green Room lounge before or after the concert, with an appetizer menu and classic bar. Note that the Showbox does offer numerous all-ages shows in the calendar. There's not a lot of seating and big-name performers sell out fast, so plan to get tickets early depending on the show—and to most likely stand during the concert.

TRACTOR TAVERN
5213 Ballard Ave. NW (North)
(206) 789-3599
www.tractortavern.com
This Ballard staple of live music comes with full historic cred and has absolutely no attitude. It's not quite a dive, but walks the edge with a completely laid-back, no-frills interior that includes hundreds of boots hanging from the ceiling. It's relatively small, and virtually every spot in the house affords a terrific view of the stage. Music tends to be bluesy, Americana folk music with acts like Left Hand Smoke and the Dusty 45s. Note that while credit cards are accepted for advance ticket purchases and at the bar, on the day of the show only cash is accepted for entrance at the door. The crowd is a diverse mix of ages, and you can find anyone there from the techie to the tattooed. Square dancing and swing dancing are featured several times a month.

TRIPLE DOOR
216 Union St. (Central)
(206) 838-4333
www.thetripledoor.net
While many favorite live music joints in Seattle are endearing dives, with surly waitstaff and dirty bathrooms that make for a fun story to tell later, Triple Door isn't one of those. This is class and luxury all the way, located in the historic 1926 Mann building; nevertheless, it is a legendary performance venue with an impressive calendar. Triple Door combines its roster of world-class entertainment in a gorgeous setting, featuring the food and wine of acclaimed restaurant Wild Ginger, next door. A fun feature is the Musicquarium lounge, surrounded by a huge 1,900-gallon freshwater tank full of exotic fish.

MARTINI BARS

MARCUS' MARTINI HEAVEN
88 Yesler Way (Central)
(206) 624-3323
www.marcusmartiniheaven.com
This Pioneer Square martini lounge boasts having served more than 100,000 martinis since 1997. The sophisticated, sexy bar offers a wide range of premium martinis, from the classic to unique concoctions like the PB&J (with Frangelico and Chambord), Key lime pie (with Stoli Vanilla, triple sec, and a graham cracker rim), and the Seattle-themed Purple Haze (with Hendrix Vodka, of course). Marcus' also offers a limited selection of seasonal wines, a decent beer list, and a small bites menu.

TINI BIGS
100 Denny Way (Central)
(206) 284-0931
www.tinibigs.com
Named after the oversize martinis that are the specialty here, Tini Bigs has the feel of a combination of a bar and a diner. The Queen Anne location is great, and the bar stools and neon pink lighting give it a retro feel. It's very dark inside, with black walls and dim lighting, which can be either romantic or disorienting. More than 25 specialty martinis as well as a large selection of single-malt

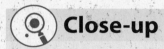

Close-up

Beyond Grunge: Seattle's Musical Progeny

Seattle has been one of the hotbeds in the United States for emerging musical talent, along with New York, Nashville, Los Angeles, and Austin. Jimi Hendrix is perhaps the most legendary individual musician to have ever come out of Seattle, and of course the city is famous for its birth of the grunge movement that spawned today's alternative music scene. (Insert sigh here—Seattleites get really tired of hearing about grunge and have retired the flannel already. Well, mostly.)

But you may not know that the Puget Sound area's spawning of musical prodigy began long before Hendrix or Nirvana. **Bing Crosby** was born in nearby Tacoma in 1903 and went on to become one of the first multimedia stars who enjoyed unrivaled commands of both the record charts and movie ticket sales for two decades. Well into the rock era, Bing Crosby was the best-selling recording artist, with a staggering half-billion-plus records in circulation.

Although **Quincy Jones** was born in Chicago in 1933, he was brought up in Seattle and lived here his entire childhood. The musician, composer, and producer went on to become the first African American to head an established, major record company (Mercury Records, 1961), and produced the best-selling album of all time, Michael Jackson's *Thriller*. He has also produced movies and television shows, including the Academy Awards, founded a magazine, and formed his own company, Quincy Jones Entertainment, in 1990.

Folk singer and political activist **Judy Collins** was born in Seattle in 1939; Bill and Hillary Clinton reportedly named their daughter after the song *Chelsea Morning*, released by Collins in 1969.

The world of music changed on November 27, 1942. That was the day **Jimi Hendrix** was born, growing up in South Seattle and attending Garfield High School. He was

scotches, and every other type of liquor and cocktail, offer plenty of choices. Try the Dirty Girl Scout martini (with crushed graham cracker rim) or the Fire Eater (pepper-infused vodka garnished with a jalapeño). There is also a nice food menu featuring varied items from sandwiches to satay.

SPORTS BARS

ALL NATIONS SOCCER BAR & RESTAURANT
930 N. 130th St. (North)
(206) 365-5165
www.allnationssoccerbar.com

If you love soccer, this is the place for you. In fact, it doesn't even call itself a "sports bar"— it is, unapologetically, a soccer bar, where soccer is the culture. All Nations celebrates the beloved sport by offering music, food, and drink that accompany soccer around the world, such as *choripan* (a bread and chorizo dish found at games in Argentina), a "meter of beer" from Rio de Janeiro, and plenty of team chants and songs from across the globe. And, of course, soccer matches are played at all times on the huge television screens.

fired from his first gig, in the basement of the Seattle synagogue Temple De Hirsch, for his "showoff" moves. Considered by fans, critics, and other musicians to be the greatest electric guitarist in history, Hendrix broke new ground with virtually everything he did. You can try to channel his memory at the large bronze statue of him playing a Stratocaster near the corner of Broadway and Pine in Capitol Hill, or at his gravesite and large memorial at Greenwood Memorial Park in nearby Renton. The Experience Music Project showcases a great Hendrix exhibit, featuring many of his guitars (including those from Woodstock and the Monterey Pop Festival), rare films, notebooks with lyrics in his handwriting, and more.

Born only a few years before Jimi's iconic Woodstock appearance, **Chris Cornell** (Seattle, 1964) would go on to form **Soundgarden,** the band largely responsible for launching an alternative music movement to counter top-40 pop, along with **Nirvana** and **Pearl Jam,** also hailing from Seattle. **Kurt Cobain**'s short, tragic life has all but overshadowed the success and influence of Nirvana. Born in Aberdeen, Washington, in 1967, Cobain seemed to reflect his own pain in his angst-filled lyrics; he was found dead in 1994 by his wife, Courtney Love, of a self-inflicted gunshot wound.

Stone Carpenter Gossard (Seattle, 1966) formed the band **Green River** in 1984. Though it was never well-known outside Seattle, Green River was hugely influential on the grunge music genre and other bands that formed, including Nirvana and Gossard's later bands, Pearl Jam and **Mudhoney.**

Other bands that come from Seattle are: Alice in Chains, Band of Horses, Death Cab for Cutie, Fleet Foxes, Foo Fighters, Heart, Mad Season, Modest Mouse, the Postal Service, the Presidents of the United States of America, Queensryche, Screaming Trees, Sir Mix-A-Lot, and the Sonics.

BALLARD LOFT

5105 Ballard Ave. NW (North)

(206) 420-2737

www.ballardloft.com

Situated in an old industrial building, this neighborhood eatery and bar is casual and embodies the soul of Ballard. A dozen microbrews on tap, house-created cocktails, and specialty sausages accompany the full menu and sport environment. The 13 flat-screen televisions play a variety of games, and there are also dartboards, video games, and pool and shuffleboard tables.

SPORT RESTAURANT & BAR

140 4th Ave. North, Suite 130 (Central)

(206) 404-7768

www.sportrestaurant.com

Located in a prime spot across the street from the Space Needle, Sport is situated in a rather nondescript building but offers an atmosphere of camaraderie, whether you're a regular or it's your first time in. Lots of television screens, a full menu, specialty drinks, and a decent wine list, along with great beer, all make this a casual, fun hangout. The real spot of interest, however, is in the huge memorabilia collection that spans 100 years of Seattle sports champions. From Gil Dobie, the University of Washington's first football coach in 1907, to the magic of the Seattle Storm's 2004 championship season, you will find an incredible array of items that cover four separate showcases.

WINE BARS

LOCAL VINE
2520 2nd Ave. (Central)
(206) 441-6000
www.thelocalvine.com

This Belltown spot is a comfortable place to enjoy wine, food, and conversation. More than 100 wines by the glass are available, along with a nice small plates selection and Wi-Fi. The owners have aimed to make it as much a comfortable place to hang out as that of a local coffee shop, and you will usually find neighborhood residents doing just that. The fireplaces are just the extra draw necessary to entice long visits on rainy Seattle days. The Local Vine also offers many wine tasting events, as well as wine and food discovery classes.

PORTALIS WINE BAR
5205 Ballard Ave. NW (North)
(206) 783-2007
www.portaliswines.com

Portalis is a great little combination of a retail wine shop and wine bar where you can sit and enjoy a glass or flight, along with a menu of small plates to nosh on. Selections from around the globe and in every price range are available, with free wine consultations. For those who are not big wine aficionados, an amazing selection of 30 artisan beers is also available.

PURPLE CAFÉ AND WINE BAR
1225 4th Ave. (Central)
(206) 829-2280
www.thepurplecafe.com

The most striking aspect of this stylish wine bar is the huge, towering column of a wine rack that stretches up to the two-story ceiling, with a curved staircase winding along it for server access. It's quite dramatic, and although Purple is less intimate than many wine bars, the sheer selection makes up for it. The seasonal Northwest cuisine almost stands up to the stellar wine varieties.

SMASH WINE BAR & BISTRO
1401 N. 45th St. (North)
(206) 547-3232
www.smashwine.com

This small neighborhood spot in the Green Lake area features a nice selection of flights and wines by the glass, and there is always a Sommelier's Selection of Washington picks. For non–wine drinkers, a nice selection of martinis and excellent beers is also available. The plates are outstanding, from crispy gingered calamari to duck and shiitake spring rolls. Various tastings and other events occur frequently.

SWIRL WINE BAR
3217 W. McGraw St. (Central)
(206) 327-9221
www.swirlmagnolia.com

Although there's generally not a lot in Magnolia outside the peaceful family neighborhoods and beloved Discovery Park, Swirl provides a cozy wine bar in the quiet area. It's a casual but elegant space with friendly service. A good selection of wines by the glass and fairly extensive bottle selection are on offer, along with a nice assortment of cheese and meat plates, as well as Theo chocolates.

SHOPPING

Like everything else in this city, shopping is an eclectic mix. Although there seem to be upscale boutiques and funky secondhand stores in every area, the various Seattle neighborhoods do have overriding shopping experience personalities.

If you are looking for designer labels and high-end department stores, downtown is where you want to start. The Nordstrom flagship store is, of course, the holy grail here; but you will also find Bon Marché, Macy's, and Barney's, as well as an entire lineup of designer shops from Betsey Johnson to Cartier. The main indoor malls are Pacific Place, City Centre, and Westlake Center. If you are looking for that special piece of artwork to add to your collection, stick around the downtown area and make your way over to either Belltown or Pioneer Square. Both neighborhoods, anchoring each end of the central business district, are rich with galleries offering a wide range of paintings, sculpture, photographic art, and Seattle's specialty, hand-blown glasswork. Pioneer Square is also an excellent spot for antiques hunting.

Foodies will want to browse the stalls of Pike Place Market, and the shops along the surrounding streets, for an astounding array of artisan foods and cooking implements. Pike Place is also the best place to shop for souvenirs for yourself or to take back home to friends and family. The International District is also a great place for foodie shoppers, particularly if your tastes run to the more exotic and international.

If trendy, independent boutiques are more your thing, you'll want to head to Ballard. The charming tree-lined brick streets are filled with small European-style shops, where you will find the absolute hippest shoes, fashion-forward clothing, local designers, and really unique home decor items. For a lot more funk, with the dial turned way down on trendy, move to next-door Fremont. This hippy, quirky, anything-goes neighborhood is full of vintage shops, tucked-away spots where you can score collectible toys or that rare vinyl LP, fun clothing boutiques, and even the occasional head shop. A refreshing aspect of Fremont is that it is virtually chain-store-free. Another neighborhood for great vintage finds is Capitol Hill, where you can also find world imports, alternative bookstores, adult toys, and plenty of shops that cater to a gay clientele.

ANTIQUES

ANTIKA
8421 Greenwood Ave. North (North)
(206) 789-6393
www.antikaantiques.com

This Greenwood shop houses a diverse selection of furniture from the late 1800s to mid-21st century, including pine, oak, and Danish teak. There are also hundreds of accessories and small items including kitchen canister sets, glassware, wrought iron, and more. Each item carried has been handpicked from the United States, England, or Europe. Antika occupies 6,500 square feet on two floors, which are broken up into five separate rooms with their own distinctive themes.

ANTIQUE LIQUIDATORS
503 Westlake North (Central)
(206) 623-2740
www.antiqueliquidators.com

This showroom is in the business of liquidating stock from all over the world, and often you will find the best deals and prices on high-quality pieces here. It specializes in English, Danish, Indonesian, and Indian antiques, although pieces from other parts of the world can be found, as well as reproductions.

ANTIQUES AT PIKE PLACE
92 Stewart St. (Central)
(206) 441-9643
www.antiquesatpikeplace.com

Less than a block from Pike Place Market, this antiques mall showcases an eclectic selection from 65-plus antiques dealers. The vendors carry furniture and other items from periods including Victorian, art deco, French country, and modern. There is also an amazing collection of estate jewelry, and an abundance of old photography that is interesting to sort through. The staff are friendly and knowledgeable, and layaway and delivery are both available.

EARTHWISE ARCHITECTURAL SALVAGE
3447 4th Ave. South (South)
(206) 624-4510
www.earthwise-salvage.com

Earthwise is a very different sort of antiques shop. Founder Kurt Petrauskas made it his mission to preserve Seattle's architectural past by salvaging reusable building materials and architectural features that would otherwise be heading for the landfill. Homeowners, renovators, and builders all frequent Earthwise for unique, historic pieces that simply aren't found anywhere else. This results in a warehouse packed with great salvage finds such as windows, doors, molding, cabinets, lighting, pillars, wrought iron, appliances, claw-foot tubs, hardware, and much more. The items are also often purchased or rented for special events and movie props.

MING'S ASIAN GALLERY
519 6th Ave. South (Central)
(206) 748-7889
www.mingsgallery.com

Ming's is a must-stop place in the International District for any lover of either antiques or Asian history and design. It is an incredible showroom representing 5,000 years of history through the imperial dynasties of China, Korea, Japan, Burma, Mongolia, Thailand, Cambodia, Nepal, Tibet, India, and Indonesia. It's like a delightful museum of exquisite artifacts and furniture—but one in which you can actually purchase anything and take it home, for a price. Historical treasures include fine furniture, rugs, bronzes, porcelains, paintings, jade, ivory, and textiles. Appraisal and design services are offered, and there are many exhibitions and lectures throughout the year. Don't be afraid to walk in to simply browse and gape at the collection; many people do, and the gracious staff welcomes browsers who simply want to appreciate the magnificent collection.

PACIFIC GALLERIES ANTIQUE MALL & AUCTION HOUSE

241 S. Lander St. (Central)
(206) 292-3999
www.pacgal.com

This is the cream of the crop when it comes to significant high-end antiques—sort of the Sotheby's of Seattle. The house is one of the most reputable antiques and fine art dealers in the West, and it enjoys an extremely loyal customer base. Pacific Galleries has its own research and appraisal department with experienced, accredited appraisers. The 30,000-square-foot antiques mall is open daily, with collections from more than 200 dealers, and a weekly estate auction is held every first and third Sun at 1 p.m.

PIONEER SQUARE ANTIQUE MALL

602 1st Ave. (Central)
(206) 624-1164
www.pioneersquareantiques.com

Located in historic Pioneer Square, this antiques mall fills 6,000 square feet of underground space with 60 dealer booths. All sorts of antique pieces and collectibles can be found here, including pottery, jewelry, dinnerware, toys, books, and memorabilia.

SEATTLE ANTIQUES MARKET

1400 Alaskan Way (Central)
(206) 623-6115
www.seattleantiquesmarket.com

This store on Seattle's historic waterfront is stocked from a 6,000-square-foot warehouse, and the selection is enormous and constantly changing. The store is a direct importer of 19th- and 20th-century European furniture and accessories, and there is also an extensive collection of American pieces. A lot of great collectibles such as books, cameras, radios and other memorabilia from the past are also available.

ARTISAN/GIFT SHOPS

CRACKERJACK CONTEMPORARY CRAFTS

1815 N. 45th St. #212 (North)
(206) 547-4983
www.crackerjackcrafts.com

Housed in the beautiful Wallingford Center, a restored 1916 schoolhouse that is a community anchor of the neighborhood, Crackerjack was the first Seattle store to showcase a wide variety of handcrafted artworks and media by Northwest and international artists. The store is known for the high quality of its inventory, specializing in jewelry, wood and glass objects, functional pottery, hats, and dolls.

GOODS FOR THE PLANET

525 Dexter Ave. North (Central)
(206) 652-2327
www.goodsfortheplanet.com

This South Lake Union store carries a wide variety of eco-friendly products, including furniture, baby supplies, toys, linens and towels, home decor, clothing, gifts, and garden supplies. The company researches all product lines carefully and carries only those that are both manufactured and packaged with the least environmental impact; many come from local sources. Check out the Seattle Coffee Shirt, an organic tee that is dyed with coffee grounds and packaged to look like a bag of coffee beans. The store also has a great calendar of events such as home canning classes, aromatherapy workshops, and sewing lessons.

PORTAGE BAY GOODS

706 N. 34th St. (North)
(206) 547-5221
www.portagebaygoods.com

Portage Bay Goods stocks an eclectic collection of whimsical, offbeat gifts and hand-crafted artisan goods, alongside a mostly hilarious card selection and children's items. You'll also find bath products, unconventional office supplies, candles, and jewelry. There's a nice collection of recycled and eco-friendly products as well. The store's Web site claims the store is the perfect place to grab a fabulous gift that says you really, really care in about five minutes, and that anyone can find something they love whether they be Democrat, Republican, gay, straight, Christian, or atheist. The Fremont shop is a really fun place to just browse with friends, while constantly calling each other over because "you've just got to see this!"

YE OLDE CURIOSITY SHOP
1001 Alaskan Way, on Pier 54 (Central)
(206) 682-5844
www.yeoldecuriosityshop.com
This shop, at more than a century old, has been around almost as long as Seattle has. The history of Ye Olde Curiosity Shop dates to the Civil War, when Joseph Standley opened the small curio shop on the waterfront in 1899, turning his childhood passion for collecting natural and Indian artifacts into a business. Joe's ethnological collection of rare Alaskan Indian and Eskimo carvings, tools, and ivories won a gold medal at the 1909 Exposition; he was active in the shop until his death in 1940. Since that time family members have taken over, and today Ye Olde Curiosity Shop is run by fourth-generation Andy, Tammy, and Debbie. It carries an amazing variety of Northwest items including totem poles, shrunken heads, blow guns, player pianos, whale and walrus *oosiks,* masks, jewelry, artwork, and much more. Terrific and unusual souvenirs

from Seattle and Washington can also be found; the shop promises your visit will be fun, educational, and entertaining.

BOOKSTORES

ELLIOTT BAY BOOK COMPANY
1521 10th Ave. (Central)
(206) 624-6600
www.elliottbaybook.com
A Seattle tradition, Elliott Bay consistently makes the lists of top bookstores around the country. For book lovers, the relocation of Elliott Bay Book Company from its long-time Pioneer Square location to Capitol Hill was traumatic. The family-owned store was founded in 1973 in the historic Globe Building, where it occupied two floors and, over the years, expanded to fill dozens of little nooks and crannies throughout the old building. However, after 36 years the owners made the difficult decision to relocate, in order to expand and afford better parking and access. The new location is another historic building, circa 1918, full of high wood ceilings, beams, and skylights. This is the sort of space where people feel at home and browse for hours. Elliott Bay is a true independent bookstore that fosters the literary community, with reading groups, author speaking series, book reviews, and other events.

GLOBE BOOKS
218 1st Ave. South (Central)
(206) 682-6882
John and Carolyn Siscoe have owned and operated the Globe for more than 30 years. The little gem of a store specializes in history and literature, and the Siscoes can enlighten you on almost anything you'd want to know about those two subjects. Regulars are greeted with books set aside just for them, and personal interaction with every customer

through the door is a given. The Globe is very clearly a labor of love, and the shelf of personal recommendations is always worth a visit.

SPINE & CROWN BOOKS
413 E. Pine St. (Central)
(206) 322-1227
www.spineandcrown.blogspot.com

This small Capitol Hill neighborhood bookstore is a treasure trove for book lovers. The quality and selection of current and popular books, combined with used, rare, and out-of-print finds, are excellent. The owner, Chris, and the staff are knowledgeable and passionate about books and can help you find or order just about anything. This is a very personable, homey place where regulars are known by name and reading preference.

CLOTHING STORES

BLACKBIRD
5410 22nd Ave. NW (North)
(206) 547-2524
www.helloblackbird.blogspot.com

This high-end Ballard men's clothing store was born because owner Nicole Miller struggled to find interesting styles in Seattle for her husband. Blackbird has since become extremely popular, offering men's fashion that goes way beyond the typical: screen-print tees, vintage-inspired materials, French classics, and everything else from preppy to surfer looks. There's also a great line of watches, shoes, belts, hats, and sunglasses. The space is urban and edgy, with concrete floors, airy loft ceilings, and a mobile metal staircase that displays shoes.

ELLA MON
5404 22nd Ave. NW (North)
(206) 297-2800
www.ellamon.com

This charming Ballard women's boutique is decorated with a wealth of unexpected architectural elements, from the gorgeous chandeliers to the intricate ironwork racks and trellis that towers over the checkout counter. Another nice touch is the original artwork on a large gallery wall; a different local artist is on display each month or two. Ella Mon aims to bring contemporary fashion to urban professional women, with friendly service. The clothes are classic and sophisticated rather than trendy—but they're anything but boring. Ella Mon caters to women over 35, and carries designer lines from Jenne Maag, James Jeans, and Isabel de Pedro, among others. Trunk shows and collection launches happen quite frequently.

DAVID LAWRENCE
1318 4th Ave. (Central)
(206) 622-2544
www.david-lawrence.com

High-profile fashion is the look here, and at David Lawrence you'll find men's and women's clothing that you probably saw at that trendy Belltown hotspot last night. Names such as Versace, Dolce & Gabbana, and John Paul Gaultier line the racks, as well as denim from Rock & Republic, Genetic, and William Rast. As you may have already surmised, the price tags reflect the labels; this is not the place for bargain shopping, but if you want high fashion you have found your nirvana.

ENCANTO BARCELONA
1406 1st Ave. (Central)
(206) 621-1941
www.encantobarcelona.com

This stylish store is the place to shop for modern men's and women's European imports, in an affordable price range. Although they don't run sales, there is always a rack of "seductively priced" merchandise. The selection is fluid and constantly changing, and there is also an assortment of accessories. The staff are very helpful and attentive, without being pushy. Check out the second location in Ballard.

FRESH
7309 35th Ave. NE (North)
(206) 522-3774
www.freshseattle.com
The spring green color scheme and beautiful displays make this shop a delight to walk into. Partners Wendy Schwartz and Julia Marconi enjoy collecting a unique assortment of clothing and accessories that you won't find in the department stores, including local designers. A fun selection of items outside the wearable fashion realm includes cards, housewares, baby items, candles, and a great gift selection.

FROCK SHOP
6500 Phinney Ave. North (North)
(206) 297-1638
www.shopfrockshop.com
Owner Suzy Fairchild describes her boutique as "Audrey Hepburn's closet," and you certainly get that vibe. The vintage-inspired collection of dresses and separates are fun, unique, and beautiful. Fairchild's background includes working as a designer for Nordstrom and in London, and it shows in both the aesthetic of the store and the eclectic styles available here. She also makes and sells her own hats and handbags that feature vintage leather belts for straps.

INDUSTRY
1826 6th Ave. (Central)
(206) 547-9961
www.theindustryseattle.com

Industry's Web site claims that it is fashion for the everyday rock star, and begs its customers to never settle for average. The hip, urban fashions found here are definitely different with a rock 'n' roll edge. Jeans and designer T-shirts are the staples, but great jackets and accessories can also be found. Owners Angela Kantanto and Megan Stokke met in Paris, and their store is clearly styled with a French creativity and that distinctly Parisian shopping experience of finding hidden treasures tucked in small corners. For men who like comfortable, basic clothing—yet want a stylish look that's different—you can't do better than Industry.

SANDYLEW
1408 1st Ave. (Central)
(206) 903-0303
www.sandylew.com
Sandylew is a refreshing find in the downtown shopping scene. The owner, Sandy Lew, is a local jeweler and metal artist, and she turns that eye for dramatic visual art to her fashion collection. The sophisticated yet sometimes wacky array of international designers runs a wide range of prices, so there is something for everyone. You'll find lots of custom-printed fabrics, Asian-inspired designs, and ruffles. Eco-friendly items and accessories are also available, and Lew's own steel and mixed-media dress sculptures adorn the walls.

COMIC BOOKS, COLLECTIBLES, AND TOYS

ARCANE COMICS & MORE
5809 15th Ave. NW (North)
(206) 781-4875
www.arcanecomics.net
Arcane carries a wide selection of new and back-issue comics, magazines, games, posters, videos, toys, collectibles, and apparel.

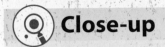

Close-up

The Nordstrom Story

It's hard to have a chapter about shopping in Seattle and not include **Nordstrom**. One of the greatest retail success stories in the world, the Seattle-based department store is known for its over-the-top customer service. And like most Seattle pioneers, its founder also has an interesting, offbeat story.

John Nordstrom left Sweden in 1887 at the age of 16, with $5 in his pocket. He landed in Manhattan, unable to speak a word of English. Over the next grueling decade, he toiled at backbreaking manual labor in mines and logging camps, crossing the country for work and eventually ending up in Washington. In 1897 he read the headlines that thousands of other people did: GOLD FOUND IN THE KLONDIKE! The next day he began planning his route north to partake in the Alaskan gold rush.

The work was no easier in this difficult terrain, but over the course of two years, the young Swedish immigrant had earned $13,000—the equivalent of more than $300,000 today.

Returning to Washington, John Nordstrom went into business with Carl Wallin, a friend he'd made in Alaska who owned a shoe repair shop in downtown Seattle. The two men opened a retail shoe store in 1901 called Wallin & Nordstrom. After opening a second store in 1923, Nordstrom retired in 1928 and sold his share of the business to his sons. A year later, Wallin also retired and sold his share to the Nordstrom sons as well.

The company continued to grow, becoming the largest independent shoe store chain in the United States, with eight stores in Washington and Oregon. Under the leadership of John's sons, Nordstrom expanded into the clothing business in the 1960s and continued to prosper. After going public in 1971, the full-service department store began expanding nationwide and adding merchandise lines including cosmetics, fragrance, jewelry, home decor, and even pet items.

In 1998 Nordstrom was perhaps single-handedly responsible for saving the downtown shopping scene—or at least infusing it with a much-needed retail giant. The Frederick & Nelson department store had abruptly folded, leaving downtown with the great gaping hole of a vacant four-story building. People worried that the central retail core would be sunk, until Nordstrom completely renovated the gorgeous building and set up shop. With the Pacific Place upscale mall soon built across the street, other national retailers began opening outlets in downtown Seattle—today a thriving shopper's mecca.

Nordstrom Downtown Seattle—Store, Spa, and Restaurant
500 Pine St.
(206) 628-2111
www.nordstrom.com

Nordstrom Rack Downtown Seattle—Clearance Items
1601 2nd Ave.
(206) 448-8522
http://shop.nordstrom.com/c/6016611

New comics arrive every Wed and are on the shelves by noon. The Best Reads program offers customers the first volume of recommended series, at a 40 percent discount. In addition to this Ballard location, there is a second store on California Avenue in West Seattle.

ARCHIE McPHEE
1300 N. 45th St. (North)
(206) 297-0240
www.archiemcpheeseattle.com
This Wallingford store is a one-stop location for gifts, party supplies, crafts, costumes, oddities, and the weirdest collection of toys and candy that you've ever seen. A mecca for connoisseurs of the strange, Archie's is reminiscent of a carnival sideshow. If you find yourself in need of a rubber chicken, punching nun, 8-foot-tall gladiator, or pickle lip balm, this is the place to come. Most of the 10,000-plus items are priced at less than $15 and are sure to bring out the kid in everyone.

GASOLINE ALLEY
6501 20th Ave. NE (North)
(206) 524-1606
www.gasolinealleyantiques.com
This is one toy store that appeals to adults much more than children. Gasoline Alley is filled with an incredible collection of thousands of vintage and collectible toys, including scale die-cast kits, out-of-production model kits, sports memorabilia and trading cards, and much more. The store stocks more than 120,000 items at any given time, including some very, very rare items.

GOLDEN AGE COLLECTABLES LTD.
1501 Pike Place Market #401 (Central)
(206) 622-9799
www.goldenagecollectables.com

Located on the lower level of Pike Place Market, this store concentrates on classic collectibles and comic books. In business since 1971, the store has a vast collection that includes pop culture merchandise like movie scripts, autographs, Japanese toys, and vintage toys. Fairly regular special events occur as well, such as visits by superheroes.

SCHMANCY
1932 2nd Ave. (Central)
(206) 728-8008
www.schmancytoys.com
Schmancy is a pretty downtown store that carries a great selection of quirky toys, collectibles, and original artwork. The owner, Kristen Rask, loves plush toys so much that she founded an annual exhibit called Plush You! that showcases plush creations from around the globe. A gallery also showcases the whimsical art of various local artists.

ZANADU COMICS
1923 3rd Ave. (Central)
(206) 443-1316
www.zanaducomics.com
A diverse selection of comics including new and back issues, mainstream, alternative, adult comics, and graphic novels. There's also a collection of T-shirts, models, videos, and more. Zanadu features regular appearances by artists and writers at both the downtown location and the second location in the University District.

GROCERS AND SPECIALTY FOOD

DeLAURENTI SPECIALTY FOOD & WINE
1435 1st Ave. (Central)
(800) 873-6685
www.delaurenti.com

This downtown store pays homage to the food and wine of Italy, from a huge selection of olive oils and handmade pastas cut to order, to the excellent deli case and numerous varieties of imported prosciutto and cheese. Upstairs you'll find racks holding more than 500 Italian wines, which could be overwhelming if it weren't for the knowledgeable staff who are happy to make recommendations based on your likes or what you're cooking. Don't pass by the sweets; DeLaurenti has some incredibly tempting chocolates, cookies, and sorbet.

EvZE WORLD GOURMET
3213 Eastlake Ave. East (Central)
(206) 709-7566
www.evze.com
Offering gourmet and hard-to-find artisan foods from around the world, EvZE specializes in independent producers who make food without artificial ingredients or hydrogenated oils. Every item is 100 percent guaranteed, and the customer service is excellent. Here you can find seafood, sauces and spices, legumes, grains, condiments, and wine, as well as gift baskets and a great assortment of culinary accessories.

MADISON MARKET
1600 E. Madison (Central)
(206) 329-1545
www.madisonmarket.com
Capitol Hill residents flock to this neighborhood co-op with an excellent deli and produce department. Ninety-five percent of the items are organic, and most come from local farms. The selection is great for anyone on a special diet, from vegans to salt- or gluten intolerance. Don't forget to stop at the smoothie counter for a refreshing pick-me-up.

PCC NATURAL MARKETS
600 N. 34th St. (North)
(206) 632-6811
www.pccnaturalmarkets.com
PCC stands for Puget Consumers Co-op, owned by 45,000 members to make it the largest consumer-owned food retail cooperative in the United States. After getting its start in 1953, today PCC has nine locations around Seattle. The cooperative is certified organic and partners with local farmers to support sustainable agriculture. Their mission, besides sustainability, is to celebrate food and educate consumers about the food industry and nutrition issues. At PCC you can find grass-fed meat, poultry without growth hormones, and ethically caught seafood, as well as some of the freshest produce around. The stores are very nice, clean, and well-lit; it's no musty hippie hole. You do not have to be a co-op member to shop here, so stop in and check out the great selection of healthy, organic food.

THE SHOP AGORA
6417-A Phinney Ave. North (North)
(206) 782-5551
www.theshopagora.com
If you like Greek and Mediterranean foods, this North Seattle store near Green Lake is the place for you. Friendly owners Nikos and Alexis Saloutos are usually around and happy to give advice or just chat. Gourmet olives and oils, unfiltered Tuscan honey and pomegranate molasses, artisanal vinegars, spices, pasta, and more can all be found here. The gift sets and baskets are incredible, and the Saloutoses host a free wine tasting every week. I particularly love the Tiny Acts of Gratitude packs: decks of cards for friendship, love, gratitude, and happiness. The purpose is that you find these traits in others and pass one of the cards to them, sort of

like the random acts of kindness. It's a nice way to make the day of a stranger or loved one, and probably your own, as well.

UNIVERSITY SEAFOOD AND POULTRY CO.

1317 NE 47th St. (North)
(206) 632-3700

Run by the Erickson family for 60 years, this old-fashioned shop sells locally farmed poultry and additive-free seafood of nearly infinite variety. Besides the typical chicken and turkey, you'll find pheasant, duck, and squab as well as other game such as venison and rabbit. A large selection of fish, as well as lobster, crab, oysters, and other shellfish, is always available, and always fresh. They also sell sauces and wine to complete your meal.

UWAJIMAYA

600 5th Ave. South (Central)
(206) 624-6248
www.uwajimaya.com

Since 1928 Uwajimaya in the International District has been Seattle's favorite place for Asian groceries and gifts. Japan native Fujimatsu Moriguchi began selling homemade fish cakes and other items from the back of his truck in Tacoma. Tragically, Moriguchi and his family were sent to an internment camp in California during World War II, after which they relocated to Seattle, where the Uwajimaya retail store was opened. Today seven family members manage the store, selling an extensive collection of fresh seafood, meat, and produce as well as imported gifts from Japan and other Asian countries. They also offer cooking classes, and the customer base is not only newly immigrated Asians but also third- and fourth-generation, as well as a large non-Asian following. Don't miss the terrific sake and Asian beer selection.

MUSIC STORES

EASY STREET RECORDS

20 Mercer St. (Central)
4559 California Ave. SW #200 (South)
(206) 691-EASY
www.easystreetonline.com

The two locations of Easy Street are everything an independent record store should be. Steeped in a history and authenticity you can almost feel, the environment is one that encourages you to rummage through new and used CDs and vinyl albums to your heart's content. Movies are also stocked, and the California Avenue location also has a cafe that serves food, beer, and wine—leading to the store's motto, "Saving the record industry one beer at a time." Plenty of free in-store concerts fill the calendar, giving another reason to love this place.

EVERYDAY MUSIC

1523 10th Ave. (Central)
(206) 568-3321
www.everydaymusic.com

EM, as it's known, used to be easy to spot due to the larger-than-life Jimi Hendrix statue right out front. Recently, however, the store moved 1 block south and a half-block east from Jimi but still carries the same incredible selection of more than 100,000 new and used CDs and records. Hundreds of titles arrive daily and EM buys from its customers, so the selection is constantly changing. Anything you can't find can be special ordered, and the staff will open any item to let you take a listen at the listening stations throughout the store. This place is completely low-tech, no-frills, and user-friendly.

JIVE TIME RECORDS

3506 Fremont Ave. North (North)
(206) 632-5483
www.jivetimerecords.com

The thing to know about Jive Time is that its focus is on vinyl—used, lovingly cared-for, collector's dream vinyl. For those who love the tactile pleasure of vinyl and obscure, hard-to-find musicians, digging through the thousands of LPs at Jive Time feels like a treasure hunt. It's well organized by genre, though, and the staff seem as if they used to work at the store in the movie *High Fidelity*. The store buys music if you have anything to unload, and new selections are rotated in daily. Used tapes, CDs, and movies can also be found, as well as a nice collection of accessories and gifts. The Jive Time logo rocks, so you may find yourself walking out with a T-shirt or album crate.

WALL OF SOUND
315 E. Pine St. (Central)
(206) 441-9880
www.wosound.com
If your taste in music runs beyond the eclectic and avant-garde, perhaps to that which very few people have even heard of, Wall of Sound was made for you. The store specializes in Japanese noise, industrial, art-rock, indie, garage punk, alternative, free-jazz, folk, experimental, world, electro-acoustic, and other non-mainstream musical genres. Selling both new and used CDs and LPs, Wall of Sound specializes in stocking hot new electronic music releases. Check out its monthly live music night at the Rendezvous/Jewelbox Theater.

> **i** It's rare to find a really great price on a quality vintage LP in Seattle's record stores. Collectors and shop owners know what they have, and most customers are serious and knowledgeable. Some rare treasures can be found, as well as decent prices—but don't count on walking out with a $3 limited-edition Jimi Hendrix or anything.

OPEN-AIR MARKETS

BALLARD SUNDAY FARMERS' MARKET
Ballard Avenue between 20th and 22nd
Avenues (North)
(206) 781-6776
www.fremontmarket.com/ballard
Enveloped in the tree-lined canopy of maritime Ballard, surrounded by historic brick buildings, this Sunday market wins acclaim for best local market. Its offerings from local farmers, culinary artists, and craftsman designers is constantly changing and expanding; you can select fruits and vegetables, artisan cheeses, jams and sauces, herbs and local plants, hormone-free meats, fresh seafood, and flowers while listening to musicians. Two wine bars and coffee shops are along the streets for taking a break while still viewing the goings-on. Crafts for sale include ceramics, handmade furniture, jewelry, soaps and lotions, and garden art. The Ballard market is held every Sun of the year, rain or shine, from 10 a.m. to 3 p.m. Free parking is available on Shilshole Avenue, 1 block away, and leashed pets are accepted.

FREMONT MARKET
34th Street, between Phinney Avenue
and Evanston (North)
(206) 781-6776
www.fremontmarket.com
Since 1990 the Fremont Market has been the epicenter of all things wild and wacky. The large, rambling Sunday flea and farmers' market is modeled after the European street markets. And true to that style, it offers a little bit of everything: food, musicians and street performers, local artists and handmade craft products, vintage finds, world imports, collectibles, and a fresh selection of produce and other foods, with around 150 vendors represented. Most of the market is held

under tents stretched along 34th Street, but at the end there is also an indoor garage-sale space with dozens of vendor booths selling everything from vintage cowboy boots to old vinyl records. It is open on Sun year-round from 10 a.m. to 4 p.m. (although many vendors stay later in the summer), except the Sun closest to Christmas and summer solstice weekend, when the Fremont Solstice Parade is on. Leashed dogs are welcome.

MADRONA FARMERS' MARKET
1126 Martin Luther King Jr. Way
Madrona Grocery Outlet (Central)
(206) 781-6776
http://madronafarmersmarket
.wordpress.com

Managed by the Seattle Farmers' Market Association, this small market is held every Fri from 3 to 7 p.m., between mid-May and the end of Sept. The location is the parking lot of the Madrona Grocery Outlet, on the eastern side of Central Seattle. The selection of produce, cheeses, meats, breads, jams, and sauces fluctuates with the season and availability from participating farmers and vendors. Cooking demonstrations are regularly presented, and a schedule can be found on the Web site. Entertainment includes street performers and musicians.

NEIGHBORHOOD FARMERS' MARKET
ALLIANCE
Seven locations throughout Seattle
(206) 547-2278
www.seattlefarmersmarkets.org

The nonprofit Neighborhood Farmers' Market Alliance (NFMA) is a community-based organization developed in response to the growing popularity and public support of the neighborhood farmers' markets in Seattle. NFMA organizes seven "producer-only"

markets in the city, where farmers sell their produce directly to shoppers, earning the full dollar value of their products, helping more than 100 of the region's small, diverse farms stay in business. Samplers, cooking demonstrations, live music, and children's activities are generally held at each market, and they all accept food stamps and have low-income shopping policies. Only the Columbia City, Magnolia, and Broadway markets allow dogs, and they must be on leashes. The locations are:

Capitol Hill—10th Avenue East and Thomas, Sun 11 a.m.–3 p.m., May–Dec

Columbia City—4801 Rainier Ave. South, Wed 3–7 p.m., Apr–Oct

Lake City—NE 125th at 28th, Thurs 3–7 p.m., June–Oct

Magnolia—2550 34th Ave. West, Sat 10 a.m.–2 p.m., June–Sept

Phinney—67th and Phinney Ave. North, Fri 3–7 p.m., May–Oct

University—50th and University Way NE, Sat 9 a.m.–2 p.m., year-round

West Seattle—California Avenue SW and Alaska, Sun 10 a.m.–2 p.m., year-round

PIKE PLACE MARKET
85 Pike St. (Central)
(206) 682-7453
www.pikeplacemarket.com

The venerable and famous market of Seattle, Pike Place Market underwent a renovation in 2010 that spruced up the nine acres that have provided much of the city's colorful history over the past century. Since 1907, when the market's first eight farmers parked here with their loaded wagons and were overwhelmed by 10,000 shoppers, Pike Place has been Seattle's most popular shopping district and is internationally recognized. It is home to approximately 200 permanent, year-round businesses, with an additional 190 craftspeople and 120 farmers who rent booth space by the day. Street performers and musicians abound, as do some of the freshest seafood in the world, amazing products, all kinds of art and craft works, and goods from around the world. This is where the famous flying fish are tossed around by the vendors at the main entrance, where you will also find a large brass pig that is often used by locals as a reference point (as in, "Meet me at the pig"). The parking garage is located at 1531 Western Ave., and the main entrance is from First Avenue and Pine, although there are many entrances throughout. You can take a tour for $10 (adults) with Market Heritage Tours, located at the information booth at First and Pike.

QUEEN ANNE FARMERS' MARKET
West Crockett Street at Queen Anne Avenue North (Central)
(206) 428-1983
www.qafma.org

Queen Anne exemplifies the little market that could, completely powered by the local community to bring a farmers' market to this neighborhood. After keeping a large Kroger grocery store out of the area in favor of the small, local Metropolitan Market, the Queen Anne Neighbors for Responsible Growth developed an association that brought the first farmers' market to the hill in 2007. You'll find street eats, farm-fresh fruits and vegetables, meats, dairy products, baked goods, herbs, and flowers. This is strictly a farm-only market; there are no craft vendors accepted, unless their items are made with farm products. Local chefs, authors, musicians, and nonprofit organizations are also represented. The market is open on Thurs from 3 to 7 p.m., between late May and early Oct.

WALLINGFORD FARMERS' MARKET
1815 N. 45th St., Wallingford Center (North)
(206) 781-6776
www.fremontmarket.com/wallingford

This outdoor street market in the quaint, family-friendly Wallingford neighborhood began in 2006, and is a little different because it is held on Wed, as opposed to the weekend. The market is open from 3 to 7 p.m. in the Wallingford Center parking lot, between the third week in May and the end of Sept. As the season progresses, the selection of just-picked natural fruits and vegetables from Washington farms and orchards changes, as well as wild honeys, jams, jellies, mushrooms, sauces, spices, and herbs. There are also specialty cheeses; pasture-finished, hormone-free pork, lamb, and beef; wild fish; free-range eggs; and dazzling arrays of flowers, rustic breads, and pastries. A small number of select craftsmen and designers offer garden art, jewelry, hand-made soaps, photography, and artwork. Cooking demonstrations and live music are also usually found. The market starts small and grows with the arc of the produce season to around 40 vendors in all. Free parking is available at the west and north ends of the Wallingford Center parking lot.

i When shopping the farmers' markets, it's helpful to bring a canvas shopping bag or tote bag. It makes it much easier to carry your purchases, of course, and saves more consumption of those dreaded plastic bags. Many places, such as the Pike Place Market, have reusable tote bags for sale—and often even the shopping bags are made from recycled materials.

OUTFITTERS/SPORTS AND RECREATION

ALPINE HUT
2215 15th Ave. West (Central)
(206) 284-3575
www.alpinehut.com

For 40 years, family-owned and -operated Alpine Hut has served Seattle skiers and bicyclists. Both the sales and service staff are made up of experts in skiing and cycling gear, and they are extremely knowledgeable and helpful. The store carries a large selection of road and mountain bikes for men, women, and children and has expert mechanics to tune them (no appointment necessary). The ski gear includes lines such as K2, Nordica, Rossignol, and Tyrolia, with technicians for tuning and fitting. There is also a good collection of clothing and accessories.

C.C. FILSON COMPANY
1555 4th Ave. South
(206) 622-3147
www.filson.com

The C.C. Filson Company has some pretty good credentials—it outfitted thousands of prospectors heading to Alaska for the Klondike gold rush in the late 1890s. After operating a small loggers' outfitting store, Filson took one look at the stampede to Yukon Territory and decided to take advantage of it, by opening C.C. Filson's Pioneer Alaska Clothing and Blanket Manufacturers in 1897 to sell clothing and equipment specially designed for the frigid, unforgiving terrain where these men were headed. After the gold rush faded into history, Filson morphed into providing gear for the timber and fishing industries, hunters, explorers, and mariners. Over the next hundred years, the company continued to produce top-quality gear for outdoors enthusiasts, and today the historic store still focuses on comfort, protection, and durability in items for men, women, and even dogs.

EVO
122 NW 36th St. (North)
(206) 973-4470
www.culture.evogear.com

A cool company with an interesting philosophy, Evo is much more than a gear shop. It's a community that explores the collaboration between sport and culture, by joining skiing, snowboarding, wakeboarding, and skateboarding enthusiasts with fashion, music, arts, and events. The staff of 40-plus team members are dedicated to building a community of people who share diverse interests, and in addition to selling a great line of gear, they also promote adventure trips, movie screenings, exhibitions, parties, and partnerships for the ski and board enthusiasts who flock here. It's all very, very cool—but avoids hipper-than-thou attitude simply by the refreshing passion that staff and customers alike show for the lifestyle.

REI
222 Yale Ave. North (Central)
(206) 223-1944
www.rei.com

REI is, of course, the mack daddy of sports and outfitters stores. The huge, three-story location on Yale is the flagship store, open since 1944, shortly after Pacific Northwest mountaineer Lloyd Anderson began a quest for a reliable ice axe at a good price. He started REI as an outdoor gear co-op for him and his climbing buddies to source gear, mostly from alpine suppliers. REI is one of those rare retail stores that also qualify as an attraction, as it consistently rates as one of

Seattle's top sightseeing destinations. There's a 65-foot climbing wall that's the focal point of the store, as well as gear-testing stations and a mountain bike test trail just outside the doors. REI also hosts a number of classes and informational meetings, and has been the site for a lot of famous pit stops, such as Greg Mortenson of *Three Cups of Tea* fame and Jon Krakauer of *Into Thin Air*. The company is a huge steward of the environment, donating millions of dollars annually to conservation efforts around the country.

SECOND ASCENT
5209 Ballard Ave. NW (North)
(206) 545-8810
www.secondascent.com

The great name of this shop was inspired by the fact that it sells quality secondhand gear for climbing, snowboarding and skiing, cycling, and other outdoor recreation. All equipment is thoroughly examined and reconditioned, and the store does sell some brand-new items as well. The prices are good, and in-store mechanics and technicians offer services to customers.

20/20 CYCLE
2020 E. Union St. (Central)
(206) 568-3090
www.2020cycle.com

This magnet for cycling enthusiasts is much more than a store—it's a community gathering place with a fireplace, DSL, and a lounge. Granted, the lounge is just a beat-up couch and coffee table, but regulars seem to always be hanging out there. Owner Alex Kostelnik services bikes and does custom installations and modifications. Repairs are done right out in the open because, according to Kostelnik, it's a great way for customers to learn how to maintain their own bikes.

SOUVENIR SHOPS
MADE IN WASHINGTON
1530 Post Alley (Central)
(206) 467-0788
www.madeinwashington.com

The first thing you are likely to notice when entering this lovely Pike Place Market shop is the gorgeous scent, which emanates from the numerous soaps, lotions, candles, and gourmet food that fill the shelves. Made In Washington offers an extensive assortment of products that are all, you guessed it, made in the state by various craftspeople, artists, and entrepreneurs. The store is dedicated to celebrating the best of Washington and to mutually beneficial vendor relationships and top-notch customer experience. Come here to get gift baskets filled with coffee, smoked salmon, jam, chocolates, Washington wines, and other gourmet food, or blown glass, mugs and pottery, jewelry, and Northwest souvenirs. There are six other locations in addition to the Pike Place store, including a shop at Sea-Tac Airport.

SIMPLY SEATTLE
1600 1st Ave. (Central)
(206) 448-2207
www.simplyseattle.com

This store is a treasure trove of gifts and artwork to commemorate Seattle and the Pacific Northwest, housed in a store with a maritime motif. From local food and wine products to T-shirts and beautiful prints, it's easy to find something that is of quality, rather than a cheesy souvenir. A second location is on Pier 56.

VINTAGE SHOPS

AREA 51
401 E. Pine St. (Central)
(206) 568-4782
www.area51seattle.com

This spacious store with high ceilings and a concrete floor is home to a collection of both vintage and new furniture, lighting, and home accessories. Most pieces are decidedly midcentury modern, although there are finds through the '70s and right up to today. Area 51 also has a great line called the Sustainable Collection, featuring pieces made from salvaged wood by local woodworkers.

ATLAS CLOTHING
1419 10th Ave. (Central)
(206) 323-0960
www.atlasclothing.net

Atlas is somewhat of a rarity in vintage shops—fairly spacious with plenty of room to browse. An oversize garage door is opened to the street scene in good weather, a nice touch. A pretty wide selection usually fills the Fremont space, with items ranging from 1950s dresses to motorcycle boots and vintage Louis Vuitton bags. There's also a good selection of both vintage T-shirts and new, handmade organic-cotton tees.

DIVA DOLLZ
624 1st Ave. (Central)
(206) 652-2299
www.thedivadollz.com

This amazing little shop near Pioneer Square specializes in, of all things, corsets and '20s–'30s burlesque-inspired items. The store was opened by New Orleans natives Shay Cemo and Steven Adams, who relocated their home and shop after Hurricane Katrina. This is a great place to get a unique dress for a special occasion. There is also an extensive collection of jewelry, gloves, and hats, which they will even custom make for you, as Cemo is an accomplished milliner.

EMMA JEAN'S CONSIGNMENTS & ANTIQUES
8554½ Greenwood Ave. North (North)
(206) 782-1926
www.emmajeansconsign.com

Although a few vintage household items and furniture pieces are thrown in, Emma Jean's is primarily about the clothing, shoes, and jewelry. It's cramped but not so much that you can't look around, and most items are reasonably priced. The selection moves through quickly, so there is always the promise of something new every week.

FREMONT VINTAGE MALL
3419 Fremont Place North (North)
(206) 329-4460
www.atlasclothing.net

This spacious store is filled with all kinds of things vintage, from clothing and furniture to home accessories, random knickknacks, and a great collection of vinyl records. After you make your way down a dark flight of steep steps to reach the showroom, prepare for the possibility of spending hours meandering around the maze of this seriously fun assortment. There's also a really great hand-painted mural that begs a Kodak moment, featuring artist renderings of everything from Wonder Woman to John Lennon in a Roy Lichtenstein style.

LAGUNA VINTAGE AMERICAN POTTERY SHOP
116 S. Washington St. (Central)
(206) 682-6162
www.lagunapottery.com

This Pioneer Square store is visually beautiful from the street, with its colorful pottery lining the shelves of the glass and black metal storefront. Laguna is one of the largest vintage pottery shops in the United States, specializing in collectible and discontinued American art pottery. Browse through the large collection of 20th-century vases, ceramics, dinnerware, and planters by makers such as Bauer, Russel Wright, Homer Laughlin (Fiesta), and Vernon Kilns.

i Are you looking for great deals on brand-new clothes, shoes, and other merchandise? If you're willing to make a trip, you may want to check out the Factory Stores at North Bend. This large outlet mall is about 30 minutes east of Seattle, and the Airporter Shuttle offers five trips every day (reservations required; call 866-235-5247). And if you have a group of 15 people or more, they will organize a private visit and tour.

LE FROCK
317 E. Pine St. (Central)
(206) 623-5339
www.lefrockonline.com
This is an amazing little shop literally jam-packed with upscale, high-quality finds from the 1920s through the 1990s. The store aims to bring back the era when "men looked more like Cary Grant and women acted more like Katharine Hepburn," and they want to help you re-create the romance of this bygone era. This really is the crème de la crème of the vintage world, and my personal favorite vintage shop in Seattle—I have bought more than a dozen pieces here. There are also some original pieces from designers such as Tawny Holt, who re-creates looks from recycled vintage material for her line Armour Sans Anguish. The keyword at this 20-year-old boutique is quality, whether it is a 1940s dress or a decade-old Prada coat.

PRETTY PARLOR
119 Summit Ave. East (Central)
(206) 405-CUTE
www.prettyparlor.com
This fun Capitol Hill shop is a frothy, girly, pink explosion of a place. The Web site describes it as a place "where Audrey Hepburn meets Judy Jetson," an apt description. It's a lot of fun just browsing in the cute store where chandeliers, parasols, and flouncy petticoats hang from the ceiling above you. Try something on if just for the fun of the boudoir-like dressing room. There are lots of dresses and accessories, as well as some current indie lines. Shoes and hats are also in plentiful supply, and there is a section for men called Manland. Owner Anna Lange—known as Anna Banana—even creates frilly fashions for her own label, House of Pretty Parlor.

RED LIGHT VINTAGE CLOTHING
312 Broadway Ave. East (Central)
4560 University Way NE (North)
(206) 329-2200
www.redlightvintage.com
Red Light is the largest vintage store in Seattle, with two locations, in Capitol Hill and the University District. The store carries items from a wide time period, ranging from Victorian era to early 1980s. This is a great place to add unique pieces to your wardrobe, but it's also an excellent costume shop with a large assortment of wigs and accessories.

SUGARTOWN
2421 NW Market St. (North)
(206) 789-1400
www.myspace.com/sugartownvintage
This Ballard shop is heavy on the '80s style, and full of satin and sequins. The prices tend to be reasonable and they always have a sale rack. It's a little less cluttered and easier to move around in than many vintage shops.

ATTRACTIONS

A lot of the major "must-see" sights of Seattle are concentrated within small geographical areas—a boon for tourists. For example, you will visit Pike Place Market, of course; in and of itself, this nine-acre open-air market—the oldest continuously operating farmers' market in the country—provides a half or whole day's worth of entertainment in its 250-plus stalls of food vendors and craftspeople. The market sits right on Elliott Bay, and from its water-facing side at Pier 62 you can access the scenic waterfront and the parks, ferries, dockside restaurants, and attractions, such as the Seattle Aquarium, that dot the shoreline.

When you come to Pier 50, you are at Pioneer Square, Seattle's most historic neighborhood and site of the original town. The six blocks that make up Pioneer Square are filled with gorgeous turn-of-the-twentieth-century buildings that are home to museums, galleries, nightspots, and fun tourist attractions like the Underground Tour. Just a few steps east from Pike Place Market is the commercial heart of Seattle, with its huge assortment of department stores, specialty shops, restaurants, and theaters. Walk 3 blocks north of the market and you've arrived in Belltown, a hip neighborhood of art galleries, trendy boutiques, and cocktail lounges.

About 5 blocks farther north past Belltown is Seattle Center, an area prized by locals and home to the iconic Space Needle. Seattle Center is 74 acres of public spaces, museums, theaters, shops, restaurants, fountains, green areas, and even an amusement park. This was the site of the 1962 World's Fair, and its pavilions and exhibition halls were turned into a cultural center where dozens of community events are found each week. From festivals and celebrations to live concerts and movie nights, much of the entertainment at Seattle Center is free or low-cost. It's easy to get to from the center of downtown via the monorail; in fact, all of these sections of Central Seattle are easily accessible via the terrific public bus system, and it's all located within the Ride Free Area, meaning you don't have to pay a fare to get around.

i Check out the self-guided tour "Points of Discovery," offered at the Seattle Center Web site. With more than 25 points of interest, the tour uncovers some of the unique features and fascinating facts that make Seattle Center a civic treasure. Download the PDF tour at http://seattlecenter.com.

Even the attractions outside of downtown are easy to get to, and fairly condensed geographically. Once in the northern neighborhoods of Ballard or Fremont, for example, you can easily stroll the main streets during events and farmers' markets, to shop and eat, or to visit some of Seattle's unique sites, such as the Chittenden Locks, or its wackier attractions, such as the Fremont Troll.

The Seattle Visitor Center is located at Pike and Seventh; the concierge desk is open from 9 a.m. to 5 p.m. daily (in winter months, Mon through Fri only). So go forth and have fun; there is so much to see and do in this city that the only concern is having enough time to do it all!

Price Code

The following price code will act as your guide to the cost of admission for one adult. Children, senior, and student prices are generally 20 percent to 50 percent less, and children under two to five years are admitted free to many attractions. Please check the Web sites for specific details.

$.........................$1 to $5
$$ ....$6 to $10
$$$ .... $11 to $15
$$$$ .... more than $15

ART MUSEUMS

FRYE ART MUSEUM
704 Terry Ave. (Central)
(206) 622-9250
www.fryemuseum.org
The area's only art museum that is completely free all the time, the Frye showcases a collection of late 19th- and early 20th-century European and American art. The Frye also hosts rotating notable exhibits by both emerging and internationally renowned artists. The museum is closed on Mon; public guided tours are available Wed through Sun at 1 p.m. Free parking is available in the parking lot across the street from the entrance on Terry Avenue.

SEATTLE ART MUSEUM $$$
1300 1st Ave. (Central)
(206) 654-3100
www.seattleartmuseum.org

This internationally renowned museum was created in 1931, when Seattle Fine Arts Society member Dr. Richard Fuller donated much of his extensive Chinese and Japanese art collection, along with a healthy endowment, so the pieces could be exhibited to the public. The SAM, as it's known, continued to grow, and the 1978 *Treasures of Tutankhamun* exhibit drew 1.3 million visitors and put the SAM on the international map. In 1991 the current downtown SAM opened and now houses about 23,000 objects from across cultures, including paintings, sculpture, decorative arts, textiles, and more. An amazing rotation of temporary exhibits is constantly evolving at the SAM, from ancient woodblock prints to dramatic contemporary photography. On the first Thurs of every month, you can enjoy free admission all day to the SAM downtown. The museum is closed Mon and Tues; first Fri are free to seniors 62 and over, and second Fri are teen nights, with free admission from 5 to 9 p.m. for ages 13–19. Members and children 12 and under are always free.

SEATTLE ASIAN ART MUSEUM $$
1400 E. Prospect St. (Central)
(206) 654-3100
www.seattleartmuseum.org/visit/
    visitSAAm.asp
Home of the original Seattle Art Museum, this gorgeous art deco building in Volunteer Park was designed by architect Carl F. Gould. When the SAM moved downtown, the Seattle Asian Art Museum opened in its former location in 1994, to showcase the museum's Asian art collection. The museum is closed Mon and Tues. Admission is free all day on the first Thurs of every month, and from 5 to 9 p.m. on the second Thurs of each month as part of the Blitz Capitol Hill art

walk. First Fri are free to seniors 62 and over, and first Sat are free for families, courtesy of Target. Members and children 12 and under are always free.

i **If you want to see all of Seattle's top attractions, don't miss out on the great value of the CityPASS. This six-attraction ticket includes admission to the Space Needle, Pacific Science Center, Seattle Aquarium, Woodland Park Zoo, Argosy Cruises Seattle Harbor Tour, and either the Experience Music Project OR the Museum of Flight. The CityPASS is $59 for adults 13 and over, $39 for ages 4–12, and free for ages 3 and under. The $111 value means that you save more than $50. And a great added benefit is that the pass allows you to skip most ticket lines and go right in. You can buy the CityPASS online or at any of the participating attractions. (888) 330-5008, www.citypass .com/seattle.**

CITY LANDMARKS

PIONEER SQUARE
201 Yesler Way (Central)
(206) 667-0687
www.pioneersquaredistrict.org
The Pioneer Square District was the birthplace of modern Seattle and the city's first downtown. Most of the Square's buildings were erected within a decade of the disastrous Great Fire of June 6, 1889. Preservationists rallied in the 1960s to save the area's exquisite ensemble of Victorian and Edwardian era architecture from demolition. Today Pioneer Square is listed on the National Register of Historic Places and is protected by both federal and local historic preservation districts. Don't miss the ornamental iron pergola, Occidental Park with its totem poles, or the Columbia

Center Observation Deck. This much cheaper alternative to the view from the Space Needle is only $5, offers 76th-floor views that are just as amazing, and seems the best undiscovered secret in Seattle—there are hardly ever any crowds here. Exercise a little caution in Pioneer Square at night, especially off the major streets.

SEATTLE SPACE NEEDLE $$$$
400 Broad St. (Central)
(800) 937-9582
www.spaceneedle.com
The Space Needle is the modern symbol of Seattle and perhaps its most recognizable landmark to visitors. Built for the 1962 World's Fair, and at that time the tallest building west of the Mississippi River, the Space Needle is part of the 74-acre Seattle Center. The German-inspired design was sketched by Edward Carlson on a coffeehouse place mat—befitting for this java-crazy city. It looms 520 feet above the city streets, with an observation deck that offers 360-degree indoor and outdoor viewing. Glass elevators speed visitors to the top at 14 feet per second, or about as fast as a raindrop falls to earth. Check out the newest installation, SkyQ. This is a system of five electronic kiosks that provide a wealth of information and hands-on interaction with the Space Needle and Seattle. For a real treat, dine at SkyCity, the revolving restaurant atop the Needle. It was added during the 2000 renovation, where $20 million in additions and restoration spruced up the Space Needle. Note that lines for the ride up the elevator to the observation deck can get long, especially on weekends or holidays; at those times it's best to get there as early as possible. Many visitors ride the monorail from the Westlake Center Mall station at Fifth and Pine, taking the

1-mile trip to Seattle Center for $4 round-trip for adults. The Space Needle and its observation deck are open 365 days a year.

SMITH TOWER $$
506 2nd Ave. (Central)
(206) 622-4004
www.smithtower.com

This 42-story, 522-foot building in the heart of historic Pioneer Square was one of the world's first skyscrapers. At the time it was built in 1914, it was an architectural feat and the tallest office building in the world outside Manhattan. Burns Lyman Smith dismissed the plans of his father, Lyman Cornelius Smith, for a mere 14-story building in favor of the far more ambitious tower that stands today—solely to gain publicity for their firm's new product, the Smith typewriter. The building is ornate, from its exterior white ornamental terra-cotta and bronze window frames to the Alaskan marble, Mexican onyx, mosaic tiles, and polished brass that adorn the interior. Doors are made of steel that was hand finished to resemble a highly grained mahogany. But the crown jewel is the legendary 35th-floor Chinese Room, which derives its name from the incredible carved wood and porcelain ceiling, and the elaborately carved blackwood furniture that was a gift from the empress of China. The observation deck on the 35th floor offers historic downtown and waterfront views, all the way to the mountains in the distance. Access to the deck is via the last manually operated elevators on the West Coast, original brass and copper cages. The observation deck is open daily Apr through Oct; weekends only Nov through Mar.

i Are you looking for the *Sleepless in Seattle* house? Everyone is, and yes—it really exists. It is one of the largest houses in the floating home community on Lake Union. Although it was painted white for the movie, today it is tan with dark green trim. To get to the community, head north on Westlake Avenue from downtown, on the west side of the lake. At around the 2400 block of Westlake you will see a marina with boats and homes, near the Kenmore Air Harbor. The home is at the end of the docks, but it is a private, gated community. The best way to see the house is from the water, with one of the tours or paddling your own kayak (plenty of rentals are available). But remember that this is a private home, and people live there!

HISTORY MUSEUMS

BURKE MUSEUM OF NATURAL HISTORY AND CULTURE $$
17th Avenue NE and NE 45th Street (North)
(206) 543-5590
www.washington.edu/burkemuseum

The Burke Museum is associated with UW and located on campus, showcasing Washington state's collection of cultural and natural wonders of the Northwest and the Pacific Rim. Its mission is to create a better understanding of the world and our place in it, and the museum shares that knowledge through its extensive changing exhibits of recent natural discoveries, historic artifacts and archives, and contemporary cultural arts. Long-term exhibits include "Life and Times of Washington State," over 500 million years of regional geological history, and "Pacific Voices," representing 17 native cultures. Don't

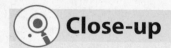 **Close-up**

Weather Be Damned—Five Great Itineraries for Rainy-Day Seattle

Yes, we all know it rains a lot in wintertime Seattle. Fortunately, the city offers an almost never-ending supply of great indoor activities. Here are my personal top-five ways to spend a rainy day.

CULTURE YOURSELF

Start at the **Seattle Art Museum** (1300 1st Ave., 206-654-3100, www.seattleartmuseum .org), where you can wander through an incredible permanent collection in a beautiful light-filled space. *Tip:* SAM is free on the first Thursday of every month. Have lunch at TASTE Restaurant, enjoying seasonal menus and award-winning desserts in the artistic setting.

Then head to **Pioneer Square** for some gallery hopping. The gorgeous Romanesque buildings are some of the oldest and most charming in the city. Start at the **Grand Central** (216 1st Ave. South, 206-623-9300), where you can visit numerous shops and art galleries under one roof. For a sweet nibble, stop in at **Grand Central Bakery.** Two blocks away, the **Tashiro-Kaplan building** (Third Avenue & Washington Street, www .tashirokaplan.com) houses many galleries, artists' lofts, and a coffee shop.

For the evening, see what's playing at the **Seattle Symphony** or the **Seattle Opera.** Or, if you just want to kick back and have a cocktail and light dinner in an artistic environment, head over to **Grey Gallery and Lounge** (1512 11th Ave., 206-325-5204, www.greygalleryandlounge.com).

BE AN UNDERGROUND TOURIST

There's a lot that can be seen by looking deeper than surface level. In Pioneer Square, the city simply rebuilt right over the rubble from the 1889 fire, leaving history and artifacts mere feet below today's streets. The city's birthplace lay virtually undisturbed, like the ruins of Pompeii, for nearly two-thirds of a century, before it occurred to anyone that it might be a good idea to preserve it. Start there, with **Bill Speidel's Underground Tour** (608 1st Ave., 206-682-4646, www.undergroundtour.com), a guided walking tour through the subterranean passages beneath old Seattle. Grab lunch at Speidel's **Underground Café** before continuing your day.

Continue your exploration beneath the surface by visiting the **Seattle Aquarium** (1483 Alaskan Way, 206-386-4320, www.seattleaquarium.org), which shows a fascinating world beneath Puget Sound's waters, with exhibits of marine mammals, local fish and birds, octopi and sharks, the Pacific Coral Reef, and other ocean oddities. For the perfect ending, take your evening meal at an underground restaurant, off-the-radar dining clubs that have no sign or permanent location and accept reserved guests only. Check out **One Pot** (onepotorg@gmail.com, www.onepot.org), an "experiment in table-making," with meandering theme dinner parties—early reservations highly recommended!

GET THE MUSIC IN YOU

Seattle is famous for its music scene, and there is simply no place like the **Experience Music Project** (325 5th Ave. North, 877-367-7361, www.empsfm.org). Opened in 2000 by that other Microsoft guy, Paul Allen, the sculpturesque building of curved metal panels was designed by Frank Gehry and houses rare artifacts and memorabilia from dozens of music legends. EPM's cutting-edge technology captures the essence and influence of rock 'n' roll icons like Eric Clapton and Seattle's own Jimi Hendrix. You can grab lunch at EPM's **Revolution Cafe**, which serves above-average fare.

Afterward, head to Capitol Hill to stock up your own music collection at **Everyday Music** (112 Broadway East, 206-568-3321, www.everydaymusic.com), one of the most beloved record stores with an overwhelming collection of vinyl. While you're there, pay homage to the Jimi Hendrix statue around the corner. End on the right note at one of the city's iconic live music venues such as **Crocodile Cafe**, played by legends from Nirvana to Yoko Ono, or **Neumos,** where a free Radiohead show nearly caused riots. Two other top places to check are **Showbox** and **The Moore.**

GET YOUR DRINK ON

Some people—not me, certainly!—believe that rainy days are simply meant for sitting in a pub and drinking. Fortunately, that is easy to do in Seattle, a city where beer rates only slightly behind coffee as nectar of the gods, and where lounges serving old-fashioned cocktails whipped up by trained mixologists have sprung up everywhere.

Start by catching an early movie at **Cinebarre** (6009 244th St. SW, 425-672-8163, http://cinebarre.com), a terrific theater with a full bar and extensive menu for ordering at your seat.

Later, Seattle's top ales with a **pub crawl. Seattle By Foot** (800-838-3006, http://seattlebyfoot.com) hosts a tour of local microbreweries on Friday and Saturday, beginning at **Pike Brewing Company.** You'll see the beer shrine that was rated the city's best museum, witness the brewing process, and of course enjoy some of the best ales in the country.

As the night wanes, check out the **Triple Door** or **Dimitrou's Jazz Alley,** both intimate venues with old-school style and great live music acts.

SHOP 'TIL YOU DROP

Another great rainy-day pastime is shopping, and Seattle provides plenty of that. Start at **Pike Place Market** (85 Pike St., 206-682-7453, www.pikeplacemarket.org), home of the legendary fish-throwing merchants. For more than a century this historic market has been where locals shop for food; You'll also find dozens of craft stalls selling everything from jewelry and clothing to ceramics, sculpture, and artwork. Most of these can be browsed without ever leaving the covered market—perfect for wet weather.

Enjoy lunch at a market spot like **Pike Place Chowder, Le Panier Bakery,** or the **Market Diner.** Afterwards, go back in time by browsing through some of Seattle's fun vintage stores. Head up to the corner of First and Pine, where you'll find **Isadora's** exquisite collection of estate jewelry; **Vintage Clothing & Collectibles** is located just a few doors down. From there, drive up Pine to Capitol Hill, where you don't want to miss **Pretty Parlor** (119 E. Summit Ave., 206-405-2883, www.prettyparlor.com) and **Le Frock** (317 E. Pine, 206-623-5339, www.lefrockonline.com).

End your day with dinner at **SkyCity,** the revolving restaurant atop the **Space Needle.** While the day views are best in clear weather, at night it doesn't matter if it's raining. The twinkling cityscape by night is spectacular, affording a dazzling show as you revolve 360 degrees during your meal.

miss a stroll through the Erna Gunther Ethnobotanical Garden. Free admission on the first Thurs of each month.

KLONDIKE GOLD RUSH NATIONAL HISTORICAL PARK

319 2nd Ave. (Central)
(206) 220-4240
www.nps.gov/klse

This park is run by the National Park Service, with sites in Canada and Alaska, and a Seattle unit located in Pioneer Square. The museum offers a glimpse into the stories of adventure and hardship during the exciting, adventurous Klondike gold rush of 1897–98. Seattle played an important part in this historical event, as the place of origin for many stampeders headed to Alaska for their riches in gold. In addition to historic exhibits from this time, there are also gold panning demonstrations, video presentations, and a Pioneer Historic District walking tour. The museum is open every day, although hours may be limited in winter months. All programs are free to the public.

MUSEUM OF HISTORY AND INDUSTRY $$

2700 24th Ave. East (Central)
(206) 324-1126
www.seattlehistory.org

The MOHAI is a dynamic and innovative center for historical exploration, and is the largest private heritage organization in the state. Its collection includes nearly 4 million artifacts from the Pacific Northwest, including archives and photographs. The main exhibit, "Essential Seattle," takes visitors on a journey through the city's 150-year history, with transformation from wilderness to pioneer town, through technology and grunge music. An exciting schedule of

rotating exhibits rounds out the collection, including regular photographic histories of the city. Open daily, with extended hours on Thurs, and the first Thurs of every month is free of charge.

NORDIC HERITAGE MUSEUM $$

3014 NW 67th St. (North)
(206) 789-5707
www.nordicmuseum.org

Since its founding in 1980 in Ballard, the heart of Seattle's Scandinavian settlement, the Nordic Heritage Museum has provided a place where the history of these countries, and their impact on Seattle, comes alive. The collection includes art, cultural objects, dioramas, folk costumes, textiles, tools, furniture, and a music library. You can trace the voyage and life of Nordic immigrants as they made their way to the Pacific Northwest and settled here. There is also a focus on the logging and fishing industries, a mainstay of Seattle's growth and prosperity in which Scandinavians played a major role. It is the only museum in the United States that honors the legacy of immigrants from Denmark, Finland, Iceland, Norway, and Sweden. Open Tues through Sun.

NORTHWEST AFRICAN AMERICAN MUSEUM $$

2300 S. Massachusetts St.
(206) 518-6000
http://naamnw.org

The NAAM is a vibrant community gathering place and museum that documents the unique historical and cultural experiences of African Americans in the Pacific Northwest. At the heart of the experience is the story of African immigrants' journey to the region and the many ways in which they survived. The museum's exhibits feature visual arts,

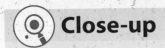 **Close-up**

Architectural Marvels in Seattle

If, like me, you are a buff of interesting buildings and architecture, here are a few more must-see places in Seattle for unique design. If you *really* like such things, check out the tours offered by the **Seattle Architecture Foundation**. From neighborhood architectural gems to green buildings and historic landmarks, you'll love the variety of guided walking tours SAF offers. Prices range from free to about $30. 1333 5th Ave., Suite 300, (206) 667-9184, www.seattlearchitecture.org/tours.html.

CENTRAL LIBRARY

The public library downtown resembles five glass boxes that were haphazardly stacked on top of one another, but staggered so that one does not sit squarely on top of the other. Inside the main entrance, the curtain of windows above casts diamond-shaped light onto the floor in a dance of shapes and shadows. 1000 4th Ave. (206) 386-4636, www.spl.org.

CHAPEL OF ST. IGNATIUS

This contemporary chapel at Seattle University was designed to resemble seven bottles of light in a stone box, and light passes through each bottle in specific areas of the building. The resulting pools of clear and colored light that define the physical and spiritual spaces are an exquisite departure from traditional stained glass. 901 12th Ave., (206) 296-5588, www.seattleu.edu/missionministry/chapel.

EXPERIENCE MUSIC PROJECT

This curving metal sculpturelike building was designed by Frank Gehry, inspired when he deconstructed several electric guitars. The 21,000 metal shingles each contort with their own unique shapes, appearing different colors depending on how the light hits them. A more detailed listing follows in the Special Interest Museums section. 325 5th Ave. North, (206) 770-2700, www.empsfm.org.

KING STREET STATION

Part of the Department of Transportation, the King Street Station links commuter rail, Amtrak, and public buses. It was designed by Reed and Stern, the architectural firm responsible for the Grand Central Terminal in New York. Highlights include the 250-foot clock tower that was modeled after the San Marco bell tower in Venice, and the ornate ceilings and mosaic tile work that are starting to emerge in a current major renovation. 303 S. Jackson St., (206) 684-3072, www.seattle.gov/transportation/kingstreet.htm.

RAINIER TOWER

This 40-story skyscraper, built in 1977, is called the "wineglass" because of its unique shape. Twenty-nine occupied floors rest on a small, inwardly curving pedestal that makes up the bottom 11 stories. The inverted-pyramid design was created partly to make more room for pedestrians, and to reduce the office building's carbon footprint. 1301 5th Ave.

crafts, music, literature, and history. Many revolving exhibits are also featured, such as those highlighting the more recent waves of East African newcomers to Seattle, particularly from Ethiopia and Sudan. The Legacy Gallery hosts myriad performances, events, and lectures on an ongoing basis. NAAM is closed Mon and Tues.

WING LUKE ASIAN MUSEUM $$$
719 S. King St. (Central)
(206) 623-5124
www.wingluke.org

This wonderful museum of Asian Pacific American history immerses visitors in its uniquely American stories of survival, success, struggle, conflict, compassion, and hope. In the heart of the vibrant International District, the Wing Luke Museum includes the historic Chinatown hotel where countless Asian immigrants found their first home in Seattle. Its namesake, Wing Luke, came to Seattle from China at six years of age. After serving in the army during WWII and then graduating from college and law school, Luke went on to become the first Asian American to hold elected office in the Pacific Northwest, winning a city council seat in 1962. He fought for civil rights and against discrimination, and was instrumental in fair housing laws. The Wing Luke Asian Museum was founded to fulfill his vision of preserving the history and important issues of Asian Americans. A Smithsonian affiliate, it is the only museum in the nation devoted to the Asian Pacific American experience. Closed Mon.

SCIENCE CENTERS

MUSEUM OF FLIGHT $$$
9404 E. Marginal Way South (South)
(206) 764-5720
www.museumofflight.org

This educational aviation museum is fascinating, with an extensive collection of preserved, historic artifacts related to air and space travel and technology. It's one of the largest and most comprehensive aviation collections in the country, containing tens of thousands of artifacts, millions of rare photographs, a world-class library, and more than 150 rare aircraft and space vehicles—including the original Air Force One and an Apollo command module. Temporary exhibits cover such endlessly popular subjects as Amelia Earhart, war fighter planes, and space exploration. You can even experience flight for yourself in a simulator, or watch the movie *Time Flies: A Century of Flight* inside the Boeing 737 Airliner Theater. The museum is open daily, and on the first Thurs of each month admission is free after 5 p.m.

i Get a self-guided **Cultural Tour** from **Destination Heritage**. These free guides invite visitors and residents to explore the vibrant character of the region by highlighting historic landmarks, museums, festivals, and scenic drives throughout King County. Download maps and audio at www.destination heritage.org.

PACIFIC SCIENCE CENTER $$$
200 2nd Ave. North (Central)
(206) 443-2001
www.pacsci.org

Located in the Seattle Center complex, the Pacific Science Center was opened as the United States Science Pavilion for the 1962 World's Fair. After the exposition, it became the first U.S. museum founded as a science and technology center. Its interactive and innovative exhibits and programs are meant to inspire interest in science, math, and technology. Permanent exhibits include animatronic dinosaurs, butterfly house, insect village, saltwater tide pool, various animal exhibits, technology exhibits, and human body works. The Willard Smith Planetarium and IMAX Theater provide great shows throughout the day, and various events and educational programs are offered constantly. Don't miss the laser light shows held on Thurs through Sun evenings, and at weekend matinees. The Pacific Science Center is closed Tues; for an additional cost, combination tickets can be purchased that include the IMAX, planetarium, or laser shows.

i Check out Seattle TourSaver, a two-for-one coupon book that includes more than a hundred offerings for buy one, get one free admission. Flightseeing, cruises, tours, hotels, museums, and cultural trips are all included. Call (888) 315-1650 or buy online at www.seattletoursaver.com. You can also purchase it locally at several Seattle locations (check the Web site).

SPECIAL INTEREST CENTERS & MUSEUMS

DUWAMISH LONGHOUSE AND CULTURAL CENTER
4705 W. Marginal Way SW (South)
(206) 431-1582
www.duwamishtribe.org

The Duwamish Longhouse now proudly sits near the mouth of the Duwamish River overlooking the Duwamish River Valley, not far from the landing site of early immigrants. The longhouse—as in ancient times—is the site where tribal business is conducted and cultural and educational events are held. In addition, the Duwamish tribe wants to share its longhouse with the public to reinforce its cultural and social traditions. Historic photographs, recordings, artifacts, a museum, and an art gallery of Seattle's first people are on-site. Monthly special events as well as ongoing workshops, demonstrations, and lectures are available to the public. The longhouse and cultural center are open Mon through Sat, and are free of charge.

EXPERIENCE MUSIC PROJECT & SCIENCE FICTION MUSEUM $$$
325 5th Ave. North (Central)
(206) 770-2700
www.empsfm.org

You simply cannot miss this place—its dramatic Frank Gehry–designed, curving metal walls rise up at the base of the Space Needle like a massive sculpture. Experience Music Project is an exploration of creativity and innovation in popular music, blending interpretative, interactive exhibitions with cutting-edge technology. EMP showcases rock 'n' roll and its roots in jazz, soul, gospel, country, and the blues; and also explores rock's own influence on punk, hip-hop, and other contemporary genres. Some of the coolest exhibits include the massive LCD screen and sound system near the lobby, and the two-story guitar sculpture. The *Northwest Passage* collection traces the development of the Northwest music scene, and famous local artists such as Jimi Hendrix and Nirvana are prominently featured. It's interesting how this music museum blends with the Science Fiction Museum, which displays memorabilia and technology; there is also a Science Fiction Hall of Fame, honoring the lives and legacies of some of the genre's greatest creators. Open daily; during the winter months, both museums are free from 5 to 8 p.m. on the first Thurs of the month and feature live music.

MARITIME EVENT CENTER
2205 Alaskan Way, Pier 66 (Central)
(206) 374-4000
www.maritimeeventcenter.com

This nautical museum also serves as a unique setting for events on the Seattle waterfront, adjacent to the Bell Harbor International Conference Center. The exhibits form the Maritime Education Initiative, serving to educate the public and youth about the vital role of the maritime industry in the Pacific Northwest. Tours and classes are available at the high-tech, high-touch museum, which features information on not only maritime history but also global trade, transportation, and fisheries. Admission is free, but the museum is only open for regular admission on certain days and hours (at this printing it was Mon only), and for special events and educational days.

SEATTLE MUSEUM OF
   THE MYSTERIES $
623 Broadway East (Central)
(206) 328-6499
www.seattlechatclub.org/museum.html

This is truly one of the most offbeat museums you're likely to ever run across. If you want to experience the weird and wacky side of Seattle, this is the place to do it. This funky little place bills itself as a library and cultural center, but it's really more of a repository for paranormal and folklore exhibits. You can see everything from casts of Bigfoot's print (and a life-size, hairy model), evidence of purported UFO activity, Seattle's only oxygen bar, crop circle exhibits from around the state, the lost city of Wellington, and the legend of D. B. Cooper. The place also does tarot readings and gives ghost tours—there's even a Ghost Communication Box, where you can connect to the other side and ask the ghost questions. The

ghost, by the way, is said to resemble Nikola Tesla. It's all great fun, and very offbeat Seattle. The small museum is very community-based and run entirely by volunteers, so hours may vary and it's closed at various times for breaks, meals, or who knows why else. Best to call first. Admission is by small suggested donation.

TOURS

A lot of different types of tours of Seattle are available, from the typical overview of major attractions, to the artistic, to the quirky and funky. If you are the kind of person who likes the latter, who wants a tour to be off-the-beaten-path and show you something you would never have otherwise discovered, here are a few recommendations you should take a close look at.

ARGOSY CRUISES $$$$
Pier 55 (Central)
(206) 623-4252
www.argosycruises.com

This one-hour Seattle Harbor cruise gives a touch of Seattle history along with breathtaking scenery. Dinner cruises are also offered in the harbor, as well as boat tours to the Hiram Chittenden Locks. Or check out the lake cruises of Lake Union, where you can see the unique houseboat communities made famous in *Sleepless in Seattle*, and Lake Washington, with its luxurious waterfront homes and Mount Rainier backdrop. Argosy Cruises are offered as an optional combination ticket at other sights such as the Space Needle, and are part of the CityPASS.

BILL SPEIDEL'S
   UNDERGROUND TOUR $$$
608 1st Ave. (Central)
(206) 682-4646
www.undergroundtour.com

See the remains of original downtown Seattle on this unique tour that is filled with humor. Walk below historic Pioneer Square sidewalks and past abandoned 1890s storefronts, with exceptional tour guides filling you in on Seattle's entertaining frontier past. Tours operate year-round and depart from Doc Maynard's Public House. For adults only, there's also the Underworld Tour, which includes a cocktail and many tales of red-light district shenanigans of graft, opium, sex, and general debauchery.

CHINATOWN DISCOVERY
TOURS $$$$
719 S. King St. (Central)
(206) 623-5124
www.seattlechinatowntour.com
Just minutes away from downtown Seattle, it's possible to discover the traditions and soul of a 7,000-year-old culture. These intimate guided tours show the daily cultural life of the Asian community in Seattle, and share the stories of their history. Tours include a sit-down presentation, leisurely walked tour, and admission to the Wing Luke Asian Museum.

EVERGREEN ESCAPES $$$$
900 1st Ave. South, Suite 412 (Central)
(866) 203-7603
www.evergreenescapes.com
The Pacific Northwest's premier sustainable travel company, Evergreen Escapes, runs a number of tours within Seattle city limits, as well as an itinerary of outdoor adventures throughout the state. The highly trained and experienced guides combine wilderness and adventure skills with sustainability concepts, great food, and camaraderie for memorable experiences. Multi-activity tours can include kayaking, hiking, rock climbing,

whitewater rafting, fishing, bird-watching, photography, beer and wine tasting, and local Seattle landmarks. From Explore Seattle walking tours to urban kayaking and paddling, you don't need to leave the city to have an outdoors adventure. Voluntourism itineraries are also available, if you want to give back with an activity such as helping with restoration efforts at Discovery Park. Half-day and full-day tours available.

FREMONT SUNDAY ICE
CREAM TOUR $$$
Valley Street and Terry Avenue North,
South Lake Union (Central)
(206) 284-2828
www.seattleferryservice.com
This is one of the most fun things to do on a Sunday in Seattle! Taking the Seattle Ferry Service, otherwise known as the party boat, on a 45-minute water tour with ice cream treats can't be beat. Once you're aboard the ancient, 50-foot steel vintage ferry, the ride takes you past the Lake Union floating homes and gives a peek at Dale Chihuly's studio, Gas Works Park, and the Sleepless in Seattle houseboat. The tour includes a humorous narration of old Seattle and some funky background music. Besides the ice cream, coffee and hot chocolate, soft drinks, and, inexplicably, a tub of tomato soup are for sale for $2–$3. Tickets are purchased as you board on a walk-on basis only (no reservations), and only cash or checks is accepted. Cruises depart year-round, on the hour from 11 a.m. to 4 p.m.

KENMORE AIR $$$$
950 Westlake Ave. North (Central)
(866) 435-9524
www.kenmoreair.com
If you really want a thrilling adventure tour that is quintessentially Seattle, opt for a

seaplane tour. These "flightseeing" excursions take off and land from the water, and offer the most spectacular way to see the Emerald City from a bird's-eye view. The 20-minute flight is narrated by your pilot as you take in the scenery below. Flights depend on weather conditions, and advance reservations are recommended.

RIDE THE DUCKS OF SEATTLE $$$$
516 Broad St. (Central)
(800) 817-1116
www.ridetheducksofseattle.com
Popular in many cities, the Duck Tours in Seattle are led by comedic captains who keep guests laughing on a fun-filled, musical tour of the Emerald City. The amphibious World War II vehicles operate on both land and water—so after you've seen downtown, Pike Place Market, and Pioneer Square, you will splash into the water for a whole new look at Seattle.

SAVOR SEATTLE FOOD TOURS $$$$
(888) 987-2867
www.savorseattletours.com
This culinary tour company is one of the top-ranked in Seattle and has been featured in *Bon Appétit Magazine* and *USA Today*. The original Pike Place Market tour takes you behind the scenes to meet some of the most talented food artisans and enjoy their savory creations. Other tours include Gourmet Seattle and Chocolate Indulgence; private and group tours are also available. It is recommended to purchase public tour tickets in advance, as they often sell out, especially during high summer season.

SEASTAR TOURS $$
3919 18th Ave. West, Fisherman's
   Terminal Dock 9 (Central)
(206) 550-2623
http://seastartours.com

You are invited aboard a real working boat used on the *Deadliest Catch* television show! The Emmy-winning series about Bering sea crab fishing only shows what visitors on this tour get to experience: what it's like to be on the actual boat. Check out the pilothouse and crab pots, take pictures with the huge crustaceans, see how the guys live on board, and hear firsthand stories straight from the fishermen shown on TV. Tours are available throughout the summer season; in winter, the working boat returns to the seas for its next catch.

SEATTLE BITES FOOD TOURS $$$$
(425) 888-8837
www.seattlebitesfoodtours.com
Local culinary and history enthusiasts lead these two-and-a-half-hour walking tours of Pike Place Market, pairing memorable stories with delicious gourmet food and drink. Each guest receives a souvenir eco-friendly reusable shopping bag and a coupon for 10 percent merchant discounts. The tour runs daily starting at 10:30 a.m., rain or shine, and is limited to a maximum of 14 guests. Advance ticket purchase is required.

SEATTLE BY FOOT $$$$
(800) 838-3006
http://seattlebyfoot.com
These entertaining and scenic guided walking tours offer four unique itineraries: a City Tour, Coffee Crawl, Pub Crawl, and Funky Fremont. These are all great fun and can show you an insiders' view of Seattle that you're unlikely to get anywhere else; the groups are small, limited to 15. All tours are between two and two and a half hours long. Group and private tours can also be arranged.

SHOW ME SEATTLE $$$$
(206) 633-CITY

www.showmeseattle.com

The claim of this tour is to see Seattle the way the locals see it. On a small shuttle bus, you will visit and learn about down-town Seattle, Pike Place Market, the Seattle waterfront, and Pioneer Square, and witness some outstanding views of the city. The tour passes through quirky neighborhoods and visits Chinatown, the Ballard Locks with ladders for the spawning salmon, the Giant Bridge Troll, and the famous *Sleepless in Seattle* floating home. "Mystery" treats are offered with each tour, and pickup at all major downtown hotels is included.

SHUTTER TOURS $$$$
(425) 516-8838

www.shuttertours.com

The ultimate tour for shutterbugs, these walking classes combine Seattle factoids with mini-lessons in photography—and some of the best subjects for film and digital shots. The award-winning, professional pho-tographer guides give instruction in compo-sition, without technical jargon, making the tours excellent for beginning to intermedi-ate photographers. You must bring your own camera, and recording/video is not allowed. The interactive walking tours to some of Seattle's most interesting out-of-the-way spots last about two hours, and are limited to eight participants.

SUB SEATTLE TOUR $$$$
608 1st Ave. (Central)

(206) 682-4646

www.subseattletour.com

Brought to you by the same folks who do the Underground Tour, this is definitely the tour for you if you like irreverence and the quirky bits of a place that typical tours don't cover. The Sub Seattle Tour is advertised as "not your father's bus ride" for rule-breakers and troublemakers. It's a humorous 90-minute bus tour of offbeat neighborhoods and sights, starting in Capitol Hill and cov-ering the city's subculture, from the Wah Mee massacre in the International District in 1983, to the unofficial memorial to Kurt Cobain at Viretta Park (and Cobain's house). The tour runs from Mar to Nov only, and is for 18 and older only.

TOURS NORTHWEST $$$$
(866) 584-1122

www.toursnorthwest.com

Tours Northwest offers several sightseeing tours to top attractions in Seattle and around the Pacific Northwest. The most popular is the three-hour City Tour, giving an over-view of Seattle in comfortable mini-coaches. Other tours include Mount Rainier National Park and the Boeing Future of Flight Aviation Center. Door-to-door pickup and dropoff to most area hotels is included.

TRAVEL TO SKETCH $$$$
(206) 353-1687

http://traveltosketch.com

This has to be one of the most fun and unique types of walking tours anywhere. Sketch your way through the architecture, art, and interesting spaces of Seattle on this cultural guided tour that provides anyone ages "12 to 112" the tools to observe, and record, aspects of a city and its culture. No artistic or drawing experience is required, and the tours start in a variety of locations and neighborhoods. Some tours are com-bined with wine tastings or visits to cafes, and most are three- to six-hour custom classes.

OTHER ATTRACTIONS

HIRAM M. CHITTENDEN LOCKS
3015 NW 54th St. (North)
(206) 783-7059
www.nws.usace.army.mil/PublicMenu/
Menu.cfm?sitename=lwsc&pagename
=mainpage

Also known locally as the Ballard Locks, this complex of locks in Salmon Bay is part of the Lake Washington Ship Canal. They are used to maintain the water level, prevent the mixing of Puget Sound seawater with the freshwater of the lakes, and move boats in and out of the connecting waterways. Free guided tours are offered from the visitor center between Mar 1 and Nov 30 (call for times). It's a fascinating place to spend a free afternoon watching the boat channel and, from June through Oct, the migration of huge salmon populations. From Aug through May you may see harbor seals or sea lions. Bring a lunch, as the attached Carl S. English Jr. Botanical Garden makes a perfect spot for a picnic; afterward you can stroll through to admire the beautiful plants and flowering gardens. The locks are open from 7 a.m. to 9 p.m. year-round, and the visitor center from 10 a.m. to 6 p.m. May 1 through Sept 30, and 10 a.m. to 4 p.m. Oct 1 through Apr 30.

OLYMPIC SCULPTURE PARK
2901 Western Ave. (Central)
(206) 654-3100
www.seattleartmuseum.org/visit/osp

This nine-acre former industrial site that was turned into a green art space makes for a great stroll dotted with contemporary sculptures by Alexander Calder, Richard Serra, and Mark di Suvero. The beauty of the Olympic Mountains and Puget Sound provide a dramatic backdrop to the permanent sculptures and rotating art installations, and a 2,200-foot Z-shape path leads from the steel-and-glass pavilion through the park and gardens. Best of all, it's open daily to the public from sunrise to sunset, with no admission fees. Free public tours with a variety of topics are also held on an ongoing basis, so check the Web site calendar for dates.

SEATTLE AQUARIUM $$$$
1483 Alaskan Way (Central)
(206) 386-4300
www.seattleaquarium.org

The Seattle Aquarium on the waterfront is not only a hands-on, fun marine experience for visitors, it's also a major marine conservation initiative that aims to educate the public about the wonders of the waters. The aquarium welcomes more than 800,000 visitors annually, helping them become aware of the impact we all have on the marine environment. Exhibits include numerous small-to-massive tanks and ponds, with Washington water life, Pacific coral reef, ocean oddities, marine mammals, fish, and birds. A diver show and dome feeding happen several times a day, as do talks on marine mammals and octopi. Many educational and preservation programs are also in place at the aquarium, which is open daily.

WASHINGTON STATE FERRIES $$
801 Alaskan Way, Pier 52 (Central)
(888) 808-7977
www.wsdot.wa.gov/ferries

Taking a ferry ride to one of many nearby Puget Sound locations is a favorite activity for visitors and locals alike. Hop aboard one of the Washington ferries for sweeping views of the Sound, Seattle skyline, and Olympic and Cascade Mountains. One of the shortest, and most popular, routes is to Bainbridge

Island, where you can stroll around the shops and galleries of the charming town or visit the Bloedel Reserve. Bremerton is another nice destination from the downtown Seattle pier, where you can visit the historic USS *Turner Joy* and Navy Museum, casinos, galleries, or Harborside Fountain Park. Vehicles, bicycles, kayaks, canoes, and pets (on leashes or in carriers) are allowed to cross on the ferry. From the Seattle Pier 52 terminal, only the ferry to Vashon Island is passenger-only (no vehicles).

SEATTLE ON A SHOESTRING: SOMETHING FOR NOTHING

Although it can be easy to do so, you don't have to spend a boatload of money when visiting Seattle. If you're short on cash, don't fret—there is an absolutely astounding amount of cool, fun things to do in this city without spending a penny! Here is a reference list of free attractions in and around the city. For more information about some of the activities, refer to the page number given for a detailed listing.

BENAROYA HALL
(see p. 173 for more information)
This gorgeous performance hall that is home to the Seattle Symphony offers free public tours, on Tues and Fri at noon and 1 p.m. at the Grand Lobby entrance. On select Mon throughout the year, you can get a real treat—Joseph Adams, the resident organist on the 4,490-pipe Watjen concert organ, gives a free 30-minute concert starting at 12:30 p.m., with tours before the performance (at noon) and afterward. For a complete schedule, go to www.seattlesymphony .org/benaroya/tour.

BLITZ ART WALK
(see p. 166 for more information)
This art walk is held in the creative Capitol Hill neighborhood, showcasing visual, literary, musical, and performing arts. Held on the second Thurs of each month from 5 to 8 p.m.

BURKE MUSEUM
(see p. 147 for more information)
Free admission all day on the first Thurs of every month, and the museum stays open until 8 p.m.

CENTER FOR WOODEN BOATS
(see p. 220 for more information)
Every Sun afternoon the center offers free boat rides on Lake Union. The rides take place at 2 and 3 p.m., weather permitting, and you can make reservations in person as early as 10 a.m. the day of (no phone or prior reservations allowed). The best bet is to get down there as close to 10 a.m. as possible, then tour the museum, do some wood carvings at the center, or have lunch in one of many nearby waterfront restaurants before your boat ride.

CITY HALL LUNCHTIME CONCERTS
Throughout the year, Seattle City Hall becomes a concert hall on the first and third Thurs. Various free live music is presented at noon, from classical and orchestra performances to percussion, Latin grooves, rock bands, American and Celtic folk music, and children's concerts. You can even get a card with a redemption code to download a limited-edition, digital music sampler featuring 12 Seattle bands. The card itself is eco-friendly; it's embedded with seeds, and when you're done with the card you can plant it and grow wildflowers! So Seattle. 600

4th Ave., (206) 684-7171, www.seattle.gov/
arts/community/seattle_presents.asp.

COAST GUARD MUSEUM

Interesting collection of Coast Guard memorabilia, uniforms, and guns, with Arctic ice-
breaker ships usually moored nearby. A slice
of Seattle maritime history and the important
role the Coast Guard plays in it. Open Mon,
Wed, and Fri from 9 a.m. to 3 p.m. 1519 Alaskan
Way South, Pier 36, (206) 217-6993, www.rex
mwess.com/cgpatchs/cogardmuseum.html.

DUWAMISH LONGHOUSE AND
CULTURAL CENTER
(see p. 153 for more information)

Experience the culture, history, and artifacts
of Seattle's first people. This Native American
cultural center is open Mon through Sat,
with free admission.

EXPERIENCE MUSIC PROJECT AND SCI-
ENCE FICTION MUSEUM
(see p. 151 for more information)

On the first Thurs of the month during the
winter season, EMP|SFM hosts All Access
Nights with free admission from 5 to 8 p.m.
Call (206) 770-2700 for the exact dates each
year that this is offered.

FARMERS' MARKETS
(see p. 137 for more information)

Seattle has a thriving community of farmers', flea, and open-air markets. At last count
there were more than a dozen, including the
huge and extremely popular Fremont Sunday Market, but loosely organized grassroots
markets spring up all the time as well. There
is no admission fee for any of the markets.
Great places to stroll and be entertained, as
well as grab some great food, for not much
money.

5TH AVENUE THEATRE

Take advantage of the popular series Spot-
light Nights, which gives behind-the-scenes
looks at upcoming shows put on by the 5th
Avenue Theatre company. Artistic Director
David Armstrong leads guest speakers and
performers through song, dance, interviews,
and more. 1308 5th Ave., (206) 625-1900,
www.5thavenue.org/education/spotlight
nights.aspx.

FIRST THURSDAY ART WALK
(see p. 167 for more information)

If you haven't figured it out yet, the first
Thurs of every month is a terrific time to be
in Seattle—particularly if you love art and/
or you don't want to spend a lot of money.
From noon to 8 p.m. you can stroll artists'
booths and galleries throughout Pioneer
Square for free; many galleries offer complimentary wine and hors d'oeuvres. You'll
notice in these freebie listings that many
Seattle museums also get in on the First
Thursday wagon with free admission.

FREMONT PUBLIC ART SCULPTURES

Fremont is a uniquely weird neighborhood
with a distinct personality all its own; it's
no wonder that it draws a lot of artists and
other creatives. The area is home to three of
the most beloved, offbeat public sculptures
in the city. The **Fremont Troll** lives under
the Aurora Avenue Bridge at N. 36th Street;
it is a large concrete troll crushing an actual
VW Beetle. Visitors climb the troll and graffiti
him, and he makes for a great photo op. Just
around the corner, at N. 34th and Fremont
Avenue, is the *Waiting for the Interurban*
statue. Six cast aluminum figures, including
a dog, wait at the bus stop located there,
for a bus that never comes. The figures are
routinely costumed and adorned by locals.

And at 600 N. 36th you'll find one of the city's more controversial landmarks—a 16-foot-tall bronze **statue of Lenin.** Yes, dictator Vladimir Lenin of the former USSR. It arrived in Seattle via Czechoslovakia, where it was found tumbled in a city dump after the fall of communism in 1989. Seattleite Lewis Carpenter mortgaged his house to buy and transport the statue to Seattle, where it has been displayed—and been the subject of constant dispute—ever since.

FRYE ART MUSEUM
(see p. 145 for more information)
The area's only art museum that is completely free all the time, the Frye showcases a collection of European and American art. Parking is also free at the downtown museum. Guided tours are available at 1 p.m. Wed through Sun, and the museum often has music concerts and other entertainment—all provided at no charge.

HIRAM M. CHITTENDEN LOCKS
(see p. 158 for more information)
The complex of water locks where salmon migrate and boats move between Puget Sound and connecting lakes is a great place to spend a pretty day, absolutely free. You can even get a free guided tour from the visitor center between Mar 1 and Nov 30. The adjacent botanical gardens are beautiful and have no admission charges; you may even be lucky enough in summer months to catch a free concert in the park.

KING COUNTY METRO TRANSIT AND SOUND TRANSIT
(see p. 19 for more information)
In the Ride Free Area consisting of most all downtown Seattle, the bus service in Seattle is free. You can hop on and off as often or as far as you like within this zone, all completely fare-free.

KLONDIKE GOLD RUSH NATIONAL HISTORICAL PARK
(see p. 150 for more information)
Located in Pioneer Square, this museum preserves the story of the 1897–98 stampede to the Yukon gold fields and Seattle's role in this event. Free admission all the time, to everyone. And between June 15 and Sept 2, they offer a free guided walking tour of historic Pioneer Square. The tours leave each day at 2 p.m. and last 60–90 minutes; reservations are not needed, but the tour is limited to 25 participants.

KUBOTA GARDEN
This tranquil public garden was founded in 1927 by Japanese immigrant Fujitaro Kubota and today is owned by the city. Its stunning 20 acres of urban refuge feature streams, waterfalls, ponds, hills, rock outcroppings, and an incredible plant collection. When the property was targeted by developers around 1980, it was declared a Historical Landmark for protection. 9817 55th Ave. South, (206) 684-4584, www.kubota.org.

LAST RESORT FIRE DEPARTMENT MUSEUM
Also in Pioneer Square, the Last Resort houses the largest collection of antique motorized fire apparatus in the Pacific Northwest. While it's not for everyone, there are some pretty cool old fire trucks here and it's worth a stroll. Open Wed and Thurs only from 11 a.m. 3 p.m. (in the winter, Wed only); free admission. 301 2nd Ave. South, (206) 783-4474, www.lastresortfd.org.

ATTRACTIONS

LIVE THEATER WEEK
Are you in Seattle during the third week of Oct? If so, take advantage of this fabulous yearly offering from the theater community. Live Theater Week features 50 free performances and more than 30 complimentary special events. http://seattleperforms.com/ltw.

MARITIME EVENT CENTER
(see p. 154 for more information)
Admission is always free to this interactive, high-tech nautical museum of maritime history in the Pacific Northwest. Opening days and hours are limited, so be sure to check the Web site first.

MUSEUM OF FLIGHT
(see p. 152 for more information)
One of the foremost flight museums in the world, the Museum of Flight houses spy planes and the original Air Force One. Free on the first Thurs of every month, from 5 to 9 p.m.

MUSEUM OF HISTORY AND INDUSTRY
(see p. 150 for more information)
Free admission all day on the first Thurs of every month, with extended hours of 10 a.m. to 8 p.m.

OLYMPIC SCULPTURE PARK
(see p. 158 for more information)
This nine-acre former industrial site that was turned into a green art space makes for a great stroll dotted with contemporary sculptures by Alexander Calder, Richard Serra, and Mark di Suvero. Best of all, it's open daily to the public, with no admission fees.

NORTHWEST FOLKLIFE FESTIVAL
(see p. 196 for more information)
Held over Memorial Day weekend each year, this completely free festival celebrates the folk, ethnic, and traditional arts of the area. There are lots of art, music, dance and theater performances, children's activities, food, and more.

PARAMOUNT THEATRE TOURS
(see p. 175 for more information)
On the first Sat of each month, free guided 90-minute tours of the grand, lovingly restored Paramount are offered to the public. Meet at the main entrance a few minutes before 10 a.m.

PIKE PLACE MARKET
(see pp. 138, 177 for more information)
Free entertainment doesn't get much better than this. Start at the pig—the large bronze swine sculpture that sits at the main entrance to the market, just down from First Avenue and Pike. This is where the famous Pike Place Fish company is located, those crazy guys who throw whole fish to each other as the customers order them. It's usually thronged with gawkers, and the vendors sometimes get a little put out when there are too many onlookers and no buyers, which just adds to the entertainment value, naturally. You can spend hours walking around here and could almost make a meal off the dozens of samples that many of the market stalls offer, while street performers entertain. Great, cheap fun any day of the week.

SEATTLE ART MUSEUM
(see p. 145 for more information)
On the first Thurs of every month, you can enjoy free admission all day to the SAM downtown. First Fri are free to seniors 62 and over, and second Fri are teen nights, with

free admission from 5 to 9 p.m. for ages 13 to 19.

SEATTLE ASIAN ART MUSEUM
(see p. 145 for more information)

Free admission all day on the first Thurs of every month; on the second Thurs of each month, admission is free from 5 to 9 p.m. as part of the Blitz Capitol Hill art walk. First Fri are free to seniors 62 and over, and first Sat are free for families, courtesy of Target.

SEATTLE CENTER
(see pp. 146, 151, 177, 184 for more information)

Seattle Center is the large, general area that includes the Space Needle, Experience Music Project, Pacific Science Center, Children's Museum, and numerous theaters. While all of the museums and rides do charge admission, the 74-acre campus is free to wander around and presents many free events throughout the year. It's a very interesting part of the city to people-watch and perhaps enjoy an outdoor lunch. The International Fountain is cool and popular, and for families, it's a place where a lot of children run through the dancing water. The Harrison Street Art Gallery in Center House presents free art exhibits open to the public, and free events held here include movie screenings, fitness classes, the Bite of Seattle Festival in July, the Concerts at the Mural summer series, and many other community events with no admission charge. Check the online calendar at www.seattlecenter.com/calendar.

SEATTLE PARKS
(see p. 219 for more information)

It almost goes without saying that the abundance of parks in the city makes for great,
free entertainment and recreation. Don't forget to check out our Parks and Recreation section for details on this surefire way to spend a terrific free day in Seattle.

SEATTLE PUBLIC LIBRARY
(see p. 307 for more information)

One of the most dramatic buildings in Seattle, the central library is one of only four major works in the United States designed by Rem Koolhaas. One-hour tours are first-come, first-served and limited to 20 participants. Library tours are Mon at 11 am, and architecture tours are Fri at noon. You can also download a podcast for your own self-guided tour. Once you're at the library, free readings and events are held all the time, for both adults and children, so be sure to check out the calendar. The Pacific Northwest Ballet also gives free preview performances on select Tues from noon to 1 p.m. www.pnb.org/Community/Audience/BalletPreviews.aspx.

SHAKESPEARE IN THE PARKS

The Seattle Shakespeare Company presents free Shakespeare in the Parks performances every July through Aug, at various parks around the city. It's a great opportunity to take a blanket and picnic lunch, as well as your family and pets, and enjoy the outdoor theater. (206) 733-8222, www.seattleshakespeare.org/woodeno.

UNIVERSITY OF WASHINGTON BOTANIC GARDENS & WASHINGTON PARK ARBORETUM

This international hub for plant science and ecosystem research contains more than 10,000 specimens. It's a hidden gem on the shores of Lake Washington; it seems that most locals don't even know about this incredible collection of plants that can't be found anywhere else. An information desk is at the Graham Visitors Center, and trails meander throughout the gardens. It's also a great place for bird-watching. Free guided tours are offered from Jan through Nov, or you can download free audio tours to your own MP3 player if you prefer to explore on your own (http://depts.washington.edu/uwbg/visit/tours.shtml#audiotour). The only charge is for the separate Japanese Garden at the south end of the arboretum. Free stories and activities for the kids are also held on Sat at 10 a.m. at the Elisabeth C. Miller Library. 3501 NE 41st St., (206) 543-8616, http://depts.washington.edu/uwbg.

VINEYARD AND BREWERY TOURS

Just outside of Seattle lie many wineries and breweries, some of which offer free tours. **Bainbridge Island Vineyards and Winery** gives a guided tour on Sun at 2 p.m. Head 15 miles northeast of the city to the Columbia Valley, where **Chateau Ste. Michelle** conducts tours with free wine sampling from 10:30 a.m. to 4:30 p.m. daily. In nearby Woodinville, **Redhook Brewery** gives a brewery walk several times a day, with beer samples and a souvenir tasting glass for just $1.

VOLUNTEER PARK CONSERVATORY

This spectacular Victorian-style greenhouse at the north end of Volunteer Park was modeled after London's Crystal Palace. View and smell the dazzling collection of bromeliads, palms, ferns, trees, cacti, and seasonal display plants. Many are very rare, and very old. The conservatory also takes in and displays confiscated or quarantined orchids, cycads, and other plants seized by U.S. Fish and Wildlife agents. Admission is free, although donations are appreciated. For the best free view in Seattle, climb the Volunteer Park water tower. 1402 E. Galer Street, (206) 322-4112, www.volunteerparkconservatory.org.

WING LUKE ASIAN MUSEUM
(see p. 152 for more information)

Admission is always free on the first Thurs of every month, at Seattle's Asian American history museum in the International District—which also makes for a great area to stroll around for free people-watching and entertainment.

WOODLAND PARK ZOO ROSE GARDEN
(see p. 190 for more information)

Free of charge since opening in 1924, the rose garden at the park boasts 280 varieties of roses in one of the best growing habitats in the world.

THE ARTS

Seattle's art community is a vibrant, eclectic, original, interactive, community-based scene; pretentious, inaccessible art is not for the residents here. For the most part it's a creative community available to everyone, and it invites exploration, which often takes it beyond the edges of imagination. This seems entirely fitting for a city that is known for innovation in so many fields.

But don't let that knowledge lead you to think that Seattleites don't retain a deep appreciation for the classical arts. The opera, symphony, and ballet companies are among the best in the country, and dozens of professional theaters enjoy strong audience support. Many have been tapped by top producers worldwide as launching pads for new productions. Seattle's cultural scene definitely mirrors its inhabitants—next to every traditionalist is the cutting-edge bad boy; for every serious piece of art, there's something whimsical that will make you laugh.

You will see the thriving, "for the people" vibe I'm talking about when you browse the listings in this chapter. From a plethora of taking-it-to-the-streets art walks that happen in almost every neighborhood around the city, to the many creative centers and support organizations that exist for the arts community here, it's hard to feel excluded from the Seattle art scene. Local artists even designed the city's manhole covers!

ART CENTERS AND COOPERATIVES

CENTER ON CONTEMPORARY ART
6413 Seaview Ave. NW (North)
(206) 728-1980
www.cocaseattle.org
Serving the Pacific Northwest as a catalyst and forum for contemporary art, the CoCA showcases all forms of contemporary art from the visual to poetry, performance art, and inventions. A dizzying array of rotating events, exhibits, and competitions comes through the center, and it's always fun to visit. CoCA is open Mon through Fri, with free entry and parking.

FREMONT ABBEY ARTS CENTER
4274 Fremont Ave. North (North)
(206) 414-8325
www.fremontabbey.org
The Fremont Abbey Arts Center is a non-profit organization that provides a creative community space for people of all ages and incomes to be supported in their artistic and social development, via interaction with new collaborative arts experiences in the 9,000-square-foot facility. The Abbey, as it's called, focuses on music, dance, visual, and literary and culinary arts in formats including multi-arts performances, group classes,

workshops, individual lessons, new exhibits, and artistic life celebrations. The Abbey is situated in a gorgeous 1914 brick building that was once a church, and still retains incredible stained-glass windows; hence, the name. Both students and the general public experience high-quality performances by artists from around the world.

SOIL COOPERATIVE ART GALLERY
112 3rd Ave. South (Central)
(206) 264-8061
http://soilart.org

SOIL began in 1995 when a small number of local artists felt a need to exhibit challenging work. They banded together and had a number of exhibitions together in a variety of locations. SOIL is a not-for-profit cooperative space in Pioneer Square that is supported and operated by local artists. SOIL exists as an alternative venue for artists to exhibit, develop, and advance their work, and is committed to exhibiting and celebrating art of diverse media and content. The cooperative has been in existence 14 years and has been consistent in showing a different exhibition each month that opens on every first Thurs.

i Want to see Seattle from an artist's viewpoint? The Artist's Guide to Seattle features insightful interviews with sixteen Seattle artists about their favorite local destinations. www.visit seattle.org.

ART MUSEUMS

Please see the Attractions chapter for details on Seattle art museums.

ART WALKS AND BAZAARS

BALLARD ARTWALK
Ballard Neighborhood (North)
(206) 784-9705
www.ballardchamber.com

Organized by the Ballard Chamber of Commerce, this is your chance to see the brightest talent in the area as Ballard galleries and businesses stay open late on the second Sat of each month from around 6 to 9 p.m. to showcase artists. Start at the south end of Ballard Avenue and work your way up the street to Market. Many of the participating venues have appetizers and drinks. Download the most recent ArtWalk Map at the Web site.

BELLTOWN ART WALK & MORE
Belltown Neighborhood (Central)
http://belltownartwalk.com

Belltown is the proud home to many unique galleries and non-gallery art venues. Held the third Thurs of each month, BAWM (pronounced "bomb," as in "it's the bomb") features art, food, music, and entertainment. Numerous buskers also roam the neighborhood with great performances. You can find a map of participating venues at the BAWM Web site; many of the sights can be found along Bell Street, between 5th and Elliott.

BLITZ ART WALK
Capitol Hill Neighborhood (Central)
(206) 817-2711
www.blitzcapitolhill.com

Not in Seattle for a First Thursday? Don't get too bummed out, because the Capitol Hill neighborhood has organized its own art walk, held on the second Thurs of each month from 5 to 8 p.m. It showcases the neighborhood's best visual, musical, literary, and performing arts in an open house format. With 40–50 participating venues each month, Blitz puts on display the breadth of creativity happening on Capitol Hill. Grab a map from any of the participating venues during the week leading up to the art walk, or print one from the Web site.

FIRST THURSDAY ART WALK
Pioneer Square Neighborhood (Central)
(206) 667-0687
www.firstthursdayseattle.com
The first Thurs of every month is a terrific time to be in Seattle—particularly if you love art and/or you don't want to spend a lot of money. The Pioneer Square Art Walk was the first one in the country and has since been copied by many cities. From noon to 8 p.m. you can stroll artists' booths and galleries throughout Pioneer Square for free. Many Seattle museums get in on the First Thursday wagon with free admission.

FREMONT FIRST FRIDAY ART WALK
Fremont Neighborhood (North)
http://fremontfirstfriday.com
On the first Fri of each month from 6 to 9 p.m., Fremont's galleries, shops and restaurants are crowded with people looking for something new, and finding just that. The many vendors have fresh, exciting art representing an eclectic mix of styles from artists both local and worldwide. You'll see not just paintings, photography, and other media, but also art cars, graffiti and mural art, live music, and more. The many unique public art installations in Fremont make walking between shops fun and exciting from "you can't miss them pieces" such as the **Lenin statue, the Fremont Troll,** and the **Rocket,** to the many often-overlooked trinkets embedded in the sidewalks.

GEORGETOWN SECOND SATURDAY ART ATTACK
Georgetown Neighborhood (South)
www.georgetownartattack.com
This South Seattle neighborhood is home to a funky art walk on the second Sat of each month, which also includes an annual film festival as part of the May event. The neighborhood is invaded by hordes of art and film aficionados for a festive evening of avant-garde entertainment at more than 30 locations in the area. The Georgetown Art Attack is intended to increase public awareness of the historic industrial arts corridor and generate sentiment toward preserving this enchanting civic asset. Each month the creative enterprises in Georgetown present diverse visual and performing arts, and many resident artists open their studios to the general public in an evening that the Web site calls "art, music, and mayhem."

i Check out the City of Seattle Public Art Walking Tours, a downloadable series of maps that explore the artistic wonders of downtown Seattle and its neighborhoods. The maps include public art from city, county, and state collections as well as corporate artworks, community gardens, significant architecture, and other cultural surprises. www.seattle.gov/arts/publicart/walking_tours.asp.

WEST SEATTLE ART WALK
West Seattle Neighborhood (South)
www.westseattleartwalk.blogspot.com
The West Seattle art walk is a monthly art event, held on the second Thurs of each month from 6 to 9 p.m. year-round. The art walk is hosted by more than 60 local West Seattle merchants and features a wide range of art to showcase

the vibrant artist community found here. From Alki Beach to the Fauntleroy District and Delridge, you can download a complete walking map at the Web site.

CLASSES AND STUDIOS

DANACA DESIGN METAL CRAFTING CENTER & GALLERY
5619 University Way NE (North)
(206) 524-0916
www.danacadesign.com

This is the gallery and studio of Dana Cassara, who began practicing the art of silversmithing at North Seattle Community College in 1992. The center is a jewelry and small-scale metalworking studio located in the University District of Seattle, offering classes for individuals in the art of decorative metalworking and jewelry design. The studio is a comfortable, well-lit, and cheerful work space fully equipped for small-scale classes (limited to 10 participants). There is also a small storefront gallery featuring local artists, both professional and amateur, as well as a limited selection of tools.

EDGE OF GLASS GALLERY AND HOTSHOP
513 N. 36th St., Suite H (North)
(206) 632-7807
www.edgeofglass.com

Resident artist James M. Curtis III is showcased at this gallery and studio for blown-glass art in Fremont, along with several other local glass artists. The gallery shop offers one-of-a-kind functional glass art in platters, vessels, lighting, and mixed media for purchase. Hot glass sculpting demonstrations and private classes are offered continually, pushing the bounds of creativity to always find something new and exciting in glass art. Open Fri through Mon.

POTTERY NORTHWEST
226 1st Ave. North (Central)
(206) 285-4421
www.potterynorthwest.org

The Pottery Northwest studio is located in the Seattle Center and is a professional clay workshop for community use. Beginners and advanced classes are offered to the public, along with major workshops by nationally recognized artists. An exhibition and sales gallery shows finished pieces for sale by studio potters.

SEATTLE GLASSBLOWING STUDIO
2227 5th Ave. (Central)
(206) 448-2181
www.seattleglassblowing.com

Located in Belltown under the monorail, this working studio provides professional glassblowing demonstrations seven days a week. There are also classes in glassblowing and bead making, and artists can rent a hot shop as well. Be sure to check out the hand-blown art glass gallery, where some of the most exquisite pieces of work can be admired and purchased.

DANCE

PACIFIC NORTHWEST BALLET
301 Mercer St. (Central)
(206) 441-2424
www.pnb.org

The Pacific Northwest Ballet is one of the largest and most highly regarded ballet companies in the United States. Founded in 1972, the company of nearly 50 dancers presents more than 100 performances each year of full-length and mixed repertory ballets at Marion Oliver McCaw Hall, as well as on tour. The annual *Nutcracker* performance has become a winter holiday tradition in Seattle.

PYROSUTRA

(206) 356-4859

www.pyrosutra.com

Pyrosutra calls itself "incendiary dance," and it certainly is. This is a fire dance collective that combines choreographed belly dance, breakdance, and stilt walking with a wide range of professional fire performance techniques and innovative tools. The result is an incredible, exciting performance unlike anything you've ever seen. Pyrosutra performs weekly at the Chapel Bar, located at 1600 Melrose Ave. in Capitol Hill. The troupe also performs at other venues and events around the city; check the Web site for performance information.

SPECTRUM DANCE THEATER

800 Lake Washington Blvd. (Central)

(206) 325-4161

www.spectrumdance.org

Since its inception in 1982, Spectrum has attracted world-class dancers and produced some of the most avant-garde works in contemporary dance. Spectrum wants to move the dance arts from the marginal, ancillary, and periphery of the community and into the center. In addition to a great performance season each year, Spectrum also operates a dance school that is highly acclaimed.

VELOCITY DANCE CENTER

1621 12th Ave. (Central)

(206) 325-8773

http://velocitydancecenter.org

This nonprofit contemporary performing arts center is located in Capitol Hill, providing opportunities and space for education, dance creation, performance, and national/international exchange. Velocity has grown along with the active Seattle dance community, serving about 3,000 dance students and 2,000 dance enthusiasts each year. After years in the Odd Fellows building, Velocity has just moved to this new location and looks forward to an exciting future of fresh performances.

Seattle Center Teen Tix

Teen Tix is a great arts-access program that allows teenagers to purchase special $5 rush tickets to dozens of art performances in dance, theater, music, film, and visual art. Anyone age 13–18 can sign up for free, whether they reside in Seattle or not. Teen Tix are sold on the day of the show on a first-come, first-served basis starting when the box office opens. On Sunday, members can purchase a companion ticket for $5 as well, that anyone of any age can use. All other days, companions must purchase their own full-price tickets. There are also contests and other fun activities. Call (206) 233-3959 or visit www .seattlecenter.com/teentix.

FILM

See the "Cinemas" section in the Nightlife chapter for listings on movie theaters in Seattle.

911 SEATTLE MEDIA ARTS CENTER

909 NE 43rd St., Suite 206 (North)

(206) 682-6552

www.911media.org

Seattle on Film

Movies and television shows set in the Seattle area:

10 Things I Hate About You (Movie, 1999)
A Guy Thing (Movie, 2003)
Agent Cody Banks (Movie, 2003)
An Officer and a Gentleman (Movie, 1982)
Battle in Seattle (Movie, 2007)
Black Widow (Movie, 1987)
Dark Angel (TV, 2000–2002)
Dead Like Me (TV, 2003–2004)
Disclosure (Movie, 1994)
Double Jeopardy (Movie, 1999)
Fear (Movie, 1996)
Firewall (Movie, 2006)
Frasier (TV, 1993–2004)
Get Carter (Movie, 2000)
Grey's Anatomy (TV, 2004–)
Harry and the Hendersons (Movie, 1987)
iCarly (TV, 2007–)
It Happened at the World's Fair (Movie, 1963)
Kyle XY (TV, 2006–)

Life or Something Like It (Movie, 2002)
Love Happens (Movie, 2009)
Mad Love (Movie, 1995)
McQ (Movie, 1974)
Paycheck (Movie, 2003)
Reaper (TV, 2007–)
Rose Red (TV miniseries, 2002)
Saving Silverman (Movie, 2001)
Say Anything (Movie, 1989)
Shoot to Kill (Movie, 1988)
Singles (Movie, 1992)
Sleepless in Seattle (Movie, 1993)
Stakeout (Movie, 1987)
The Fabulous Baker Boys (Movie, 1989)
The Hand that Rocks the Cradle (Movie, 1992)
The Last Mimzy (Movie, 2007)
The Parallax View (Movie, 1974)
The Ring (Movie, 2002)
War Games (Movie, 1983)

This University District media arts center focuses primarily on film, video, and multimedia, supporting independent voices in an environment that fosters diversity, innovation, and artistic excellence. 911 offers a wide range of classes and resources, a gallery of multimedia exhibits open to the public, and an ongoing calendar of events and programs from across the spectrum of media arts. The center also produces *On Screen Magazine*, created for a community of independent filmmakers and digital media artists.

NORTHWEST FILM FORUM
1515 12th Ave. (Central)
(206) 829-7863
www.nwfilmforum.org
Northwest Film Forum (NWFF) is Seattle's premier film arts organization, screening more than 200 independently made and classic films annually, offering a year-round schedule of filmmaking classes for all ages, and supporting filmmakers at all stages of their careers. Founded in 1995 by filmmakers Jamie Hook and Deborah Girdwood, NWFF operates the region's first and only nonprofit center for the film arts. NWFF programs a

true cinematheque, embracing film production as well as film exhibition in its two cinemas, showcasing the best in American and international cinema, as well as unique live multimedia performances.

GALLERIES

ARTXCHANGE GALLERY
512 First Ave. South (Central)
(206) 839-0377
www.artxchange.org

Gallery director Cora Edmonds's international background, combined with her love of art, travel, and photography, influenced her to establish ArtXchange in 1995 as a way to raise cultural awareness and promote global understanding through art. ArtXchange participates in First Thursdays at Pioneer Square and also hosts unique events such as art auctions, book signings, and tea tastings. Edmonds has a very interesting story; it was a chance encounter with a little boy in a remote village in Nepal that led her to open ArtXchange, wanting to really cross cultures through art.

GREG KUCERA GALLERY
212 3rd Ave. South (Central)
(206) 624-0770
http://gregkucera.com

In visiting this gallery today, you would hardly know the modest beginnings Kucera started this gallery with, given that he's a high roller in the Seattle art world now. Opening in a dilapidated storefront in 1983, the new gallery received a three-line paragraph at the end of a *Seattle Times* arts column as its only press. It was when Kucera began working with Roger Shimomura, an established and widely acclaimed artist, that the gallery began making a name for itself. Since that time the Greg Kucera Gallery has shown

exhibitions rotating between emerging artists and internationally known artists of all genres, including filmmaker John Waters. Don't miss the outdoor sculpture loft.

HENRY ART GALLERY
15th Avenue NE and NE 41st Street (North)
(206) 543-2280
www.henryart.org

Part of the University of Washington, the Henry serves as a catalyst for the creation of new work that challenges and inspires, and aims to deliver a direct experience of the art of our time. The exhibits reflect a record of modern artistic inquiry from the advent of photography in the mid-19th century to the multidisciplinary art of today. But the heart of the Henry is its innovative programming, lecture series, and educational opportunities, as well as community groups and collaborations. The gallery is closed Mon, Tues, and Wed. Admission is always free for any students from kindergarten through university.

HOWARD HOUSE
604 2nd Ave. (Central)
(206) 256-6399
www.howardhouse.net

Howard House is a contemporary fine art gallery with an emphasis on cultivating emerging artists, and a unique reputation for identifying and showing artists at the tipping point of their career. This pioneering spirit is evident by awards won and important exhibitions in which Howard House artists have been included.

PLATFORM GALLERY
114 3rd Ave. South (Central)
(206) 323-2808
www.platformgallery.com

The *Seattle Post–Intelligencer* noted that Platform Gallery "is giving Seattle a much-needed infusion of rigor." Since 2004 Platform Gallery has exhibited challenging contemporary art including sculpture, painting, works on paper, photography, and installations by artists from around the world. The exhibition space is located on the East Edge of historic Pioneer Square in the Tashiro-Kaplan arts complex.

PUNCH GALLERY
119 Prefontaine Place South (Central)
(206) 621-1945
www.punchgallery.org

PUNCH was founded in Mar 2006 by a group of artists eager to participate in the dynamic cultural exchange resulting from the emergence of other artist-run galleries in Seattle. PUNCH seeks to exhibit work that is honest, thoughtful, vocal, fearless, and fresh—it has some of the most looked-forward-to openings of any gallery in Seattle. The gallery maintains excitement in its exhibition schedule with a revolving roster of contributing member artists, guest artists, and curated group shows. PUNCH Gallery is located in the Pioneer Square area of downtown Seattle in the Tashiro-Kaplan building.

ROQ LA RUE GALLERY
2316 2nd Ave. (Central)
(206) 374-8977
www.roqlarue.com

This Belltown gallery delights in pushing the boundaries, with its unconventional openings of pop surrealism and contemporary underground art that feel more like rock shows. Roq La Rue delights in being provocative, exhibiting established artists in the genre as well as fostering emerging artists who offer fantastical imagery and visually dynamic narratives.

i There are hundreds of galleries in Seattle, and it's impossible to cover them all, especially when individual interests are so subjective. Get a handle on the gallery scene with resources such as the Art Guide Northwest (www.artguidenw.com). This comprehensive online guide to the Pacific Northwest art scene features links to hundreds of galleries, museums, antiques, artists, and cultural events, along with contact information for all listings. You can also visit Seattle Art Blog (www.seattleartblog.com) for timely updates to gallery shows and art events in the Seattle and Puget Sound areas.

LITERARY ARTS

RICHARD HUGO HOUSE
1634 11th Ave. (Central)
(206) 322-7030
www.hugohouse.org

Richard Hugo House is a home for writers and readers, a center for the literary arts that supports writers of all ages and backgrounds and promotes the creation of new writing. Hugo House nurtures writers and readers and brings innovative writing classes to people from every background. A new initiative was started in 2006, the Hugo Literary Series featuring brave new writing commissioned by Hugo House from some of the most exciting local and national writers and musicians working today.

SEATTLE ARTS & LECTURES
105 S. Main St., Suite 201 (Central)
(206) 621-2230
www.lectures.org

In addition to presenting today's foremost fiction and nonfiction writers, Seattle Arts

& Lectures' events and courses illuminate arts, culture, and a world of ideas. Programs include a Literary Arts Series, American Voices Series, Poetry Series, and Writers in the Schools. Visiting lecturers have included John Updike, Isabel Allende, Michael Dorris, and Louise Erdrich. Events are held at Benaroya Hall, with courses at the University of Washington and throughout various public schools in Puget Sound.

MUSIC

Seattle has a thriving music scene, from contemporary popular music to classical. The listings in this chapter are classical and arts-oriented; for rock and popular concerts and venues, see the Live Music section of the Nightlife chapter.

SEATTLE OPERA
McCaw Hall, 321 Mercer St. (Central)
(206) 389-7676
www.seattleopera.org
Founded in 1963, Seattle Opera is a leading American opera company. The company presents the classics of the European repertoire as well as new works of American opera, performing five operas per year. For a regional opera company, it is intrepid about tackling weighty and nontraditional works, and is noted for its innovative staging of the classics. Some of the top singers in the world have performed with the Seattle Opera, and its new Wagner productions are always eagerly anticipated. Most shows sell out early.

SEATTLE SYMPHONY
Benaroya Hall, 200 University St.
  (Central)
(866) 833-4747
www.seattlesymphony.org

The Seattle Symphony has been an important part of Pacific Northwest culture since its inception in 1903. From its first performance on December 29, 1903, Seattle Symphony has held a unique place in the world of symphonic music. It is internationally recognized for its adventurous programming of contemporary works, its devotion to the classics, and its extensive recording history. Seattle Symphony has made more than 125 recordings, garnered 12 Grammy nominations and received two Emmy awards. The orchestra is also known for its extensive education programming, which annually serves 100,000 people of all ages.

PERFORMING ARTS—MIXED REPERTORY

ON THE BOARDS—BEHNKE CENTER FOR CONTEMPORARY PERFORMANCE
100 W. Roy St. (Central)
(206) 217-9888
www.ontheboards.org
This nonprofit contemporary performing arts organization located in the Queen Anne neighborhood introduces Northwest audiences to international innovators in contemporary dance, theater, and music, while developing and presenting new work by promising performing artists in the region. Showcasing artists and companies who are defining the future of dance, theater, music, and new media, OtB presents 70–80 performance nights each season as well as a host of outreach and educational programs. OtB features groundbreaking new work that would otherwise not be seen in Seattle. Performances are held in the 300-seat Merrill Wright Mainstage Theater and the intimate 84-seat Studio Theater.

UW WORLD SERIES

Meany Hall, 4001 University Way NE
  (North)
(206) 543-4880
www.uwworldseries.org

The World Music Series at the University of Washington brings musical, dance, and theater talent from all over the world, including theater artists, dance troupes, world music, pianists, and chamber music ensembles. Featured performers have included the very popular Emerson String Quartet, as well as Gamelan Çudamani, the Vienna Piano Trio, Compañía Nacional de Danza of Mexico, the Paul Taylor Dance Company, and Trio con Brio Copenhagen. Performances are held at Meany Hall on the UW campus.

THEATER

5TH AVENUE THEATRE

1308 5th Ave. (Central)
(206) 625-1900
www.5thavenue.org

Since 1926 the magnificent 5th Avenue Theatre has captivated audiences with music, drama, and laughter. In the early days, people eagerly lined up for first-class vaudeville shows, featuring top entertainers. The theater later transformed itself into a popular movie palace. The 5th fell on hard times in the late '70s but fortunately was saved from the wrecking ball. Following a spectacular $2.6 million renovation, the theater reopened in 1980, more beautiful than ever. Today it proudly produces top-quality musical revivals, premieres of bound-for-Broadway shows, and touring Broadway musicals. A special feature is that the 5th Avenue Theatre is perhaps the most magnificent of all Seattle theaters, with an elaborate interior inspired by Imperial China's Forbidden City. The craftsmanship is breathtaking, with intricately carved

ceilings and a chandelier that dangles from the mouth of a giant dragon. Free guided tours are given each Mon at noon (advance registration online is recommended).

ACT—A CONTEMPORARY THEATRE

700 Union St. (Central)
(206) 292-7676
www.acttheatre.org

ACT is housed in a wonderful space in a converted old building downtown and produces adventurous and avant-garde contemporary works. Its mission is to dare, excite, and enrich audiences, and it made history as the first theater in Seattle dedicated to producing contemporary plays. It believes in "theater of the moment" and seeks to create a conversation among those who experience it.

ARTSWEST PLAYHOUSE AND GALLERY

4711 California Ave. SW (South)
(206) 938-0339
www.artswest.org

ArtsWest is a cool, unique combination of a theater and art gallery. Its mission is to produce artistic events so compelling that they require conversation, improve the imagination, and promote cultural vibrancy as a core value for the communities of West Seattle. The auditorium is a three-quarter thrust with excellent stage views, which has presented plays by Andrew Lloyd Webber and performances such as *The Vertical Hour* and *A Tuna Christmas*. In addition to the theater, ArtsWest's Seattle Playwrights Studio has established a studio space for local playwrights to develop works in progress. The gallery showcases stimulating visual art to go alongside the compelling performances, and has an artists' association.

BOOK-IT REPERTORY THEATRE
305 Harrison St. (Central)
(206) 216-0833
www.book-it.org

Celebrating twenty years of novel theater in 2010, Book-It is a nonprofit theater that transforms great works of literature into theater, with a mission of inspiring its audience to read and to nourish literacy and artistic vitality in the community. In King County, where illiteracy is an obstacle for one-third of residents, Book-It recognizes the need to go beyond mere entertainment in which the audience does not participate. The theater group creates adaptations of classic and contemporary literature for the stage, where the characters from the adapted works narrate the text. Some of the performances have included *Emma, The Cider House Rules, Peter Pan,* and *A Tale of Two Cities.* Book-It is located in the Center House Theatre at Seattle Center.

i Seattle Performs (www.seattle performs.com) is the home of Seattle theater, plays, dance, and performance, featuring Seattle theater listings including the greater Puget Sound region, theater reviews written by users, and links to play reviews by professional stage critics. Up-to-date stage performance listings include cast lists, theater venue information (including directions and maps), detailed and accurate schedule information, and show openings and closings.

INTIMAN THEATRE
201 Mercer St. (Central)
(206) 269-1900
www.intiman.org

The Intiman Theatre is one of Seattle's most popular theaters, producing prestigious and critically acclaimed shows. Intiman produces classics and new plays—exceptional theater created by Seattle artists and those from across the country, recognized masters of their craft, and exciting new voices. These great stories encourage civic dialogue and personal reflections about issues we face as a community, in our country, and on the planet. The Intiman philosophy is that there is a connection between what we choose as entertainment and the questions we ask about what it means to be human; that connection is the foundation of every play in its season. Intiman fosters conversation and debate among its audiences, students and people with limited access to the arts. Previous performances have included *Paradise Lost, Ruined,* and *Three Sisters;* it also produces Langston Hughes's *Black Nativity* every year.

PARAMOUNT THEATRE
911 Pine St. (Central)
(206) 467-5510
www.stgpresents.org/paramount

For 77 years, Washington residents and visitors have been entertained at Seattle's magnificent Paramount Theatre. Millions have delighted in the theater's architectural majesty, viewed countless films, and enjoyed thousands of performers from all corners of the globe. During the Roaring Twenties, the Paramount was Seattle's most opulent movie house and vaudeville stage. The lavish Beaux Arts interior included a four-tiered lobby, French baroque plaster moldings, gold-leaf-encrusted wall medallions, rich paint colors, beaded chandeliers, and lacy ironwork. Although it had sadly become quite shabby by the 1980s, the Paramount enjoyed a major multimillion-dollar renovation in the mid '90s and has been showing a variety of performances ever since, from plays and musicals to movies, stand-up comedic acts, and live radio recordings.

SEATTLE REPERTORY THEATRE
155 Mercer St. (Central)
(206) 443-2210
www.seattlerep.org

One of the largest and most renowned regional theaters in the country, SRT produces a mix of classic comedies, Broadway hits, and cutting-edge new dramas. Some of the actors who have graced the stages here include Meryl Streep, Laurence Fishburne, Lily Tomlin, Samuel L. Jackson, Richard Chamberlain, Jessica Tandy, Richard Gere, and Christopher Walken. There are three separate theaters at the SRT, a lobby cafe, and the Rep Bar for a beer, cocktail, or glass of wine. Many shows offer preview dish sessions and postplay discussions, all of which are included with tickets. Performances are generally Wed through Sun, and parking is available nearby.

KIDSTUFF

Seattle is a great place for a family vacation. The entire Pacific Northwest serves as your backyard, offering an endless range of options for outdoor fun such as hiking, kayaking, fishing, or simply exploring. It's incredibly easy to scale any outdoor recreational activity for children of all ages, and people of any physical or ability level.

So many of the general attractions for adults in Seattle are also extremely interesting and enjoyable to children as well. Following are a few of the attractions mentioned in the other sections of this book (because they are not specifically targeted to kids and families) that are must-see sights for your family vacation.

PIKE PLACE MARKET

Don't miss bringing your kids to what is perhaps the most famous market in the world. The fish-throwing, vendor-hawking, busker-entertaining, food explosion of Pike Place will delight all ages, from months-old infants to hard-to-impress teenagers. Be sure to go by the Gum Wall outside the Market Theatre at 1428 Post Alley. Over the years, the wads of chewed gum that have been deposited here have taken on a life of their own, and today it's become a giant "gum art" mural that your children will likely be thrilled to add to.

SPACE NEEDLE

It almost goes without saying that children will love the shot up the glass-walled elevator to the top of Seattle's icon, and peering down at the city through high-powered telescopes once they're on the observation deck. The large gift shop at the base of the Needle is a great place to get souvenirs, and the location in the midst of thriving Seattle Center provides plenty of other fun and attractions.

SEATTLE AQUARIUM

Kids and adults will equally enjoy the excellent aquarium in Seattle. There are lots of great animals and exhibits, plus educational and interesting shows from diving to feeding. The touch pool is especially tantalizing to youngsters, where they can stick their hands in the water and actually feel starfish, rays, and other ocean life.

PACIFIC SCIENCE CENTER

There's really something to do here for kids of varying ages, making it a great family stop if you have children who span a wide age range. Older kids and teenagers should find plenty to keep them intrigued in the museum, while younger children will delight in the planetarium and butterfly house. The laser show and IMAX theater will please everyone—including Mom and Dad.

RIDE THE DUCKS

Of all the tours highlighted and described in the Attractions chapter, the one that children under the age of about 12 are likely to enjoy the most is the Duck ride. This tour is conducted by funny guides, there's always lots of laughter and singing, and the kids will love when the previously rolling vehicle splashes into the water for the floating portion of the tour.

Unlike most of the other sections of this book on attractions, restaurants, and arts that focus specifically on the city of Seattle, the Kidstuff section features attractions both in Seattle and nearby, within a half-hour drive. There are many fun things for children and families to do in the greater Seattle/ Puget Sound area, and we don't want you to miss any of them.

Price Code

Although admission prices change, the following price code will act as your guide to the cost per person. Please check the Web sites for specific details.

$.........................	$1 to $5
$$	$6 to $10
$$$	$11 to $15
$$$$	$16 and more

AMUSEMENT AND WATER PARKS

FUN FOREST
 AMUSEMENT PARK $–$$$$
305 Harrison St. (Central)
(206) 728-1586
www.funforest.com

Located in the Seattle Center campus, this old-fashioned, carnival-style amusement park lies at the crossroads of the Space Needle, monorail, and Experience Music Project. The 19 rides include a carousel and roller coaster, and the entertainment pavilion offers a multitude of prize games, laser tag, mini-golf, climbing wall, and a full video arcade. There's a "kiddie ride" area for tots, as well as a huge inflatable castle with obstacle course and an inflatable super slide. All rides and games are ticket-based, meaning that you can spend a little money, or a lot. If it's hot, head on over to the International Fountain afterward, a popular place for kids to dart through the dancing waters. Fun Forest is open daily year-round.

FUNTASIA FAMILY FUN PARK $$$$
7217 220th St. SW (Edmonds)
(425) 775-2174
www.familyfunpark.com/home.html

Funtasia is a seven-acre indoor/outdoor family fun park, located in Edmonds about a half-hour drive north of Seattle. Indoors more than 25,000 square feet of fun offer an adventure-themed miniature golf course, laser tag, bumper cars, state-of-the-art video games, and a restaurant, Cafe Funtasia. Outside are gas-powered go-karts, bumper boats with water cannons, a pirate-themed miniature golf course, and the largest nine-station batting cage in Washington state. There is also a 4,000 square-foot play land for the youngest children. The park is open daily, with extended hours on Fri and Sat nights.

WILD WAVES WATER PARK AND
 ENCHANTED VILLAGE $$$$
36201 Enchanted Pkwy. South (Federal
 Way)
(253) 925-8000
www.wildwaves.com

This 70-acre combination theme park and water park is located approximately a half-hour south of Seattle. Enchanted Village theme park features 32 amusement rides including a double-corkscrew, single-inversion roller coaster and a 1906 hand-carved carousel. TimberHawk, the biggest roller coaster in the state, is also here. Wild Waves is the largest water park in the Northwest, with nine water slides, a 24,000-square-foot wave pool, two speed slides, a raging river ride, and a four-story, interactive water tree house. The main attraction in the water park is Zooma Falls, a mammoth water adventure towering five stories tall with a crossover curve out of the shoot, four wicked turns, and five jaw-dropping acceleration zones. Special events are also held here, from outdoor classroom days to holiday special themes, such as Frightfest in Oct. The park is open every day from mid-June through Aug, and select weekends and special event days in the off-season; be sure to check the calendar on the Web site.

ARCADES

FUN FOREST AMUSEMENT PARK

See section above; a large video arcade can be found at this Seattle Center amusement park.

GAMEWORKS $$$–$$$$
1511 7th Ave. (Central)
(206) 521-0952
www.gameworks.com

The downtown Seattle location was the first site of this entertainment company cofounded by Steven Spielberg. Operated by SEGA, GameWorks offers an overwhelming arcade of interactive play designed to challenge the skills. Simulators and non-video games like pool and darts are also available. A restaurant serves basic fare such as salads, burgers, pizza, sandwiches, and hot dogs, making GameWorks a complete destination for kids.

SEATTLE WATERFRONT
ARCADE $$–$$$$
1301 Alaskan Way (Central)
(206) 903-1081
www.seattlewaterfrontarcade.com

The location at Pier 57 can't be beat, and the philosophy here is that nobody is too old to be a kid. This arcade has a wide variety of games and stays current with the latest technology and video game entertainment. Classics like air hockey, basket shooting, crane machines, Skee-Ball, and photo booths are found here—there's even a fortune-telling machine! All games are played by purchasing tickets, so the total expenditure can vary widely.

HISTORIC SITES AND LANDMARKS

FREMONT TROLL
Troll Avenue at N. 36th Street, under the
Aurora Bridge (North)
www.arfarfarf.com/troll

This is one of Seattle's more bizarre attractions, located appropriately enough in the wonderfully wacky neighborhood of Fremont. It's a whimsical, huge sculpture of a troll crushing a real Volkswagen Beetle; the troll lives, as all trolls do, under the bridge. He was created in 1990 by four local artists, as a project for the Fremont Arts Council, and is made of steel and wire covered with concrete. It's fine to crawl and climb all over the troll, and you'll also see plenty of chalk and paint graffiti. The sculpture makes one of the more interesting photo backdrops you're likely to find. FYI: Very small children may find the troll a little scary. Free.

SEATTLE ARCHITECTURE FOUNDATION $$$
1333 5th Ave., Third Level (Central)
(206) 667-9184
www.seattlearchitecture.org/youth_family_tours.html

For a great way to get up close and personal with Seattle landmarks, take advantage of the family tour Eye Spy Seattle, offered by the Seattle Architecture Foundation. Discover a kid's-eye view of architecture and design downtown. Tour stops include the 5th Avenue Theatre, Seattle Central Library, and the Rainier Tower. Tours are two hours long and generally begin at 10 a.m. on Sat. This activity-driven tour and interactive experience is best suited for children ages 5 to 10, and siblings are welcome. Strollers are not recommended on this tour given the amount of stairs. Check the Web site for upcoming tour dates.

SEATTLE MONORAIL $
370 Thomas St. (Central)
(206) 905-2620
www.seattlemonorail.com

This is a quick but fun ride that kids will enjoy. The monorail was built for the 1962 World's Fair and provides a great view of the city along its elevated platform. Trains depart every ten minutes, making the 1-mile, two-minute trip between the stations at Seattle Center and Westlake Center Mall, at 5th and Pine Street.

TILLICUM VILLAGE $$$$
Blake Island (Transport from Pier 55, Seattle Waterfront)
(888) 623-1445
www.tillicumvillage.com

This Native American village and cultural center is a fun and interesting destination for the whole family. Tillicum is located on Blake Island, believed to be the birthplace of Chief Sealth, 8 miles from the downtown Seattle waterfront. Your visit begins with the 45-minute narrated cruise to the island, where you are greeted with an appetizer of steamed clams, a local delicacy. Inside the traditional Indian longhouse at Tillicum Village, view whole salmon cooked over an alderwood fire, in the traditional Northwest Native American style. The salmon is served along with rice, stew, Tillicum bread, salads, and dessert. A performance of Dance on the Wind showcases coastal tribal dancing, and a gift gallery features works by local artisans. Blake Island offers plenty of forested trails and pristine beaches, and it's easy to spend an entire day here. You can purchase a four-hour full ticket that includes the cruise, meal, and show, or you can pay a la carte as you go. You can even camp on Blake Island overnight. Tillicum Village is open from Mar through Oct.

KID-FRIENDLY EATS

ALL PURPOSE PIZZA $$
2901 S. Jackson St. (Central)
(206) 324-8646
www.allpurposepizza.com

Not only do most kids love pizza, but they really love All Purpose because of the play kitchen in the restaurant. While parents wait for the pizza, their kids can play with pizza dough, rolling pins, and other toys in full view of the adults.

CHINOOK'S $$-$$$$
1900 W. Nickerson St. (Central)
(206) 283-4665
www.anthonys.com/restaurants/info/chinooks.html

Located on Salmon Bay in Fishermen's Terminal, Chinook's is a casual seafood restaurant with an interesting location that hundreds of fishing vessels have called home since the early 1900s. It is a fun family dining establishment on the water, with complimentary vehicle and boat parking. The outside deck is a great place to eat during nice weather and provides even more sightseeing for the kids as the boats go by.

DICK'S DRIVE-IN $-$$
500 Queen Anne Ave. North (Central)
(206) 285-5155
www.ddir.com
This place is heaps of old-timey fun, as well as a cheap place to bring a big family. Dick's is a drive-in burger joint straight out of *American Graffiti*, although walk-up windows and sit-down booths are also available. The hamburgers are made with quality, never-frozen beef and the milkshakes are to die for—never machine-made, but hand dipped and whipped. The fries are sliced daily from whole potatoes and fried in 100 percent vegetable oil. It's not exactly health food, but it's fast food made with good ingredients by hand—and I dare you to find a burger like this in any restaurant for less than $3. Dick's has been around since 1954 and has four other locations in addition to the Queen Anne restaurant.

EATS MARKET CAFÉ $$-$$$
2600 SW Barton St. (South)
(206) 933-1200
http://eatsmarket.com
Voted Best Family-Friendly Dining on Citysearch for several years, Eats is run by the husband-and-wife duo of Evan Handler and Toby Matasar, both culinary school grads who like to say they were born as foodies. The couple opened Eats to provide a

neighborhood bakery and cafe that offers homemade, seasonal comfort foods in a casual, relaxing environment. Desserts are fabulous and varied, from the delectable baked goods you may expect, to kid-pleasing root beer floats and ice cream sandwiches.

5 SPOT $$-$$$
1502 Queen Anne Ave. North (Central)
(206) 285-SPOT
www.chowfoods.com/five
This retro diner-style restaurant in the historic Queen Anne neighborhood services flavorful home cooking with an inspired presentation; it's far more than a basic cafe, and the adults in the group will like it much more than a lot of family dining establishments. The renovated 1912 building is decorated with fun kitsch from all over the United States. The menu also comes from around the country, from the Texas Longhorn burger to Louisiana Cajun dishes to New England fish-and-chips.

GAMEWORKS (SEE P. 179)

See the Arcade section above—GameWorks serves food, and the combination of restaurant and entertainment makes it a contender for family dining.

LUNA PARK CAFE $$
2918 SW Avalon Way (South)
(206) 935-7250
www.lunaparkcafe.com
The 1950s jukebox decor and menu lend nostalgia to this West Seattle diner. Luna Park was once the Coney Island of the west, built on pilings over the water and home to an amusement park in the early 20th century. A great collection of bygone memorabilia gives diners plenty to look at, and the outdoor patio is nice. Small children

will be kept occupied by the vintage Batmobile ride, clown vending machine, and temporary tattoos. Breakfast is served all day, and lunch and dinner menus are heavy on down-home comfort food. All the locals know about Luna's thick, rich malts. Portions are very large, and there is a decent selection of healthy and vegetarian options. This is a popular breakfast spot, and weekend waits can get long.

MONTLAKE ALE HOUSE $$
2307 24th Ave. East (Central)
(206) 726-5968
www.montlakealehouse.net

This family-friendly spot gets that delicate balance between family restaurant and adult-satisfying pub just right. Children are welcomed, service is upbeat, and the sunken, carpeted play pit is a hit with the young customers. Stocked with toys and books, the play area is encircled by a wide railing, so parents can drink, eat, and watch their kids. The only thing to be aware of is that parking is not always easy on the residential zoned streets.

THEO CHOCOLATE FACTORY $$
3400 Phinney Ave. North (North)
(206) 632-5100
www.theochocolate.com

Theo is the only organic, fair trade, bean-to-bar chocolate factory in the United States. The delicious award-winning chocolates are made daily in the Seattle factory, which offers tours to the public seven days a week. The staff entertain visitors with the story of cacao and explain its extraordinary transformation from a fruit into chocolate. Best of all, at the end of the tour you get to sample the goods. Tours are held every day, but the factory is usually only open Mon through

Fri—meaning that on weekend tours, you won't get to see the machines actually in operation.

VIOS CAFÉ & MARKETPLACE $$–$$$
903 19th Ave. East (Central)
(206) 329-3236
www.vioscafe.com

This Greek *taverna* is a great place for families, with its long rustic pine tables that are ideal for communal dining—and best of all, its kids' play area, fully stocked with books and toys. Food is celebrated at Vios, with authentic Greek dishes served in an atmosphere with the comforts of home. In addition to the Capitol Hill restaurant, a second location is in the Ravenna neighborhood of North Seattle, at 6504 20th Ave. NE.

MOVIES AND THE ARTS

BOOK-IT REPERTORY THEATRE $$$$
305 Harrison St. (Central)
(206) 216-0833
www.book-it.org/public-performance-
     packages.php

Book-It is a nonprofit theater that adapts classic and contemporary literature for the stage, where the characters from the adapted works narrate the text. On Target Family Fun Days throughout the year, both the performance and an all-ages book fair and craft workshop are offered free of charge. Family performances have included *Johnny Appleseed* and *Catching the Moon*. Book-It is located in the Center House Theatre at Seattle Center.

BROADWAY BOUND CHILDREN'S
THEATRE $$–$$$
5031 University Way NE (North)
(206) 526-KIDS
www.broadwaybound.org

This performing arts school and theater provides classes for active participation in theater arts for children 5–18, as well as great productions for the public. For over 14 years the Broadway Bound young performers have put on productions such as *Guys and Dolls, Peter Pan, CATS, Little Shop of Horrors,* and many others. Broadway Bound productions are held at the Broadway Performance Hall at 1625 Broadway in Seattle.

IMAX AT PACIFIC SCIENCE CENTER $$
200 Second Ave. North (Central)
(800) 664-8775
www.pacsci.org/imax

Seattle's biggest screen always has a list of several movies that are showing, from science and nature to some of Hollywood's biggest hits. The IMAX is a cinematic experience like no other, and films for all ages are shown. Many of the films come with companion PDF guides that can be downloaded from the Web site. The 405-seat theater is plush and comfortable, with a concession stand. Combine it with a visit to the Pacific Science Center or other Seattle Center attractions for a great day.

NESHOLM FAMILY LECTURE HALL AT MARION OLIVER McCAW HALL $$
321 Mercer St. (Central)
(206) 733-9725
www.mccawhall.com

Located at Seattle Center, the Marion Oliver McCaw Hall is the region's premier performance venue. Numerous performances and events of all kinds are held here every week, so it's always worth checking the calendar during your visit. Particularly of interest are the Saturday family film screenings and the ongoing series of animated and short films.

SEATTLE CHILDREN'S THEATRE $$$$
201 Thomas St. (Central)
(206) 443-0807
www.sct.org

During the academic year of Sept through June, the Seattle Children's Theatre develops and presents a variety of plays for children of all ages. It is the second-largest resident theater for young audiences in North America, and allows young people to make new discoveries about themselves and the world while building a lifelong interest in the arts. This is one of the most well-respected children's theater programs in the country. The theater also offers a wide variety of classes and workshops for ages 3–21.

SECOND STORY REPERTORY CHILDREN'S THEATRE $$
16587 NE 74th St. (Redmond)
(425) 881-6777
www.secondstoryrep.org/childrens theatre/season.html

Redmond's first full-time theater group has been around since 1999, offering a variety of plays and musicals for adults and children. Second Story's Children's Theatre Series is specially produced for grade school–age children, and some all-ages performances are appropriate for even younger kids. Many of the performances are adaptations of beloved children's books. Performances take place on Fri nights, and Sat and Sun afternoons.

THISTLE THEATRE $$
6344 NE 74th St., Suite 103 (North)
(206) 524-3388
www.thistletheatre.org

This puppet theater offers one of the most affordable performance experiences in Seattle. Using a traditional style of Japanese puppetry called *Bunraku*, the puppeteers bring the handcrafted puppets to life, for the delight of the audience. Good storytelling, realistic movement, and excellent manipulation are the hallmarks of Thistle Theatre productions. Each 45-minute play is appropriate for ages three and older. Performances are held at the Magnuson Park Theatre (7110 62nd Ave. NE) and Sunset Hill Community Club (3003 NW 66th St.) in Seattle, and the Bellevue Youth Theater (16661 Northup Way) in Bellevue.

VERA PROJECT $$$
Warren Avenue North and Republican Street (Central)
(206) 956-8372
www.theveraproject.org
This Seattle Center venue is a music-arts center run by and for youth. Its mission is to fuel personal and community transformation through popular music shows, produced in partnership with young people in Seattle. Vera offers music shows for all ages every week, as well as an art gallery and a variety of classes including art, breakdancing, silk-screening, and sound engineering. Most concerts are around $10, and all classes are $25.

MUSEUMS

CHILDREN'S MUSEUM $$
305 Harrison St. (Central)
(206) 441-1768
www.thechildrensmuseum.org
Seattle's Children's Museum is a delightful place, aiming to bring to life the joy of discovery for kids and their families through fun, creative, hands-on exploration. Each month a new theme inspires the activities, from light and animals to the planet and medieval times. This museum is great

for children from infants through about 10 years old; the Discovery Bay section is meant for ages birth through three years old, and is a mini-adventure of slides and an aquarium that little ones can easily crawl or toddle through. Imagination Station is a creative kid-size art studio, while Cog City inspires the engineer within at its maze of lifts, levers, and pipes. Other special areas include books, math, the mountains, and a mini–neighborhood village. The Children's Museum is open daily.

KIDSQUEST CHILDREN'S MUSEUM $$
4091 Factoria Mall SE (Bellevue)
(425) 637-8100
www.kidsquestmuseum.org
Although KidsQuest is located in Bellevue, it is very close to Seattle and a great destination for those with young children. The interactive, hands-on museum encourages a love of learning through play, with an emphasis on science, art, and technology. The exhibits encourage whole-family learning, and are geared toward children from birth through age 10. Throughout the day various activities are going on, such as science experiments, story times, and art projects. The museum is generally closed Mon (although occasionally open on school holidays), and open Tues through Sun. KidsQuest is free of charge for everyone on Fri from 5 to 8 p.m.

ROSALIE WHYEL MUSEUM OF DOLL ART $$
221 106th Ave. NE (Bellevue)
(425) 455-0363
www.dollart.com
Just fifteen minutes east of downtown Seattle is this doll museum, which is sure to delight children. Throughout human history, dolls have reflected our images and

been the most popular children's toys. The Rosalie Whyel museum is one of the world's foremost collections of dolls, housed in an exquisite setting. More than 1,200 dolls are on permanent display, from antique to modern, as well as dollhouses, teddy bears, and other memorabilia. A nice English garden provides a nice place to stroll or rest. A couple of blocks from the museum is Rosie's Too, a companion store that carries a wide assortment of dolls, toys, stuffed animals, clothes, and accessories. The Museum of Doll Art is open daily.

PARKS, PLAYGROUNDS, AND PLAY CENTERS

EARTH'S MINERALS SCRATCH PATCH $
6410 Latona Ave. NE (North)
(206) 523-6164
www.scratchpatchusa.com

Visualize a cozy European-style indoor play center, combined with the earth-digging scratch patches that are common in South Africa, and you have Earth's Minerals. Here, two small rooms are covered 3 inches deep with more than two tons of tumbled gemstones from all over the world, where kids can go treasure hunting. Using a mineral and rock guide provided by Earth's Minerals, children play and dig through the rocks to identify different stones. It's a fun and low-key activity, and the kids can fill up a bag of stones to take with them. Open Fri through Mon.

GREEN LAKE PARK
7201 E. Green Lake Dr. North (North)
(206) 684-4075
www.seattle.gov/Parks/park_detail.
  asp?ID=307

Possibly Seattle's most beloved park, Green Lake is huge and offers plenty to do. Miles of paths for walking, jogging, in-line skating, and bike riding surround the lake, and there is a very large children's playground. For swimming, a beach with lifeguards as well as an indoor pool give year-round accessibility, and a large wading pool for small children is at the north end of the park. Tennis courts, sports fields, boat rentals, and fishing docks round out the recreational opportunities. Free (except for equipment rental).

INTERNATIONAL CHILDREN'S PARK
700 S. Lane St. (Central)
(206) 684-4075
www.seattle.gov/parks/park_detail
  .asp?ID=364

Located in the fun and fascinating International District, this park is also known locally as the "dragon park" due to the landmark dragon sculpture that children can climb on. The center of the park is a yin-yang symbol formed from grass and sand. Elderly residents of the I.D. also frequent this park as a quiet refuge to stroll or sit. A grassroots movement has been working over several years to improve and update the park, and significant funding in 2010 has been dedicated to this. The park makes a nice starting or ending point for a family day in the I.D., which provides a lot of interesting sightseeing, eating, and shopping for all ages. Free.

NEOTOTEMS CHILDREN'S GARDEN
Seattle Center, east end of Children's
  Museum (Central)

This sweet garden was designed by Gloria Bornstein and features sculptures of whimsical sea creatures set amid rocks and native plants. The inspiration for the garden was the Native American legend of whales swimming underground. A maze of paths leads throughout the landscaped gardens, to create a place of discovery. The whale's tail fountain is a favorite among kids. Free.

SEATTLE CENTER SKATEPARK
305 Harrison St. (Central)
www.seattlecenter.com/skatepark
Completed in 2009, the skate park at Seattle Center features a surface area of 10,000 square feet, with a flowing street plaza, ledges, stairs, transitions, and state-of-the-art skating elements for all skill levels and abilities. There are even skateable sculptures and structural glass riding surfaces. Sea Sk8, as it's known to locals, is open daily during daylight hours. Free.

POOLS AND BEACHES

ALKI BEACH PARK
1702 Alki Ave. SW (South)
(206) 684-4075
www.seattle.gov/parks/park_detail
.asp?ID=445
This little slice of Southern California makes for a great family destination on warm days. The 2.5-mile beach in the West Seattle neighborhood runs from Alki Point to Duwamish Head, and in the summer months is filled with joggers, in-line skaters, kids, bicyclists, beachcombers, and sunbathers. Picnic tables, fire pits, and restrooms are fairly plentiful, although on perfect summer weekends it's advised to arrive early for prime spots. There's also a bathhouse that is now an art studio, and the monument to the arrival of Seattle's first European settlers in 1851 can be found at the south point. The entire beach faces incredible views of Puget Sound and the Olympic Mountains in the distance. Plenty of casual, inexpensive, family-friendly restaurants and stores line the street facing Alki Beach. Free; street parking is plentiful, though it can fill up on weekends. You can

also take the water taxi across; it leaves the downtown Seattle waterfront between Piers 55 and 56, taking you on the 12-minute journey across the bay for $2. A free shuttle to the beach is available at the West Seattle water taxi landing. Open year-round.

MADISON PARK BEACH
E. Madison Street and Howe (Central)
(206) 684-4075
www.seattle.gov/Parks/beach_detail
.asp?id=369
One of Seattle's most popular swimming beaches, Madison Park has a large grassy area for sunbathing and picnicking, with beautiful Lake Washington opening wide and blue before you. There is a designated swimming area in the lake with floating raft, diving board, and lifeguards, as well as a play area on land. Parking, water fountains, and public restrooms are available. Open from late June through Labor Day weekend. Free.

SEATTLE PARKS & RECREATION POOLS
206-684-4075
www.seattle.gov/parks/pools.asp
The City of Seattle operates a number of swimming pools situated in all neighborhoods and locations, including eight indoor pools and 30 wading pools. The two most highly recommended pools for kids five and up are Colman Pool (8603 Fauntleroy Way SW), an amazing heated saltwater pool located in a great beach setting that features a giant tube slide. The Pop Mounger Pool (2535 32nd Ave. West) has a big pool with a 50-foot corkscrew slide, and a little pool that is warmer and shallower, for small children. Admission fees are nominal, $4 for adults and less than $3 for kids. Lockers and family changing rooms are available, and admittance fees must be paid for everyone entering, whether they are swimming or not.

SEASONAL EVENTS/ANNUAL VENUES

CHILDREN'S FILM
FESTIVAL SEATTLE $$$
1515 12th Ave. (Central)
(206) 329-2629
www.nwfilmforum.org/go/childrensfilm
fest

The largest children's film festival in the Pacific Northwest, CFFS is a 10-day extravaganza of films from more than 25 countries. Held in Jan, programs include feature films, shorts, animation, historical films, live performances, and fantastic hands-on workshops for tomorrow's filmmakers. The festival is really crafted with all ages of children in mind, with gentle programs for the youngest and chills and adventures for the older kids. Sponsored by the Northwest Film Forum.

FAMILY 4TH AT LAKE UNION
Gasworks Park, 2101 N. Northlake Way
(North)
(206) 281-7788
http://family4th.org

Crowds gather on the grassy hill of Gasworks Park and in boats on the waters of Lake Union for this family-friendly "Celebration for the People, by the People," and to ooh and ahh over one of the most spectacular fireworks displays. The event kicks off at noon with family activities, entertainment, and food vendors. The Playfield offers free kids' activities such as kite making, face painting, climbing walls, a giant inflatable slide, an obstacle course, and a bungee trampoline platform. There is also a KidSafe program providing free numbered wristbands upon registration, to expedite reuniting lost children with their parents. Free.

PAX $$$$
Washington State Convention Center
800 Convention Place (Central)
www.paxsite.com

PAX, the Penny Arcade Expo, is a three-day gaming festival of tabletop, video, and computer games. Over the three days in Sept, a variety of exhibitions, tournaments, free-play areas, and panel discussions fills the exhibit halls. Single-day and full festival passes are available, and children age six and under are free with a paying adult. On Fri and Sat night the festival winds down with a concert.

SEATTLE INTERNATIONAL CHILDREN'S
FESTIVAL $$$
158 Thomas St. #26 (Central)
(206) 684-7338
www.seattleinternational.org

If you are planning to visit Seattle in mid-May, don't miss this huge and exciting festival for children. SICF is one of the only major cultural events focused on young audiences in the Pacific Northwest, with more than 35,000 attendees annually. Its innovative programming was called "one of the most far-reaching arts festivals for young people in the country" by the New York Times. The highlight of the five-day festival is the performance calendar, from music and dancing to circus acts, comedy routines, and puppeteering. A variety of activities is also offered including kite- and button-making, origami, drawing, learning to skateboard, interactive games, hula hooping, face painting, and more.

UMOJAFEST CHILDREN'S DAY
Judkins Park, 2150 S. Norman St.
(Central)
(877) 505-6306
www.umojafamilyfest.com/Website/
childrensday.php

KIDSTUFF

This African Heritage Festival & Parade spans three days in late July/early Aug, and dedicates one as a Children's Day. Recognizing and celebrating children and youth in the community, the free Children's Day features fun and educational activities including arts and crafts, drum, dance, storytelling, face painting, martial arts demonstrations, interactive exhibits, an art showcase, and a talent showcase. Free books and school supplies are also given out.

WHIRLIGIG! $$
Seattle Center, 305 Harrison St. (Central)
(206) 684-7200
http://seattlecenter.com/programs/
detail.asp?EV_EventNum=23
Seattle Center Whirligig! is an annual phenomenon of fun for kids. This wacky world of child-size action transforms Center House into a vibrant House of Bounce for two weeks during spring break, in late Mar to early Apr. Whirligig! offers amusement aplenty for all preteen ages; kids can glide, slide, and ride on super-cool, super-size inflatable rides. Eye-popping colors, roaming clowns, face painters, and free entertainment add to the mix of nonstop fun. A special Toddler Zone is also available, and free art-making workshops are offered. Whirligig! is open from 11 a.m. to 6 p.m. every day while it runs; an all-day pass is $7.50 and single ride tickets are $1.50—but if you come on Thurs, kids ride free all day. It is, of course, also much more crowded than other days.

WINTERFEST AT SEATTLE
CENTER $–$$
305 Harrison St. (Central)
(206) 684-7200
www.seattlecenter.com/winterfest
During the entire month of Dec, Seattle Center is aglow and abuzz with winter holiday festivities. Kids will love the ice-skating rink,

winter train and village, ice sculpting, and the many visits by Santa Claus throughout the month. Most activities are free; admission charges apply for ice-skating and theater/dance performances. See the Annual Events and Festivals chapter for more details.

SHOPS AND TOY STORES

Be sure to check the Comic Books, Collectibles, and Toy Stores section of the Shopping chapter, as well.

ARCHIE McPHEE
1300 N. 45th St. (North)
(206) 297-0240
www.archiemcpheeseattle.com
This Wallingford store is a one-stop location for gifts, party supplies, crafts, costumes, oddities, and the weirdest collection of toys and candy you've ever seen. A mecca for connoisseurs of the strange, Archie's is reminiscent of a carnival sideshow. If you find yourself in need of a rubber chicken, punching nun, 8-foot tall gladiator, or pickle lip balm, this is the place to come. Most of the 10,000-plus items are priced less than $15.

BOOTYLAND
1317 E. Pine St. (Central)
(206) 328-0636
www.bootylandkids.com
Despite the fact that this store's name sounds like it contains X-rated paraphernalia for adults, in fact its selection is mostly for babies and children: eco-conscious clothing, natural and wooden toys, baby supplies including organic diapers, and a great line of locally screen-printed T-shirts. There is also some clothing for women and men as well, and a small selection of vintage and consignment items. Most things are modern and offbeat, making it a fun place to browse.

CLOVER
5335 Ballard Ave. NW (North)
(206) 782-0715
www.clovertoys.com

This quaint Ballard shop is filled with wooden toys, stuffed animals, dolls, puppets, and baby clothes. It has a warm European feel, housed in a pretty century-old building. There's also a really nice selection of room decor accessories, featuring unique locally made items such as heirloom quilts by Rebecca Hewitt and original paintings and vintage reproductions by Seattle artists Matthew Porter and Molly Brett.

IZILLA TOYS & BOOKS
1429 12th Ave., Suite D (Central)
(206) 322-TOYS
www.izillatoys.com

Billing itself as Seattle's most unique toy store, Izilla is the kind of family-owned place that reaffirms your commitment to patronizing independent businesses. The Capitol Hill store specializes in a unique selection of quality toys from all over the world, and each item carried in the inventory is carefully selected. The store's mission is to encourage play that is imaginative and nonviolent, and the selection of toys reflects that. The children's bookstore has recently expanded, and Izilla offers kids two special clubs. The Birthday Club sends a card and present to everyone who has registered, on their birthday. Allowance Days, usually held on the last Sun of the month, are a fun way for kids to get a bargain and help the community at the same time; kids making their own purchase get a 15 percent discount, and 10 percent of all sales are donated to children's organizations in Seattle. The store has a lot of great free events as well, such as story times, game nights, crafts, and music classes.

MAGIC MOUSE TOYS
603 First Ave. (Central)
(877) 262-0486
www.magicmousetoys.net

A self-professed "toy store run by a professional child," Magic Mouse is a huge store at the corner of First and Yesler in Pioneer Square. The 7,000 square feet are stocked with toys, games, books, kites, model kits, dolls, and other items sure to bring out the childlike wonder and merriment in all of us. Shipping and gift wrapping services are also available.

SECRET GARDEN BOOKSHOP
2214 NW Market St. (North)
(206) 789-5006
www.secretgarden.indiebound.com

The Secret Garden is a delightful independent bookstore that focuses on children's books. It is heavily involved in the community, featuring numerous author events, school book fairs, and cultural programs throughout the city. It's a full-service bookstore that stocks all genres of books for everyone, but the specialization is definitely children and young adult readers.

ZOOS/ANIMALS/WILDLIFE

BLOEDEL RESERVE $$$
7571 NE Dolphin Dr. (Bainbridge Island)
(206) 842-7631
www.bloedelreserve.org

This 150-acre nature preserve and garden is located on charming Bainbridge Island, a 20-minute ferry ride across Puget Sound from downtown Seattle. The former private residential estate was once the home of the Bloedel family, and their vision has been extended by the Arbor Fund to create the wonderful preserve that it is today. Eighty-four of its acres are second-growth forest, and meandering through the woods, you'll find a variety of ponds, gardens, and meadows. There is a quite large bird refuge, where you may spot kingfishers and great blue herons, in addition to ducks, geese, and swans. To get there, catch the ferry at Pier 52 on the waterfront, for the fun 20-minute ride with great views of the Sound and city skyline. You can also drive via the Agate Pass Bridge. Bainbridge Island is a terrific place to spend the whole day when you're finished with the reserve; check out the many family-friendly restaurants and shops, or rent bikes to discover the island. The Bloedel Reserve is open Wed through Sun, with shorter winter hours.

SEATTLE BUG SAFARI $$
1501 Western Ave., Suite 304 (Central)
(206) 285-BUGS
http://seattlebugsafari.com

Kids of all ages can experience the exotic world of insects, at the city's only live bug zoo. The Safari Guides lead a fun, educational journey through the natural habitats of bugs from all over the world. Seattle Bug Safari

is open Tues through Sun (except major holidays). Mon opening hours vary with the season, so be sure to check the Web site.

WOODLAND PARK ZOO $$$
750 N. 50th St. (North)
(206) 684-4800
www.zoo.org

The 92-acre Woodland Park Zoo is one of the oldest zoos on the West Coast, and it houses the largest live animal collection in Washington state. More than 300 species are represented here, and Woodland Park has won five major exhibit awards. The grounds and displays are divided into different bio-climatic zones, from tropical rain forests to coastal deserts. There is an animal contact farm, Zoomazium play space for toddlers to eight-year-olds, a historic 1918 carousel, bug world, and an African village re-creation. The zoo is open 364 days a year (closed only on Christmas); parking is available for an extra charge. While you're here, you may want to check out the Rose Garden, 2.5 gorgeous acres with no admission charge.

ANNUAL EVENTS
AND FESTIVALS

Seattle is a place that likes to celebrate and party, and it seems the people here will use virtually any excuse to do so. Festivals and special events are held throughout the year, and just about every culture is celebrated. The city is not afraid of sexuality or its bawdy side, either—there are festivals that celebrate burlesque (Moisture Festival) and the erotic (Erotic Arts Festival). Some festivals include plenty of nakedness as well, such as the Fremont Summer Solstice Parade that is full of painted, nude participants. If that's not enough for you, you can head to Snoqualmie, where Nudestock is held every August. This one-day nudist festival is not listed here, as it's outside Seattle, but if you want to learn more about it, go to www.fraternitysnoqualmie.com/nudestock .html.

Of course, all the major holidays are celebrated, and plenty of festivals center on food, music, or movies—favorite festival themes anywhere. This being Puget Sound, several festivals are focused or take place on the water. The small neighborhood and cultural festivals are great ways to get a real sense of place in Seattle, and to get to know its inhabitants better. If you are here between June and August, you can't miss Seafair, the annual summer celebration that features dozens of events all over town.

JANUARY

**MARTIN LUTHER KING JR. DAY
  PARADE & EVENTS**
Various locations
(206) 296-1002
www.mlkseattle.org
Seattle has one of the largest annual Martin Luther King Day celebrations in the United States. The central celebration of Dr. King and his work begins with the parade from 4th Avenue and Pine downtown, starting at 11 a.m. The MLK Celebration Committee holds a march (usually starting at Garfield High School), with rallies before and after. During the day, various workshops are held on issues such as homelessness, HIV and health care, education, race and gender, housing, and others. At Seattle Center, the Dr. Martin Luther King Jr. Holiday Celebration honors Dr. King's dream by promoting the principles of peace, unity, and equality, providing an opportunity for Seattle citizens to remember his dream and vision, and recognizing citizens who are energizing the MLK dream in their communities. A full afternoon of awards, activities, and entertainment included glee clubs, vocalists, multicultural dances, peace awards, and more. Throughout the city many service projects and other commemorations are going on as well. Most events are free.

SEATTLE BOAT SHOW

Qwest Field Event Center—800
  Occidental Ave. South
South Lake Union—901 Fairview Ave.
  North
(206) 634-0911
www.boatsafloatshow.com

Seattle's premier show for boating is held from the end of Jan through early Feb each year. Highlights include appearances by famous sailors, explorers, adventurers, and other boaters, as well as contests, more than 400 exhibitors of various types of boats and services, and the world's largest toy boat collection on display. Tickets are $12 for adults and $5 for ages 11–17 (10 and under are free). A five-day pass can be purchased for $24, and all online orders include a day of free parking and one-year magazine subscription.

SEATTLE CHAMBER MUSIC SOCIETY WINTER FESTIVAL

Benaroya Hall, 200 University St.
  (Central)
(206) 283-8808
www.seattlechambermusic.org

The Seattle Chamber Music Society has presented its Winter Festival for more than 30 years. The festival consists of four main concerts, three preconcert recitals, a family concert, and a preview lecture. Ticket prices range from $8 for the family concert to $45, and three- and four-concert packages from $115.

FEBRUARY

MARDI GRAS

www.mardigrasseattle.org

Mardi Gras is definitely celebrated in Seattle. The main event is held on Fat Tuesday, the day before Ash Wednesday in early Feb.

Pioneer Square gets rowdy with a party that spills from the bars and restaurants into the streets. A Spam-Carving Contest adds a quirky touch, and there are also mambo contests and carnival-style events. Seattleites still remember the 2001 celebration, however, when things got out of hand and turned into a riot. Chaos consumed Pioneer Square and one man was mortally wounded before police dispelled the crowds.

NORTHWEST FLOWER & GARDEN SHOW

Washington State Convention Center
800 Convention Place (Central)
(253) 756-2121
www.gardenshow.com/seattle

This annual floral funfest is six acres of inspiring gardens, many thousands of flowers and plants, free seminars for all gardening levels, and shopping at 350 garden-related exhibits. Internationally known speakers who have presented at the show include Suzy Bales, Rich Darke, John Greenlee, and Valerie Easton. Other attractions include the Sproutopia children's area, the handiwork of high school horticulture students in the Funky Junk display, floral display competitions, and a container-garden exhibition. Held on a Wed through Sun in early Feb; admission is $20 at the door and $16 in advance, with discounts for youth, groups, and half-day tickets. Children 12 and under are admitted free.

TET FESTIVAL—VIETNAMESE LUNAR NEW YEAR

Seattle Center, Fisher Pavilion, 305
  Harrison St. (Central)
(206) 706-2658
www.tetinseattle.org

Vietnamese culture and traditions come together at this festival, to reflect on the past and celebrate the renewal of life. This annual Lunar New Year celebration welcomes the return of spring and chases out evil winter spirits with a traditional roaring lion dance and firecrackers. Wear your gold and red, the royal colors of Vietnam, and come eat Pho noodle soup, spring rolls, rice cakes, and shrimp pancakes while you enjoy the celebration and performances. The festival features mixes of professional performers and talented local artists. Attendees will also have a chance to explore and immerse in Vietnam's culture through workshops, visual art exhibits, and hands-on children's activities. Free.

MARCH

BEST OF THE NORTHWEST
Warren G. Magnuson Park, 7400 Sand
  Point Way NE (North)
(206) 525-5926
www.nwartalliance.com/events/
  Spring_Best_of_the_Northwest
The Best of the Northwest art shows happen several times a year, with the first in Mar. This juried show will feature more than 110 regional artists spanning every medium— great garden art, fine paintings, beautiful artist-designed clothing and jewelry, glass, wood, metal, ceramic, and more. Spend the day enjoying the art, music, and tasty food! Free event; plenty of free parking.

EMERALD CITY COMICON
Washington State Convention Center,
  800 Convention Place (Central)
(206) 694-5000
www.emeraldcitycomicon.com
The premier comic book and pop culture convention in the Pacific Northwest features a wide array of activities and programming including industry guests, various discussion panels, celebrity signings and photo opportunities, prize drawings, and costume contests. It features a large exhibit hall with comics retailers from across the Northwest, bringing a large stock of modern and vintage comics, as well as statues, action figures, models, and other items of interest to comic collectors.

IRISH FESTIVAL
Seattle Center, Fisher Pavilion, 305
  Harrison St. (Central)
(206) 427-3027
www.irishclub.org/center.htm
Held around St. Patrick's Day, this is a weekend of nonstop Irish music, dancing, children's activities, Irish genealogy and Irish language workshops, cultural exhibits, short films, and many booths selling Irish and Celtic products. Events for children include the Smilingest Irish Eyes Contest and the Most Irish-Looking Face Contest, and other activities in the children's activities center. Wear green, white, and orange to get in the spirit, and munch on traditional Irish stew and delicious homemade scones with jam and cream. Presented by the Irish Heritage Club. Free.

MOISTURE FESTIVAL
Various venues in Seattle
(206) 297-1405
www.moisturefestival.com
The Moisture Festival is a gathering and celebration of burlesque, comedy, and variety performance, including aerialists, jugglers, bubble acts, can-can girls, and more, to keep the tradition of vaudeville alive. Since 2004 the Moisture Festival has presented this exhilarating form of theater to celebrate spring. Most shows are held at Hale's Palladium, 4301 Leary Way NW, or the ACT Contemporary

Theatre downtown at 7th and Union. Tickets are $5–$25, and several shows at the festival are always performed as benefits, with the performers donating their talents and the proceeds going to nonprofit organizations.

ST. PATRICK'S DAY PARADE
Downtown, starting from 4th Avenue and Jefferson (Central)
(206) 427-3027
www.irishclub.org/parade.htm
This traditional celebration parade for St. Patrick travels north on 4th Avenue, from Jefferson to Seattle Center. The parade is held in conjunction with the Irish Festival, and during the parade and festival the monorail is free between 1:30 and 2:30 p.m. Bagpipes, bands, schools, and clubs march along Seattle's downtown streets; you can view a parade route on the Web site. Free.

SEATTLE JEWISH FILM FESTIVAL
Various venues around Seattle
(206) 324-9996
www.seattlejewishfilmfestival.org
The annual Seattle Jewish Film Festival (SJFF) is a 10-day international cinematic exploration and celebration of Jewish life, culture, identity, and history. SJFF uses the magical medium of film to both entertain and educate the Jewish and general communities about complex issues facing Jewish people and world communities alike, while challenging conventional perspectives. Screenings are supplemented by guest speakers, providing a dynamic forum for dialogue with actors, filmmakers, academics, and expert panelists from near and far. In recent years, SJFF offerings have included musical and comedy performances, curated exhibits, and thematic educational opportunities and special events. Some 8,000 attendees cast their ballots for Best Feature, Best Documentary, and Best Short Film, with winners receiving the SJFF Audience Choice Award on Closing Night. Individual screening tickets are $8–$18, with passes from $65 to $200. The Tom Douglas pre-party, Matzoh Momma Sunday brunch, and Closing Night are all sold separately. For the most part, screenings are held at the Cinerama Theatre and the SIFF Cinema at McCaw Hall; special events are at various locations.

TASTE WASHINGTON
Various locations
(206) 367-2420
www.tastewashington.org/seattle
Taste Washington, the ultimate wine experience, is a weekend of wine and food tasting at one of the nation's premier wine and food events, taking place in both Seattle and Spokane. The Seattle event kicks off with the annual Winemakers Dinner at the Washington Athletic Club. Seminars and the Grand Tasting are held at conference centers and/or the Qwest Field Event Center. If you're new to wine, or an old hand at swirling and spitting, Taste Washington Seattle is the ideal event to learn what wines you'll love to drink. Come to Taste Washington and try them all! Hip, new restaurants and historic establishments alike will tempt you with delicious fare. Seminars, sommelier blind tastings, exhibit tables, and celebrity chef cooking demonstrations are all part of the festival. Tickets are $75 for general admission to $125 for VIP.

APRIL

LANGSTON HUGHES AFRICAN AMERICAN FILM FESTIVAL
Langston Hughes Performing Arts Center, 104 17th Ave. South (Central)
(206) 684-4758
www.langstonblackfilmfest.org

This annual event provides provocative films from independent black filmmakers and works about the African American experience. The festival features panel discussions, screenplay readings, matinee screenings for middle and high school youth, and in-depth chats with filmmakers, industry professionals, and local community leaders. The festival began in 2004 as a weekend series and has grown to nine days of film, workshops, filmmaker events, and community celebrations. Films are selected from entries screened by panels, and curated from current and vintage offerings worldwide. Individual screening/event tickets cost from $10 to $20 depending on the event.

NATIONAL FILM FESTIVAL FOR TALENTED YOUTH
Various venues around Seattle
(206) 905-8400
www.nffty.org
Over a four-day weekend in late Apr and/ or early May, the NFFTY presents the largest and most influential film festivals for young filmmakers, ages 22 and under. Brought to you by the same people who put on the Seattle International Film Festival, NFFTY includes more than 150 film screenings as well as filmmaking panels, concerts by youth bands, and opportunities for young filmmakers to network with industry professionals. Most screenings are held at the SIFF Cinema at 321 Mercer St., or the Experience Music Project theater at 325 5th Ave. Individual film tickets can be purchased for $10 each, tickets to the Opening Night Gala for $50, single-day passes for $20, and three-day festival passes for $50–$75.

SEATTLE CHERRY BLOSSOM & JAPANESE CULTURAL FESTIVAL
Seattle Center, Fisher Pavilion, 305 Harrison St. (Central)
(206) 723-2003
www.jcccw.org
Explore Seattle's deep connections with Japan and celebrate the beauty of spring at the Seattle Cherry Blossom & Japanese Cultural Festival. From the booms of *taiko* drums to the silence of ikebana flowers, the event is a feast for the senses. Delicious Japanese food, tea ceremony demonstrations, and artwork present both a modern and ancient view of this complex culture. Free.

SEATTLE EROTIC ART FESTIVAL
Seattle Center, Exhibition Hall, 305 Harrison St. (Central)
www.seattleerotic.org
This festival is a vibrant and colorful event showcasing world-class art and creative expression of many forms that will delight your senses. It started as a fabulous vision of a place where art evoked the erotic energy of intimate human expression. A place where art that was rarely seen in mainstream galleries and museums could be celebrated, discussed, and supported. An event where tired clichés of "sexiness" could be replaced with intriguing explorations of eroticism. Whether you stroll through the visual art exhibition, delight in performances and interactive installations, indulge in erotic literary art, peruse the expansive Festival Store, or dance until the wee hours, this is one unique arts festival. Ticket prices range from $25 for one-day passes and $40 for two-day passes, to $500 for an immersive weekend "Velvet" VIP package. There are also several workshops available that can be purchased separately. Gallery hours from noon to 6 p.m. are for ages

18 and over; from that time until the festival closes at 4 a.m., it's 21 and over only.

MAY

A GLIMPSE OF CHINA—CHINESE CULTURE AND ARTS FESTIVAL
Seattle Center, Center House, 305
   Harrison St. (Central)
(206) 818-8680
www.chinaartandculture.org
Enter a virtual Chinese garden and partake in cultural traditions covering 5,000 years of Chinese history in this celebration of one of the world's oldest cultures. The festival showcases the unique traditional art and culture of China through visual and performing arts and gift booth exhibitions including Chinese music, dance, Wushu performances, works by nationally acclaimed artists, seminars, and interactive activities.

ASIAN-PACIFIC ISLANDER HERITAGE MONTH CELEBRATION
Seattle Center, Center House, 305
   Harrison St. (Central)
206-228-6871
www.seattleapi.com/index.html
With rich stories and cultures, the Asian Pacific Islander community of the greater Puget Sound area gathers to celebrate the diverse community and history within the United States. In 1992 Congress designated May as Asian Pacific Islander Heritage Month to celebrate the stories and history of the Asian Pacific American community. Enjoy and experience the rich cultures of the Asian Pacific Islander communities through song, dance, music, art, and displays. The festival launches Asian Pacific Islander Heritage Month in Seattle with spectacular lion dances, youth drill teams, martial arts, taiko drums, and incredible artists from around

the state. This daylong celebration at the first of May kicks off the month's events, such as tea ceremonies, immigration ceremonies, family fun days at Wing Luke Asian Museum, and much more. You can download a full schedule of the month's events at the Web site. Presented by the Asian-Pacific Directors Coalition. Free.

NORTHWEST FOLKLIFE FESTIVAL
Seattle Center, 305 Harrison St. (Central)
(206) 684-7300
www.nwfolklife.org
Held over Memorial Day weekend, the Northwest Folklife Festival celebrates, shares, and sustains the vitality of folk, ethnic, and traditional arts. The four-day festival attracts about a quarter of a million visitors, with over 7,000 volunteer performers from more than 100 countries. It is a major focal point for many traditional and ethnic performing groups and communities, and provides a forum for sharing and revitalizing these communities. Music, visual art, dance, theater, film, literary arts, and a family area are all part of the festival, as well as merchants selling all variety of arts and crafts. The Living Green Courtyard focuses on sustainability, serving as an area for the recycling of all food and trash waste as well as showcasing environmentally friendly goods. The Northwest Folklife Festival is completely free of charge, although a $10 donation is appreciated to keep the festival going.

PIKE PLACE MARKET STREET FESTIVAL
Pike Street and First Avenue, and
   throughout the market (Central)
(206) 682-7453
www.pikeplacemarketstreetfestival.com
This big festival at the historic Pike Place Market is a benefit for the Market Foundation,

started in 1971 as a way to say thanks to Seattle citizens for voting to save the market. The festival includes an eclectic mix of live music, local artisans, and of course, lots of food. A kickoff parade down Pike Street features local drill teams. Suggested $1 donation at the entrance; funds are used for renovations and improvements to the market.

SEATTLE CHEESE FESTIVAL
Pike Place Market, between Pine and Virginia Streets (Central)
(206) 622-0141
www.seattlecheesefestival.com
The Seattle Cheese Festival is an annual destination artisanal cheese festival for the general public and the food-service industry to taste, celebrate, and better understand artisanal cheese made locally and around the world. The event includes two days of cheese sampling from local and international artisanal producers, seminars and panel discussions, pairings, a wine and beer garden, and area restaurants that offer a "Cheese Fest Best" special dish. The wine and beer garden is $10 for five tastings, and seminars are $35; the rest of the festival is free.

SEATTLE INTERNATIONAL CHILDREN'S FESTIVAL
Seattle Center, 305 Harrison St. (Central)
(206) 684-7338
www.seattleinternational.org
Presented by Giant Magnet, SICF is one of the only major cultural events focused on young audiences in the Pacific Northwest, with more than 35,000 attendees annually. The five-day festival includes music, dancing, circus acts, comedy routines, puppeteering, arts and crafts, skateboarding, games, face painting, and more. Tickets are $10–$15. See the Kidstuff chapter for more details.

SEATTLE INTERNATIONAL FILM FESTIVAL
Various venues around Seattle
(206) 324-9996
www.siff.net
This festival is highly anticipated every year and brings filmmakers and -lovers from all over the world. With a reputation as more of an "audience" festival than an industry one, SIFF is held from late May through mid-June. SIFF is typically kicked off with a big Opening Night Gala at Benaroya Hall. Screenings and other events over the following three weeks are held in theaters in various neighborhoods around the city, as well as Kirkland and Everett. All together, more than 170 feature films and 100 shorts are presented to an audience of over 130,000. Ticket and pass prices vary greatly, depending on which events or screenings you wish to attend: from a $45 pass that will get you into four Sun morning screenings, to several hundred dollars for passes that entitle you to numerous screenings and parties, to full-series yearly and platinum passes that can cost $600–$2,750.

SEATTLE MARITIME FESTIVAL
Downtown Seattle Waterfront/Pier 66
(206) 282-6858
www.SeattlePropellerClub.org
In cooperation with the Port of Seattle, this free celebration of Seattle's maritime industry brings a cargo ship of free family fun to the waterfront. A highlight is the world's biggest tugboat race, with more than 40 tugboats and workboats participating. There is also a boat parade, chowder cook-off, boatbuilding competition, survival-suit races, harbor tours, and kids' activities.

SPIRIT OF WEST AFRICA

Seattle Center, Center House, 305
 Harrison St. (Central)
(206) 290-5560
www.thionediop.com

The Spirit of West Africa celebrates life through music, dance, art, and culture. This festival, produced by local Senegalese griot musician Thione Diop, showcases the sizzling talents of West African musicians, dancers, and artists in the Seattle area and from around the country. Watch while the traditions of six West African countries come to life through live music, dance performances, exhibits, film, art, games, and an African market. Take part in ritual and celebratory African drumming and dance, and witness the healing powers of musicians trained since birth to serve their communities. Free.

UNIVERSITY DISTRICT STREETFAIR

University Way NE (North)
(206) 547-4417
www.udistrictstreetfair.org

The U District StreetFair is the kickoff event for the festival season in the Seattle region, and the longest-running street festival in the nation! Self-described as "country fair meets urban retail corridor," the StreetFair attracts more than 50,000 people and over 300 craft and food booths to the district on the third weekend of May each year. You'll find a whirl of color and creativity. The StreetFair is an energetic and exciting celebration of arts and crafts, community information, music, and food. There are two main stages featuring music, dance performance, comedy, and more; a special children's area with age-appropriate events; a wonderful medley of street performers; and much more. The unique local and regional arts and crafts and an array of international food will delight you. Free.

JUNE

FESTIVAL SUNDIATA

Seattle Center, Fisher Pavilion, 305
 Harrison St. (Central)
(206) 329-8086
www.festivalsundiata.org

This special festival weekend is put on by the African American Cultural Association, and showcases dance workshops, hip-hop experiences, drill team exhibitions, gospel music, skateboarding exhibitions, and other entertainment. Also represented are the Pacific NW African American Quilters Association, Children's African Village–Crafts, Zulu Nation, and more. There is always plenty of entertainment and food vendors. Festival Sundiata is named in honor of Sundiata Keita, legendary *mansa* (king of kings) of the Mali Empire in West Africa, and celebrates the popular traditions of this national hero. Festival Sundiata celebrated its 30th year in 2010. Open Sat and Sun in mid-June from 11 a.m. to 8 p.m. Free admission.

14/48, THE WORLD'S QUICKEST THEATER FESTIVAL

ACT Theatre, 700 Union St. (Central)
(206) 292-7676
www.1448fest.com

The world's quickest theater festival is a creative process and an exercise in community, with an assemblage of artists dedicated to pushing the nature of theater to the breaking point. On the first night of the festival, around 80 artists gather and make introductions. Theme ideas are thrown around and tossed in a hat, and one is drawn. Writers receive the theme and number of actors that they will now write a 10-minute play for. The next morning, the finished plays are due, rehearsals begin, and that night is the world premiere of seven brand-new plays. This is done all over again the next day. It's madness, it's brilliant, and it's a hell of a lot of fun.

FREMONT FAIR
Fremont Avenue North and 36th, and surrounding streets (North)
(206) 632-1500
www.fremontfair.org

Founded in 1972, the Fremont Fair is one of Seattle's most beloved neighborhood street festivals, featuring a weekend of eclectic activities that celebrate the quirky community of Fremont, the self-proclaimed "center of the universe." Held annually in mid-June to coincide with the summer solstice, the event draws more than 100,000 people to shop, eat, drink, mingle, groove, and enjoy all manners of creative expression. Artistic highlights include craft and art booths, street performers, local bands, beer garden, wacky decorated art cars, the Solstice Parade (below), and many other oddities that personify Fremont's official motto, "Delibertus Quirkus"—Freedom to Be Peculiar. The Fremont Arts Abbey Kids' Area on 35th Street offers a full program of children's activities, and there is also the Big Purple Slide and face painters, ice cream, and other cool stuff for kids. The Fremont Fair is produced by the Fremont Chamber of Commerce, and funds raised benefit a number of area nonprofits including Solid Ground, which focuses on local poverty and originated and produced the fair for nearly 40 years. Activities primarily take place west of Fremont Avenue North on N. 35th Street and North 34th Street/Canal Street. Parking is very limited during the fair; it's suggested that you take the bus or bicycle (a short and easy ride from downtown). The fair is completely free, although you can purchase vendor items such as food, beer, and crafts.

FREMONT OUTDOOR MOVIES
3501 Phinney Ave. North (North)
(206) 352-8291
http://fremontoutdoormovies.com

What started out as a few Fremont residents getting together on summer nights to watch campy B movies outside has turned into a full-fledged weekly event. Every Sat night from June through Aug, a couple hundred people gather to watch cult classics such as *Raising Arizona, Thelma & Louise,* and *Pulp Fiction.* You can bring your leashed pets, food and beverages, and lawn chairs (or other seating—you'll see everything from bean bag chairs to couches). Feel free to dress in costume as well; many people do, either whatever random costumes they wish to wear, or something in keeping with the film being shown that night. There's also a fun photo booth, with a winning photograph announced in *Seattle* magazine. It's a fun and funky summer night in Fremont. Suggested donation of $5.

FREMONT SOLSTICE PARADE
Begins at Leary Way and N. 36th Street (North)
(206) 547-7440
http://fremontartscouncil.org/ ?page_id=79

Held in conjunction with and on the same day as the Fremont Fair, the free-spirited Solstice Parade is produced by the Fremont Arts Council to celebrate the arrival of the summer solstice. The Solstice Parade is family-friendly and there are always lots of kids, but be aware that the majority of the parade participants—marchers, dancers, bicyclists, and performers—are fully or partially nude, covered only with highly artistic body paint. The parade begins at noon, at the intersection of N. 36th Street and Leary Way, and winds through downtown Fremont, ending at Gasworks Park. Free.

IRANIAN FESTIVAL
Seattle Center, Center House, 305
  Harrison St. (Central)
(206) 652-4222
http://iaca-seattle.org/category/
  iranian-festival

The region's premier Iranian cultural event celebrates one of the most hospitable cultures in the world. The festival offers a melting pot of new experiences as it unites a multifaceted community—young and old from all walks of life. Music and dance performances, Rumi poetry, food and libations, puppet shows, and face painting provide a glimpse into this rich and diverse culture. Presented by the Iranian American Community Alliance. Free.

NW NEW WORKS FESTIVAL
100 W. Roy St. (Central)
(206) 217-9886
www.ontheboards.org/index.php?page=
  nwnw_detail&perfID=270

Produced by On the Boards performance center, the New Works Festival commissions, produces, and presents evening-length performances by the most innovative artists in the region. Over two weekends in two different theaters, several dance, music, and theater performances are offered.

PAGDIRIWANG PHILIPPINE FESTIVAL
Seattle Center, Center House, 305
  Harrison St. (Central)
(206) 527-8605
www.pagdiriwang.2x.nu/fchsw/index
  .html

Celebrate Philippine Independence at Pagdiriwang, the annual celebration of arts and culture of the Philippines at the Seattle Center. The festival commemorates the end of Spanish rule in 1898 with pageantry, music, dance, food, children's activities, drill teams, rock bands, art and photo exhibits, and martial arts. It also features contemporary Filipino literature, performance, and thought.

ROCK 'N' ROLL SEATTLE MARATHON & HALF MARATHON
Starting line—Tukwila's Gateway
  Corporate Center (South)
Finish line—Qwest Field (Central)
(800) 311-1255
http://seattle.competitor.com

The Rock 'n' Roll Series offers marathons and half marathons that meld the excitement of a rock concert into an endurance event. Each unique city on the tour hosts a world-class event infused with live music at every mile, scenic courses, screaming spectators, a headliner concert, and a great sense of accomplishment. Recognized throughout the running industry for its professionally organized events, the series continues to rock the socks off of participants at every skill level. The Seattle Rock 'n' Roll Marathon was first held in 2009, kicking off the Seafair season and solidifying its place as a signature summer event in the Pacific Northwest. Runners from all 50 states and 14 countries participated in the race, which highlighted some of the area's most scenic locations, including Lake Washington, awe-inspiring Mount Rainier and Seattle's downtown skyline. $25 entry fee, plus a fund-raising commitment for the American Cancer Society.

SEAFAIR, SEATTLE'S SUMMER CELEBRATION
Various locations around Seattle
(206) 728-0123
www.seafair.com

This is the biggest annual community celebration of Seattle and the Puget Sound area, held since the 1950s. The huge festival is over a month long, kicking off the last weekend in June and going through Aug. The celebration of summer features parades, art and music festivals, fun runs and marathons, triathlons, and amazing shows of skill including the U.S. Navy Blue Angels air show and the Seafair Unlimited Hydroplane Race. One of the most dramatic events is the Torchlight Parade, following a 2.5-mile route beginning at dusk, with bands, clowns, pirates, drill teams, giant helium balloons, dragon dances, equestrian units, and more—you may even see Elvis. Seafair also sponsors an academic scholarship program for women, ending with the winner's coronation at the Torchlight Parade. Most events are completely free and open to the public, although you can purchase premium-seating tickets for some of the shows and competitions. If you are in Seattle during this period of time, Seafair events are not to be missed.

SEATTLE PRIDEFEST
Various locations around Seattle
(877) PRIDE-82
http://seattlepridefest.org

This festival is one of Seattle's biggest parties—it's the Northwest's largest LGBT gathering, and the biggest free Pride festival in the country. Spanning several days, the grandest event of the festival is the Seattle Pride Parade, when the streets of downtown Seattle are packed as the parade moves along 4th Avenue for more than two hours (www.seattlepride.org/parade.php). After the parade, the party moves to Seattle Center, where tens of thousands of revelers come to dance, drink, eat, shop, and party. But it doesn't stop there—the official PrideFest after-party is called the Momo Pride Street Party ($5). Get on the free shuttle from the EMP turnabout and go directly to the gates of Momo, in front of Neumos. There you can dance and party to DJs and a headliner musical performer. The parade and PrideFest at Seattle Center are free; the Momo party and other events require tickets that range from $5 to $25. Don't miss PrideFeast, a one-day benefit where you eat at participating restaurants, and a portion of your bill is donated to local nonprofits who support LGBT health and wellness (www.pridefeast.org).

JULY

BALLARD SEAFOOD FEST
2208 NW Market St. (North)
(206) 784-9705
www.seafoodfest.org

Sponsored by the Ballard Chamber of Commerce, the Seafood Fest started in 1974 as a one-day community salmon barbecue and has evolved into a weekend-long event in July in the middle of historic Ballard. Two entertainment stages, a beer garden, vendors, a salmon barbecue, and, of course, food vendors each offering a unique seafood item attract people to celebrate this maritime tradition in Ballard. Free.

BASTILLE DAY
Seattle Center, Fisher Pavilion, 305
   Harrison St. (Central)
(206) 443-4703
www.seattle-bastille.org

Commemorate France's democratic beginnings at this annual celebration of French culture and presence in the Puget Sound area. The festival marks the French national holiday in memory of the liberation of the infamous Bastille prison and the start of the

French Revolution. This two-day festival kicks off with the Bal des Pompiers dinner and dance (21 and over), followed by a full day of French wine and pastries, cooking demonstrations, children's games, music, and more. The trade and economic section features booths representing French companies in the area. Entry to the event is free, although the restaurant booths do charge for food (most are under $5), and the Bal des Pompiers dinner and concert is $45–$65, with alcohol sold separately.

BEST OF MAGNUSON PARK

Warren G. Magnuson Park, 7400 Sand
   Point Way NE (North)
(206) 525-5926
www.nwartalliance.com/events/
   Best_of_Magnuson_Park

Held over a weekend in July, this Best of the Northwest arts and crafts show takes place in Magnuson Park. About 150 local and regional artists display their work in the park from 10 a.m. to 6 p.m.

BITE OF SEATTLE

Seattle Center, 305 Harrison St. (Central)
(425) 283-5050
www.biteofseattle.com

The premier food festival of the Northwest, Bite of Seattle showcases restaurant owners and their chefs. The region's culinary arts are in glorious display—and taste!—from more than 50 Seattle-area restaurants and 30-plus food product companies. Restaurant booths line the festival, offering plates and bites for small charges, while special exhibition areas include beer and wine gardens, cooking demonstrations, and The Alley hosted by Tom Douglas, celebrity chef of Seattle. The Alley features various dishes from Douglas's many area restaurants, with proceeds from

the $10 admission benefiting Food Lifeline, a local food distribution nonprofit. While you nosh, there is plenty to entertain you on six stages featuring all genres of music, from rock and funk to blues and R&B. Held in mid-July over a full weekend; admission is free, with small charges per plate and tasting.

CAPITOL HILL BLOCK PARTY

12th Avenue and E. Pike Street (Central)
(206) 388-1440
www.capitolhillblockparty.com

This Capitol Hill party is about independent music and culture, thought, and progressive politics. Over two days, on three stages, more than 50 bands—both Northwest and national independent bands—play live music. A number of craft booths, food vendors, and local nonprofits also set up in the area. The event raises money for the Vera Project and Home Alive. This great music event is also very affordable, for so many bands—$23 for a single-day ticket and $42 for a two-day pass (advance-sales prices). Children all ages are welcome at the Vera Stage and Mainstage, and under 10 are free with paying adult. The Neumos Stage is 21 and over.

CHINATOWN–INTERNATIONAL
   DISTRICT SUMMERFEST

Hing Hay Park, 423 Maynard Ave. South
   (Central)
(206) 382-1197
www.cidbia.org/events

Come enjoy lively lion and dragon dances, rhythmic taiko drumming, and award-winning drill teams. This annual two-day event includes kids' and family activities, cultural dances, musical performance, karaoke contest, and more than 100 booths featuring arts and crafts, local business, community organizations, and much more. Don't miss out on the largest pan-Asian street festival in the Pacific Northwest, with some of the best arts, entertainment, and food. Always held on the second weekend of July, Sat 11 a.m.–7 p.m. and Sun 11 a.m.–6 p.m. Free.

FAMILY 4TH AT LAKE UNION
Gasworks Park, 2101 N. Northlake Way
(North)
(206) 281-7788
http://family4th.org
This annual Independence Day celebration almost died, and the story of its saving is a true Seattle grassroots saga. Without a corporate sponsor after the 2009 event, the nonprofit production company One Reel announced that the 2010 celebration would be canceled. Local radio host Dave Ross announced the predicament, and within 24 hours individual citizens and local businesses had pledged to contribute the entire cost of the iconic 4th of July event. Crowds gather on the grassy hill of Gasworks Park and in boats on the waters of Lake Union to watch one of the most spectacular fireworks displays to celebrate the country's independence. Free.

LAKE UNION WOODEN BOAT FESTIVAL
1010 Valley St. (Central)
(206) 382-2628
www.cwb.org
Held over the Fourth of July weekend, the Center for Wooden Boats on Lake Union puts on this festival with the theme of heritage wooden boats. The ambience is that of an old-fashioned, down-home waterfront festival where everything is fun, almost everything is free, and nothing much is fancy. It's as authentically grassroots American as you can get and has been for the past 33 years.

Events include visiting vessels from all over the world on exhibit; public rides on Lake Union by sail, row, paddle, steam, or electric boats; demonstrations in tools, ropes, and navigation; live music; and activities for kids that include toy boatbuilding, chalk art, coloring contests, and a treasure hunt. A really fun aspect is the regatta, where teams build boats in 24 hours and then launch and race them on Sun.

SEATTLE CHAMBER MUSIC SOCIETY SUMMER FESTIVAL
Benaroya Hall, 200 University St.
(Central)
(206) 283-8808
www.seattlechambermusic.org
The Seattle Chamber Music Society has presented its Summer Festival for more than 25 years. The festival consists of 12 concerts: each Mon, Wed, and Fri at 8 p.m. throughout July. Emerging artists and family concert tickets are $10–$12; single-ticket prices for other concerts are $38–$44 (with special $10 tickets for those 25 and under). Series packages range from $120 to $480 depending on how many concerts are included.

SEATTLE INTERNATIONAL BEERFEST
Seattle Center, Mural Amphitheatre, 305 Harrison St. (Central)
www.seattlebeerfest.com
Billed as the "ultimate world beer experience," this three-day festival is a must for anyone who loves a good brew. BeerFest celebrates the world's most legendary brewing styles and the nations that made them famous. Come taste over 150 world-class beers from more than 15 countries, including some very rare, obscure brews. There's also a cigar bar, live music, and areas for free darts, chess, checkers, and backgammon.

Beer drinkers pay $20 for 10 beer tickets and official SIB glass. Additional tickets are just $1 each; each serving is four ounces. There is a $5 entry charge for anyone not drinking beer. 21 and over only.

SEATTLE OUTDOOR
THEATER FESTIVAL
Volunteer Park, 1247 15th Ave. East
  (Central)
(206) 748-1551
www.greenstage.org/sotf
Two days in July brings 14 live theater performances in Capitol Hill's beautiful Volunteer Park. This completely free festival includes performances from the Seattle Shakespeare Company, Theater Shmeater, Open Circle Theater, Last Leaf Productions, GreenStage, and more. There is a generous sprinkling of the Bard, as well as several other classic and contemporary plays. Bring your blankets and lawn chairs for this popular family-friendly event. GreenStage also puts on two Shakespeare in the Park productions every July through Aug; check the Web site for details.

SEATTLE SHAKESPEARE COMPANY IN
THE PARKS
Various parks around Seattle
(206) 733-8228
www.seattleshakespeare.org/woodeno
The Seattle Shakespeare Company presents two Shakespeare productions every July through Aug, performed at various parks throughout the region. It's a great opportunity to take a blanket and food, as well as your family and pets, and enjoy the outdoor theater. These "Wooden O" productions appeal to a wide range of people because of the innovative approach that also remains true to the classic, poetic nature of the text. Audiences at the summer shows can picnic

with their friends and family while enjoying some of the greatest drama history offers in a way that is exciting, immediate, and relevant. These performances are free to the public, but donations are always welcome.

THREE DOLLAR BILL
OUTDOOR CINEMA
Cal Anderson Park, 1635 11th Ave.
  (Central)
(206) 323-4274
http://threedollarbillcinema.org/
  programs/outdoor-cinema
Enjoy this campy outdoor film series that presents fun and free movies under the stars every summer. From foot-stomping favorites like *Hairspray* to thrills and chills with *Creature from the Black Lagoon* in 3-D, the fun silver-screen selections make for hot summer nights that everyone can enjoy. Free.

UMOJAFEST
Judkins Park, 2150 S. Norman St.
  (Central)
(877) 505-6306
www.umojafamilyfest.com
This African Heritage Festival and Parade spans three days in late July/early Aug, with many celebrations and activities that not only entertain, but also educate and empower the community. *Umoja* is a Swahili word meaning unity, which is the theme of Umojafest. The festival is the premier outreach program of the African American Heritage Museum & Cultural Center, as part of its "Museum Without Walls" program. The tradition of the festival spans more than five decades and includes varied musical entertainment (reggae, jazz, soul, hip-hop), children's group performances, dance, drumming, oration, national recording artists, Bite of Africa food booths, and much more. Other

activities include basketball and soccer tournaments, gospel music, fashion expo, green/sustainability expo, spoken word, and poetry, as well as voter registration booths and a host of community organizations. Free.

URBAN CRAFT UPRISING SUMMER SHOW
Seattle Center, Exhibition Hall, 305 Harrison St. (Central)
www.urbancraftuprising.com

Urban Craft Uprising was started in 2004 to showcase the work of independent crafters, artists, and designers, providing a unique, high-quality, handcrafted alternative to "big box" stores and mass-produced goods. At UCU shows, fans can choose from a wide variety of goods including clothing of all types, jewelry, gifts, bags, wallets, buttons, accessories, aprons, children's goods, toys, housewares, paper goods, candles, journals, art, food, and much, much more. UCU aims to build a local (and beyond) community of artists, crafters, and designers and to promote other community-building including showcases, classes, events, and other local activities. Since its early beginnings at its first winter holiday show with just 50 craft booths and overflow crowds, Urban Craft Uprising now holds the largest indie craft event in the Pacific Northwest. In 2009 UCU held its first summer show.

WEST SEATTLE SUMMER FEST
California Avenue SW and SW Edmunds (South)
(206) 297-6801
www.westseattlefestival.com

West Seattle Summer Fest is a free three-day street fair, hosted by an organization of local area merchants. Now in its 28th year, West Seattle Summer Fest is host to dozens of bands, hundreds of merchants and artists, and more than 30,000 attendees. Complete with a food court, beer gardens, and family activities, this is a true community celebration in the heart of West Seattle. Stores open up their doors and spill out onto the sidewalks to display all the wonderful products and services they offer year-round, while artists and artisans display in the streets. Junction restaurants and a delectable selection of cross-cultural food vendors satisfy your hunger along the way. Live music on two stages, a skateboard exhibition, and a large, kid-friendly family activity area make each day special. And don't forget the annual Saturday night street dance (now on two stages!) and, of course, West Seattle's own Sunday farmers' market.

AUGUST

BRASILFEST
Seattle Center, Fisher Pavilion and Mural Amphitheatre, 305 Harrison St. (Central)
(206) 684-7200
www.brasilfest.com

This festival fills Seattle Center with a sultry display of South American soul and Brazilian style, and celebrates Brazilian cultural diversity through traditional and contemporary expressions beyond bossa nova and samba. This one-day extravaganza will offer continuous music, dance, workshops, and performance that represent a broad repertoire of traditional and contemporary Brazilian expressions as well as traditional folkloric performers. Experience all this exuberant and vivid culture has to offer, from capoeira (Brazilian martial arts) demonstrations and workshops for all ages, s1amba workshops, children's activities (mask-making, painting), Brazilian instruments, arts and crafts, photo exhibits, and films. BrasilFest is the first annual celebration of Brazilian culture in Washington state, drawing a significant audience. Free.

CAMBODIAN CULTURAL HERITAGE CELEBRATION

Seattle Center, Center House, 305 Harrison St. (Central)
(206) 760-0539
http://seattlecenter.com/events/festivals/festal/detail.asp?EV_EventNum=5

Experience Cambodia's beautiful culture with traditional and classical dance and music, handmade crafts, games, and storytelling. Explore and learn about the customs and heritage of Cambodia at this free and open event.

CONCERTS AT THE MURAL

Seattle Center, Mural Amphitheatre, 305 Harrison St. (Central)
(206) 684-7200
http://seattlecenter.com/programs/detail.asp?EV_EventNum=52

KEXP 90.3FM and Seattle Center have teamed up to present Concerts at the Mural, a series of eclectic concerts on some of the summer's sultriest weekends in Aug. Take advantage of the warm summer nights and take in the tunes from some of KEXP's favorite artists. The five free all-ages shows are tailored to the culturally curious who seek to discover the best of the area's independent music scene. Come early to get your seats, listen to KEXP DJs, and enjoy the beer/wine garden. The concerts are free, and at one or more of them KEXP sponsors a barbecue dinner, which is also free.

MOVIES AT THE MURAL

Seattle Center, Mural Amphitheatre, 305 Harrison St. (Central)
(206) 684-7200
http://seattlecenter.com/programs/detail.asp?EV_EventNum=41

Experience free movies by moonlight at Seattle Center. Picnic on the gently sloping Mural Amphitheatre lawn, in front of a state-of-the-art giant screen, with the Space Needle standing sentry in the starry skies above you. Movies at the Mural is an outdoor cinema experience like no other! Lineup is usually announced in late spring.

TIBET FEST

Seattle Center, Fisher Pavilion, 305 Harrison St. (Central)
(206) 542-3774
www.washingtontibet.org

Tibet's ancient and modern history is woven through Tibet Fest through a synthesis of traditional performance with modern song and music and discussions of the Tibetan people. Symbolic masks, arts and crafts, children's activities, and traditional foods, along with prayer flags and expert speakers, illuminate the culture's foundation in Buddhism. Presented by the Tibetan Association. Free.

SEPTEMBER

BUMBERSHOOT

Seattle Center, 305 Harrison St. (Central)
(206) 816-6444
http://bumbershoot.org

This is the music festival. Now in its 40th year, Bumbershoot is a must-go for any serious music aficionado, drawing more than 150,000 visitors each year. Held over Labor Day weekend, it is North America's largest urban arts festival, featuring not only incredible music performances but also film, comedy, spoken word, dance, theater, and visual arts. Seven stages each have their own distinct personality, showcasing a lineup of cutting-edge and legendary musical talent in rock, pop, hip-hop, jazz, funk, global, indie, and more. Regional favorites and international superstars have performed at Bumbershoot, including Modest Mouse,

Franz Ferdinand, The Yeah Yeah Yeahs, Sheryl Crow, and the Black Eyed Peas. The street boundaries for the large festival are between Mercer Street and Denny Way, and 1st and 5th Avenues. Single-day tickets, full festival passes, and platinum/gold packages are all available, ranging from $22 to $250.

DECIBEL FESTIVAL
Various venues
(206) 905-1026
www.dbfestival.com
This music festival is all about electronic music, digital art, and new media. The four-day event bridges the gap between technology and creativity through visual art, workshops, panel discussions and cutting-edge electronic music performances. By assembling a diverse selection of international talent, Decibel Festival provides a forum for musicians, industry professionals, and educators alike. The core of the festival comprises several concerts and live performances in a variety of locations throughout Seattle's hip Capitol Hill neighborhood. In addition to these performance programs, Decibel includes a professional section featuring panels and workshops. Since its inception, Decibel has hosted over 400 acts ranging from underground dance and experimental electronic music to transmedial art. The festival is a nonprofit organization, with proceeds benefiting the Shunpike Partner Artist program. A pass for the entire festival is around $100; no one under 16 years old is admitted.

FREMONT OKTOBERFEST
Phinney Avenue and N. 35th Street (North)
(206) 633-0422
www.fremontoktoberfest.com

What would an Oktoberfest be without a gala festival street fair, full of amazing craftsmen, colorful world imports, and irresistible flea market treasures from across the land? (Probably just another frat party!) Almost 200 years after the start of the event in Germany, Fremont carries on the tradition with a colorful microbrew festival that is Seattle's only weekend Oktoberfest. The event spans a Fri, Sat, and Sun in late Sept and features more than 25 microbreweries, nonstop music from local bands, a street fair, traditional German food, a variety of acts, and zany contests in keeping with the offbeat Fremont tradition. So bring the tiny youngsters to the kids' area and enjoy the fun, great music, and gobs of food. Oh, and by the way, enjoy sampling some of the best beer in Washington at the Microbrew Garden. Tickets are $20–$25 in advance (including 6–10 tasting tokens and souvenir mug), or $25–$30 on the day of the event. Special $15 tickets for non-drinking attendees are available, including four water tickets.

ITALIAN FESTIVAL
Seattle Center, Fisher Pavilion, 305 Harrison St. (Central)
(206) 282-0627
www.festaseattle.com
The Italian Festival, inaugurated in 1988, celebrates the joy of "all things Italian"—from opera and popular music to pasta and wine. Festa Italiana is a series of events held in late Sept that culminates in a major Italian Festival at Seattle Center. The festival celebrates the cultural roots of Italians and Italian Americans by presenting and promoting the arts, the food, and the spirit that are uniquely Italian. Food vendors, cooking demonstrations, crafts, Sicilian puppet theater, an all-ages concert, Italian films, a grape-stomping

contest, and a bocce ball tournament honor the "old country" and recognize the remarkable contemporary contributions of this dynamic and artful culture. Presented by Festa Italiana. Free.

KOREAN CULTURAL CELEBRATION
Seattle Center, Center House, 305
   Harrison St. (Central)
(206) 354-0853
www.koamartists.org/KCF.htm
Korea's traditional Harvest Festival Day offers festivalgoers insight into this country's cultural evolution and contemporary culture through folk songs, dance, tae kwon do demonstrations, traditional harvest foods, films, and exhibits. On this day, tradition holds that a feast is prepared and families hold memorial services at the family gravesite. Viewing the full moon is a feature of the evening. Presented by the Korean-American Art & Cultural Association of the Pacific Northwest. Free.

LIVE ALOHA HAWAIIAN CULTURAL FESTIVAL
Seattle Center, Mural Amphitheatre, 305
   Harrison St. (Central)
(206) 851-4411
www.seattlelivealohafestival.com
The Live Aloha Hawaiian Cultural Festival serves to promote, perpetuate, and share the Hawaiian culture in the Pacific Northwest by enriching and strengthening the Hawaiian community and celebrating Hawaii's arts and culture. The festival provides a feast for the senses as visitors journey through Hawaii's sights, sounds, and tastes with workshops, crafts, *keiki* floral activities, exhibits, and *ono* food. Join many of the more than 50,000 Hawaiian Islanders who call Washington their home as they share their

homeland's colorful history through live performances of the hula and *mele*. Free.

SEATTLE FIESTAS PATRIAS
Seattle Center, Fisher Pavilion, 305
   Harrison St. (Central)
(206) 764-8051
www.seattlefiestaspatrias.com
This celebration of the independence from colonial rule of countries in Central and South America recognizes the diversity of the Latino culture in western Washington. Join Seattle Fiestas Patrias, "Patriotic Holidays," for this festive holiday filled with Hispanic foods, dance, mariachi music, exhibition of ethnic garments and crafts, and children's activities—all in celebration of the unique Latin American cultures and their shared language. On Sat night, there is a big dance with live music and DJ. Free.

OCTOBER

CROATIAFEST
Seattle Center, Center House, 305
   Harrison St. (Central)
(206) 443-1410
www.croatiafest.org
CroatiaFest celebrates the vitality and distinctiveness of the Croatia homeland and provides a glimpse inside one of the last undiscovered treasures of Europe. Acclaimed dance ensembles and musicians, visiting artists, intricate costumes, art exhibits, foods, tourist information, and historical displays showcase Croatia's rich past and exciting possibilities. Free.

DIA DE MUERTOS
Seattle Center, Center House, 305
   Harrison St. (Central)
(206) 356-6673
www.tallermexicano.org

Dia de Muertos, or "Day of the Dead," is the traditional day in Mexican culture for remembering the departed, to remember history. Dia de Muertos joins together tradition, culture, and art to keep alive the very deepest of indigenous and Spanish roots that intertwine in traditional community altars, sugar skulls, sand painting, special foods, candles, processions, music, and dance. Numerous altars and *ofrendas* are available, as well as lectures and short films. There are craft demonstrations, and numerous activities for both children and adults. The highlight of the remembrance portion of Dia de Muertos is the procession, with music and candles, from Center House to the International Fountain. At the fountain, participants say out loud the names of their loved ones being honored. Free.

EARSHOT JAZZ FESTIVAL
Various locations
(206) 547-6763
www.earshot.org/Festival/festival.html
For more than 20 years, the Earshot Jazz Festival has presented the full spectrum of jazz—from high-profile concerts in Seattle's fine halls, to cutting-edge creations that move the art form ever forward. The event is respected for honoring the deep heritage of jazz while celebrating the genre's leading edges. Hundreds of the most important artists of our day play in more than 60 events in venues all around Seattle. In addition to concert performances, the festival includes educational programs and panels, a film series, poetry and author readings, and art exhibits. Held from mid-Oct through early Nov. Tickets for individual performances range from $10–40, with a couple of free concerts thrown into the schedule. Jazz Festival Gold Card passes can also be purchased for $350 ($300 for members).

LIVE THEATRE WEEK
Various venues
(206) 770-0370
http://seattleperforms.com/ltw
Live Theatre Week is an open invitation to the public, exposing new audiences to new theaters. It's your all-access pass to Seattle's performing arts during the third week of Oct. Connect with local theaters at more than 30 complimentary special events and 50 free performances. The festival also includes Free Night of Theater, to encourage anyone who does not go to the theater to give it a try, while asking current theatergoers to experience a theater they've never been to before. Check the schedule and reserve your free tickets on the Web site; they cannot be booked by telephone or directly with the theaters. The week also includes many special events—community-driven, informal events hosted by specific theater companies. They can be anything including open rehearsals, tours, receptions, workshops, parties, or play readings. Live Theatre Week Special Events are free, open to the public, and, unlike Free Night of Theater events, do not require reservations.

SEATTLE LESBIAN AND GAY FILM FESTIVAL
Various venues
(206) 323-4274
http://threedollarbillcinema.org/programs/SLGFF
One of the most respected and well-attended alternative film festivals in the country, this weeklong event in late Oct features full-length and short films by and about the LGBT community. Since 1996 the festival has gained industry and audience recognition for showcasing the latest and greatest in queer film, from major motion

picture premieres to emerging talent. An important venue in the Seattle film scene—and the social event of the season—the festival provides unique opportunities for visiting and local filmmakers to engage and entertain more than 10,000 attendees. Both American and international films are shown at various theaters, including the Egyptian and Little Theater. Average ticket price is $10, but $15–$30 passes and gala screenings are also available.

SOUTH ASIAN PERFORMING ARTS FESTIVAL
Various locations
www.ragamala.org/utsav.htm
This feast of music and dance from India is presented by Ragamala, an organization for the advancement of traditional performing arts of South Asia. South Indian classical vocal concerts, Bharatanatyam dances, Hindustani flutes, violinists, percussion performances, and many talented Seattle community performers are featured. There are also *tabla* percussion workshops and other demonstrations. Most activities are at Seattle Center, although several performances are usually held at the Brechemin Auditorium on the UW campus or other locations. All performances are free; check the Web site for the current year's schedule and locations.

TURKFEST
Seattle Center, Center House, 305
   Harrison St. (Central)
www.turkfest.org
TurkFest celebrates the multiple cultures that link modern Turkey to the East and West. This educationally enriching, entertaining, and engaging festival of friendship showcases Turkish culture and heritage. The festival takes place in Oct every year to commemorate the founding of the Republic of Turkey on October 29, 1923. Each year TurkFest invites dancers, musicians, and artists from around the country to share their artistic forms of expression with local audiences. Free.

NOVEMBER

BEST OF THE NORTHWEST
Seattle Center, Exhibition Hall, 305
   Harrison St. (Central)
(206) 525-5926
http://nwartalliance.com/events/
   Best_of_the_Northwest
More than 200 Northwest artists display their handcrafted goods at this holiday art and fine craft show each Nov. Tickets are $7.

HMONG NEW YEAR CELEBRATION
Seattle Center, Center House, 305
   Harrison St. (Central)
(425) 241-2085
www.hmongassociationofwa.org
The Lunar New Year is a time to welcome the prosperity of the coming year and the passing of the previous year. The Hmong New Year Celebration helps preserve the unique culture of this Southeast Asian highland culture that originates in the mountains of China, Laos, and Thailand. Dance, traditional music, historical exhibits, and the customary courtship ritual of ball-tossing demonstrate this culture's compelling legacy. Presented by the Hmong Association of Washington. Free.

SEATTLE MARATHON & HALF MARATHON
Seattle Center, 305 Harrison St. (Central)
(206) 729-3660
www.seattlemarathon.org

Run the first Sun after Thanksgiving, this annual marathon also includes a half marathon, 5K, and kids' run. One of the top 15 races in the country, the marathon starts at 5th Avenue and Mercer, winding through downtown and ending up at Memorial Stadium for the exciting finish. More than 10,000 people run in the Seattle Marathon each year. Registration is from $25 to $70.

TREE LIGHTING CEREMONY & HOLIDAY PARADE

Westlake Center, 1601 5th Ave. (Central)
(206) 467-1600
www1.macys.com/store/event/index
.ognc?action=search&storeId=411

This full-day holiday tradition is held every year in downtown Seattle the day after Thanksgiving, beginning at 8:45 a.m. with the parade, marching down Pine and University Streets before heading north to Macy's, where the official tree-lighting ceremony takes place at 5 p.m. A spectacular fireworks display ends the evening dramatically.

WINTERFEST AT SEATTLE CENTER

305 Harrison St. (Central)
(206) 684-7200
www.seattlecenter.com/winterfest

From the day after Thanksgiving through the entire month of Dec, Seattle Center is aglow and abuzz with winter holiday festivities. Incorporating many different traditions, this celebration offers fun including an ice rink, winter train and village, ice sculpting, and lots of live music. Many Seattle Center venues get into the holiday spirit, from the Festival of Light at the Pacific Science Center to performances such as *The Nutcracker* ballet and *A Christmas Carol*. Most activities are free; admission charges apply for ice-skating and theater/dance performances.

DECEMBER

ARGOSY CRUISES CHRISTMAS SHIP FESTIVAL

Pier 56, 1201 Alaskan Way (Central)
(206) 622-8687
www.argosycruises.com/themecruises/
xmasSchedule.cfm

This is the largest holiday floating parade in the world. The Argosy Christmas Ship festival is a holiday celebration that has been a Northwest tradition for 60 years. From the flotilla of Argosy ships to the crowds of people who gather on shore, this celebration is one of the gems of the holiday season. Each Dec night through the 23rd, the Argosy Christmas Ship sails to different Puget Sound waterfront communities, more than 45 total. Choirs onboard sing 20-minute performances to these communities, all broadcast via a state-of-the-art speaker system. On shore, thousands of people gather around roaring bonfires anticipating the arrival of the ship. You can join on board the Argosy lead ship, *Spirit of Seattle,* and have dinner there, take one of the parade ships that follow, use your own boat, or join with friends and neighbors to gather together on land to watch the parade. In addition to good cheer, family, and friends, a portion of all ticket sales benefits the *Seattle Times* Fund for the Needy, an annual program that raises money for several charitable organizations in the Puget Sound area. Christmas Ship tickets are $35 for adults, $19 for kids 5–12, and free for kids 4 and under. Dinner rates are $59 for adults and $10 for children ages 5–12.

COMMUNITY HANUKKAH CELEBRATION

Stroum Jewish Community Center, 3801 Mercer Way
(206) 526-8073
www.sjcc.org

Come celebrate the Festival of Lights during one of the largest community Hanukkah celebrations in Seattle. Everyone is invited to join in the fun, which includes arts and crafts and a workshop to make your own holiday decorations. Festive food and music add to the cheer. More than 1,250 people participate in the SJCC's Purim Carnival and Hanukkah Celebration each year.

NEW YEAR'S EVE AT THE SPACE NEEDLE
400 Broad St. (Central)
(206) 905-2100
www.spaceneedle.com

The famous Space Needle displays the world's tallest structure-launched fireworks show every New Year's Eve, with more than 2,000 pyrotechnic effects. The base of the Space Needle hosts the West Coast version of New York's Times Square as more than 50,000 people gather below to watch the fireworks shoot across the midnight sky, with an estimated 400,000 viewing the show from surrounding neighborhoods. Numerous parties around the city boast views of the Space Needle fireworks. Free display.

URBAN CRAFT UPRISING WINTER SHOW
Seattle Center, Exhibition Hall, 305 Harrison St. (Central)
www.urbancraftuprising.com

Urban Craft Uprising was started in 2004 to showcase the work of independent crafters, artists, and designers to provide a unique, high-quality alternative to "big box" stores and mass-produced goods. At UCU shows, fans can choose from a wide variety of handcrafted goods including clothing of all types, jewelry, gifts, bags, wallets, buttons, accessories, aprons, children's goods, toys, housewares, paper goods, candles, journals, art, food, and much, much more. UCU aims to build a local (and beyond) community of artists, crafters, and designers and to promote other community-building, including showcases, classes, events, and other local activities. Since its early beginnings at its first holiday show with just 50 craft booths and overflow crowds, UCU now holds the largest indie craft event in Seattle and the Pacific Northwest with its annual winter show. In 2008 the winter show saw more than 8,000 attendees and over 130 crafters, artists, and designers from around the world.

THE PACIFIC NORTHWEST

Puget Sound and the entire Pacific Northwest remain largely influenced by the man from whom Seattle received its name. Duwamish Chief Sealth delivered a speech in 1855 to an audience of white settlers and area tribe members, as territorial governor Isaac Stevens was negotiating the purchase of Puget Sound from its original inhabitants. Chief Sealth's address, considered one of the most important in Native American history, delivered in part the following message:

"The earth does not belong to human beings; human beings belong to the earth. This we know. All things are connected like the blood that unites one family. Whatever befalls the earth befalls the sons and daughters of the earth. How can you buy or sell the sky, the warmth of the land? If we do not own the freshness of the air and the sparkle of the water, how can you buy them? Every part of this earth is sacred to my people. Every shining pine needle, every sandy shore, every mist in the dark woods, every clearing and humming insect is holy in the memory and experience of my people."

The peaceful Duwamish led by Chief Sealth cooperated with the newcomers to help them build their settlement and exist in their new environment, but sadly relations eventually broke down as the growing white population forced the Duwamish and other area tribes out of their own lands. Although the ensuing history was full of violence and the decimation of Native American communities, something of Chief Sealth's wisdom seems to have been internalized and handed down through the generations, for the modern people of Puget Sound embrace the beliefs expressed in his speech as an abiding philosophy.

It may have taken a long time and come at great expense, but the Pacific Northwest today is one of the most environmentally conscious areas of the country, perhaps the world, with a strong feeling of this sacredness for the land and a reverence for nature and its preservation. For a city founded on industries exploitative of natural resources, such as lumber and fishing, this turnabout is quite remarkable.

Before we get into Seattle-specific parks and recreation in the next chapter, let's take a look at some of the magnificent natural resources in the greater Pacific Northwest region. One of the things Seattleites love best about their habitat is that within an hour or so you can be in complete wilderness, where it is possible to hike or camp for days without encountering another person.

IN THE MOUNTAINS

You can't miss them. They rise majestically from the surrounding landscape and loom above Puget Sound. The largest and most visible of these from Seattle is **Mount Rainier,** to the south of the city. At 14,410 feet it is the highest peak in the Cascade Mountain Range, formed eons ago from a combination of shifting tectonic plates, dramatic volcanic eruptions, and massive Ice Age glacial movement and flooding. Thirty-five square miles of glaciers still shroud the dormant volcano, remnants of the Cordilleran ice sheet—the largest freshwater discharge known on Earth—that carved a fantastic landscape of deep, steep-walled coulees to create a spectacular alpine scenery completely unique to the planet. It is a landscape forged by fire and ice, destruction and renewal—here long before us and very possibly to outlast us.

Other nearby mountains include Adams, Baker, Jefferson, Washington, Hood, and St. Helens, famous for its 1980 eruption that shed two-thirds of a cubic mile from its peak in the largest landslide in recorded history. The eruption of **Mount St. Helens** leveled forests 18 miles away and forcibly relocated Spirit Lake, a high alpine lake, with no surviving life. Despite three decades of regeneration, it remains a stunning spectacle of a volcano's raw power; a log mat still drifts on the lake's surface today, bearing witness to the lasting effects of the blast. St. Helens continues to be a work in progress; the wildflower-studded landscape of today is already well on its way to becoming the lush forests and meadows of tomorrow.

The region boasts some of the most diverse ecosystems within the United States, from the high, glaciated slopes of Mount Rainier National Park down to the lush, forested valleys of Diamond Peak wilderness.

Old-growth groves of giant western red cedars and Douglas firs provide food and shelter for abundant wildlife and sustain the mountain ecosystem. The uniqueness of the Central Cascades landscape is that it is constantly changing, from the geography to the vegetation; no two areas are the same. While Mount Washington and Three Sisters wilderness are separated by only 20 miles, they feel like completely different worlds.

Naturalist and author Russ Mohney calls the Pacific Northwest a "moveable season"— as you climb the mountains foot by foot, you can pass through the equivalent of every season in a matter of hours. The ranges offer limitless mountaineering possibilities to both beginning and experienced climbers, and have presented an irresistible lure for adventure junkies from around the world.

Washington Mountain Highlights

Mount Rainier National Park (see more details on p. 258 in the Day Trips section). Begin at either the Sunrise Lodge or the Henry M. Jackson Visitor Center for an overview of the park—or Rainier Base Camp, if you want to climb the massive peak known to climbing enthusiasts simply as "The Mountain." Keep in mind that only 65 percent of those who attempt to summit each year succeed, and Rainier claims the life of two or three climbers each year—yet its allure has been calling them for decades. The naturalist John Muir apparently couldn't help himself when he encountered the giant. In 1888 he wrote, "I did not mean to climb it, but got excited and soon was on top."

Permits are required to climb Rainier or camp overnight, but many day hiking trails are available. Constantly changing weather patterns heavily affect the park and Mount Rainier's accessibility, and during the winter roads and vehicle access can be blocked for weeks. Always check the status of roads and park accessibility before visiting.

North Cascades National Park lies in the northernmost region of the Cascade Mountains amid wild, virtually impenetrable mountains full of glaciers and sheer cliff walls. These far northern Cascades peaks are so formidable that they inspired such names as Mount Terror, Mount Despair, and Desolation Peak. Popular with hikers, backpackers, and rock climbers, the park receives half a million visitors per year.

Mount St. Helens National Volcanic Monument Park (see more details on p. 260 in the Day Trips section). Begin at the Johnston Ridge Observatory, or the Forest Learning Center, where you can walk through a life-size replica of the pre-1980 forest and watch actual eruption footage in a re-created blast zone. At Coldwater Lake there is an interpretive trail that gives a close-up look at the impact of the 1980 eruption. You can climb to the rim of the 8,366-foot crater, take a helicopter tour above the volcano, and walk through a nearly 2.5-mile lava tube at Ape Cave, to the south of St. Helens.

Mount Baker is the most isolated of the Cascade volcanoes, in a region that is largely nonvolcanic in origin. Although the upper reaches of the mountain are heavily mantled with snow and ice, the area around it is largely ice-free. The best view of Mount Baker is from Glacier Creek Road off Highway 542, where a 10-kilometer hike offers closer views.

Mount Adams is considered the "forgotten giant," as the least-visited mountain in the Cascades range. Wildlife and solitude are abundant, and the ice caves and volcanic bridges near Trout Lake are fascinating. Climbing permits can be obtained at the ranger station, and the steep 1.4-mile climb to the "Sleeping Beauty" peak is rewarded with expansive vistas. Alpine lake fishing, whitewater rafting on the White Salmon River, and five spectacular waterfalls at the Lewis River Falls are also nearby.

ON THE WATER

With the grand mountains as a backdrop, it's often the size and majesty of the snow-capped peaks that demand attention—but if you pay attention to the smaller things that deserve to be seen, you'll find hidden gems that are as big as the mountains. While massive glaciers and volcanic eruptions created dramatic, overnight change in the Pacific Northwest, water has been the master architect, carving the landscape with an intricate finesse. Get down close to the ground and observe the wildlife, look up in the trees, turn over the rocks in a creek, and you'll discover an opportunity to see wildlife big and small.

The mountain peaks block Pacific Ocean storms and hold in the clouds, creating a large temperate rain forest that covers the valleys and feeds rivers full of salmon that date to the last Ice Age. The Columbia River, which acts as the border between Washington and Oregon, is the only river to have ever smashed through the Cascade Mountains, draining an area nearly the size of France and emptying more water into the Pacific than any other in the Western Hemisphere.

Washington State Water Highlights

Ross Lake National Recreation Area is the most accessible part of the North Cascades National Park and includes three reservoirs: Ross Lake, Diablo Lake, and Gorge Lake, as well as the Skagit River. Ringed by mountains, the recreation area offers breathtaking

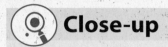

Close-up

Mountaineers of the Northwest

Ashford, Washington, native **Jim Whittaker**, who became the first American to summit Mount Everest in 1963, started out as a guide on Mount Rainier and is eloquent about the appeal of mountaineering. "It is in the wild places—in the damp, clean air of an ancient forest, on a snowy summit at the top of the world—that I enter my own personal cathedral and know where I fit in the vastness of creation," says Whittaker. "The Cascade Mountains have been compared to the Swiss Alps; however, the Cascades are higher, more glaciated, and cover a larger area than the much admired Alps. Both areas are beautiful examples of the natural world and deserve to be kept as natural as possible so that future generations can enjoy wildlife and wilderness and the silence of the upper air."

Whittaker's respect and love for the Pacific Northwest are shared by many, including his twin brother, Lou, and nephew Peter, both of whom are also climbers. Many of the top names in American mountaineering hail from the region, which provides a complex geology, rugged approaches, Himalayan characteristics, and, with Mount Rainier, the toughest endurance climb in the lower 48 states. Jim Whittaker's 1963 Everest team trained on Rainier, attempting and failing a summit bid three separate times; yet they went on to ultimately stand on top of the highest mountain in the world.

Peter Whittaker inherited a love for the sport in his blood, it seems. "I grew up with an uncle and a father who were larger than life—they were living legends," he explains. "I wasn't asked *if* I was going to climb mountains. My father pretty much just tied a rope around me and hauled me up." The younger Whittaker also points out that the Pacific Northwest is a great place for beginners to learn mountaineering. He estimates that 60 percent to 70 percent of clients of RMI, the guiding company started by his father Lou, are first-timers. "I love taking people into our mountains for the first time, and showing them that world."

alpine scenery and plentiful wildlife habitats including those of black and grizzly bears, timber wolves, eagles, black-tailed deer, beaver, and otters. It is a play land for outdoor enthusiasts, with recreation opportunities such as boating, fishing, and hiking. Happy Creek Forest Walk is a short trail through old-growth forest. Rainy Pass, near the crest of the Cascades, offers rest stop and picnic facilities and a 1-mile, barrier-free trail to Lake Ann.

Lake Chelan National Recreation Area surrounds the third-deepest lake in the United States, the fjord-like Lake Chelan. Located in the Stehekin Valley, Lake Chelan is a glacially carved trough that reaches a depth of 1,500 feet. Boating, fishing, and lakeshore camping are popular activities here, and it's also a splendid place to simply soak in the incredible natural beauty, commune with nature, and snap some amazing photographs. Try the 2.5-mile Coon Lake Trail, 5-mile Agnes Gorge Trail, or 6-mile Rainbow Loop Trail. Don't miss Rainbow Falls, at 312 feet high easily the most impressive waterfalls in the state, and accessible by boat, foot, or a bus tour offered by North Cascades Stehekin Lodge.

Yakima River Canyon provides 15 miles of scenic river waters that are perfect for

One of Whittaker's fellow guides at RMI is **Ed Viesturs,** one of America's most famous climbers. To those outside the mountaineering community, Viesturs is perhaps best known for being on the IMAX team filming on Mount Everest when the 1996 disaster happened, as chronicled in Jon Krakauer's book *Into Thin Air*. Viesturs's team decided to turn back from the summit that fateful day because of weather conditions; for others who proceeded forward, the death toll would eventually be eight, including Viesturs's good friends Rob Hall and Scott Fischer.

Viesturs is known for his focus on safety and an often cautious approach. "For me, how I reach the top is more important than whether I do," he says. "Reaching the summit is optional. Getting down is mandatory." Today he spends a lot of time guiding primarily beginning alpinists on Rainier. "They may have hiked some mountains or climbed smaller peaks, but for the most part it's their first time putting on crampons and using ice axes and harnesses. When we do some of the more lengthy seminars, such as the six-day treks on Rainier, then it's people who may have already climbed Rainier with us on a two-day ascent and want a bigger challenge."

Viesturs loves the Northwest because of the wide range of opportunities it provides. "In the whole Cascades range, you have the simpler glacier ascents on some of the smaller volcanoes, and then you've got the whole gamut in the North Cascades, where approaches are one- to two-day events. There's a huge variety, from the stuff that novices can do to the other end of it, where alpinists can have some really hard and amazing climbs. There's a lot of places here you can climb just on the weekend— they're great stepping stones to gain the experience. You can do whatever you want right here and never have to leave."

rafting, fly fishing, or simply admiring the 2,000-foot basalt canyon walls that are home to nesting eagles, hawks, and falcons. A rare plant, the endangered basalt daisy, grows only in this area. The Oak Creek Wildlife Area covers 47,200 acres in Yakima County, including more than 90 miles of stream waterfront. These streams flow into large sub-basins in the Upper Yakima River watershed that support endangered salmonids, including bull trout.

Kitsap Peninsula is centrally located between the Olympic and Cascade Mountain ranges and is surrounded by 236 miles of saltwater shoreline. Spectacular mountain and water views extend in every direction, and the communities are a fascinating combination of Native American and Scandinavian pioneer history. Nine state parks are on Kitsap Peninsula, offering activities such as scuba diving, boating, kayaking, swimming, hiking, bicycling, and beach combing.

Olympic Peninsula juts out of the state's northwest corner, with some of the richest and most undeveloped rain forestland in the Pacific Northwest. A diverse blend of climates and natural wonders mixes with small towns that serve as the region's commercial hubs. The Olympic National Park and National Forest span nearly a million acres that are open to camping and hiking, with more than 500 miles of trails. On the Olympic Peninsula you can traverse easily between the alpine scenery of Mount Olympus, to sandy beachfront, to the Hoh Rain Forest's jungle atmosphere.

Puget Sound Islands dot the waterways of the Pacific Northwest, from the 170 islands that compose the San Juan archipelago to the islands of Whidbey, Camano, Fidalgo, and Bainbridge. Only about 40 of the total islands are inhabited, and only a few are reachable by ferry. Boating, hiking, whale watching, bird-watching, fishing, and numerous other outdoor activities can be found here.

PARKS AND RECREATION

The natural beauty found in the entire Pacific Northwest is also here in Seattle, lending itself to a nearly endless list of recreation, sports, and outdoors adventures. The local community is full of avid cyclists, hikers, climbers, boaters, and just plain active, health-oriented people who love to take advantage of nature's bounty that we have been given.

Whether you are here for a day or forever, it's easy to get outdoors in Seattle. This chapter is meant to give you a great resource for finding the places you can go for recreation, as well as important details such as where to rent a bicycle or boat, how to take an exciting thrill ride in a hot-air balloon or seaplane, where to hit the beach or pool, and even a few indoor activities for those rainy days (yes, we do have a few from time to time). This chapter will also tell you where to find gyms and fitness facilities with day pass privileges during your stay, and where to smack a few golf or tennis balls.

BALLOONING

SEATTLE HOT AIR BALLOONS
(800) 791-5867
http://1800skyride.com/HotAirBalloons/
   seattle-wa

Experience the freedom and tranquility of floating across the sky, with a bird's-eye view of places you may have seen before, but never as you will see them from above. Balloon rides are taken from launching points around the Seattle area, and generally flown around sunrise or sunset when air conditions are traditionally calm, cool, and stable. Once you are aboard the wicker basket, your magical flight begins. As you drift along with the breeze, the scenery slowly changes until, after approximately an hour in the air, it is time to land. The successful completion of the flight is celebrated with a special toast.

SOARING ADVENTURES OF AMERICA
(206) 241-0098
www.800soaring.com

This national company with locations all over the United States offers hot-air balloon flights in Seattle. The Great American Hot Air Balloon Ride has room for one to four people. After the balloon is inflated and boarded at the launch site, you will gently ascend and float between 500 and 1,000 feet, traveling wherever the wind takes you. The balloon flies above the treetops and below the clouds for about an hour, covering 5 to 10 miles. Upon landing, celebrate with a champagne or fruit juice toast, an old ballooning tradition. The whole experience takes about three hours. The company also provides glider and skydiving experiences.

BEACHES

ALKI BEACH PARK
1702 Alki Ave. SW (South)
(206) 684-4075
www.seattle.gov/parks/park_detail
   .asp?ID=445
This 2.5-mile beach in the West Seattle neighborhood runs from Alki Point to Duwamish Head, and in the summer months is filled with joggers, in-line skaters, kids, bicyclists, beachcombers, and sunbathers. Picnic tables, fire pits, and restrooms are fairly plentiful, although on perfect summer weekends it's advised to arrive early for prime spots. The entire beach faces incredible views of Puget Sound and the Olympic Mountains in the distance. Free; street parking is plentiful, though can fill up on weekends. You can also take the water taxi across; it leaves the downtown Seattle waterfront between Piers 55 and 56, taking you on the 12-minute journey across the bay for $2. A free shuttle to the beach is available at the West Seattle water taxi landing. Open year-round.

GOLDEN GARDENS PARK
8498 Seaview Place NW (North)
(206) 684-4075
www.seattle.gov/parks/park_detail
   .asp?ID=243
Located in Ballard on Puget Sound, this popular park offers extraordinary views of Puget Sound and the Olympic Mountains. The gardens were named in 1907 by Harry Treat, a real-estate baron whose trolley brought Ballard residents here each weekend. Roads were built in later decades, and soon came the bumper-to-bumper traffic that's part of the experience today. A recent project restored two wetlands, established a short loop trail, and restored the northern beach. Golden Gardens offers strolls along a rugged coastline, hikes through forest trails, sunbathing on sandy beaches, fishing from a pier, and a boat launch. The park is also home to an off-leash area for dogs in the upper northern portion. Don't miss the sunset—one of the most amazing viewing points in Seattle, and you can make a bonfire to go with it.

SEATTLE PARKS & RECREATION BEACHES
(206) 684-4075
www.seattle.gov/parks/ beaches.asp
The City of Seattle operates nine safe beaches at different locations, on the shores of area lakes. All beaches have lifeguards and are family-friendly. Amenities at all beaches include swimming rafts, drinking fountains, public restrooms, and parking. Some beaches also have play areas for children, picnic areas with grills, fishing piers, diving boards, and sports courts. Note that dogs are not allowed at city beaches. Admission fees are nominal.

BOATING AND SAILING

CENTER FOR WOODEN BOATS
1010 Valley St. (Central)
(206) 382-2628
www.cwb.org
Both a sailing club with lessons and rentals, and a museum of the artifacts and history of wind- and human-powered boats, the Center for Wooden Boats are free to the public all the time. In addition, while lessons and rentals are available for a fee, every Sun afternoon the center offers free boat rides on Lake Union. The rides take place at 2 and 3 p.m., weather permitting, and you can make reservations in person as early as 10 a.m. on the day of (no phone or prior reservations allowed).

GREEN LAKE BOAT RENTAL

NE corner of Green Lake, near Evans Pool
  (North)
(206) 527-0171
www.seattle.gov/parks/boats/Mooring
  .htm

Green Lake Boat Rental, a private company located on the northeast corner of the lake near Evans Pool and Green Lake Community Center, offers a variety of boats to rent to the general public including canoes, paddle boats, and rowboats.

GREEN LAKE SMALL CRAFT CENTER

5900 W. Green Lake Way North (North)
(206) 684-4074
www.seattle.gov/parks/Boats/Grnlake
  .htm

Green Lake Small Craft Center is located at the southwest corner of Green Lake in North Seattle, a popular lake totally surrounded by parkland. Here rowing, canoeing, kayaking, and sailing classes for children and adults are taught during daylight hours. Annual events include the Green Lake Spring Regatta in Apr, the Summer Rowing Extravaganza in Aug, and the Frostbite Regatta in Nov.

ELECTRIC BOAT COMPANY

2046 Westlake Ave. North, Suite 102
  (Central)
(206) 223-7476
www.theelectricboatco.com

This is a different sort of boating experience. The Electric Boat Company rents 21-foot electric Duffy boats on Lake Union. Each boat seats a maximum of 10 adults comfortably, with plush leather seats, two tables, and a sound system with CD player. They are fully enclosed and heated for even chilly days. Open seven days a week; two-hour minimum rental.

MOSS BAY ROWING CLUB

1001 Fairview Ave. North, Suite 1900
  (Central)
(877) 244-8896
www.mossbay.net

Boating enthusiasts of all ages, sizes, and abilities can enjoy access to the water and take in the sights on Lake Union. Within minutes of your arrival at the easy-access marina, the folks at Moss Bay will get you out on the lake to row, sail, or kayak. Boats can be rented from 8 a.m. to 8 p.m. during the summer (more limited winter hours), and they also do take-away kayak rentals, which enables you to rent for a weekend and take it to another location. In addition, Moss Bay offers instruction in rowing and sailing, and offers two-and-a-half-hour and half-day guided boat tours.

MOUNT BAKER ROWING & SAILING CENTER

3800 Lake Washington Blvd. South
  (South)
(206) 386-1913
www.seattle.gov/parks/Boats/Mtbaker
  .htm

Mount Baker Rowing & Sailing Center is located on Lake Washington at Stan Sayres Park, about midway between Seward Park and the I-90 floating bridge in southeast Seattle. The center offers programs for ages 8–100 in rowing, sailing, kayaking, and windsurfing for all ability levels. Because Stan Sayres Park features a boat-launching ramp, as well as several piers for power or sailboats, one could arrive by water to take a class!

NORTHWEST OUTDOOR CENTER

2100 Westlake Ave. North, Suite 1
  (Central)
(800) 683-0637
www.nwoc.com

The NWOC is the place to rent kayaks or, if you're feeling brave, a stand-up paddle board. The center has around 100 kayaks available for immediate use, right from its docks into Lake Union. The center also offers lessons and classes for all skill levels. Lake Union makes a great place to kayak, with its great view of the Seattle skyline and Space Needle. You can paddle around the unique and charming floating home community there, while seaplanes take off and land in the middle of the lake.

PUGET SOUND SAILING INSTITUTE
2203 Alaskan Way, Bell Harbor Marina (Central)
(800) 487-2454
www.pugetsoundsailing.com
This organization charters out skippered sailboats, with a capacity of four to six people. The institute is run by highly experienced director Michael Rice, who has won ASA Instructor of the Year an unprecedented six times. You can sail yourself if you know how (under the skipper's supervision), learn to sail, or just sit back and enjoy. You are welcome to bring your own food and beverages on board. The fleet for charter includes boats from 22 to 38 feet.

SEATTLE PARKS & RECREATION MOTORIZED BOAT LAUNCHES
(206) 684-7249
www.seattle.gov/parks/boats/motorized
.htm
Seattle has more pleasure boats per capita than anywhere else in the U.S. Seattle Parks & Recreation manages seven motorized boat launches on Puget Sound, Lake Washington, and the Ship Canal. A permit is required for anybody using a ramp lane regardless of where you park your vehicle and trailer.

A single-day launch permit costs $7 and is good until midnight of the date purchased. Overnight permits are $8 per night and can be purchased for a maximum of four nights. You can buy permits at yellow fee machines and kiosks at each boat launch location. Visit the Web site to locate one.

SHILSHOLE BAY MARINA
7001 Seaview Ave. NW (North)
(206) 787-3006
www.portseattle.org/seaport/marinas/
shilshole
Located just a few blocks from the Hiram M. Chittenden Locks in Ballard, Shilshole Bay Marina is only 20 minutes from downtown Seattle. Shilshole's stunning setting and convenient saltwater location make boating easy. The premier sailing center of the Northwest, Shilshole Bay Marina provides 2,700 linear feet of guest moorage, serving kayaks to mega yachts, 24-hour staffing, and a fuel dock with gas, groceries, and ice. The marina also features a public fishing pier and more than a mile of public promenade to enjoy the breathtaking views of the Olympic Mountains and Puget Sound. Located to the north of the marina is a public boat ramp, another fishing pier, and beautiful Golden Gardens Park.

WATERFRONT ACTIVITIES CENTER AT UNIVERSITY OF WASHINGTON
3900 Montlake Blvd. NE (North)
(206) 543-9433
http://depts.washington.edu/ima/
IMA_wac.php
The Waterfront Activities Center, located directly behind Husky Stadium on Union Bay and the Montlake Cut, offers canoe and rowboat rentals to the general public, as well as students and faculty. Open May

through Aug; rentals are available to those 18 and older.

WINDWORKS SAILING CENTER
7001 Seaview Ave. NW, Shilshole Bay
   Marina (North)
(206) 784-9386
www.windworkssailing.com

Windworks has a fleet of 30 vessels, ranging from 25-foot basic day-sailing vessels up to 43-foot cruising sailboats and catamarans. Windworks rents sailboat charters to non-members for half-day to multiday use, but nonmembers must include a qualified skipper (no single-handed sailing rentals).

BOWLING

GARAGE
1130 Broadway (Central)
(206) 322-2296
www.garagebilliards.com

Deriving its name from the auto repair shop that was once housed in the 1928 building, Garage offers a 70s style bowling experience. The bowling alley is one of a kind, three stories high and the first to open within Seattle city limits. There is also billiards, a full-service restaurant and a bar.

JEFFERSON PARK LAWN BOWLING
   CLUB
4103 Beacon Ave. South (South)
(206) 938-2805
http://seattlebowls.org

Lawn bowling is a fun sport that's gaining quite a following in Seattle, so if you're 10 or older, come to one of the city's two public lawn bowling greens and see what it's all about. Anyone can bowl at Jefferson Park Lawn Bowling Club; no experience is necessary. Annual memberships are offered, but first-time visitors can come by during

"open bowl" for $5 nonmember entry and free lessons. A second lawn bowling green can be found at Lower Woodland Park, at N. 63rd Street and Whitman Place North; open to the public at all times, with free lessons and bocce and croquet in addition to lawn bowling.

MAGIC LANES
10612 15th Ave. SW (South)
(206) 244-5060
www.magiclanesbowl.com

"Bowling is back," proclaims Magic Lanes—an interesting place with a bowling alley, sports bar, restaurant, and Magic Casino featuring poker, Pai Gow, and blackjack. A special "kids bowl free" promotion gives children two free games during the summer.

WEST SEATTLE BOWL
4505 39th Ave. SW (South)
(206) 932-3731
www.westseattlebowl.com

This bowling alley near Alki Beach offers a nonsmoking environment, food, shoe rental, and online reservations. Sat nights are particularly fun, with GlowZone bowling. Black lights, club lighting, and music give a fun disco feel to your bowling game. A bar serves beer, wine, and nonalcoholic beverages. All ages welcome.

CAMPING, BACKPACKING, AND HIKING (OVERNIGHT)

BLAKE ISLAND STATE PARK
Between Vashon and Bainbridge Islands,
   8 miles west of Seattle
(888) CAMPOUT (226-7688)
www.parks.wa.gov/
   parks/?selectedpark=Blake Island

Blake Island State Park is a 475-acre marine camping park with 5 miles of saltwater beach shoreline providing magnificent views of the Olympic Mountains and the Seattle skyline. The park is reachable only by tour boat or private boat (try Argosy Cruises). Blake Island was an ancestral camping ground of the Suquamish Indian tribe, and legend has it Chief Sealth was born there. It is believed the island was named by naval explorer Captain Charles Wilkes in honor of George Smith Blake, who commanded U.S. Coast Survey vessels from 1837 to 1848. Indian-style salmon dinners and demonstrations of Northwest Indian dancing are offered at **Tillicum Village,** a concession on the island. The campground has 44 tent spaces, two primitive sites, one dump station, four restrooms (one ADA compliant), and one shower area. Three **Cascadia Marine Trail** sites are located on the west end of the island. These sites are for use by canoers and kayakers only. The primitive sites are available on the south side. All campsites are first-come, first-served.

CAMP LONG

5200 35th Ave. SW (South)
(206) 684-7434
www.seattle.gov/parks/Environment/
camplong.htm
Camp Long is one of Seattle's best-kept secrets. Located in West Seattle, this 68-acre park offers visitors an opportunity to enjoy nature, hike in the forest, camp overnight in rustic cabins, rock climb, and learn about natural history. Rental facilities include a lodge with one meeting room, kitchen space, 10 cabins, two covered picnic areas, group fire ring, and climbing rock. A talented staff of naturalists lead group environmental education and rock climbing classes. Programs at Camp Long are fun, interactive experiences for all ages.

FAY BAINBRIDGE STATE PARK

15446 Sunrise Dr. (Bainbridge Island)
(888) CAMPOUT
www.parks.wa.gov/parks/?selected
park=Fay Bainbridge
Fay Bainbridge State Park is a 17-acre marine camping park with 1,420 feet of saltwater shoreline on the northeast corner of Bainbridge Island. The park offers sweeping views of Puget Sound, the Cascade Mountains, and two volcanoes, and features sandy beaches. The park has 10 tent sites, 26 utility sites, one dump station, two restrooms, and two showers. There are two kitchen shelters with electricity, one overlooking Puget Sound, plus 11 sheltered and 80 unsheltered picnic tables. The utility sites have water only and will accommodate RVs up to 30 feet in length. Some of the sites will take RVs larger than 30 feet. All camping is first-come, first-served.

Hike Metro

If you are not planning to rent a car in Seattle but still want to go hiking, you should check out the terrific **Hike Metro Web site** (http://sites.google.com/site/seattlemetrobushiking/main-page). This great resource pulls together an organized list, by geographic area, of hikes and outdoor adventures in the Seattle area that you can get to by bus or public transportation. A great way to go even greener on your commune with nature!

CITY PARKS, DAY HIKES, AND RUNNING TRAILS

Seattle is a city rich with parkland of all kinds. Parks have been divided into various categories depending on the amenities and activities offered. The parks highlighted in this section are day parks and make good partial-day visits for hiking, biking, picnicking, etc. Other city parks can be found under sections such as Beaches (for those whose primary feature is a beach), Camping (for those that allow overnight camping and hiking), and even Boating, Fishing, and Golfing for those parks offering such facilities. Therefore, you may want to take a look at the other parks detailed throughout this chapter, categorized by recreational interest.

CARKEEK PARK
950 NW Carkeek Park Rd. (North)
(206) 684-0877
www.seattle.gov/Parks/environment/ carkeek.htm
Historic 186-acre Carkeek Park offers spectacular views of Puget Sound. More than 6 miles of trails wind through stream, beach, and forest habitat, providing opportunities for natural exploration and recreation. Playground and picnic tables provide a perfect location for gatherings. The award-winning **Carkeek Park Environmental Learning Center** is the perfect location for retreats, community events, evening classes, ceremonies, receptions, memorials, birthday parties, and family gatherings. If the tide is low, a visit to Carkeek Park can be turned into an all-day adventure by walking the Puget Sound shore from Carkeek's fine beach to the Chittenden Locks.

DISCOVERY PARK
3801 W. Government Way (Central)
(206) 386-4236
www.seattle.gov/parks/Environment/ discovparkindex.htm
Discovery Park is absolutely the gem of the Seattle park system, and a favorite of locals. The 534-acre natural-area park is the largest city park in Seattle and occupies most of the former Fort Lawton site. The site is one of breathtaking majesty. Situated on Magnolia Bluff overlooking Puget Sound, Discovery Park offers spectacular views of both the Cascade and the Olympic mountain ranges. The secluded site includes 2 miles of protected tidal beaches as well as open meadowlands, dramatic sea cliffs, forest groves, active sand dunes, thickets, and streams. Be sure to walk the 2.8-mile Nature Loop Trail, and visit the beach at low tide, when the tidal pools reveal crabs, mussels, and tiny fish. Discovery Park is also home to the **Daybreak Star Indian Cultural Center.** Don't miss the **Salmon Bay Wildlife Corridor,** a rich estuary where freshwater merges with saltwater. Despite human intervention that has highly altered the estuary, Salmon Bay shelters a multitude of birds, mammals, and insects in addition to salmon and other fish.

GAS WORKS PARK
2101 N. Northlake Way (North)
(206) 684-4075
www.seattle.gov/parks/park_detail .asp?ID=293
On the north end of Lake Union is Gas Works Park, with a spectacular view of the lake and the city beyond. In case you're wondering about the name—yes, the site used to be a plant that manufactured gas from coal. The plant closed down in the 1950s, and the city acquired the site in 1962. Throughout

the summer, Gas Works Park hosts all kinds of festivals: a 4th of July celebration, Seattle Peace Concerts, and even live performances of Shakespeare. When there is not a festival going on, Gas Works is a great place to have a picnic or fly a kite, and there is a play area with a large play barn (in the former compressor building of the factory) for kids. A beautiful sundial is situated at the top of the hill within the park.

HISTORYLINK.ORG PRINTABLE WALK-ING TOURS
1411 4th Ave., Suite 803 (Central)
(206) 447-8140
www.historylink.org/index
    .cfm?DisplayPage=results
    .cfm&keyword=cybertour
History Link is an amazing resource, a virtual community encyclopedia of Washington state history. A terrific aspect for walkers is the section of interactive cyber tours, which introduce you to the history and background of various Seattle neighborhoods, and also provides a printable map in PDF format for do-it-yourself walking tours. Neighborhoods covered include Ballard, Lake Union, the International District, the Lewis and Clark Expedition, the Burke-Gilman Trail, Pike Place Market, Pioneer Square, and many more.

JAPANESE GARDEN
1075 Lake Washington Blvd. East (North)
(206) 684-4725
www.seattle.gov/tour/gardens.htm
This gem of a park is tucked away in the center of the city, stretching along one side of Lake Washington Boulevard, within the Washington Park Arboretum. The Japanese Garden represents a compressed world of mountains, forests, lakes, rivers, meadows, and a village, each with a quiet message of

its own. You need not be an expert to enjoy the beauty of the garden, but some understanding of its color, symbolism, and tradition may add to your appreciation and make your visit more meaningful. Activities include festivals, music, storytelling, workshops, and tea ceremonies.

LINCOLN PARK
8011 Fauntleroy Way SW (South)
(206) 684-4075
www.seattle.gov/parks/park_detail
    .asp?ID=460
Lincoln Park is one of Seattle's largest and most popular parks. Its 135 acres of open space provide a broad range of landscape types and a rich variety of recreational opportunities. The park was put together piecemeal over the years as West Seattle developed: a shelter in 1925; parking areas in 1928; a playground in 1930; seawalls, trails, fireplaces, and horseshoe pits during the Depression; and major additions just after WWII, as people streamed into the area to work in the burgeoning Boeing aircraft plant in the Duwamish Valley. Today Lincoln Park offers beach access to Puget Sound, a paved walking path along the water, ball fields, tennis courts, horseshoe pits, children's play areas, wading pool and Colman Pool—a heated outdoor, saltwater pool operated during the summer months.

MAGNUSON PARK
7400 Sand Point Way NE (North)
(206) 684-4946
www.seattle.gov/parks/magnuson
Warren G. Magnuson Park sits on a splendid mile-long stretch of Lake Washington's shoreline in northeastern Seattle. At 350 acres, it is Seattle's second-largest park. This former navy facility is rapidly becoming

home to a unique combination of features and activities for you to enjoy: recreation and leisure—boating, swimming, walks, kite flying, to name a few; sports fields; natural areas; and a community campus. In addition, you can take part in shaping the new and expanded park features now in the planning process.

SEATTLE PARKS & RECREATION RUNNING & JOGGING TRACKS
(206) 684-4075
www.seattle.gov/parks/athletics/
running.htm

Seattle Parks & Recreation has a wide range of facilities available for runners and joggers, ranging from rough trails to Cintrex-surfaced tracks. The best of these include **Discovery Park,** which offers a 2.8-mile loop trail through the forest, and **Green Lake,** a 2.8-mile paved path around the lake. The **Burke-Gilman Trail** is also very popular, with its 12.5 miles of asphalt path that leads from Gas Works Park all the way north to Kirkland. Several 400-meter synthetic running tracks are also available at three area high schools, and the West Seattle Stadium. The Web site gives a complete listing, along with maps of trails, for every public park and jogging track in the city.

SEWARD PARK
5895 Lake Washington Blvd. South
(South)
(206) 684-4396
www.seattle.gov/parks/environment/
seward.htm

Within the Seattle city limits, Seward park boasts 300 acres of beautiful forestland— home to eagles' nests, old-growth forest, a 2.4-mile bike and walking path, an amphitheater, a native plant garden, an art studio, miles of hiking trails, and more.

CYCLING AND MOUNTAIN BIKING

BIKESTATION
311 3rd Ave. South (Central)
(206) 224-9252
www.bikestation.com/seattle/index.asp

This nonprofit organization is modeled after European and Japanese examples, and was the first of its kind to open in the United States. Bikestation plans, designs, and operates bike-transit centers, enabling bicycling and other alternatives to be an integral part of the transportation system. Its facilities offer secure bicycle parking and related services to make cyclists' lives easier. Park your bike at a Bikestation and you can be assured that your vehicle is secure and covered. Many Bikestations offer free parking during their hours of operation, and paid memberships for 24-hour access to secure parking. Rentals are also available inside Bikestation Seattle; for more information on rentals, call (206) 307-1179.

BURKE-GILMAN TRAIL
Access Point at Gas Works Park, 2101 N.
Northlake Way (North)
(206) 684-7583
www.kingcounty.gov/recreation/parks/
trails/regionaltrailssystem/burkegil
man.aspx

The Burke-Gilman Trail runs more than 18 miles from Shilshole Bay in Seattle to the city of Bothell, where it intersects the Sammamish River Trail. The trail is perhaps the most popular for cyclists; as part of the Locks to Lakes Corridor, the BGT is a paved, off-road facility over its entire length with the exception of an on-road segment in Ballard. The trail follows a historic railroad route near the Lake Washington Ship Canal and north along Lake Washington to the Sammamish

River. Along the way it passes the Hiram Chittenden Locks, Fremont Canal Park, Gas Works Park, the University of Washington, Magnuson Park, Log Boom Park in Kenmore, Wayne Golf Course in Bothell, and Blyth Park in Bothell. The trail is managed by Seattle within the city limits south of NE 145th Street and by King County outside Seattle.

CASCADE BICYCLE CLUB
7400 Sand Point Way NE (North)
(206) 522-BIKE
www.cascade.org

Cycling is serious business in Seattle, and this community club with more than 12,000 members proves it. As a visitor, you can take advantage of the wealth of information and resources provided by its Web site; also, the club offers free rides every day of the year, more than 1,300 annually, ranging from leisurely 10-mile jaunts to strenuous endurance events to multiday rides. Cascade Bicycle Club also partners with the city for Bicycle Sunday, a weekly community ride between June and Sept that goes along Lake Washington to the Seward Park entrance. Members and nonmembers are welcome to attend rides.

DUTCH BIKE COMPANY
4421 Shilshole Ave. NW (North)
(206) 789-1678
www.dutchbikeseattle.com

Although this bike shop rents your typical three-speed classic city bike, the reason it is worth a mention is because of its crazy Conference Bike available for rent. This contraption seats seven people, and believe me, if you rent it you will not go unnoticed on the streets of Seattle. On the Web site, you can even watch a video of the Conference Bike in action.

MARYMOOR PARK VELODROME
6046 W. Lake Sammamish Pkwy. NE
(Redmond)
(206) 205-3661
http://velodrome.org

Marymoor Park, in nearby Redmond, is home to the state's only velodrome, a 400-meter track dedicated to bicycle racing. Operated by the Marymoor Velodrome Association, this top-notch facility hosts programs for riders of all levels, including youth classes, the popular Friday Night Racing series, and even national racing championships. Marymoor is King County's most popular park, and more than three million people visit annually to explore its 640 acres of recreational activities.

MONTLAKE BIKE SHOP
2223 24th Ave. East (Central)
(206) 329-7333
www.montlakebike.com

This shop, in addition to repairing bikes, sells and rents a full range of mountain bikes, hybrids, touring bikes, racing bikes, tandems, recumbents—plus Burley trailers and trail-a-bikes, and travel cases. Rent by the hour, day, week, or month, and you can walk in or make advance reservations. All rentals require a credit card (not debit card) for security deposit.

RECYCLED CYCLES
1007 NE Boat St. (North)
(877) 298-4683
www.recycledcycles.com

Recycled Cycles is an alternative to the "typical" bike shop, offering lower prices through the sale of pre-owned bicycles, parts, and accessories. They also rent hybrids, road bikes, Burley trailers, and trail-a-bikes. Helmets are free, if you don't have your own. Located conveniently near the Burke-Gilman Trail in the University District.

i Get a free *Seattle Bicycling Guide Map* from the Department of Transportation. In 2009 SDOT distributed more than 30,000 maps. To receive a printed copy, call Bike Alliance of Washington at (206) 224-9252, or use the online form at www.seattle.gov/transportation/bikemapform.htm. You can also download a PDF copy at www.seattle.gov/transportation/docs/bike100221_mainmap.pdf.

DOG PARKS AND PLAYGROUNDS

DOWNTOWN DOG LOUNGE
1405 Elliott Ave. West (Central)
(206) 213-0019
www.downtowndoglounge.com
A happening place for dogs that offers the standard boarding and grooming services, as well as phenomenal doggy day care facilities. Your dog can roam around the puppy palace, upper deck, and south or north playground, with or without you.

FUZZY BUDDY'S DOG DAYCARE
10907 Aurora Ave. North (North)
(206) 782-4321
www.fuzzybuddys.com
A playground and day care for dogs catering to small pooches, with a 6,000-square-foot facility with rubber floors, kiddie pools, and worn couches for naps when the playing just gets to be too much. There's even aromatherapy for nervous dogs! Weekly small dog meet-ups and monthly parties are nice, and your dog's first visit is free.

HOUNDS ABOUND DAYCARE
307 N. 103rd St. (North)
(206) 297-7387
http://houndsaboundseattle.com

A full-service playground for dogs, complete with a play house, rubber flooring, outside play yard, wading pools, and comprehensive fencing system. There is a separate area for smaller dogs, as well. Shuttle service is provided.

SEATTLE PARKS & RECREATION OFF-LEASH AREAS
(206) 684-4075
www.seattle.gov/PARKS/offleash.asp
For a city that has 45 percent more dogs than children, dog parks are a must. This section of the Seattle government Web site gives information about the city's 11 designated off-leash areas for dogs, from downtown to surrounding neighborhoods throughout the city. For visitors not familiar with Seattle, it's worth noting that some dog parks are very busy and popular, while others are downright desolate. The best are **Magnuson** (Disneyland for dogs, even with a doggy beach), **Genesee,** and **Golden Garden.** The I-5 Colonnade is rarely used and, quite frankly, a little scary; the off-leash area at Jose Rizal Park is nearly impossible to find.

FISHING

A SPOT TAIL SALMON GUIDE
(206) 295-7031
www.salmonguide.com
A Spot Tail Salmon Guide is the only charter guide in Seattle that offers light tackle saltwater fishing, called mooching or fly fishing. Light tackle mooching is a fun, active, hands-on fishing technique as opposed to trolling, which is passive. This is a good charter if you're interested in learning this technique and doing a different kind of fishing. They also offer saltwater fly fishing with casting and stripping for the more experienced fisherman. Captain Keith Robbins maintains

extremely high fishing standards and has more than 19 years of experience.

ALL STAR CHARTERS
720 Waverly Ave. (Everett)
(800) 214-1595
www.allstarfishing.com

These guys offer great fishing charters around Seattle and Puget Sound. Catch halibut, lingcod, or All Star Charters' specialty, salmon. At the same time you're enjoying calm-water fishing on the Sound, you can also admire the mountains in the background and probably spot seals, sea lions, birds, and maybe an orca. The skippers are Coast Guard licensed, friendly, and extremely knowledgeable, and will teach you innovative Seattle fishing methods. They operate year-round, and most trips are six to seven hours long; excursions include the cleaning and bagging of your fish.

ELLIOTT BAY FISHING PIER
Pier 86, W. Galer and 16th Avenue West
**   (Central)**
(206) 787-3654
www.portseattle.org/community/
**   resources/parks/index.shtml**

Located at the gorgeous, 11-acre Elliott Bay Park on the Seattle waterfront, this 400-foot pier goes right over the bay and provides some of the best fishing in the city. Locals report it being a good spot for Seattle Blackmouth and squid. There is also a tackle shop and 4,100 linear feet of shorelines. Picnic tables, benches, and restrooms are available. The pier is run by the Port of Seattle, and open from 6 a.m. to 11 p.m. daily.

SEATTLE PARKS & RECREATION FISH-
ING PIERS
(206) 684-4075
www.seattle.gov/parks/Boats/Fishpier
**   .htm**

The City of Seattle operates many public fishing piers throughout the city. Before you fish, make sure to view the Washington Department of Fish and Wildlife Fishing Regulations, available at the Web site above. Visit the Web site to find the location of fishing piers in the North, Central, and South areas of Seattle. Specifically, check out **Seacrest Park;** it has a brand-new floating dock that is very nice.

SHILSHOLE BAY MARINA
7001 Seaview Ave. NW (North)
(206) 787-3006
www.portseattle.org/seaport/marinas/
**   shilshole**

Located just a few blocks from the Hiram M. Chittenden Locks in Ballard, Shilshole Bay Marina is only 20 minutes from downtown Seattle. The marina features a public fishing pier and more than a mile of public promenade to enjoy the breathtaking views of the Olympic Mountains and Puget Sound. Located to the north of the marina is a public boat ramp, another fishing pier, and beautiful Golden Gardens Park.

TERMINAL 105 PARK
4260 W. Marginal Way SW (South)
(206) 787-3654
www.portseattle.org/community/
**   resources/parks/index.shtml**

This small park, run by the Port of Seattle, has 220 feet of shoreline access and a 50-foot fishing pier, as well as a boat launch. The main draw of this pier is that the area is a salmon habitat. Restrooms and parking are also available; open from 6 a.m. to 9 p.m. daily.

ICE-SKATING

HIGHLAND ICE ARENA
18005 Aurora Ave. North (Shoreline)
(206) 546-2431
www.highlandice.com

Open since 1962, Highland has the largest heated lobby in the Northwest, full rubber flooring in the lobby, glass windows for viewing both inside and out, and a computer-controlled air-quality management system. This system is monitored continuously and supplies fresh, dry, pre-warmed air for skaters. Rental skates are available in a wide range of sizes from tiny tot (size 7) through adult (size 14), and the rink features shadow-free lighting, a state-of-the-art sound system, and an up-to-date video arcade. There is a morning and afternoon public skate session daily; Sun from 1:30 to 8 p.m. is Family Session, where parents and kids can all skate for $13. Located 15 minutes north of Seattle.

LYNWOOD ICE CENTER
19803 68th Ave. West (Lynnwood)
(425) 640-9999
www.lynnwoodicecenter.com

Public skating sessions are offered every day, and Wed is Cheap Skate Night, with $5 skating from 7 to 8:30 p.m. The Lynwood Ice Center is a nonprofit organization dedicated to providing affordable family entertainment. The rink features a state-of-the-art surround sound system, private party rooms, and plenty of new rental skates, both figure and hockey. There is a warm, comfortable lobby, snack bar, and pro shop, all managed and operated by an experienced staff. Located about 25 minutes north of Seattle.

GOLF

GREEN LAKE PITCH & PUTT
5701 W. Green Lake Way North (North)
(206) 632-2280
www.seattle.gov/parks/athletics/golfcrse
  .htm#green

Located at the south end of the lake, Green Lake Pitch & Putt offers fun and affordable golf for individuals and families. This is a nine-hole, par three course for pitching and putting only. The course is open from 9 a.m. until dusk from Mar through Oct 31.

PUETZ GOLF
11762 Aurora Ave. North (North)
(206) 36202272
www.puetzgolf.com

In 1945 the two Puetz brothers opened a golf driving range; it was the first golf facility in the northwest to sell pro-line clubs at a discount. Today Puetz Golf still carries a great selection of quality merchandise, but it also has a driving range with 30 practice tees and a putting green. Lessons are also available, including ladies' and juniors' lessons, by PGA teaching professionals.

SEATTLE GOLF INSTRUCTION
4209 Mary Gates Memorial Dr. NE
  (North)
(206) 328-3164
www.seattlegolfinstruction.com

Instructor Corey Waggoner provides customized golf plans and lessons to singles and couples, using video technology and a wealth of experience. He is the golf instructor at the University of Washington, and lessons are held at the UW Golf Range. Waggoner will also accompany you as you play on any Seattle or Bellevue course, acting as your caddie to assist and teach course management, strategy, and shot selection.

SEATTLE PARKS & RECREATION GOLF COURSES

(206) 285-2200

http://premiergc.com

Golfing opportunities are available for all skill levels at City of Seattle courses. Seattle Parks & Recreation owns and maintains four really nice golf courses: **Interbay, Jackson Park, Jefferson Park,** and **West Seattle.** Premier Golf operates them under a contract with the city. Golf instruction is available for any level, and the pro shops have a great selection and competitive pricing and covered heated driving ranges for those rainy days. Be sure to look at the course descriptions, as each one has its own challenges.

UNIVERSITY OF WASHINGTON GOLF RANGE

4209 Mary Gates Memorial Dr. NE (North)

(206) 543-8759

http://depts.washington.edu/ima/IMA_golf.php

The UW golf range is open to the general public, as well as faculty and students. The range is night-lighted and has 43 tees (20 covered), two chipping and putting greens, and target greens. Open May 1 through Aug 31 from 9 a.m. to 10 p.m.

GYMS AND FITNESS FACILITIES

BALLARD HEALTH CLUB

2208 NW Market St. (North)

(206) 706-4882

www.ballardhealthclub.com

This great little neighborhood fitness center offers $10 drop-in visits, making it an excellent choice for visitors. It is a family-owned business located in the heart of historic downtown Ballard. Since 1998 BHC has provided a community-oriented, supportive atmosphere in which to exercise and relax. There is no sales staff, and the certified personal trainers are all friendly and helpful. In addition to full weight equipment and fitness machines, there are also roughly 45 classes from which to choose, ranging from Ab Lab to zumba to many styles of yoga, including hatha, vinyasa, ashtanga, and combination yoga/Pilates.

COMMUNITY FITNESS

2113 NE 65th St. (North)

(206) 523-1534

www.communityfitness.com

This is a great company that offers drop-in pricing as well as 10-class passes. The uniquely designed health club for group exercise is set in a casual atmosphere with local instructors. Classes include yoga, zumba, cycling, body pump, sculpting, dance fitness, and more. Check the Web site for classes and facilities; brand-new members are asked to arrive 15 minutes prior to class start times. A second location also opened at 6108 Roosevelt Way NE.

SEATTLE ATHLETIC CLUB

2020 Western Ave. (Central)

(206) 443-1111

www.sacdt.com

Seattle Athletic Club offers all of the services and amenities of a world-class sports and fitness center, in a great location 1 block north of Pike Place Market. The 62,000-square-foot facility offers all state-of-the-art equipment. In recent years the club has undertaken a complete renovation of the locker rooms, addition of a group exercise studio, international-style softball squash courts, indoor cycling studio, private Pilates studio, and expansion of the cardio and strength training facilities. It also offers yoga, personal training, martial arts, wellness services including massage, and an aquatics program. The club is known for its top-notch squash program, under internationally renowned squash pro Yusuf Khan. Although it is a membership-based club, they do offer complimentary trial passes.

SEATTLE CENTRAL COMMUNITY
   COLLEGE
1718 Broadway (Central)
(206) 587-6315
www.seattlecentral.edu/mac/programs
   .php

Seattle's community college offers drop-in, noncredit Total Body Conditioning classes on Mon, Wed, and Fri at noon. The unique class incorporates various exercise equipment to give you a great full-body workout. Hand weights, large exercise balls, and floor-based exercises are combined to challenge strength, flexibility, and balance. The fundamental aspects of self-defense are also taught. The classes are held at the Charles H. Mitchell Activity Center and anyone is welcome to join any class.

SEATTLE PARKS & RECREATION
   GYMNASIUMS
(206) 684-4075
www.seattle.gov/parks/centers.asp

The city operates more than two dozen community centers in neighborhoods around Seattle, and many of these have full-service gymnasiums and/or fitness centers. The facilities often include weight equipment and machines, and sports courts. Some of the centrally located community centers with gyms or fitness facilities include Yesler, Queen Anne, and Northgate. Entrance fees are just a few dollars for adults and generally free for children 17 and under. Check the Web site for exact locations and facilities.

YMCA OF GREATER SEATTLE
909 4th Ave. (Central)
(206) 382-5003
www.seattleymca.org

The Seattle branch of the YMCA operates 12 branches in King and Snohomish Counties, which offer full fitness facilities including gymnasiums with sports courts, indoor running tracks, strength training center with weights, workout machines, power cycling studios, and cardiovascular centers. The YMCA centers also have swimming pools, recreation rooms, locker facilities, and often massage therapy. The downtown YMCA is at this address, but others are located in the south and north parts of town. If you are a member of another YMCA outside Washington state, you will be recognized as a full member at Seattle YMCAs for up to 21 days in a calendar year, by presenting a current membership card. For additional visits, you will be expected to pay the daily membership rate. Nonmembers can still access the swimming pools and other facilities by providing valid photo identification, filling out an information card, and paying a day-use fee of $10 for adults 21 and over, and $5 for ages 13–20 (free for 12 and under).

IHRSA Passport

Are you a member of a health/ fitness club at home? If so, you may check to see if it belongs to the IHRSA. The IHRSA Passport Program gives members of participating clubs access to a worldwide network of health clubs when traveling. After checking the Web site to see if your gym is a member, *you must ask at your current home fitness facility* for a valid IHRSA passport to take with you when you travel. Some of the Seattle clubs that participate include 24 Hour Fitness, the Seattle Athletic Club, PRO Sports Club, and LA Fitness. Call (800) 228-4772 or visit the Web site at www.healthclubs.com.

IN-LINE AND ROLLER-SKATING

ALASKAN WAY TRAIL
3130 Alaskan Way West (Central)
(206) 684-4075
www.seattle.gov/parks/park_detail
.asp?ID=311

The 3-mile Alaskan Way Trail runs along Seattle's waterfront from Myrtle Edwards Park at Pier 70 to Safeco Field and points south. The surface is fairly good, but there are numerous obstacles such as intersections, train tracks, and pedestrians that require good stopping skills. This trail is flat and very scenic, adjacent to the Olympic Sculpture Park.

FAST GIRL SKATES
252 NE 45th St. (North)
(206) 274-8250
www.fastgirlskates.com

This cool roller-skate shop is where the Seattle roller derby chicks get their gear. The flagship store is the first of its kind in the world, carrying a large stock of traditional four-wheel roller skates and the gear to go with them, as well as skate fashions and jewelry. And these fashions aren't like the flouncy, sequined skating skirts. Fast Girl is more the thigh-high-stocking type.

GREEN LAKE PARK
7201 E. Green Lake Dr. North (North)
(206) 684-4075
www.seattle.gov/parks/park_detail
.asp?ID=307

This huge public park that goes all around Green Lake is one of Seattle's most beloved. The newly reconstructed 2.8-mile path around the lake provides a perfect recreational spot for skaters. The crushed-granite path for walkers and joggers runs closest to the lake, and alongside it is the 13.5-foot-wide asphalt path for wheeled users.

INNER SPACE INDOOR SKATEPARK
3506 Stone Way North (North)
(206) 634-9090
www.innerspaceskateboarding.com

This indoor skatepark is also for in-line skaters; see details under the Skateboarding section.

MOUNTAINEERING AND CLIMBING WALLS

MOUNTAINEERS CLUB CLIMBING WALL
Magnuson Park, 7700 Sand Point Way NE
(North)
(206) 521-6000
www.seattlemountaineers.org

The Mountaineers Club Seattle is headquartered at Magnuson Park, and here they have built an excellent bouldering and top-roping wall that was donated to the city. Climb without a rope for 12 feet or under, and with a rope for over 12 feet. Features include crags, chimneys, and small holds. The view overlooking Lake Washington is magnificent.

REI
222 Yale Ave. North (Central)
(206) 223-1944
www.rei.com/stores/seattle/climbclass
.html
The downtown Seattle REI is the flagship store, and its focal point is the 65-foot climbing wall right in the center, called the Pinnacle. This is the world's third tallest indoor climbing structure, with routes ranging from 5.4 to 5.11, with gear and belay provided by store staff. The Pinnacle is open Sat and Sun, and advance reservations are strongly recommended. All climbers must complete and turn in an REI release of liability form prior to climbing. Minors (18 and under) must have this form signed by their legal guardian. For REI members and their immediate family members, each Pinnacle climb is $7. Nonmembers can climb for $20 per person, per climb, or join REI at the store and receive a coupon for a free climb. The Pinnacle is closed during sales and certain special events.

STONE GARDENS
2839 NW Market St. (North)
(206) 781-9828
www.stonegardens.com
Known as the climber's gym, this Ballard facility offers over 16,000 square feet of climbing surface, with textured walls and natural features. There is a 40-foot outdoor wall and a 65-foot indoor lead roof, with a selection of quality routes from 5.4 to 5.13 and boulder problems from V-0 to V-12. On-site amenities include weight and exercise equipment, a pro shop, showers, and loft space that can be rented for parties. Open daily.

VERTICAL WORLD
2123 W. Elmore St. (Central)
(206) 283-4497
www.verticalworld.com
Seattle is home to the first U.S. climbing gym, Vertical World. They opened the very first rock climbing gym in America in 1987 on Elliott Avenue in Seattle. The gym was no more than rocks glued to painted plywood panels. Today, with more advanced facilities, Vertical World offers memberships and daily rates for non-members, as well as handling corporate functions, private parties, kids' camps, and a variety of custom group climbing programs. Learn to climb classes are also available. Contact for hours and rates.

SCUBA DIVING

ALKI BEACH PARK
1702 Alki Ave. SW (South)
(206) 684-4075
www.seattle.gov/parks/park_detail
.asp?ID=445
Just off the laid-back shore of Alki Beach lies a great diving opportunity. The sandy bottom, wharf pilings, and eelgrass habitats are home to a large variety of animals. Depth ranges from 22 to 78 feet, and you're likely to see sea stars, sun stars, nudibranchs, crabs, sea pens, plumose anemones, cabezon, lingcod, copper rockfish, kelp greenling, and perch. Access hours are 5 a.m. to 11 p.m. The park also has restrooms and picnic tables.

EDMONDS UNDERWATER PARK
Main Street at the Edmonds-Kingston
Ferry Landing (Edmonds)
(425) 771-0227
www.ci.edmonds.wa.us/Discovery_pro
grams_Website/Underwater_Park.html
This spot just a few miles north of Seattle is simply amazing. The park includes more

than 27 acres of tide and bottom lands, of which approximately half have been developed with features and trails specifically for divers. It was established in 1970 as a marine preserve and sanctuary, and is the most popular of Washington's 10 underwater parks. The underwater park itself is a series of man-made reef structures interspersed with sunken vessels in various states of decay, which together create an artificial habitat for a wide variety of marine life. These features are connected by an extensive network of fixed guide ropes anchored to the bottom that make it easy for divers to get around the park. The man-made reefs are made from concrete blocks, tractor tires, PVC pipes of various sizes, sunken navigation buoys, an old tree trunk, sunken boats and ships, old pieces of the 520 floating bridge, and much, much more. There is even a cash register and the bed of a pickup truck. Surface facilities include parking, restrooms, dry changing area, and showers. Air can be purchased as well.

SCUBA SCHOOLS GROUP
2000 Westlake Ave. North, Suite 210 (Central)
(206) 284-2350
www.seattlescuba.com
In addition to diving and CPR/first aid classes, one of the best things about the Scuba Schools Group is that they don't require any membership, fees, or meetings in order to go on their dives. They host a wide variety of local dives, and they are open to anyone at no cost (unless the dive site has its own entry fee). Divers need to be certified and have experience in cold-water dives, and need to bring all necessary gear. Rental equipment and gear are available. Divers can also meet at the shop to pick up tanks and weights,

and carpool to the dive site. Some of the spots the club dives include Blake Island Reef, West Seattle Reef, and Edmonds Underwater Park, with both day and night dives.

UNDERWATER SPORTS
10545 Aurora Ave. North (North)
(206) 362-3310
www.underwatersports.com
The Seattle location is only one of Underwater Sport's eight locations around Puget Sound. They have one of the largest instructional teams anywhere and offer classes, an equipment store, rental and repair, and local dive trips for certified divers.

SEAPLANES

KENMORE AIR
950 Westlake Ave. North (Central)
(866) 435-9524
www.kenmoreair.com
Kenmore is the largest seaplane operator in the United States. On its fleet of more than 20 seaplanes, Kenmore offers sightseeing flights that return to the original departure port, as well as pilot lessons. Kenmore Air's City Explorer seaplane flightseeing excursions are offered several times daily from beautiful Lake Union just a mile north of downtown. The terminal is an inexpensive cab ride from popular downtown hotels, or take the Seattle streetcar from Westlake Center to the South Lake Union stop. During your 20-minute flight, you'll enjoy a professionally produced, GPS-triggered narration system that describes points of interest below you based on aircraft position and direction of flight. Kenmore also offers flights to such destinations as the San Juan Islands; Victoria, British Columbia; and Port Angeles.

NORTHWEST SEAPLANES
860 W. Perimeter Rd. (Renton)
(800) 690-0086
www.nwseaplanes.com
Northwest Seaplanes provides scheduled and charter seaplane service from South Lake Washington to various boating, fishing, and eco-tourism destinations such as the San Juan Islands, Vancouver Island, and British Columbia's Inside Passage. Northwest's fleet includes five Dehavilland Beavers, each of which accommodates six passengers. The family-owned business has been around for more than 37 years.

SEATTLE SEAPLANES
1325 Fairview Ave. East (Central)
(800) 637-5553
www.seattleseaplanes.com
Seattle Seaplanes offers 20-minute scenic flights, dinner flights to restaurants on neighboring islands, charter float-plane rides, and flight instruction. Take off from Lake Union and enjoy an eagle's-eye view of the University of Washington, Bill Gates's estate, Lake Washington, Bustling Elliott Bay, the Ballard Locks, and the spectacular Cascade and Olympic mountain ranges. Jim Chrysler has over 30 years of piloting experience and has owned and operated Seattle Seaplanes (formerly Chrysler Air) for more than 15 years.

SKATEBOARDING

BALLARD COMMONS PARK
5701 22nd Ave. NW (North)
(206) 684-4075
www.seattle.gov/parks/park_detail
  .asp?ID=4278
This public park in Ballard features a large skate bowl, in addition to seating areas, public art, and a water feature. Open from 4 a.m. to 11:30 p.m.

GOODS
1112 Pike St. (Central)
(206) 621-1307
www.needgoods.com
Goods is a hip store in downtown Seattle that caters to the skateboarding crowd. The store also carries a large line of clothing, hats, and shoes—particularly a huge inventory of sneakers. It can have a lot of attitude and is heavy on the young crowd.

INNER SPACE INDOOR SKATEPARK
3506 Stone Way North (North)
(206) 634-9090
www.innerspaceskateboarding.com
Seattle's only indoor skatepark, Inner Space has about 7,000 square feet of skateable indoor space, including a shop with skateboards, accessories, food, and sodas. Open daily, with $5 admission after 6:30 p.m. Everyone must sign a waiver, and those under 18 must have a parent sign. In-line skates are allowed as well as skateboards. It can be a little hard to find; the skatepark is underneath Hard Hat Tool & Supply, and the entrance is at the back of the building on 35th Street. There are very few parking spots.

SEATTLE CENTER SKATEPARK
305 Harrison St. (Central)
www.seattlecenter.com/skatepark
Completed in 2009, the skatepark at Seattle Center features a surface area of 10,000 square feet, with a flowing street plaza, ledges, stairs, transitions, and state-of-the-art skating elements for all skill levels and abilities. There are even skateable sculptures and structural glass riding surfaces. Sea Sk8, as it's known to locals, is open daily during daylight hours.

SKIING, SNOWBOARDING, AND SNOWMOBILING

See the Mountains section of the Day Trips and Weekend Getaways chapter.

SWIMMING POOLS

SEATTLE PARKS & RECREATION POOLS

(206) 684-4075

www.seattle.gov/parks/pools.asp

The City of Seattle operates a number of swimming pools situated in all neighborhoods and locations, including eight indoor pools and 30 wading pools. Several of these have beach areas as well, either on the shore of a lake or Puget Sound. Most pools offer a wide variety of aquatics programs, including lessons, water exercise classes, aqua jogging, family swim, and lap swim times. Many pools also have spas or warm water pools, saunas, diving boards, slides, and rope swings. For families, don't miss Colman Pool, an amazing heated saltwater pool located in a great beach setting, and featuring the giant tube slide that kids will love. Admission fees are nominal, $4 for adults and less than $3 for youth. Lockers and changing areas are available, and admittance fees must be paid for everyone entering, whether they are swimming or not.

YMCA OF GREATER SEATTLE

909 4th Ave. (Central)

(206) 382-5003

www.seattleymca.org

The Seattle YMCA operates 12 branches in King and Snohomish Counties, which offer pools that often include lap lanes, heated water, and other features. The downtown YMCA is at this address, but others are located in the south and north parts of town. If you are a member of another YMCA outside Washington state, you will be recognized as a full member at Seattle YMCAs for up to 21 days in a calendar year, by presenting a current membership card. For additional visits, you will be expected to pay the daily membership rate. Nonmembers can still access the swimming pools and other facilities by providing valid photo identification, filling out an information card, and paying a day-use fee of $10 for adults 21 and over, and $5 for ages 13–20 (free for 12 and under).

Brrr...

If you are visiting Seattle over the New Year and are just plain crazy, you may want to participate in the annual **New Year's Day Polar Bear Plunge.** The event is held every January 1 at noon at Matthews Beach Park for the past eight years, with many participants forsaking plain old bathing suits to dress up in costumes. Afterward, enjoy a warm beverage and receive the official Polar Bear Plunge Patch of courage. Around 1,000 people do this, and if you are like me and wouldn't jump in that cold water if a polar bear actually were chasing you, it's great fun to witness as a spectator sport. NE 93rd Street and Sand Point Way NE, (206) 684-4989, www.seattle.gov/Parks/aquatics/PolarBearPlunge.htm.

TENNIS

SEATTLE PARKS & RECREATION TENNIS COURTS
(206) 684-4062
www.seattle.gov/parks/tennis.asp

The City of Seattle operates several dozen outdoor tennis courts at parks all over the city. To conserve energy, from the last Sun in Oct until the first Sun in Apr only the five major tennis courts are lighted: Bobby Morris, Meadowbrook, Rainier, Solstice, and Lower Woodland. For indoor tennis, visit the excellent **Amy Yee Tennis Center** (2000 Martin Luther King Jr. Way South). It offers 10 indoor courts, four outdoor courts, and a wide array of programs, including junior and adult group lessons, tiny tot programs, junior and adult camps, and adult play—classes and flights. Same-day reservations can be made over the phone at (206) 684-4764 or in person. Fees are $25 for singles and $30 for doubles, per one-and-a-quarter-hour court usage. Discounts and free days are available for seniors and youth ages 10–18.

YOGA/PILATES

This section specifically lists studios that offer only yoga or Pilates; however, in the Gyms and Fitness Centers section, you will find that many of the facilities listed there also have classes including yoga and Pilates.

8 LIMBS YOGA CENTERS
500 E. Pike St. (Central)
(206) 325-8221
www.8limbsyoga.com

8 Limbs has been voted the best yoga by *Seattle* magazine, *Seattle Weekly,* and CitySearch. The studios offer group hatha yoga classes for all levels, pre- and postnatal yoga, kids' yoga, workshops, and more in Capitol Hill, Wedgwood, and West Seattle. All 8 Limbs studios offer drop-in rates per class, as well as lower-priced community classes and free Yoga 101 classes on the first Sat of each month. You can also buy passes for five, 10, or 20 classes if you think you'll be going often enough.

CENTER FOR YOGA OF SEATTLE
2261 NE 65th St. (North)
(206) 526-9642
www.yogaseattle.com

This is a BKS Iyengar yoga study center that began in a church basement in 1975. Visitors to Seattle who are looking for a place to take a yoga class may drop in to the regular, reserved-space classes (fee is $20 per class). If you have not studied Iyengar yoga in the recent past, you should take only level 1 and 2 or slow-beginning classes. Please arrive 10–15 minutes early, let the instructor know that you are a visitor, and you will need to fill out a brief form.

MIND AND BODY STUDIO
2022 E. Union St. (Central)
(206) 325-3328
www.seattlepilates.com

This wellness studio provides clients with Pilates, yoga, gravity training system (GTS), massage, physical therapy, and other body-work services. Centrally located in Seattle and with more than 2,000 square feet of space, the studio offers a large exercise room with 16-foot ceilings, a fully equipped Pilates studio, a private treatment room with a skylight for massage, physical therapy, yoga classes, and three GTS machines. Drop-ins are welcome at all classes. Previous experience is necessary for intermediate/advanced Pilates classes; all yoga classes are basic level and open to all experience levels.

SEATTLE CENTRAL COMMUNITY COLLEGE

1718 Broadway (Central)

(206) 587-6315

www.seattlecentral.edu/mac/programs
.php

Seattle's community college offers drop-in, noncredit yoga classes on Thurs at 5 p.m. The classes are held at the Charles H. Mitchell Activity Center, anyone is welcome to join any class, and they are appropriate for all levels of fitness.

URBAN YOGA SPA

1900 4th Ave. (Central)

(206) 420-0222

www.urbanyogaspa.com

This place is so much more than a yoga studio. The space is incredibly beautiful, designed by the award-winning Olson Sundberg Kundig Allen Architects team, with soothing interior design by Ted Tuttle. Numerous styles of yoga classes are offered, including donation-based classes. You can get one week of unlimited yoga for $25, a great opportunity for visitors. In addition to the yoga classes, there is also a full-service spa with wellness treatments including massage, facials, and manicures.

SPECTATOR SPORTS

The mild weather and some of the most phenomenal sports stadiums to be found anywhere make Seattle a great place to catch a game. The Mariners and the Seahawks both flirt with glory, though never quite seem to attain it; nevertheless, they have a loyal following and gorgeous digs. One of the best things about both Safeco and Qwest Fields is their location on the south end of downtown, on the outskirts of Pioneer Square. From a game, there are a number of great restaurants, bars, and brewpubs you can walk to for a celebratory (or commiserating) drink—especially good to know because you do not want to be mired in the postgame traffic trying to get out of the area.

With the departure of the NBA Seattle SuperSonics team in 2008, the city no longer has a professional basketball team. However, the WNBA is still playing pro b-ball, and the UW Huskies women's basketball team is very popular in Seattle. Even the Thunderbirds, a WHL hockey team, enjoy a small but enthusiastic fan base. Catching a game of some sort also makes a good rainy-day activity; the retractable roofs of venues like Safeco and Qwest Fields mean that games don't get rained out.

BASEBALL

SEATTLE MARINERS
Safeco Field, 1250 1st Ave. South
  (Central)
(206) 346-4000
http://seattle.mariners.mlb.com

The Mariners are the most popular sports team in Seattle. The MLB team has a devoted following, and tickets can sell out early—especially for big games and when they play against certain teams. The Mariners play at Safeco Field, one of the prettiest ballparks in the country. It's also one of the only ones with a retractable roof—almost a necessity in rain-soaked Seattle. The roof can open or close in just 20 minutes, allowing the team to play on a real grass field without the worry of getting rained out. Sweeping views of Seattle's downtown skyline

and breathtaking sunsets over Puget Sound, combined with excellent views of game action from all angles, give fans at Safeco Field an experience unequaled in Major League Baseball. Tours are offered, including areas of the ballpark that are not normally open to the public, such as the press box, private suites, field, dugouts, and visitors' clubhouse (all areas are subject to availability depending on activities within the ballpark). Tours are given several times throughout the day when there are no games, and cost $9 for adults and $7 for children ages 3–12 (2 and under are free). Check the Web site for seasonal tour schedules.

Tickets for games start at $7 for center-field bleachers and go up to $65 for lower box and terrace seats. You can buy tickets online, at the stadium box office, or at Mariners Team Store locations around town, including downtown, Bellevue, Lynnwood, and Tukwila. As far as parking goes on game days, with the location on the outskirts of central downtown, parking is difficult. You can purchase parking tickets ahead of time for the Safeco Field garage or Qwest Event Center garage for $15–$30. Expect heavy traffic getting into and out of the area. The best bet is to take public transportation—the "Metro to the Mariners" service runs special routes to the game for $5, and regular Metro and Sound Transit routes stop within a few blocks of the stadium at regular fares.

UNIVERSITY OF WASHINGTON HUSKIES
Husky Ballpark, 3800 Montlake Blvd. NE (North)
(206) 543-2200
www.gohuskies.com
UW has only a men's baseball team, called the Diamond Dawgs by fans. Tickets can be purchased at the Huskies Web site, on www.StubHub.com, or at the Husky ticket office; prices are $6 for adults, with a $15 family plan available that admits four. Most games are played at the Husky Ballpark, which opened in 1998. Occasionally the Dawgs will play special games at Safeco Field, and those tickets are $8 for adults. Adequate parking is available at Husky Ballpark, and public transportation is also plentiful and easy.

BASKETBALL

SEATTLE STORM
Key Arena, 305 Harrison St. (Central)
(206) 217-WNBA
www.wnba.com/storm
The Seattle Storm WNBA team came to Seattle in 1999, as one of four new expansion

teams for the 2000 season. The Storm play at Key Arena at Seattle Center. Single-game ticket prices generally range from $14 to $55 for stadium seating and can go up to as much as several hundred for courtside seats. Tickets can be purchased online through Ticketmaster or at the Key Arena box office. Parking garages are available around Key Arena and Seattle Center, but due to its downtown location, public transportation is usually the easiest way to get there. The monorail goes from Westlake Center, at Pine and 4th, directly to Seattle Center.

UNIVERSITY OF WASHINGTON HUSKIES
Bank of America Arena, 3800 Montlake Blvd. NE (North)
(206) 543-2200
www.gohuskies.com
Many Seattle residents are big Huskies fans, and UW has both a men's and a women's basketball team. Tickets can be purchased at the Huskies Web site, on www.StubHub.com, or at the Husky ticket office; prices are $3–$35. Both basketball teams play at the Bank of America Arena at Hec Edmundson Pavilion, which underwent a massive $40 million renovation from 1999 to 2000. Parking is available at the arena, and of course public buses run regular routes there as well.

FOOTBALL

SEATTLE SEAHAWKS
Qwest Field, 800 Occidental Ave. South (Central)
(888) 635-4295
www.seahawks.com
The Seahawks have been playing in Seattle since 1976, and during that time the team has certainly had its ups and downs. The Seahawks made one Super Bowl appearance,

in 2006 when they lost to the Pittsburgh Steelers 21–10. Currently owned by Paul Allen (of Microsoft), the Seahawks play at Qwest Field just south of Pioneer Square, adjacent to the Mariners' Safeco Field. Public tours are given at 12:30 and 2:30 p.m. Fri and Sat from Sept 1 to May 30, for $7. On home game days, the team is led onto the field by Taima, an Augur hawk, flying majestically out of the tunnel.

Qwest Field has a seating capacity of 67,000, with expansive concourses, comfortable seats, cutting-edge technology, and upper-end concession and dining options. Tickets can be purchased online through Ticketmaster or at the stadium box office. Prices start at around $50 and can range up to $300 for charter seating and suites. As with baseball games at Safeco, football game days offer garage parking at both facilities, but parking can be expensive, and getting in and out of the area is a nightmare. Taking public transportation is highly recommended, and the Seahawks Web site has a comprehensive Transportation Guide section that will tell you all you need to know about getting there via bus and light rail.

UNIVERSITY OF WASHINGTON HUSKIES
Bank of America Arena, 3800 Montlake Blvd. NE (North)
(206) 543-2200
www.gohuskies.com

The Husky football team has a loyal following; they are often called the Dawgs, and there is even a Dawg Blog and a Dawg Channel. Tickets can be purchased at the Huskies Web site, on www.StubHub.com, or at the Husky ticket office; prices are $32–$72. Big games, like Nebraska or Washington State,

will just about always sell out quickly. The football team plays at Husky Stadium, annually voted the most scenic football structure in the nation, proving a huge obstacle for opposing teams. With nearly 70 percent of the seats located between the end zones, Husky Stadium can be one of the loudest in the nation. Sound Transit light rail has been approved to Husky Stadium; construction began in early 2010 and is scheduled for completion in 2016. Until that time, parking at UW sporting events will undergo periods of change. Check the Web site for current parking information before driving to a UW sporting event. Bus service also runs regularly to the stadium.

HOCKEY

SEATTLE THUNDERBIRDS
ShoWare Center, 625 W. James (Kent)
(253) 239-7825
www.seattlethunderbirds.com

Part of the Western Hockey League, the Thunderbirds have been smacking the puck around the ice in Seattle since 1977, when they were called the Breakers. The WHL is a member of the Canadian Hockey League, and comprises the junior hockey teams. Players are scouted for the CHL and NHL from these teams. Tickets can be purchased at the Thunderbirds Web site, starting at around $12–$18. The team plays at ShoWare arena in the Kent Events Center, located 18 miles south of downtown Seattle. If you are driving, it's a straight shot south on I-5 to exit 149; plenty of free parking is available. More than 20 local and regional bus routes also serve the transit center at Kent Station, in addition to Sounder commuter rail; check the Web site for specific transit information.

HORSE RACING

EMERALD DOWNS
2300 Emerald Downs Dr. (Auburn)
(888) 931-8400
www.emeralddowns.com

Apr through Sept is horse racing season, and this track is just a few miles south of Seattle in Auburn. A day at the Emerald Downs races comes in many forms. You can simply pay admission and hang out on the track level with your friends, or bring a blanket and relax in the park. If you want to have a "home base" at the track, reserve a seat in the grandstand or a table in the Rainier Restaurant. Numerous special events are held throughout the season, including a Fireworks Spectacular around the Fourth of July. General admission tickets are $7 and include access to the first five levels of the grandstand, paddock, and park. Children 17 and under are admitted free, as are military personnel with valid ID. General parking is free, and valet is offered for $10. To get to the racetrack, drive south on I-5 to exit 147 (272nd Street), turning east for 3 miles. Then turn right on West Valley Highway for 1 mile, then left at 37th Street NW to Emerald Downs. Sound Transit Express bus routes 564 and 565 and Sounder commuter rail all go directly to the track from downtown Seattle on race days.

ROLLER DERBY

RAT CITY ROLLERGIRLS
Key Arena, 305 Harrison St. (Central)
http://ratcityrollergirls.com

With a motto like "You win some, you bruise some," this is not your traditional spectator sport! If you haven't caught wind of the revival of women's roller derby over the past few years, you're really missing out. It's back

in a big way, it's fast, and it's a lot of fun. The Rat City Rollergirls (RCRG) is Seattle's premier all-female, flat-track roller derby league. RCRG is composed of about 80 active skaters and many more retired skaters who are still involved. The team got rolling in Apr 2004 after a group of good friends with glasses of good wine sat around a lamb stir-fry and Minute Rice dinner swapping wild stories about a roller derby resurgence in Texas. Within weeks, that dinner party conversation led to the formation of the RCRG, the first flat-track derby league in the Northwest. Within months the league—named, after a fashion, for the South Seattle neighborhood where it got its start—had grown to four teams: Derby Liberation Front, Grave Danger, Sockit Wenches, and Throttle Rockets. If you want to join the "Rat Pack" fans and see a game, check out the RCRG Web site for a schedule and more details.

SOCCER

SEATTLE SOUNDERS
Qwest Field, 800 Occidental Ave. South
   (Central)
(206) 622-3415
www.soundersfc.com

The Seattle Sounders FC is Major League Soccer's 15th team. Actor, comedian, and soccer fan Drew Carey owns the team and was also instrumental in forming the team's 53-piece marching band, the Sound Wave— the only soccer marching band in the United States. The Sounders play at Qwest Field, and tickets range from $25 to $95. Parking is available at and around the stadium, but both parking and traffic can be difficult. Public transportation options are easy and numerous.

UNIVERSITY OF WASHINGTON HUSKIES

Husky Soccer Stadium, 3800 Montlake
  Blvd. NE (North)
(206) 543-2200
www.gohuskies.com

There are both men's and women's soccer teams at UW, and on the field at Husky Soccer Stadium the Huskies annually rank among the nation's leaders in women's soccer attendance. Tickets can be purchased online, by phone, or at the Husky ticket office; single-game tickets are $6 for adults, with a $15 family plan available that admits four. Both teams play at the Husky Soccer Stadium, a soccer-only facility that opened in 1997. Plans and fund-raising are currently in place for building a new, covered 3,000-seat stadium. Parking and public transportation are available.

DAY TRIPS AND WEEKEND GETAWAYS

If you have more than a few days in Seattle, there are a lot of great destinations that are nearby and easy to get to. Whether your interest is the mountains, islands, or valleys of the Pacific Northwest, or you want to check out the state's fabulous wine regions, this chapter will give you a great overview. A number of cruise ships leave from Seattle's ports, and there are also a large number of casino and spa resorts to choose from if that's your thing. You may even want to take advantage of Seattle's location, so close to the Canadian border, to cross over into beautiful British Columbia. This chapter highlights destinations within about a three-hour drive from Seattle, with recommendations for overnight stays and must-see attractions.

BRITISH COLUMBIA

British Columbia is Canada's westernmost province, set between the Pacific Ocean to the west and the magnificent Rocky Mountains to the east. Blessed with breathtaking landscapes, BC is home to a geographical diversity that lends itself to a vast array of activities and adventures. There are mountains to climb, rivers to run, beaches to comb, forests to hike, parks to stroll, and warm summer lakes to laze about on. Although there are many places in BC well worth visiting and exploring, two destinations in particular make great short getaways from Seattle.

Vancouver

VISITOR CENTER
Plaza Level, 200 Burrard St., Vancouver
(604) 683-2000
www.tourismvancouver.com
This bustling cosmopolitan city across the Canadian border to the north of Seattle is juxtaposed with the dramatic natural scenery in its background. Ringed by water and the mountains, much like Seattle itself, Vancouver is rugged and outdoorsy, yet stylish and sophisticated all at the same time.

Vancouver definitely has an international vibe, with a blend of European and Asian cultures that, similar to Seattle, creates an exciting fusion of cuisine, traditions, and arts. Shopping and nightlife are both plentiful and varied; it's hard to imagine anyone ever getting bored in Vancouver. Many new structures and improvements to existing infrastructure were put in place for the 2010 Olympics, improving the visitability of the world-class city even more.

Robson Street is the place to go for shopping and people-watching. Several galleries are also located on Robson, including the highly-acclaimed **Vancouver Art Gallery** (750 Hornby St., 604-662-4700, www .vanartgallery.bc/ca), where you can find works by the popular British Columbian artist Emily Carr. Another great place to stroll and shop is **Granville Island** (1689 Johnston St., 604-666-5784, www.granvilleisland.com), a charming public market with narrow lanes, situated on a little island just across from downtown. Vendor stalls of produce, fresh-baked bread, and seafood will tempt you, as well as the artisan wares and unique shops all over the island.

For nature lovers and those seeking outdoor recreation, begin at **Stanley Park** (Georgia Street, www.vancouver.ca/Parks/park/stanley). This 1,000-acre green space lies along one of the city's busiest streets, separating the edge of downtown from the water. It's a great place to walk, run, bring your dog, play Frisbee, have a picnic, or just enjoy a beautiful day at the park. A seawall path provides a terrific walking route, with totem poles lending visual interest throughout the park. The **Vancouver Aquarium** (843 Avison Way, 604-659-3474, www.vanaqua.org) is also found here.

From Stanley Park, drive across the Lions Gate Bridge to Vancouver's oldest tourist attraction, the **Capilano Suspension Bridge** (3735 Capilano Rd., 604-985-7474, www.capbridge.com). This amazing 450-foot, swaying bridge is suspended 230 feet above the Capilano River; the 27 acres of surrounding park and exhibits make for a terrific half-day. Later, head up **Grouse Mountain** (6400 Nancy Greene Way, 604-980-9311, www.grousemountain.com) on the 15-minute **Skyride** from downtown Vancouver for some of the best views of the city. You can also ski, zipline, and paraglide from Grouse Mountain, if you're in the mood for an adrenaline rush.

The **Vancouver Trolley** (875 Terminal Ave., 604-801-5515, www.vancouvertrolley

.com) is a great way to both take in the major attractions of the city, as well as get around. For $20–$45 depending on the type of ticket, you can hop on and hop off the trolley loop as many times as you want in a one- or two-day period. The trolley takes riders to all the major points in the city, with driver guides who give a running tour as you go.

Getting There

The drive north on I-5 from Seattle will take about three hours; buses are also available between the cities. Flights take about an hour, although by the time you factor in time for check-in, security, and boarding, the total travel time is about the same as driving. Amtrak has a train service called the Cascades that provides a four-hour ride with stunning views from its panoramic window coaches—I recommend this travel option the most, as the trip is beautiful and for the most part you can get around Vancouver quite easily with public transportation and taxis. Princess Cruise Lines also offers a one-way sailing from Seattle to Vancouver, for $100–$150, which is a beautiful way to get there if you have the time. It's important to remember that whichever way you travel to British Columbia, a valid passport is required for U.S. citizens to enter and leave Canada.

Where to Eat

For amazing views, the **Top of Vancouver Revolving Restaurant (**555 West Hastings St., 604-669-2220, www.topofvancouver.com**)** is at the top of the Harbour Centre Tower. Glass elevators whisk you 553 feet to the restaurant, where your table features an unobstructed view of the city; the revolving floor turns a full 360 degrees every hour. Vancouver has great ethnic food—try **Tojo's** for sushi, **Vij's** for upscale Indian food, or

Provence Marinaside for a Northwest take on French Mediterranean dishes.

Where to Stay

The **Wedgewood Hotel & Spa** (845 Hornby St., 604-689-7777, www.wedge woodhotel.com) is the landmark luxury property in Vancouver, with opulent rooms that feature fireplaces and jetted bathtubs. For something a little more cutting-edge, the **Moda** (900 Seymour St., 604-683-4251, www.modahotel.ca) is a 1908 building that has been transformed into chic modern design, in the middle of the arts district.

Victoria

VISITOR CENTER
812 Wharf St., Victoria
(800) 663-3883
www.tourismvictoria.com

Victoria is a historic, utterly charming town just across the Strait of Juan de Fuca from Washington, on Vancouver Island. The capital city of British Columbia boasts a wealth of historic buildings and some of the most fascinating museums in western Canada. Start with the downtown Inner Harbour area, home to the **Royal British Columbia Museum** (675 Belleville St., 250-356-7226, www.royalbcmuseum.bc.ca), magnificent **Parliament** buildings, and **Thunderbird Park,** with its display of totem poles.

Craidarroch Castle (1050 Joan Cres, 250-592-5352, www.craidarrochcastle.com) is simply amazing, with 39 rooms lavishly furnished in the late 1890s period in which it was built. Take a stroll through the historic **James Bay neighborhood** to see stunning original homes; or **Johnson Street** and **Trounce Alley** for boutiques filled with designer goods. Take high tea at the

incredible **Empress Hotel** (721 Government St., 250-384-811), once the queen's palace, for a step back to an elegant time. Don't miss the century-old **Butchart Gardens** (800 Benvenuto Ave., 250-652-5256, www.butch artgardens.com), 55 acres of lush, botanic show gardens. Victoria also has a **Chinatown** district with bustling markets, bakeries, and boutiques that make for an interesting stroll.

No description of Victoria would be complete without mentioning the water. Smooth-as-glass bays reflect the Olympic Mountains towering in the distance. Pods of whales swim off the shores, while eagles soar above them. Every beach is unique, some full of rocks and tidal pools waiting to be explored; others have long sandy stretches with views that rival the Mediterranean.

Getting There

Because you must traverse the Strait of Juan de Fuca to get to Victoria, there is no really direct, easy way. The **Victoria Clipper** (250-382-8100) provides the best bet, with ferry service departing from Pier 69 on the downtown Seattle waterfront to Victoria's Inner Harbour. The ferries run regularly during the summer, but in the off-season be sure to check ahead of time for schedules. **Washington State Ferries** (www.wsdot.wa .gov/ferries) leave from Anacortes, about an hour north of Seattle, if you want to drive up and take the shorter water route. Both ferries accept vehicles and passengers on foot. If you want to go by air, you can take a **Kenmore Air** (www.kenmoreair.com) float plane from Lake Union or King County International Airport.

Where to Eat

The internationally renowned **Sooke Harbour House** (1528 Whiffen Spit Rd.,

250-642-3421, www.sookeharbourhouse .com), 40 minutes west of Victoria in Sooke, sets the bar for West Coast cuisine. The menu changes daily, with seafood usually served the day it is caught and greens and herbs coming from the resort's own gardens. Sooke Harbour House has one of the country's finest wine cellars, and the restaurant has been named the best on Vancouver Island by prestigious *Vancouver Magazine* for 20 consecutive years.

Where to Stay

Try the **Humboldt House Bed & Breakfast** (867 Humboldt St., 888-383-0327, www .humboldthouse.com), which is filled with antiques and beautiful classic decor everywhere you look. Each room is themed, from the Oriental Room to the Gazebo Room.

CASINO RESORTS

Like many states, the casinos in Washington are run by First Nations tribes. There are a number of different casinos throughout the state, 28 at the time of this writing, but some are so complete that they are truly destinations in themselves. Many are also very family-friendly. I have included the cream of the crop here.

QUINAULT BEACH RESORT
78 SR 115, Ocean Shores
(888) 461-2214
www.quinaultbeachresort.com
More than just a resort or a casino, this is a place where you can take a hike along the dunes and dig your toes in the sand at the Pacific Ocean's edge. Olympic National Park and Washington State Park are nearby; despite the fact that it's a casino resort, this is a great place for family fun. The rooms and suites are comfortable and warm, with a very homey vibe that's refreshingly absent of cutting-edge interior decor. All rooms have a fireplace, which is a nice touch, and most have a majestic ocean view. On-site amenities include a day spa, fitness center, indoor pool, and Jacuzzi.

The Quinault Indian Nation runs this resort, and its 1,300 members live nearby on a reservation of more than 200,000 acres of unspoiled lakes and pristine wilderness. Guests of the resort are invited to visit the reservation, led by an Indian guide who will take you on a tour of untouched coastal beaches, tell you about native birds and mammals, or lead you on a fishing expedition.

There's plenty of nightlife and several restaurants, and of course the full casino. Many special events and entertaining performances are held here constantly, from powwows and Native American festivals with dancing and arts, to fireworks displays and concerts. The town of Ocean Shores, where the resort is located, is a relaxed little ocean-side town with plenty for families to do, including free sand-sculpting lessons and sand-castle competitions. If you're there in Mar, don't miss the annual Razor Clam Festival.

Getting There
By car, the resort is a little over two hours from Seattle, south on I-5 to Olympia. From there, you take Highway 101 (at exit 104) north toward Hoquiam and Ocean Beaches. After crossing the Hoquiam Bridge, turn left onto Highway 109 for 18 miles. There is no public transportation.

Where to Eat
Kids will love the local favorite, **Sand Castle Drive-In** (788 Point Brown Ave. NE,

360-289-2777). The very basic joint is similar to the old-time burger joints where you drive up, park, and receive car-side service—only the Sand Castle serves fish burgers, fish-and-chips, chowder, and clam strips. For the adults, the **Galway Bay Irish Pub and Restaurant** (880 Point Brown Ave. NE, 360-289-2300, www.galwaybayirishpub.com) is a warm tavern that does pub food justice—don't miss the soda bread.

Where to Stay

For families, the **Parlor Suite** is a great home away from home. A separate living room and bedroom with two queen beds offers plenty of space, and the jetted bathtub and fabulous ocean views will spoil you.

SUQUAMISH CLEARWATER CASINO RESORT

15347 Suquamish Way NE, Suquamish
(360) 598-8700, (866) 609-8700
www.clearwatercasino.com

This casino-themed resort is about 30 minutes from downtown Seattle. The site is breathtaking, nestled among pines and cedars. The casino, of course, is a main attraction, offering a multitude of video slot machines, blackjack, poker, craps, keno, and roulette tables. But the resort offers many more attractions than the casino, and there is truly something for the whole family. The array of indoor and outdoor pleasures includes the full-service **Angeline Spa** (360-598-1420, www.clearwatercasino.com/spa), zero-entry pool with Jacuzzi, art gallery, sports lounge, and the award-winning **White Horse Golf Course** (22795 Three Lions Place NE, 360-297-4468, www.white horsegolf.com). The resort also offers plenty of entertainment, such as live music in the Beach Rock Lounge, and free concerts on the lawn in the summer. The 85 guest rooms overlook either the Agate Passage or Northwest forest landscape, and feature a king bed and sleeper sofa or two queen beds, luxurious bedding from the local Pacific Down Company, 32-inch televisions with premium cable, and high-speed Internet access. Suites and two spacious, fully furnished rental houses are also available. Sixteen rooms allow smoking, and pets are welcome with a $200 refundable deposit. Complimentary breakfast is offered to all guests.

Getting There

The resort is located on the scenic Kitsap Peninsula, between Poulsbo and Bainbridge Island at the Agate Pass Bridge. Follow Highway 305 North toward Poulsbo approximately 6 miles; the resort is located just across the Agate Pass Bridge. It is also accessible via the Bainbridge Island ferry, and a free courtesy shuttle is available from the ferry landing.

Where to Eat

The **Cedar Steakhouse** (www.clearwater casino.com/dining/cedar) offers a fixed-price, four-course gourmet dinner Mon through Wed.

Where to Stay

The **Salt Aire Cottage** is a darling two-bedroom waterfront homes with amazing views and a great patio for barbecuing or relaxing. The **Beach House** is a three-bedroom waterfront home with a sloping lawn down to the shore.

TULALIP RESORT CASINO

10200 Quil Ceda Blvd., Tulalip
(888) 272-1111
www.tulalipresort.com

Located 37 miles north of Seattle, Tulalip Resort Casino is run by the Tulalip tribes. It is a complete destination in its own right, with a luxury hotel, numerous dining options, entertainment, shopping, meeting facilities, a full-service spa, and of course the casino. Arrival at the front entrance is pretty show-stopping, with a dramatically overdone water feature including fountains and water-falls, Tulalip tribe life re-creations, and an orca whale jumping out of the small lake (not real!). Don't let the fairly nondescript build-ing exterior fool you, though—the inside and amenities are just as dramatic.

While the casino is Vegas-style lights, nonstop action, and the familiar *ca-ching* of slot machines, the hotel is laid-back and soothing, with natural materials and Coast Salish art throughout. Guest rooms and suites are pan-Asian chic with luxury amenities including flat-screen televisions and included wireless Internet. There is also a fitness center and the lush indoor Oasis Pool and waterfall. It would be hard to get bored here, with several cool lounges, a cabaret and outdoor amphi-theater on-site. Tulalip has a fantastic summer concert series, that features big names in music such as Billy Idol, Buddy Guy, Chicago, Lynyrd Skynyrd, and The Temptations.

Getting There

The drive to Tulalip Resort Casino will take less than an hour. Travel on I-5 north to exit 200, turning left onto 88th Street NE and then right onto Quil Ceda Boulevard. There is no public transportation.

Where to Eat

Catch one of the monthly **Winemakers Din-ners** (www.winemakersdinners.com) if you can—sommelier and wine buyer Tommy Thompson leads guests in exploring flavors from some of Washington's most influential wineries, paired with artistically prepared dishes of the same region.

Where to Stay

The ultimate bachelor pad can be found in the resort's **Players Suite.** The 1,500-square-foot suite is dedicated to sports of all kinds, not just casino gaming—there is a custom steel and copper pool table, a dartboard, and an arcade-style Golden Tee video golf-ing game. The full multimedia and sound system, double-sided fireplace, and mas-saging whirlpool tub make this a decadent indulgence.

CRUISES

Due to its location on Puget Sound near the Pacific Ocean, and its excellent ports, Seattle is a prime departure city for many cruise lines headed to Alaska. More than 220 cruises, carrying over 850,000 passengers, depart from Seattle ports each year. At the time of this writing, six major cruise lines were operating weekly service out of Seattle, offering seven- to fourteen-day round-trip itineraries. The ships depart on the weekend and Monday, and occasionally special itin-eraries for repositioning ships are offered. In addition to the large cruise lines, Seattle also benefits from small-ship sailings to the San Juan Islands, British Columbia, and North-west rivers, generally on one- to four-day cruises. In addition to the round-trip cruises that depart from and return to Seattle, sev-eral lines also offer long one-way itineraries to exotic destinations such as the Panama Canal, South America, Hawaii, and the Poly-nesian islands. These cruises are anywhere from 16 to 65 days in length and depart from Seattle with final destinations such as San Diego and Fort Lauderdale, Florida.

AMERICAN SAFARI CRUISES
(888) 862-8881
http://americansafaricruises.com

This small-ship yacht explores the famed Alaskan Inside Passage, in a one-way cruise from Seattle to Juneau that lasts 15 days. Embrace exhilarating closeness to snow-capped mountains, wildlife and birds far too numerous to keep count, waterfalls, tree-lined narrow passageways, and surprises at just about every "gunkholing" turn. Choose May or Sept—either is an excellent time for cruising along British Columbia's coast and Alaska's Inside Passage. At these times of the year the foliage is vivid, there are fewer boats and people, and bears and other animals are likely foraging along the shoreline. Then your second choice is which yacht best fits you: the *Safari Explorer, Safari Quest,* or *Safari Spirit.* The ship leaves from the Fishermen's Terminal, and the crew also offers complimentary airport pickup and transportation. There is also a seven-night Northwest Passage cruise sailing round-trip from Friday Harbor in the San Juan Islands. Here, orca whales move silently through the water in search of salmon. Seals and sea lions lounge on rocky islets, black bears and deer flourish in the deep evergreen forests, and snowcapped mountains fall steeply to the waters. American Safari yachts accommodate just 12, 22, or 36 guests, which also makes them perfect for a group of friends or family to charter.

CARNIVAL
(888) CARNIVAL (227-6482)
www.carnival.com

Carnival offers weekly seven-day Alaska cruises on the *Carnival Spirit,* departing Tues from the new Smith Cove Cruise Terminal at Pier 91. A destination eons in the making,

Glacier Bay's pristine landscape makes the top spot on most travelers' must-see lists. Your Glacier Bay Alaska cruise takes you to this protected national park that is spread across 3.2 million acres in southeast Alaska, home to 15 active glaciers, numerous sea-birds, otters, humpback whales, and count-less sights.

CELEBRITY CRUISES
(800) 722-5941
www.celebritycruises.com

Celebrity offers 7- and 10-night departures to Alaska on board the *Celebrity Infinity,* and new 16- or 17-night, one-way Panama Canal cruises. Alaska ports of call include Ketchikan, Juneau, Tracy Arm Fjord, Skagway, and the Inside Passage—one of the most famously beautiful passages in the world. It features virtually everything you go to Alaska hoping to see, including rain forests, glaciers, fjords, and white-capped peaks—all of which create a setting that's perfect for viewing whales and sea lions. The longer Alaskan cruises also go to the Hubbard Glacier and Icy Strait Point. The Panama Canal cruises head south to San Diego, then make stops in Mexico at Cabo San Lucas, Acapulco, and Huatulco before continuing on to Costa Rica. After spending a couple of days cruising through the Panama Canal, a stop is made in Cartagena, Colombia, before continuing on to the debarkation port of Fort Lauderdale. Celebrity Cruises depart from the Bell Street Pier Cruise Terminal at Pier 66 on the downtown waterfront.

CRUISE WEST
(888) 851-8133
www.cruisewest.com

The small ships of Cruise West (138 guests maximum) can forsake the wider shipping lanes for channels just a few hundred feet wide, tie up to inner piers in tiny villages, and share waterways with local fishermen and perhaps a few private yachts. The ships also carry inflatable excursion craft to take you directly to the action. The seven-night Pacific Northwest Coastal Escape cruises from Seattle to retrace Captain Vancouver's footsteps through the scenic waterways of the San Juan and Gulf Islands on this voyage of contrasts—rich in wildlife, culture, and scenery. Meander the picturesque streets of Victoria, wander Butchart Gardens, and learn the stories behind the totem poles in Stanley Park. Explore the quaint seaports of Friday Harbor and Port Townsend. Cruise West also offers an exciting 10-night Gold Rush Inside Passage itinerary, one-way from Seattle to Juneau, Alaska. Follow the Seattle to Juneau route of the original stampeders from the 1898 Klondike gold rush. From dense, forested shores to stunning fjords, immense glaciers, and unspoiled waterways, the Inside Passage is a world of spectacular beauty. Cruise the pristine waters of the San Juan Islands, the Strait of Georgia, Glacier Bay National Park and Preserve, Frederick Sound, and Tracy Arm, and visit the towns of Sitka, Petersburg, and Skagway, the jumping-off points for thousands of early gold seekers.

HOLLAND AMERICA LINE
(877) 932-4259
www.hollandamerica.com

Holland America Line offers seven- and 14-day cruises from Seattle to Alaska, departing from the Smith Cove Cruise Terminal at Pier 91. Seven-day sailings go to Juneau, Glacier Bay, Sitka, and Ketchikan in Alaska, and Victoria, British Columbia. These deep-water fjords left by retreating glaciers resulted in granite cliffs towering thousands of feet above the sea and countless waterfalls cascading into placid waters. The 14-day cruises also go through the Inside Passage and visit Skagway, Anchorage, Homer, and Kodiak. Holland America also offers extensive one-way cruises that leave Seattle for numerous Pacific Ocean and South American ports of call, and end up in San Diego for debarkation. These 35- to 65-day cruises go to places such as Hawaii, French Polynesia, Mexico, Costa Rica, Nicaragua, Panama, Peru, and Ecuador.

NORWEGIAN CRUISE LINE
(800) 327-7030
www.ncl.com

Norwegian Cruise Line has made Seattle its home port for seven-day summer cruises to Alaska on board the *Norwegian Star* and *Norwegian Pearl,* with both round-trip itineraries and seven-day cruises that leave from Seattle and end up in Vancouver, British Columbia. These cruises visit Alaska's Inside Passage, Juneau, Skagway, Glacier Bay, Prince Rupert, Ketchikan, and Victoria, BC. Passengers depart from the Bell Street Pier Cruise Terminal at Pier 66 on Sat and Sun.

PRINCESS CRUISES
(800) 421-1700
www.princess.com

Princess Cruises offers 4-, 7-, and 14-day cruises from Seattle to Alaska. Sail the gorgeous waterways and granite cliffs of the Inside Passage, home to whales, seals, eagles, and more. On seven-day cruises you'll visit Skagway, Juneau, and Ketchikan while sailing in Glacier Bay or Tracy Arm Fjord, depending on your itinerary. The 14-day cruises include visits to Glacier Bay National Park and Tracy Arm Fjord for unbelievable glacier viewing opportunities, plus Kodiak, home to the famous bears, Icy Point, Seward, and other frontier-flavored ports. The four-day Northwest Sampler visits Vancouver and Victoria in British Columbia, before returning to Seattle; and there is also a one-way, one-day coastal cruise from Seattle to Vancouver. The South Pacific Grand Adventure is a 33-day cruise that goes to Hawaii, Tahiti, French Polynesia, Samoa, and New Zealand, with Sydney as the final debarkation port. Princess Cruises depart Mon, Sat, and Sun from the Smith Cove Cruise Terminal at Pier 91.

ROYAL CARIBBEAN
(866) 562-7625

Royal Caribbean offers seven-night cruises to Alaska on the *Rhapsody of the Seas,* departing from the Smith Cove Cruise Terminal at Pier 91 every Fri. From the awe-inspiring blue ice of a massive glacial field to the expansive grandeur of its wildlife and nature, Alaska is a land of natural wonders, and this cruise sails through the Inside Passage to Juneau, Skagway, Tracy Arm Fjord, and Victoria, British Columbia, before returning to Seattle.

ISLANDS

One of the main attractions of Seattle's gorgeous location on Puget Sound is the water, which is firmly rooted in the area's identity and lifestyle. It's almost a crime to be here and not get on the water. The numerous islands that dot these waterways make fantastic escapes from the city, providing an entirely different experience. On the islands of Puget Sound you can kayak, see wildlife habitats, browse art galleries and boutiques, bicycle, pick berries, and visit small wineries. One of the best things about traveling to the islands is the trip—unlike many trips, the journey really is half the fun as you take in the astounding scenery from a ferry or look down in amazement from a float plane.

BAINBRIDGE ISLAND
Chamber of Commerce, 395 Winslow Way East, Bainbridge Island
(866) 805-3700
www.bainbridgechamber.com/default.aspx?SS=3

This quaint town on the Kitsap Peninsula is only a half-hour ferry ride from downtown Seattle, making it a perfect place for a day or half-day trip. Just over 20,000 call the 36-square-mile island home and enjoy its convenient access to Seattle, gently rolling hills, pristine seashore, and rustic charm. In July 2005, CNN/Money and *Money* magazine named Bainbridge Island the second-best place to live in the United States. It's a small island town that offers big things—acres of parks, a variety of trailheads, fascinating historical sites, and dozens of attractions and annual events. The **Bloedel Reserve** (7571 NE Dolphin Dr., 206-842-7631, www.bloedelreserve.org) is a 150-acre nature preserve and garden that is well worth a visit (more details on p. 189).

Known for its lively artistic community, Bainbridge Island has its own **Performing Arts Center** (Box Office: 206-842-8569, www.bainbridgeperformingarts.com), movie complex, and arts and crafts galleries featuring local and regional artists. Enjoy shopping in historic **Winslow** and a visit to the **Bainbridge Island Vineyard & Winery** (8989 Day Rd. East, 206-842-9463, www.bainbridgevineyards.com), as well as some of Kitsap's trendiest cafes and restaurants. Don't miss the concerts on Wed evenings in **Waterfront Park** or the **farmers' market** on Sat. Fourth of July celebrations are big in the small town, with a fun parade and all kinds of festivities. A bridge over Agate Pass connects Bainbridge to the rest of the Kitsap Peninsula via Highway 305; Bainbridge Island is a great starting point for exploring other parts of the peninsula. The Chamber of Commerce visitor information center is located at the ferry exit.

Getting There

Take the Washington State Ferry from the main Seattle terminal at Pier 52; ferries depart about every 50 minutes from 6 a.m. to midnight. A 20-minute advance arrival time is recommended for non-peak travel, but on summer weekends and holidays you should allow 30–60 minutes. This also goes for weekday commuting times, as many people who live on Bainbridge work in Seattle; however, if you're taking a day trip from Seattle to Bainbridge, you will be going against the commuter crowd. The ferry accepts vehicles and foot passengers, and you can take your bike, kayak, and leashed pets. If you're staying in the town, a car isn't really necessary and can be hard to park. Winslow is very easy to walk or bike (rentals available), and Kitsap Transit also provides bus service.

Where to Eat

Café Nola (101 Winslow Way East, 206-842-3822, www.cafenola.com) is a perennial favorite. The European-style bistro serves innovative, eclectic cuisine by chef/owner Kevin Warren using seasonal and local ingredients. It's just as good for lunch as it is for its romantic, candlelit dinner scene. Specialty cocktails, Northwest microbrews, and an extensive wine list round out the offerings.

Where to Stay

To really take advantage of the beautiful Puget Sound water setting between Seattle and Bainbridge Island, why not stay at a boat and breakfast? The **SV Lille Danser** (871 Wyatt Way NW, 206-855-4108, www.whozyamama.com/id5.html) is a 50-foot sailboat docked at the island; once on board the skippered charter, you can take a sunset sail and then settle in for the night, as the water rocks you gently. It's actually quite a good deal; for $250 you get a two-hour sail and overnight stay for up to six people, and continental breakfast.

SAN JUAN ISLANDS
Visitors Bureau, 640 Mullis St., Friday Harbor
(888) 468-3701
www.visitsanjuans.com

This archipelago of 457 islands is a favorite weekend getaway for Seattleites. Only a handful of these islands are inhabited, however, and many of them are just tiny outcroppings of rocks that aren't even named. The main island, **San Juan,** consists of the decent-size town of **Friday Harbor,** which offers lots of options for lodging, dining, activities, and entertainment. Both the town and the picturesque farmlands surrounding it are close enough for walking, and the wealth of outdoor recreation that the islands are known for includes their excellent whale-watching excursions (there's a reason one of the islands is named Orcas Island).

The four main islands—San Juan, Orcas, Shaw, and Lopez—are still largely undeveloped, with a bucolic charm that is fascinating to explore. **Orcas Island** is the largest, with a beautiful fjord and a thriving art community. **Shaw** is the smallest, and its most notable feature for visitors is the ferry landing, which is operated by Franciscan nuns who also sell gas and operate a general store. **Lopez Island** is a cyclist's paradise, and the most agricultural with acres of rolling farmland. Cycling and sea kayaking are two popular ways to see the beauty of the islands and their wildlife, on the water and the land. Birds, seals, sea lions, otters, and the orca whales are abundant along the coastline.

Numerous whale-watching tours operate, offering visitors the best up-close-and-personal opportunities for sightings during the whale season from May to Sept. One of the best is the **San Juan Safaris Whale Watching & Wildlife Tours** (10 Front St., 800-450-6858, 360-378-1323, www.sanjuansafaris .com), which has its own ecotourism consultant and operates small group excursions. Their philosophy is to guide rather than herd, and the company operates with respect for the wildlife and its environment. For multi-day cruises on a yacht, try **American Safari Cruises** (3826 18th Ave. W, 888-862-8881, www.americansafaricruises.com). They operate a seven-night, round-trip itinerary from Friday Harbor that explores Victoria, British Columbia, the Harmony Islands, coastal fjords, Princess Louisa Inlet, Vancouver, and Roche Harbor.

Getting There

There are two main ways to get to the San Juan Islands. You can take the **Washington State Ferries** to one of the four main islands from the town of Anacortes, about a 90-minute drive north from Seattle. You can leave your car parked at the ferry landing or take it across on the ferry with you. The second option is to take a float plane from Seattle to San Juan Island. At the time of this writing, flight service on this route was available from **Kenmore Air** and **Northwest Seaplanes;** it is a popular route, so not likely to change. Besides a float plane, you can also take a regular, small chartered land plane from Boeing Field with **San Juan Airlines** or **Westwind Aviation.**

Where to Eat

The **Bluff Restaurant at Friday Harbor House Hotel** (130 West St., 360-378-8455, www.fridayharborhouse.com) offers a small but tempting menu of Northwest fare, served in an intimate dining room with a cozy fireplace and outstanding views.

Where to Stay

For the fun factor, the **Earthbox Motel & Spa** (410 Spring St., 360-378-4000, www.earth boxmotel.com) on San Juan Island can't be beat. It's a retro 1950s-era motor inn that has been completely renovated in a playful contemporary style with Pacific Northwest elements, and its has a wellness spa. You can even use the fun beach cruiser bikes for free. For ultimate luxury, **Rosario Resort and Spa on Orcas Island** (1400 Rosario Rd., 360-376-2222, www.rosarioresort.com) is centered on a magnificent 1909 mansion built by a shipbuilding magnate. You can get there only by seaplane or boat (ferries and water taxis are available).

WHIDBEY AND CAMANO ISLANDS
Visitor Center, 23 Front St., Coupeville
   (several other locations also)
(888) 747-7777
www.whidbeycamanoislands.com
In Puget Sound, 25 miles north of Seattle, lie these islands that offer a great weekend getaway. They are an especially big draw for anyone interested in the creative arts, as they are a mecca of art galleries, writer and artist retreats, and working artists' studios. **Whidbey Island** is particularly known for its glass artists such as John de Wit, and is often called the "Isle of Murano" of Puget Sound. Outside of cultural interests, the islands are great for scuba diving, kayaking, cycling, and whale watching. Canada's first National

Historical Reserve, **Ebey's Landing** (360-678-6084, www.nps.gov/ebla) is also here.

Whidbey Island's **Scenic Isle Way** was the first Washington State Scenic Byway on an island, and it makes for an amazing coastal drive. Many of the artists who live on the island take much of their inspiration from the beauty found along this route. The **Deception Pass Bridge** is also worth a visit; it started as a dream and became a huge inconvenience (taking more than 50 years to build), but now it crowns the second-most-visited park in the state, after Mount Rainier. The islands offer Island Transit buses that are completely free and go all around the islands—so just hop on and off, and enjoy!

Getting There

Both bridge and ferry connect the islands with the mainland, and barring traffic (or a line for the ferry, which often happens on Friday afternoon), you can reach them from Seattle in an hour or less. Take the **Clinton–Mukilteo or Keystone-Port Townsend ferries**, or drive across Deception Pass Bridge—an incredibly scenic route. The Amtrak Cascades train also makes two morning and two evening stops daily.

Where to Eat

The culinary agritourism scene on the islands is thriving. Check out **Gordon's on Blueberry Hill** (5438 Woodard Ave., 360-331-7515) , where grilled wild salmon is served with a salad of local greens and edible flowers. **Christopher's** in Coupeville (103 NW Coveland St., 360-678-5480, www.christophersonwhidbey.com) barbecues the salmon and tops it with a fresh raspberry sauce, but the Penn Cove mussel stew with local herbs is hard to pass up.

Where to Stay

The **Inn at Langley** (400 1st St., 360-221-3033, www.innatlangley.com) is luxurious, comfortable, and elegant, right in the midst of the galleries and restaurants of Langley, on the southern end of Whidbey Island. The Zen-inspired decor and water views make for an incredibly relaxing experience. For artists and writers, check out the **Whidbey Island Writer's Refuge** (P.O. Box 1392, 888-643-6191, www.writersrefuge.com), a cabin getaway to awaken the creative spirit.

MOUNTAINS

Just like the water, in Seattle there is no escaping the mountains, which are an indelible part of the landscape and a major reason why many Seattleites choose to live here. Mount Rainier, in particular, appears to loom over the city on clear days, even though it is nearly 100 miles away. Although Seattle enjoys a mild Pacific Ocean climate, where there are mountains, there is snow, and the Cascade and Olympic mountain ranges located just a short drive from the city make for excellent winter recreation, from skiing and snowboarding to sledding and snowmobiling. The national parks, visitor centers with park rangers, observatories, and many trails for hiking, skiing, and climbing make the nearby ranges accessible for both day trips and multinight getaways into nature. For more information about area peaks and famous Northwest mountaineers, see the Pacific Northwest chapter.

CRYSTAL MOUNTAIN SKI RESORT
33914 Crystal Mountain Blvd., Crystal
  Mountain
(888) 754-6199
www.skicrystal.com

Washington's largest ski area, Crystal Mountain, encompasses 2,600 acres and more than 50 named runs. The base sits at 4,400 feet of altitude, and the summit is 7,012 feet. Gentle cruising groomers to challenging steeps and backcountry trails offer something for every ability level. Add to that the top-of-the-line lifts, including two six-person and two high-speed quads, grooming machines, lodges, and restaurants, and you have a world-class destination for winter sports. Snowboarding and night skiing are popular here, and alpine snowshoe tours and guided mountain tours are also available.

Getting There

About 105 minutes from Seattle, by car you drive south on I-5 to Highway 164 toward Enumclaw. From there take Highway 410 East and enter Mount Rainier National Park, and continue 6 miles up Crystal Mountain Boulevard. On Sat, Sun, and select holidays during ski season, the **Gray Line Express Bus** takes passengers from downtown Seattle to the resort for around $80, adult round-trip.

Where to Eat

At the top of the Rainier Express Chairlift perches the **Summit House Bistro** (360-663-3085), serving up gourmet food along with the breathtaking views. At 6,872 feet, the mountaintop restaurant is an experience. In addition to exciting Northwest cuisine, you can also find a great selection of bratwurst and traditional Swiss fondue. After dinner, check out the **Snorting Elk Cellar** (360-663-7798). Besides having a funny moniker, this ski-in Bavarian rathskeller bar was voted the Top Ski Bar in the West by *Snow Country Magazine*.

Where to Stay

The resort offers five different accommodations to choose from: the Lodge with fully-equipped condominiums, including full kitchens and fireplaces; the Crystal Resort with charming chalet suites and a romantic honeymoon cabin; and three traditional hotels with all amenities. All lodging options offer transportation to the lifts.

MOUNT RAINIER NATIONAL PARK
Visitor Center, 30027 SE 706 East, Ashford
   (inside Whittaker Mountaineering)
(877) 617-9950
www.visitrainier.com

The most prominent mountain in the contiguous United States, Rainier can be easily seen from Seattle on a clear day, its peak jutting more than 14,000 imposing feet into the sky. It's also the most heavily glaciated peak in the lower 48 states, and not one but two volcanic craters top its summit, forming the world's largest glacier cave network. The mountain and surrounding area are part of Mount Rainier National Park, established in 1899 to protect 36 square miles of permanent snowfields, old-growth forests, and alpine meadows, and 26 major glaciers. Although Rainier is considered an active volcano, unlike St. Helens there is no major activity or evidence of a possible eruption; the last one recorded was in 1854.

Mount Rainier National Park provides experiences that can be enjoyed by anyone, at any skill level. Starting with the easiest, you can simply drive on the vehicle roadways that surround the mountain, with numerous rest stops, picnic areas, and lookout points. Choose from four loops, all of which can be completed easily in a day. SR 706, through Ashford, leads to the park's Nisqually entrance and then on up to the

Paradise Viewpoint. From here you can follow the Skyline Trail on foot, if you wish, for great views of the Nisqually Glacier. Sunrise is also a beautiful area, its open meadows offering great views of the mountain and Emmons Glacier. On Sun afternoons, park naturalists lead a 1.5-mile hike to explore a mountain goat habitat. Note that during the winter, many roads may well be closed due to snow and weather conditions.

For more physical adventures, the lower parts of Mount Rainier and the surrounding range provide excellent hiking, camping, and low-level climbing, as well as back-country and cross-country skiing, sledding, snowmobiling, and snowshoeing in the winter. Check out the Wonderland Trail in summer, perfect for a day trip or a challenging circumnavigation of the mountain along its full 93-mile course that will take you over ridges and valleys, and through forests and wildflower meadows. From mid-Dec through Mar, park rangers offer a guided 1.2-mile snowshoe walk through the Paradise area.

For the more adventurous, it is one of the most popular—and challenging—peaks for mountain climbers. The climbing on Rainier is extremely difficult, requiring two or three days to reach the summit, and the mountain allows the success of less than two-thirds of all attempts. Several deaths occur each year from falls, avalanche or rock falls, and hypothermia; while climbing the lower portions of the mountain could be done by those with intermediate experience, a summit attempt should be undertaken only by very proficient climbers or with the assistance of a highly qualified guide. The most dangerous factor is the weather, which constantly changes and can turn lethal at almost any time.

Summer is the driest, warmest time of the year in the area, but even then the weather can still be wet and cool. Bringing jackets and appropriate clothing, including hiking boots, is recommended if you plan to do any outdoor activities at all. Mount Rainier National Park is a climate-friendly park, with a goal of becoming carbon neutral by 2016.

Getting There

Mount Rainier National Park is located in the west-central portion of Washington state, about two to three hours from Seattle. It really is accessible only by driving; take I-5 south from the city, and once you get to the area, the route you take will depend on where you want to visit. Year-round access is via SR 706 to the Nisqually Entrance in the SW corner of the park. Limited winter access is available via Highway 123 in the southeast corner of the park. The Carbon River/Mowich Lake area (northwest corner) is accessed via SR 165 through Wilkeson. Visit the Web site for specific directions, road closures, trails, and other visitor information. There is no public transportation, but private bus and tour companies do run packages to Mount Rainier.

Where to Eat

It's hard to find a dining experience more unusual, kitschy, or historically accurate than that of the **Mount Rainier Railroad Dining Company** (54106 Mountain Hwy. East, 888-773-4637, www.rrdiner.com). Here, you can eat on an authentic railroad car right next door to a scenic, historic train station.

Where to Stay

Mount Rainier National Park has six campgrounds, with running water and toilets but no RV facilities. If you plan to camp overnight, you will need a permit, which can be obtained free at visitor centers and ranger stations. Or head to the **Paradise Inn** (360-569-2275, www.mtrainierguestservices.com/accommodations/paradise-inn), a fantastic log lodge that gives a true, old-fashioned mountain retreat experience. For a truly unique experience, stay in the **Cedar Creek Treehouse** (P.O. Box 204, 360-569-2991, www.cedarcreektreehouse.com), perched 50 feet up in a giant cedar tree and offering incredible views for miles around. The Rainbow Bridge connects the private tree house to an observatory 100 feet above the forest floor, for even more spectacular views.

MOUNT ST. HELENS NATIONAL VOLCANIC MONUMENT

Monument headquarters, 42218 NE Yale Bridge Rd., Amboy
(360) 449-7800
www.fs.fed.us/gpnf/mshnvm

Everyone surely remembers the devastation of the May 1980 Mount St. Helens eruption. After lying dormant for more than 100 years, the volcano rumbled with a 5.1-magnitude earthquake that caused the north face to collapse, in one of the largest landslides in recorded history that brought with it explosive magma and volcanic ash. Fifty-seven people were killed, and the eruption completely destroyed hundreds of square miles of forest and alpine lakes.

More than a quarter-century later, life is starting to return to the landscape that St. Helens rendered barren, although the threat of another eruption remains very real. The **National Volcanic Monument** (42218 NE Yale Bridge Rd., 360-449-7800, www.fs.fed .us/mshnvm) at Mount St. Helens allows visitors to learn about the eruption firsthand,

witness the result of its catastrophic devastation, and discover the natural rebirth that is occurring in the surrounding land today. The **Johnston Ridge Observatory** (21500 Spirit Lake Hwy., 360-274-2143) gives unparalleled views of the area and points of interest. Single-day tickets to the monument are $3, with free admission for those 15 years and younger. Other worthwhile area visitor centers include the visitor center at **Silver Lake** (admission fee), **Mount St. Helens Forest Learning Center** (www.weyerhaeuser .com/Sustainability/MtStHelens), and the **Hoffstadt Bluffs visitor center** (www.mt-st-helens.com) (both free).

Around the area, many trails provide great hiking and climbing—check out the astonishing **Loowit Falls,** a waterfall that emerges as meltwater from a glacier within the crater. The **Ape Caves** are also pretty cool, consisting of mile-long lava tubes formed by long-ago eruptions. Rangers lead tours in the summer, and you should bring a flashlight; it's an easy hike from there to **Lahar Viewpoint.** Climbing permits are required above 4,800 feet and can be purchased online from the Mount St. Helens Institute (www.mshinstitute.org). Most hiking trails and camping facilities are open from June through Oct, although note that they can sometimes be closed depending on the volcanic activity of St. Helens. In the winter, snowshoeing and cross-country skiing are popular activities here. Several companies offer helicopter tours, which provide an exciting (though expensive) way to see the volcano.

Getting There

You really must drive here, unless you take a guided excursion with a tour company. It's about two hours from Seattle, taking WA

504 from I-5. July through Sept are the best months to visit, offering the clearest viewing of the volcano; also, the Johnston Ridge Observatory is closed from Nov through Apr.

Where to Eat

Dining is limited in the National Monument and right around Mount St. Helens itself. The **Fire Mountain Grill** (15000 Spirit Lake Hwy., 360-957-1025, www.hoffstadtbluffs.com/restaurant.html) at Hoffstadt Bluffs offers casual, family-friendly dining. For more options, you'll need to go to the nearby towns of Longview, Castle Rock, or Kelso.

Where to Stay

Many people come to the mountains to camp; if this is you, the **Seaquest State Park** (3030 Spirit Lake Hwy., 888-226-7688, www.parks.wa.gov) and **Eco Park Resort** (14000 Spirit Lake Hwy., 877-255-1980, www.ecoparkresort.com) both offer great camping sites. If you're the kind who wants a little more comfort, the closest nice lodging is the **Blue Heron Inn Bed & Breakfast** (2846 Spirit Lake Hwy., 360-274-9595, www.blueheroninn.com) in Castle Rock.

STEVENS PASS
Summit Stevens Pass, US 2, Skykomish
(206) 634-1645
www.stevenspass.com

Located on the crest of the Cascade Range, the Stevens Pass ski area receives abundant and frequent snowfall, and due to the cool air of the region, the snow tends to stay dry and powdery. And the pass gets lots of it—an average 450 inches per year. Stevens is located on two national forests, the Mount Baker–Snoqualmie on the west side of the crest and the Wenatchee National Forest on the east. The ski resort has a base

elevation of 4,061 feet, and the top elevation is at Cowboy Mountain, 5,845 feet. There are more than 1,100 acres of skiable terrain with 37 major runs. The night skiing here is great, with six lifts lit and operating from Thurs through Mon nights.

The resort is run by a locally owned company and believes in careful stewardship of the mountain. Skiing and snowboarding are just about equally popular here, as well as Nordic cross-country and backcountry skiing and snowshoeing. A free shuttle is offered between the summit and the Stevens Pass Nordic Center, for easy access to the backcountry from the alpine area.

Getting There

Stevens Pass is 78 miles east of Seattle, in the Skykomish Valley; driving time is approximately two hours, depending on weather conditions. To get there, take I-405 north to Highway 522 toward Monroe. Turn left at Highway 2 and follow it 50 miles to Stevens Pass Resort.

Where to Eat

Located in the Granite Peaks Lodge, the **Bull's Tooth Pub and Eatery** (Stevens Pass) is a great place to refresh after a few runs on the hill. Hearty grilled entrees, salads, and fresh soups are prepared to order With 10 tap beers and a nice selection of fine wines and spirits, this is a great place to relax and unwind. Families sit fireside in our dining area, while the lounge area is reserved for those over 21.

Where to Stay

Check out the **Harmony Lodge at the Skykomish River** (206-650-5390, www.harmony-lodge.com). Built in 1929 by a renowned architect as a hunting lodge for senators, it was purchased in the 1960s and turned into an exquisite rental cabin. Extremely secluded and private, it is nevertheless close to the Stevens Pass ski area. The 1,000-square-foot cabin with panoramic windows looks over 2,000 feet of privately owned Index Creek, where the water dances in waterfalls over rocks.

OLYMPIC PENINSULA

This land of contrasts has been inhabited by Native Americans for thousands of years. Here you will find Pacific Ocean beaches, rain forest valleys, glacier-capped peaks and a stunning variety of plants and animals. Only one road, US 101, circles the peninsula, and much of it is remote and rugged, with wild coastlines and old-growth forests. Influenced by both the mountains and the sea, the area has a wide range of climate conditions and a temperate rain forest. In addition to great swaths of remote wilderness and federally protected parklands, the peninsula is also dotted with historic towns that are great fun to explore.

OLYMPIC NATIONAL PARK
Visitor Center, 3002 Mount Angeles Rd.,
  Port Angeles
(360) 565-3130
www.nps.gov/olym
Olympic National Park offers great hiking, backpacking, and fishing, with 95 percent of its land designated as wilderness. Roads provide access to the outer edges of the park, but the heart of Olympic is wilderness; a primeval sanctuary for humans and wild creatures alike. The park protects the largest unmanaged herd of Roosevelt elk in the world. A 45-minute drive from Port Angeles to Hurricane Ridge brings you from the lowlands blanketed with old-growth forests to tree line, where clumps of subalpine firs give

way to open meadows. On a clear day, views of the Olympic Mountains and the Strait of Juan de Fuca are spectacular.

You can also visit the **Hoh River Rain Forest,** isolated on the Pacific coast by both inclement weather and distance. The rain forest receives between 12 and 14 feet of precipitation each year (though summers are fairly dry), with trails winding nearly 20 miles up Hoh River Road and plunging into thick clusters of mossy, old-growth trees. Don't miss the **Hall of Mosses.** The entrance fee to Olympic National Park is $15 per vehicle and $5 for each person on foot, bike, or motorcycle. Entrance passes are good for up to seven consecutive days.

Getting There
All park destinations can be reached by US 101, which circumnavigates the Olympic Peninsula. From Seattle, take I-5 north to WA-104 West. At Edmonds, you will take the **Washington State Ferry** to Kingston, and then drive across the Hood Canal Floating Bridge to US-101 North, the Olympic Highway that leads to the park.

Where to Eat
Within the park, check out **Creekside Restaurant** in Kalalach Lodge (157151 Hwy. 101, 360-962-2271, www.olympicnational parks.com/activities/dining.aspx). The grilled king salmon, crab cakes, and wild mushroom strudel are incredible, but you may want to have breakfast here—the lodge is known for its crunchy French toast. Just outside the south perimeter of the park, you can dine at **Roosevelt Dining Room** in the Lake Quinault Lodge (345 South Shore Rd., 888-896-3818, www.olympicnationalparks .com/activities/dining.aspx), named after FDR, who did indeed eat there. Outstanding

cuisine is served alongside the panoramic lake and mountain views.

Where to Stay

Sixteen campgrounds are available, offering toilets, picnic tables, fire pits, and some RV facilities. The nightly camping fees range from $10 to $18, depending on location and season. Permits are required for all overnight trips in the Olympic wilderness backcountry, at $5 per group plus $2 per person, per night. Wilderness permits may be obtained at the **Wilderness Information Center** (600 E. Park Ave., Port Angeles, 360-565-3100, www.nps.gov/olym/planyourvisit/wic.htm) or at ranger stations. The park also offers the **Log Cabin Resort, Lake Crescent Lodge, Kalaloch Lodge**, and **Sol Duc Hot Springs Resort,** all of which rent cabins or lodge hotel rooms and offer amenities such as grocery stores, dining rooms, or pools.

PORT TOWNSEND

Visitor Center, 440 12th St., Port Townsend
(888) ENJOYPT or (360) 385-2722
www.enjoypt.com

At the northeastern point of the peninsula lies Port Townsend, one of the best-preserved Victorian-era seaports in the country. The town makes you feel as if you've stepped back in time, with a largely intact, historic architectural legacy and a main street filled with quaint shops and art galleries. Its maritime past is a constant presence, but the thriving community has a distinctly urban chic today. MSN City Guide named it one of the Top 8 Port Cities in the United States.

As with many places in Washington, Port Townsend offers a wide range of things to do, from the museums, art galleries, and live music of town, to the parks, beaches, and trails that provide hours of outdoor adventure. The first Sat of every month there is a **Gallery Walk,** where galleries in the downtown waterfront district are open from 5:30 to 8 p.m., along with artist interaction and lots happening on the historic surrounding streets. **The Festival of American Fiddle Tunes** happens in July, going strong for more than 30 years. Port Townsend is a great spot for sailing, and many sailboat rentals and lessons are available.

Getting There

Driving is what most people do, because it's quite easy and enjoyable to combine a visit to Port Townsend with exploration of other parts of the Olympic Peninsula and National Park. However, if you come to Port Townsend alone, it is fairly easy to get here and get around via public transportation. Take the Bainbridge Island ferry, and from there pick up the Kitsap Transit bus #90 to Poulsbo. Transfer to Jefferson Transit bus #7 to Port Townsend. Once there, downtown is easily walkable, and Jefferson Transit provides extensive bus service.

Where to Eat

The **Upstage Restaurant & Entertainment** (923 Washington, 360-385-2216, www.upstagerestaurant.com) is next door to the famous Rose Theatre, offering a restaurant and sunny, secluded patio with an herb garden. As the name implies, there is also a bar and live entertainment—two floors center on the stage with a rand piano, where musical acts, dances, and comedy shows are performed regularly.

Where to Stay

The **Manresa Castle** (651 Cleveland St., 360-385-5750, www.manresacastle.com) is unexpected grandeur, built in 1892 with a Prussian-influenced architecture. The private residence—the largest ever built in Port Townsend—was purchased in 1927 by Jesuit priests and used as a training college for many years. Today it is a charming inn with incredible gardens, where many couples come to get married.

SNOQUALMIE VALLEY

Nestled in the western foothills of the Cascade Mountains, Snoqualmie Valley is approximately 30 miles east of Seattle. The valley became a popular tourist destination on July 4, 1889, with the arrival of the first excursion train running from Seattle. This area was the setting of the 1990s hit movie and television series *Twin Peaks*. With an elevation of over 4,100 feet, **Mount Si** dominates the skyline of the Upper Valley and is a popular destination for hikers of all skill levels. Atop Mount Si, hikers enjoy expansive views of the valley and wildflowers during the spring and summer months and on clear days, distant views of Mount Rainier, the Seattle skyline, and Olympic Mountains complete the landscape. In fact, Mount Si has become Washington's second-most-popular hiking trail.

SNOQUALMIE FALLS
WA 202 at Railroad Avenue SE
(425) 985-6906
www.snoqualmiefalls.com
At one of Washington's most popular scenic attractions, more than 1.5 million visitors a year come to view the powerful 270-foot waterfalls—more than 100 feet higher than Niagara Falls. Located only 29 miles east of downtown Seattle, it makes an easy day trip. The falls were created about 5,000 years ago, after the glaciers receded and left a fertile

Twilight Sightings

If you are a fan of the *Twilight* book and movie series, you will love the western edge of the Olympic Peninsula. Along the northwest side of Olympic National Park, you will find the towns of Port Angeles, Forks, and La Push, the setting for the books by Stephenie Meyer and where most of the movie filming took place. Discover the homes and hangouts of Edward, Bella, Jacob, and all your other favorite *Twilight* characters. Visit Bella and Edward's high school in Forks. Stake out the scenic beach at La Push where Bella learns the truth about Edward. Do a little werewolf spotting in the forests. Or grab a bite at the restaurant in Port Angeles where they have their first date. Local stores and restaurants offer menu items and memorabilia for fans with a thirst for all things *Twilight*. There are many tours and guides that will point out sites from the movies such as Bella's truck, Bella Italia restaurant, and the Lincoln cinema. Check out the Web site www .twilightontheolympicpeninsula .com, or download a free Washington state *Twilight* road-trip map at www.experiencewa.com/plan-a-trip/printed-guides-and-maps/twilight-map.pdf.

plain and the magnificent waterfalls. The park includes two acres of hiking trails with an observation deck and picnic areas.

For a great trip through history and beautiful excursion through the Upper Snoqualmie

Valley, visit the **Northwest Railway Museum** (38625 Southeast King St., 425-888-3030, www .trainmuseum.org). You can tour the Victorian-era train depot and then take the trip on an antique railroad coach, offering stunning views of the valley. If you want to make your trip more than a day getaway, the old frontier town is full of stories, with unique shops and a vibrant restaurant scene. There tend to be quite a few art events and festivals, and the outdoor recreation is abundant.

Getting There

Driving is really the only way to get to Snoqualmie Falls; take I-90 toward Portland to the Highway 18 West exit; follow that to WA 202, to the falls. Many tour companies also offer a day trip or overnight camping at the falls; check out **Evergreen Escape** (www.evergreenescapes.com) or **Customized Tours** (1129 S. 220th St., 206-878-3965, www.toursofseattle.com).

Where to Eat

Check out the **Woodman Steakhouse and Saloon** (38601 SE King St., 425-888-4441, www.woodmanlodge.com), where modern dining meets history. The original Woodman Lodge was a social community gathering house during pioneer days, and its restoration celebrates that spirit. After dinner, keep in the spirit with a drink at **Finaghty's Irish Pub** (7726 Center Blvd. SE #110, 425-888-8833, www.finaghtys.com).

Where to Stay

Salish Lodge & Spa (6501 Railroad Ave. SE, 425-888-2556, www.salishlodge.com) enjoys an unbeatable location, overlooking the falls. From your room, you can hear the roar of the whitewater tumbling over granite cliffs into the river canyon below. Many scenes from *Twin Peaks* were filmed here. Don't miss the famed country breakfast that many locals and nonguests come for. More details on p. 266.

SNOQUALMIE PASS
(425) 434-6111
www.fs.fed.us/r6/mbs

With an elevation of 3,022 feet, this is the lowest and most heavily traveled east–west highway crossing in the state. It is one of four Washington east–west highways with mountain passes open year-round. Snoqualmie Pass offers easy access to a variety of recreational opportunities including hiking, backpacking, skiing, snowboarding, and cross-country skiing. Shuttle buses connect the several ski areas populating the pass.

The most popular of these is **The Summit at Snoqualmie** (1001 SR 906, 425-434-7669, www.summitatsnoqualmie.com), a ski resort less than an hour from Seattle. The Northwest tradition of skiing on Snoqualmie Pass began in the 1920s and '30s, pre-dating the 1937 opening of the Snoqualmie Summit Ski Area. The earliest skiers were a hardy group of world-class ski jumpers who hiked up the hill and competed on a jump built by the Seattle Ski Club, near Beaver Lake Hill. Interest in the sport by both jumpers and spectators grew rapidly, and in 1933 the Seattle Parks Department applied for a permit from the U.S. Forest Service to establish a ski hill at Snoqualmie Pass.

Getting There

From Seattle, take I-90 east to exits 52 through 54, depending on what part of the Snoqualmie Pass you are going to.

Where to Eat

Do you happen to remember the 1990s television series *Northern Exposure*? If you were a fan, then you've seen **Roslyn Café** (201 West Pennsylvania Ave., 509-649-2763, www.roslyncafe.com) on the small screen. Although the show was set in the fictional town of Cicely, Alaska, the filming was actually done in the Snoqualmie town of Roslyn. The café, where you will undoubtedly recognize the painted mural, is a few doors down from Dr. Fleischman's office, and along the main street you can also see Ruth-Anne's store and the KBHR radio studio.

Where to Stay

To be honest, there aren't a whole lot of very special accommodations in the pass/ski resort area. There's a Howard Johnson and . . . well, you get the picture. The **Summit Lodge** (603 SR 906, 800-557-7829, www.snoqualmiesummitlodge.com) is probably the best choice if you want to be very near the pass and the ski area, and it's a pretty nice little place. Comfortable accommodations are added to with the outdoor heated pool as well as an indoor pool. It's convenience and decent accommodations in a beautiful mountain environment.

SPA RESORTS

Washington spas make the most of the great outdoors, and a spa getaway provides respite from the urban pace of the city. Renewal comes in the form of massage and wellness treatments, fresh regional food, and the serene beauty of Pacific Northwest forests and waters.

SALISH LODGE & SPA

6501 Railroad Ave. SE, Snoqualmie
(425) 888-2556
www.salishlodge.com
Perched atop the majestic Snoqualmie Falls at the base of the Cascade Mountains, the resort offers gorgeous guided hikes. Listen to the roar of whitewater tumbling over granite cliffs nearly 300 feet into the emerald river canyon below. Breathe in the scent of evergreens and firs. Dine on innovative and indigenous cuisine, savor the serenity of the eucalyptus spa, then drift off to sleep in front of your room's wood-burning fireplace. The 89 guest rooms reflect the calm, contemplative environment of the Pacific Northwest and come with featherbeds and two-person whirlpool tubs. The Asian-inspired spa has the feeling of a Japanese bathhouse, with a pair of hydrotherapy pools set into natural rock. The lodge makes a special effort to cater to couples, and dogs are welcome.

Getting There

Just a thirty minute drive from Seattle, merge onto Highway 518 East from Sea-Tac Airport, then take I-405 North to Bellevue for 10 miles. At exit 11 head east on I-90 toward Spokane to Highway-18/Snoqualmie Parkway, where you will exit and turn left, then continue for 3.5 miles, until you can turn left on Railroad Avenue SE.

Where to Eat

The full-service restaurant has exquisite meals, but don't overlook **The Attic** (4226 E. Madison St., 206-323-3131, www.atticalehouse.com). This cozy spot with leather couches that you sink into makes for a romantic place to have a cocktail and small meal, featuring the same type of cuisine as the restaurant. On Fri and Sat nights you'll be treated to live music from a local musician.

Where to Stay

Ask for a river-view room or suite, for stunning vistas of the falls and canyon.

SKAMANIA LODGE

1131 SW Skamania Lodge Way,
   Stevenson
(800) 221-7117
www.skamania.com

This magnificent mountain resort, nestled on 175 wooded acres, is located in the spectacular Columbia River Gorge National Scenic Area. It's the perfect stop for travelers who are planning to continue on to Oregon from Seattle, and it's also a spa getaway that really offers something for everyone. The 18-hole golf course has a pro shop, rental equipment, driving range, putting greens, and restaurant. The fitness center includes an indoor heated swimming pool, dry saunas and indoor and outdoor whirlpools, tennis, basketball, volleyball, and hiking trails. The resort gets its name from the Chinook Indian word for "swift water" and is aptly named, with its Columbia River location and the 70 nearby waterfalls, including the famous 620-foot Multnomah Falls.

Getting There

About three hours south of Seattle, Skamania Lodge is located just before you cross the Columbia River into Oregon. Drive south on I-5 to I-205 South, until you reach Highway 14. Head east for a scenic drive. Immediately after entering Stevenson city limits, turn left on Rock Creek Drive to Skamania Lodge Way.

Where to Eat

The award-winning **Cascade Room** (2616 Main St., 604-709-8650, www.thecascade.ca) offers fine dining alongside panoramic windows overlooking the incredible Columbia Gorge. The restaurant's wood floors are more than 200 years old, and much of the menu offerings are cooked in the wood-fired oven.

Where to Stay

Some rooms have gas fireplaces, which lend a nice touch on all but the warmest summer evenings.

SOLSTICE SPA & SUITES

925 Commercial St., Leavenworth
(888) 548-4772
www.solsticespa.net

This very small, tranquil resort is situated in the Cascade Mountains, and the nature theme spreads throughout the entire place, from the outdoor-inspired guest suites to the wellness treatments. Even the name is taken from the area—Solstice is the owner's favorite Cascades hiking trail. Try an Anjou Pear Foot Therapy or Body Treatment, a Lavender Relaxation Massage, or the Columbia River Hot Rock Massage. The suites are carefully appointed, with attention to details such as the hypoallergenic silk duvets and handcrafted iron furnishings. Each suite also has a professional hydrotherapy tub and a rock-lined outdoor soaking pool. The large rooms are perfect for couples or girls' getaways, and many of the spa packages also cater to those guests. Really want to live it up? Add a limousine wine tour and tasting to your stay.

Getting There

Solstice is about a two-hour drive from Seattle. From I-5 North, take I-405 North to WA 522 East. After 13 miles, turn left at US 2 East and drive for about 85 miles to Leavenworth. Turn left on 12th Street and then right on Commercial Street. You can also take the Amtrak Cascades train to Leavenworth direct from the King Street Station in Seattle. Solstice can arrange a hotel transfer from the train station for you.

Where to Eat

Try **Visconti's Italian Restaurant** (636 Front St., 509-548-1213, www.viscontis.com) for a romantic ambience with gourmet cuisine and an award-winning wine selection that even *Wine Spectator* magazine has commented on. Ask about the assortment of vintage Italian wines.

Where to Stay

There are only three suites, each of them large and amazing, so your choice may come down to availability. If you are a couple, the Augusta Mountain Suite is perhaps the most romantic, with a large king bed.

TACOMA

TACOMA REGIONAL CONVENTION & VISITORS BUREAU
**Visitor Center, 1516 Pacific Ave., Tacoma
(800) 272-2662
www.traveltacoma.com**

Just 18 miles south of Sea-Tac Airport, Tacoma is an easy day trip—but there is so much to do here, you may want to make a weekend of it if you have the time. Attractions run the gamut from distinctive museums to historical sites and wildlife parks. Explore Tacoma's Museum District where the **Museum of Glass** (1801 Dock St., 253-396-1768, www.museumofglass.org), **Tacoma Art Museum** (1701 Pacific Ave., 253-272-4258, www.tacomaartmuseum .org), and Washington State History Museum form a triangle around the stunning **Chihuly Bridge of Glass.** The 500-foot span, created by famed Washington glass artist Dale Chihuly, includes a Seaform Pavilion, Venetian Wall, and two Crystal Towers. You can see more amazing Chihuly work at the historic

Union Station (1717 Pacific Ave., 253-863-5173), where five installations are displayed beneath the landmark's great dome. If you want to try your hand at this incredible artistry, you can take a class at the Museum of Glass.

The **Washington State History Museum** (1911 Pacific Ave., 888-BE-THERE, www.wshm.org/wshm) is not to be missed, and other historic attractions include the **1890 Meeker Mansion** (312 Spring St., 253-848-1770, www.meekermansion.org) and **Fort Nisqually Living History Museum** (5400 North Pearl St., 253-591-5339, www .fortnisqually.org), a restored 1855 Hudson Bay trading post. There are plenty of outdoor activities as well; take the kids to **Northwest Trek Wildlife Park** (11610 Trek Dr. East, 360-832-6117, www.nwtrek.org), where they can take a tram tour through dozens of natural habitats filled with bison, grizzly bears, cougars, and otters, as well as experience up-close-and-personal encounters with experienced park guides. The **Point Defiance Zoo & Aquarium** (5400 North Pearl St., 253-591-5337, www.pzda.org) is another great family outing. Watch polar bears swim and eat, admire the majesty of the Sumatran tiger family, and see one of the world's most elusive animals, the clouded leopard.

Getting There

Driving a car is quick and easy, just a straight shot down I-5 and you're in Tacoma in under half an hour. Or take the Sounder commuter train, which offers weekday service every half-hour from King Street Station in downtown Seattle to Tacoma in less than an hour. On the weekend, take the Amtrak train (available weekdays as well). Once you're in Tacoma, you can get around on the city's free light rail line, which runs between the theater district, convention center, Union Station, and Tacoma Dome.

Where to Eat

The historic **Swiss Tavern** (1904 Jefferson Ave., 253-572-2821, www.theswisspub.com) is a fun place in the Union Station district and has been around since 1913, when it was a meeting place for Swiss immigrants. The tavern is also a showcase for local artists; you can gaze at the eight Venetian glass sculptures by Dale Chihuly while you eat; 21 and over.

Where to Stay

If you want to really embrace the glass art that Tacoma is famous for, check out the **Hotel Murano** (1320 Broadway Plaza, 877-986-8083, www.hotelmuranotacoma.com). This very unique hotel in downtown Tacoma greets you with a world-class art collection, and each floor features works by a different artist, with their sketches hanging in the guest rooms. You're guaranteed to wake up feeling inspired.

WINE COUNTRY

There is a reason Washington wines have grown so popular and prolific—with lush, volcanic soil that creates nearly perfect conditions for vines, a climate that gets plenty of rain yet also receives more than 17 hours of sunlight daily in prime growing season, and the ingenuity of Washington entrepreneurs, you have the perfect recipe for a successful wine-producing region. Leading grape varietals include Chardonnay, Merlot, Cabernet Sauvignon, Syrah, and Riesling. The grapes here are never grafted, as in many other vineyards of the world, but instead they all grow on their own roots, enabling a pure and rich varietal flavor.

All of this makes for not only excellent wine, but also a great destination for wine tours and tasting, and to simply admire and enjoy the beautiful wine valley country of Washington state. This distinctive experience can take you anywhere from the smallest mom-and-pop winery to expansive state-of-the-art vineyards that are run like a well-oiled machine, and lets you sample some of the most talked-about wines, as well as discover hidden gems. If you visit in March, you can take advantage of **Washington Wine Month,** celebrated by local retailers and restaurants as well as wineries.

Washington is home to several distinct wine regions, profiled below. The best way to get to any of them is by car, as there's not any very convenient public transportation options, and you will really need a car to get around the region and between the wineries while there; www.washingtonwine.org.

COLUMBIA VALLEY
I-82, between WA 221 and WA 395
www.columbiavalleywine.com
This is the largest viticultural region in the state, with approximately 150 wineries on some 7,000 vineyard acres. Whether you are looking for a small boutique winery or one of the largest in Washington, you will find it here. If you are traveling in Sept, be sure to catch the annual harvest festival, called Catch the Crush.

One of the most well-known wineries in the area is **Columbia Crest** (Hwy 221, Columbia Crest Drive, 509-875-4227, www.columbiacrest.com), fashioned after a French chateau. The largest winery in Washington state, Columbia Crest is best known for its popular Chardonnay and the outstanding Merlot that helped establish Washington's reputation for the varietal. The tasting room and gift shop are open from 10 a.m. to 4:30 p.m. daily, and guided tours are available on the weekends. Other wineries in Columbia Valley include **Buckmaster Cellars** (509-628-8474, www.buckmastercellars .com), **Terra Blanca** (34715 N. Demoss Rd., 509-588-6082, www.terrablanca.com), **Oakwood Cellars** (40504 N. Demoss Rd., 509-588-5332, www.oakwoodcellars.com), **Kiona Vineyards** (44615 N. Sunset Rd., 509-588-6716, www.kionawine.com), and **Sandhill Winery** (48313 N. Sunset Rd., 509-588-2699, www.columbiavalleywine.com/sandhill).

Where to Eat

Try **Roots Restaurant and Bar** in Camas (19215 SE 34th St., 360-260-3001, www.roots restaurantandbar.com), featuring local farm products with an impressive wine list, or the wine bar and cafe at Bunnell Family Cellar in Prosser, called **Wine O'Clock** (548 Cabernet Court, 509-786-2197, www.bunnellfamilycellar.com).

Where to Stay

The very unique **Cave B Inn** (344 Silica Rd. NW, 888-785-2283, www.cavebinn.com) is situated amid the scenic vineyards of SageCliffe Estate, offering 30 rooms with a pool and spa. The Cliffehouses are individual cottages overlooking the Columbia Gorge with towering stone fireplaces and incredible sunset views.

WALLA WALLA

Tourism Office, 8 S. 2nd Ave., Suite 603, Walla Walla
(877) WWVISIT
www.wallawalla.org
The town so nice they named it twice, Walla Walla is not only fun to visit, it's just fun to say. About 270 miles southeast of the city, it's the most remote wine region in the state; but considering some of the absolutely stellar wines produced here, it's an unbeatable destination for oenophiles. The college town has a rich cultural community, with art galleries and a theater around the historic downtown, and a superb selection of restaurants. On the first Fri of every month, **Dunham Cellars** (150 E. Boeing Ave., 509-529-4685, www.dunhamcellars.com) conducts **Art Walk Walla Walla.**

Many of the wineries in this region are small operations, so it's best to call ahead of time for opening hours and times for tours. With more than 1,600 vineyard acres and around 100 wineries, you are sure to have plenty to choose from, suiting every palate. If you visit in the summer, be sure to check out the Summer Sounds on the Plaza concerts. **Woodward Canyon** (11920 W Hwy 12, 509-525-4129, www.woodwardcanyon.com) and **L'Ecole 41** (509-525-2775, www.lecole41 .com) were two of the pioneering wineries; others worth noting are **Pepper Bridge** (1704 J B George Rd., 509-525-6502, www .pepperbridge.com), **Walla Walla Vintners** (225 Vineyard Ln., 509-525-4724, www.wallawallavitners.com), and **Seven Hills Winery** (212 N. 3rd Ave., 509-529-7198, www.sevenhillswinery.com).

Where to Eat

Whitehouse Crawford (55 W. Cherry St., 509-525-2222, www.whitehousecrawford .com) is located in a 100-year-old planning mill, with old brick walls and wood beams. For a Mediterranean twist, check out **Saffron** (125 W. Alder Street, 509-525-2112, www .saffronmediterraneankitchen.com), with its organic, seasonal menu.

Where to Stay

Abeja (2014 Mill Creek Rd., 509-522-1234, www.abeja.net) is a winery and inn, where you can stay in a stunning turn-of-the-twentieth-century farmhouse that has been restored to lovely guest accommodations.

WOODINVILLE
East of I-405 and south of WA 522
(425) 205-4394
www.woodinvillewinecountry.com

Just 25 minutes northeast of the city limits, the Woodinville area is the closest wine region to Seattle. Woodinville is home to about 40 vineyards and wineries, including major names such as Chateau Ste. Michelle and Columbia Winery. Small wineries and family-run operations are also plentiful, and many offer formal or informal tours and tastings.

Chateau Ste. Michelle (1411 NE 145th St., 425-488-1133, www.ste-michelle.com) was the founding winery in Washington state and still provides one of the best visits, with a variety of different tasting experiences offered every day from 10 a.m. to 4:30 p.m. If you're visiting during the summer, don't miss the popular outdoor concert series. A diverse lineup of jazz, rock, blues, and contemporary artists plays on the expansive grounds—and wine, of course, is served.

Columbia Winery (14030 NE 145 St., 425-488-2776, www.columbiawinery.com) is another major winery, producing distinctive Washington wines from European vinifera grapes since 1962. Columbia's late wine-maker David Lake was deemed the "Dean of Washington winemakers" by *Wine Spectator* magazine. The Victorian mansion and its surrounding vineyards are open daily, and for $5 you can be guided through a tasting of five wines by a knowledgeable wine educator.

In early Dec the Woodinville region holds the popular **Saint Nicholas Day,** during which most area wineries host open houses with tastings in a fun holiday celebration.

Where to Eat

If a splurge is in your budget, the famous **Herbfarm Restaurant** (14590 NE 145th St., 425-485-5300, www.theherbfarm.com) is located here (see p. 81). This is a true culinary treat, and a dining experience you are not likely to forget. Highly recommended—but make reservations well in advance.

Where to Stay

Willows Lodge (14580 NE 145th St., 877-424-3930, www.willowslodge.com) is a beautiful place that appears as if it naturally arose from the surrounding landscape. The spa offers Carita facials, a French line available in only a small number of spas in the United States. Willows is within walking distance of Chateau Ste. Michelle, Columbia Winery, and Red Hook Brewery.

YAKIMA VALLEY
Visitor Information Center, 101 N. Fair
Ave., Yakima
(800) 221-0751
www.visityakimavalley.org

About 140 miles southeast of Seattle lies the sunny **Yakima Valley wine region.** It makes a terrific weekend getaway not only for the multitude of wineries located here, but also for the naturally beautiful area that offers plenty of outdoor recreation. The **Yakima River** is gorgeous and serene, known as one of the state's blue-ribbon trout streams with excellent fly fishing; rafting and kayaking are great options as well. Hiking and wildlife-watching throughout the Yakima Valley are top-notch, with breathtaking scenery in a pristine natural environment.

There are more than 60 wineries on 12,000 vineyard acres, in the state's first federally recognized appellation, established in 1983. Most wineries here are small family operations where unpretentious hospitality is the norm. You can enjoy a glass of wine while gazing at the beautiful snowcapped Mount Adams or overlooking the diverse agricultural abundance of the Yakima Valley. For shoppers and treasure hunters, the area offers numerous antiques shops that dot the towns. Families will enjoy a tour of the **Darigold Dairy** (www.darigold.com).

Where to Eat

Try recurring favorite **Gasperetti's** (1013 N. 1st St., 509-248-0628, http://gasperettis restaurant.com), a gourmet Italian restaurant that's been around since 1966, or the much-raved-about **Sage Restaurant & Wine Bar** (4000 W. Creekside Loop, 509-853-1057, www.sageyakima.com), both in Yakima.

Where to Stay

The Yakima Valley is home to many charming, historic bed-and-breakfast inns, such as **Outlook Inn Guest House at Tefft Cellars** (1320 Independence Rd., 888-549-7244, www.tefftcellars.com/aboutus/Guest.htm) and the **4Seasons River Inn** (16202 S. Griffin Road, 509-786-1694, www.4seasonsriver inn.com). If a new, luxury hotel is more your thing, check out **Ledgestone Hotel** in Yakima (107 N. Fair Ave., 509-453-3151, http://ledgestonehotel.com).

Other Wine Regions

Smaller wine-growing regions you may want to check out include **Columbia Gorge,** on the Washington-Oregon border with about 20 wineries; **Lake Chelan,** due east from Seattle with 15 wineries that also produce Pinot Gris and Gewürztraminer; **Rattlesnake Hills**, with 17 wineries; and **Red Mountain,** with 15, including production of Sangiovese and Petit Verdot (both just east of Yakima Valley).

Appendix

LIVING HERE

In this section we feature specific information for residents or those planning to relocate here. Topics include real estate, education, health care, and much more.

RELOCATION

Seattle may have come a long way since Arthur Denny and his group of less than two dozen settlers landed at Alki Point in 1851, but its pioneering spirit and stubborn insistence on doing things a little differently are definitely still with us. Despite the overly gray and soggy winters, people of all backgrounds and from all over the world have chosen to live here, in droves. The modern relocation boom started in the 1980s, a period that saw the population double. By July 2007, Seattle had seen more population growth in the preceding year than at any time in the previous four decades.

This huge influx of people has impacted the city in many ways—some good, some not so good. Property taxes have risen drastically, as have housing costs. Though this puts a strain on many residents and invites suburban sprawl as people move outward in search of affordable homes, these spiraling housing costs must also be looked at from all angles. Because Washington has no state income tax, higher property taxes, in effect, compensate for that (along with higher sales tax). And although the average cost of a home or condominium has indeed risen over the past decade, the Seattle real estate market also held pretty steady during the recent economic downturn and housing bust, and remained one of the healthiest real estate markets in the nation. Local housing prices did take a hit, but as the area has started to come out the other side of the downturn more Seattle neighborhoods have been deemed affordable (in comparison with the county's median household income), according to a *Seattle Times* analysis.

Decreased market values for homes also significantly depended on location—suburban properties definitely were hit harder, whereas urban homes in inner Seattle did not lose nearly the value. City living also means better access to public transportation, and in some ways a more active lifestyle, as residents tend to walk much more than those in suburban neighborhoods. The Web site www.WalkScore.com, which ranks cities across the country for their "walkability" and allows individuals to receive the walkable score for their own neighborhoods, puts Seattle as the sixth-most-walkable city in the country.

Seattle came in as the seventh-healthiest housing market in a 2009 report by *Builder* magazine, in which real estate markets that had outperformed the norm were evaluated. "The healthiest markets have many things in common," the report stated. "Most of them are great places to live, either close to the ocean, mountains, or major universities"—a description that fits Seattle to a T. The bottom line, according to economists, is that a growing city means a better economy.

In Seattle's case the growing city has led to another problem: traffic. The traffic situation in the city has reached epic proportions—depending on where you are moving from. To someone from Los Angeles, Washington, D.C., or Houston, Seattle traffic may seem like nothing. But trust me; it's much worse than it was a decade ago and is maddening to its residents. Good thing we have that walkability thing going for us.

Of course, despite the high cost of housing and the increased traffic, there are a million reasons people want to move to Seattle. There is the fact that it's a great place to do business; there is no state income tax, the healthy Washington economy outperforms the national economy, and Seattle has been ranked as one of the best places in the country to locate a business. The schools are good and the populace is one of the most educated in the country. There is a wealth of cultural institutions and attractions, as well as a decidedly international influence. Despite the appreciation for culture and the arts, it is a completely unpretentious place. There is the progressive mind-set, coupled with just plain friendliness, that embraces all lifestyles with open arms. And certainly not least, there is all that astounding natural beauty that fills and surrounds the Emerald City at every turn, and which in fact led to the nickname.

WHERE TO LIVE

Once you have decided to move to Seattle, the first thing to decide is in what part of the city you want to live. Many factors usually go into this decision, from affordability and schools to the distinctly different personalities of the various neighborhoods. Which one suits you best? We'll take a look at the neighborhoods described in the Area

Overview chapter, from the perspective of a potential resident—meaning information on home prices, population, crime, commuting time to downtown Seattle, and what it's like to live there. All data are based on the latest attainable figures compiled by Seattle magazine.

i For a wealth of information and resources about moving to Seattle, check out the *Northwest Newcomer Guide*. The official greater Seattle relocation and neighborhood guide for dozens of chambers, cities, libraries, and corporations, the free publication is designed to introduce and familiarize relocating employees, families, and residents to the most beautiful and vibrant community in the world. Download your free copy and access more resources at http://nwnewcomer.com.

North Seattle

Ballard

This originally Scandinavian community still reflects its Nordic heritage and is full of historic buildings and an old-fashioned, small-town charm. At the same time, it's a very hip place full of trendy restaurants and boutiques, particularly along Ballard Avenue and NW Market Street.

The median home price in Ballard is $417,500. With a population of 17,491, the area has a crime rate of 18 per 1,000 residents. Commuting time to downtown Seattle is 11 minutes without traffic.

Fremont

As you may have inferred from the rest of this book, Fremont is a quirky place all its own. With a definite eccentric, hippy, artsy vibe, the neighborhood also has a sense of humor and refuses to take itself too seriously—despite its self-proclaimed motto as the "Center of the Universe." While it is certainly a neighborhood that appeals to artists, young, unconventional working people, and students, it is also home to a lot of older hippies and rebels as well as a pretty good number of families. Really, it seems that everyone is welcome to this place, where a tattoo parlor may be found next to a toy store, and where people bring their kids to a parade featuring naked, painted folks dancing around.

Fremont's median home price is $453,500, with an estimated population of about 7,900. The crime rate per 1,000 residents is 88, and commuting time to downtown is 10 minutes.

Green Lake

Very much a family enclave, the areas around the prized jewel of Green Lake are spacious, largely single-family, and low-key. The large park and lake make up the central hub of the neighborhood, where residents from all over the city come for recreational activities. The commercial streets are heavy with athletic stores, yoga studios, and family-friendly restaurants.

With nearly 10,000 residents, the area has a crime rate of 78 per 1,000 residents, and the median home price is $494,500. Downtown commute time is 11 minutes.

Greenwood/Phinney Ridge

These neighborhoods offer a warm, tight-knit community, with residential areas filled with bungalows and Tudor-style homes that enjoy strong neighborhood associations. That said, this is Seattle, and so the area is anything but boring. Along the commercial streets you will find an eclectic mix of businesses, from belly-dance restaurants to a space-travel supply store.

The combined population of the two adjacent neighborhoods is a little over 19,000, with a commuting time of 12 minutes to downtown Seattle. The median home price in Greenwood is $329,936, with a crime rate of 71; in Phinney Ridge the homes are a much higher $529,000 and the crime rate is 50 per 1,000 residents.

Northgate

Northgate was once a fairly sleepy little single-family residential neighborhood that was mainly known for its mall and big-box stores. Thanks to a recently revitalized shopping district, it's a little more hip today, though it still has more of a suburban feel than other North Seattle neighborhoods.

The median home price here is $254,950, making it one of the more affordable close-in neighborhoods. A population of around 8,500 enjoys a downtown commute time of 11 minutes. The crime rate is 111 per 1,000.

University District/Roosevelt

The U District, not surprisingly, is home to a large number of students and is an off-campus haven for many more. A wide streetscape makeover in the early 2000s revitalized a lot of the infrastructure, and small business has boomed here since. The shops and affordable restaurants in the area draw the postcollegiate crowd as well, and many alternative enterprises such as astrology and meditation can be found here.

The combined population is about 25,000, with an average crime rate of 88. The median home price is $388,000 in the University District and $303,250 in Roosevelt, and downtown can be reached in seven to eight minutes.

Wallingford

The midcentury, Craftsman architectural vibe of Wallingford makes it feel as if you're in a small town; the largely family-owned businesses that know all the regulars reinforce that impression. The restaurant and shopping scene here is decidedly multicultural, and the town square–like Wallingford Center is the heart of the neighborhood.

The median home price here is a surprisingly affordable $303,250, with a population of about 7,700. It takes seven minutes to reach downtown, and the crime rate is 92 per 1,000 residents.

Central Seattle

Belltown

This is pretty much the hipster haven of Seattle, and Belltown enjoys a great location in the heart of downtown that is chock-full of art galleries and happening restaurants. The nightlife scene is excellent here as well. But Belltown also enjoys a little grittiness, which the locals seem to relish; despite its revitalization and trendy factor of recent years, the homeless still loiter here, and coming across a needle in the gutter would not be out of the question. This is the neighborhood where those who want to live as urban as possible come; it's not a place to be if music at 2 a.m. will bother you.

The residences are high-rise condominiums and apartments, with a median price of $404,000. With an estimated population of around 9,000 in Belltown itself, the area has a crime rate of 152.

Capitol Hill/First Hill

The location of Seattle's original Millionaires' Row still boasts some of the most amazing mansions in the city, as well as a modern mix of all sorts of residents. As a center point for the gay community, there is a fair-size LGBT population here, as well as a lot of professionals alongside artists and musicians. Some of the best restaurants are found here and the nightlife is always hopping. Housing is a real mix between single-family homes, apartments, condos, and mixed-use developments.

The median home price between the two areas is $333,212, and the total population is a staggering 39,000-plus, for a relatively contained geographic area. Commuting time to downtown, just across I-5, is three minutes; crime rates are 87–100.

Central District

This classically pretty neighborhood is lined with bungalows full of character, and more homes are being restored along with more businesses continuing to move to the area. This was Seattle's historic African American neighborhood, home to one of the city's top public high schools, Garfield. The district has provided one of the hottest real estate investments in recent years.

The median home price is right at $400,000 and the population is 2,791. The crime rate is 76, and time to commute to central downtown clocks in at five minutes.

Chinatown/International District

This neighborhood on the edge of the downtown core is truly multicultural, with a diverse mix of restaurants and shops including the famed Uwajimaya Village. It's easy to get to the central business district, the waterfront, ferries, and sports stadiums from here, and the large King Street Station with buses and light rail is in the heart of the International District.

The median home price is on the low end of downtown's scale at $285,000, with just under 3,000 residents. The crime rate is

208 per 1,000 residents, and the commute time to the center of downtown is three to four minutes.

Downtown

This area encompasses the residential living, outside of Belltown, in the core of Seattle's central district. Mostly luxury high-rise buildings are found here, with doormen and all the amenities, and you're close to the offices and shopping that are situated around Westlake, 5th Avenue, and Pike/Pine. Top dining and an easy walk to Pike Place Market round out the appeal, particularly for those who want to live in the city with everything at their fingertips.

Buying property at the median price will cost $369,500 in this area, which has a current residential population of about 8,000. The crime rate is 372 per 1,000 residents—this is the urban core, after all.

Eastlake/Lake Union/Portage Bay

These waterfront communities along Lake Union, on the north end of downtown, offer single-family homes, condos, and the unique floating homes made famous in the movie *Sleepless in Seattle* (and yes, that house can be found here as well). These neighborhoods are fairly cohesive, and some of the best new restaurants can be found here. South Lake Union in particular has received a building boom in recent years, with some of the snazziest new urban condos and lofts going up among the original warehouses and industrial properties.

The median home price is around $430,000, with population figures of about 8,000. Commute time to downtown is three to four minutes, with a crime rate that ranges from 113 in Eastlake to 232 in South Lake Union.

i A floating home is a house on a raft semipermanently moored to a dock. It is always attached to city utilities, including the sewer. These features, and a slew of government regulations, distinguish floating homes from live-aboards and other kinds of boats. There are about 500 legal floating home moorages left in Seattle, from a high of several thousand after World War II. The floating homes of Seattle have an association all their own, where you can find out more information about this very different lifestyle: www .seattlefloatinghomes.org.

Madison Park/Madrona

This may be the most young family–friendly neighborhood in Seattle. At its heart is Madrona Park, surrounded by gated communities that line Lake Washington and less imposing, but charming, streets filled with single-family bungalows. Strollers rule the sidewalks here, with eateries and stores that will make kids happy lining every commercial block. A 1,400-member "Madrona Mom" online group demonstrates how tightly the community tries to knit itself together.

The population is about 6,900 with pricey median homes of $760,000 in Madison Park and $575,000 in Madrona. Crime rate is a low 52 per 1,000 residents, and the commuting time downtown is eight to 14 minutes, depending on what end of the area you live in.

Magnolia/Interbay

This is a neighborhood that, for being very close to downtown, has a very far-removed feel. Wedged between Puget Sound and Discovery Park, the quiet residential areas have rolling expanses of lawn set along winding streets. The views and sunsets are amazing, which partly explains the housing costs. Plenty of neighborhood businesses keep residents supplied with the basics, and the downtown core is close by for a more lively scene.

The median home price is $567,000 and the population is estimated to be 21,591. It's a seven-minute commute downtown, and the crime rate is 35.

Queen Anne

A very Victorian feel defines Queen Anne, set up on a hill overlooking Seattle with spectacular skyline, water, and mountain views. The curving, narrow streets are lined with gorgeous, restored historic homes and a vibrant business community that includes some great restaurants, bookstores, and boutiques. You will hear references to Lower and Upper Queen Anne, which simply indicate how far up the hill you are.

The population here is a healthy 33,239 and the median home price is $455,000. Crime is a low rate of 28, and it takes about four minutes to get to the center of downtown.

South Seattle

Alki Beach/West Seattle

This is as close as Seattle gets to a true beach town, with its stretch of sand and beachfront businesses. It's also the historic site of the first European settlers' landing at what would become the city of Seattle. The area had gotten a bit run-down for a while, but revitalizations and an influx of new, remodeling residents in recent years have infused West Seattle with a new charm and energy. Single-family homes and a large inventory of townhomes, many of which are on the waterfront, are available to choose from. There is good shopping available, and the area has a youthful, family-oriented vibe.

The population is a little over 13,000, with a median home price of $420,000. Crime is 59 per 1,000 residents, and the commute downtown is nine minutes.

Columbia City

You will often hear Columbia City referred to as if it is, indeed, a city that is not part of Seattle. It certainly has the feel of a town all its own, but residents do have a Seattle city address. Residents here are fiercely loyal to the neighborhood, for the most part, and it's a place where the restaurants are full of regulars and people stop on street corners to chat. Many of the brick buildings that line the main streets are historic, lending a quaint charm that feels a bit like a less hip, more low-key Ballard.

The median price of a home is right at $400,000 and the population is 8,664. The commute downtown is 14 minutes, and the crime rate in Columbia City is 72.

Georgetown/SoDo

What was once an industrial wasteland has slowly been transforming itself, due to the urban pioneers who began flocking here over the past decade. Now it's a popular place for the cool kids, with a level of funkiness that may have matched early Fremont—without the self-consciousness. Many of the residents are artists who have made homes and studios out of old warehouses along the train tracks, and a whole new crop of glitzy townhomes threatens further gentrification.

The current population of residents is around 2,700 but growing, and the median home price is $319,500. Crime rates are still a very high 369 per 1,000 residents, due largely to the still scruffy environment. It's eight minutes to downtown.

Rainier Valley

This neighborhood is working-class and ethnically diverse; you can find food from barbecue to Mexican to Ethiopian to Vietnamese. The community center here is a neighborhood hub, and outside the largely Asian International District, Rainier Valley is really the melting pot of Seattle.

A home at the median price range will cost $365,000 here, and the crime rate is 51. Population figures are estimated to be about 35,000 and the commute downtown will take you eight minutes.

Suburbs

Eastside

The Eastside communities of Bellevue, Issaquah, Redmond, Mercer Island, Kirkland, and Woodinville are very popular suburban alternatives to Seattle, and all a relatively easy commute to the city (depending, of course, on that pesky traffic). Despite the combined average median home price from all Eastside neighborhoods of over $586,000, there are some affordable areas here. Keep in mind that the median price means the point at which half of the homes cost more and half cost less—and there are some major multi-million-dollar estates here, including that of Bill Gates (whose annual property taxes alone are nearly $1 million). Although Gates lives in Medina, **Mercer Island** is home to some of Seattle's wealthiest executives, including Paul Allen of Microsoft, Alan Mulally of Ford, and many Starbucks and Amazon suits—and its median price reflects that.

Bellevue offers the city downtown of the Eastside suburbs, with a hip restaurant and nightlife scene, and a vibrant cultural community with a number of quality museums and art galleries. **Redmond** is home to the sprawling Microsoft campus, and **Woodinville** is Washington's answer to Napa Valley. Throughout all of the Eastside communities, you will find countless miles of hiking and biking trails, the pristine Cougar Mountain Wilderness, and many parks. Depending on the city, commuting times to downtown Seattle are between 15 and 25 minutes.

Puget Sound Islands

The neighboring islands of **Bainbridge** and **Vashon** are both just a short ferry ride to downtown Seattle, but offer a quiet island lifestyle that seems much farther away. Commuting time is 45–50 minutes by Washington State Ferry. The ferry is the only way to get from Seattle to Bainbridge or Vashon Island, and so is the main inconvenience of living here; for instance, if you go for a late night on the town in Seattle, you may want to get a hotel room, as the ferry runs may have stopped by the time you get to the landing.

Neighborhood	Median Home Price	Population	Crime Rate
Bellevue	$510,000	118,100	38/1,000
Issaquah	$480,450	24,710	47/1,000
Kirkland/Juanita	$479,950	47,890	42/1,000
Mercer Island	$950,000	22,380	22/1,000
Redmond	$513,700	50,680	36/1,000
Woodinville	$494,000	11,430	45/1,000

Neighborhood	Median Home Price	Population	Crime Rate
Bainbridge	$612,000	23,080	24/1,000
Vashon	$530,000	11,003	58/1,000

That said, the islands offer just about everything the residents need on a day-to-day basis, from a wide variety of great restaurants to dozens of boutiques and shopping centers. There is a thriving arts scene on Bainbridge, while Vashon is filled with fruit orchards and strawberry farms. And don't underestimate the pull of the water and the endless recreational, outdoor adventures offered here—nor the incredible views that many homes enjoy.

South King County

This region offers perhaps the most affordable housing in all the greater Seattle metropolitan area. In the aforementioned *Seattle Times* article about affordable neighborhoods mentioned at the beginning of this chapter, all of the King County neighborhoods with affordable median prices in 2008 were south of Seattle. **Auburn** topped the list, with a median home price of $248,450,

followed by **North Burien, Des Moines/ West Kent, Algona/Pacific, Enumclaw,** and **Federal Way/Twin Lakes.** Commuting times from these communities to downtown Seattle ranges between 18 and 33 minutes.

In addition to affordability, South King County offers spectacular parks and water views, neighborhoods with community centers and a small-town feel, and far less traffic than Seattle—factors that have been bringing families here in droves. In fact, local residents like to call SR 509, which connects Burien to downtown Seattle, the "Secret Highway." New revitalization has been breathed into towns like Kent, Burien, Des Moines, and Renton; in fact, Burien has recently received a $200 million infusion into its city hall, libraries, shops, parks, and a performance center. Much of South King County seems like a welcome throwback to the days before malls ruled the earth.

Neighborhood	Median Home Price	Population	Crime Rate
Algona	$256,943	2,731	25/1,000
Auburn	$248,450	55,426	96/1,000
Burien	$349,900	31,410	68/1,000
Des Moines	$283,000	29,090	45/1,000
Enumclaw	$287,935	10,684	31/1,000
Federal Way	$290,150	87,390	64/1,000
Kent	$332,000	86,660	80/1000
Pacific	$275,090	6,040	33/1,000
Renton	$372,000	60,290	80/1,000
Seatac	$299,000	25,530	86/1,000
Tukwila	$279,950	18,000	190/1,000

REAL ESTATE

As previously mentioned, the Seattle housing market is fairly expensive, after home values and taxes have risen drastically over past years. The median price for a single-family home in Seattle was $399,000 in February 2010, according to the *Seattle Post–Intelligencer*—a slight increase over the February 2009 numbers. Condominium prices increased more over the one-year period, by more than 6 percent to a median price of $290,500 in February 2010. Most important, however, in predictions for a housing upswing are the numbers of pending and closed sales, which were up 60 percent and 41 percent, respectively, from the year before.

The rental market can be tight and expensive, but some good news here is that the recent economic downturn led to rents in the Seattle metro area dropping by more than 13 percent in 2009. The average monthly rent for apartments in Seattle at the end of 2009 was $1,023, according to *Bloomberg Business Week*.

A Realtor is a member of the local, state, and national real estate associations, and agrees to uphold a strict code of ethics and professional standards. The Seattle–King County Association of Realtors (SKCAR) is the local association governing King County Realtors and also exists to help protect the rights of local citizens in owning, transferring, and using real property.

i The SKCAR Web site offers an entire section just for consumers that provides a full list of member Realtors, as well as resources for first-time home buyers and multicultural home buyers, consumer tips, and a property search function for all MLS-listed properties in King County: www.nwrealtor.com.

When consulting a professional Realtor in the buying or selling of one of your most important investments, it is advised that you interview several agents at different firms. The top real estate firms in Seattle, in terms of number of agents, are:

COLDWELL BANKER BAIN
1200 Westlake Ave. North, Suite 406
(888) 283-2221
www.cbbain.com

Coldwell Banker Bain in Washington is a leader in Northwest real estate. The company's extensive network of tools and knowledgeable professionals allow for the first-class service you expect during the very personal experience of buying or selling a home. In addition, a property management team offers full services. Out of more than 3,800 Coldwell Banker companies around the world, Coldwell Banker Bain is the number-one company internationally for the past five years in a row.

JOHN L. SCOTT
1700 NW Gilman Blvd., Suite 305, Issaquah
(888) 854-1547
www.johnlscott.com

John L. Scott Real Estate was founded in 1931 and is currently led by third-generation chairman and CEO J. Lennox Scott. John L. Scott has 130 offices and more than 3,200 sales associates in Washington, Oregon, and Idaho. Last year John L. Scott closed over 25,000 transactions for more than $7 billion in volume sales, making it one of the most productive regional real estate companies in the nation. The Washington headquarters are in Issaquah, but there are four offices in Seattle.

PRUDENTIAL NORTHWEST REALTY ASSOCIATES

4700 42nd Ave. SW, Suite 470
(800) 718-7413
http://pnwrealty.com

Prudential Northwest Realty Associates has established itself as an industry leader by upholding the principles of the agent-customer relationship. One of the most respected names in business, the Prudential tradition dates back more than 130 years and enjoys a 98 percent name recognition factor across the greater Seattle area. With relocation accounting for over 30 percent of all transactions in the Puget Sound marketplace, Prudential's highly trained relocation specialists are committed to delivering the highest standards of professional integrity and customer service.

RE/MAX NORTHWEST REALTORS

300 NE 97th St.
(800) 522-5650
www.northwestrealtors.com

With offices in four locations including Bothell, Kirkland, Seattle, and Mill Creek, RE/MAX Northwest Realtors is ideally located to serve the entire Puget Sound region. With hundreds of skilled and experienced agents, RE/MAX Northwest offices have been a highly productive part of the Puget Sound real estate industry for years. The average agent has over 12 years' experience in the real estate industry. In addition to caring agents, RE/MAX Northwest offers top-notch tools of the trade through its local and international resources within the RE/MAX network.

WINDERMERE REAL ESTATE

5424 Sand Point Way NE
(206) 527-3801
www.windermere.com

What began as an eight-agent office in 1972, in the Seattle neighborhood of Windermere, has grown to a dedicated network over 300 offices and 8,000 agents strong. While residential real estate is the mainstay of its business, Windermere also has offices and associates who specialize in new construction, commercial real estate, relocation, and property management. To further facilitate the home-buying process, Windermere has affiliated resources in certain regions to provide mortgage, title, and escrow services.

i You can search for Seattle-area home builders and access resources at the Master Builders Association Web site, www.mba-ks.com. For Built Green information, go to www.builtgreen.net.

THE BUSINESS OF MOVING TO SEATTLE

Whenever you move to a new city or state, there are a lot of little details that must be attended to. Here we will go over some of the things that will help facilitate your move to Seattle.

Voter Registration

In Washington state, elections are administered at the local level by county auditors (except King County, which has the Records, Elections, and Licensing Services Division). These offices are available to help you with registering to vote, requesting an absentee ballot, and other elections-related services. You must complete a voter registration form if you are registering for the first time in Washington or if you have moved to a new county. If you have moved within the same county, you may transfer your registration by completing a new form or by contacting your county auditor by mail, e-mail, or phone. There is no registration by political party in Washington state.

To register, you can download the form from the Washington Secretary of State Web site, www.secstate.wa.gov/elections/register.aspx, or call the Secretary of State's toll-free Voter Information Hotline at (800) 448-4881.

Vehicle Registration

When you move to Washington state, you have 30 days to title and register your vehicle by mail or in person at a local vehicle licensing office. Fees start at $30 and go up from there depending on vehicle weight. To complete your vehicle registration, call (360) 902-3770, option 5, or go to the Washington State Department of Licensing Web site fee page, www.dol.wa.gov/vehicleregistration/fees.html.

Driver's License

Once residency is established, you have 30 days to get a Washington driver license if you plan to drive. Those with a valid out-of-state driver's license must visit a licensing office; written and drive testing are waived unless there is a medical or physical condition that indicates that testing is required. Out-of-state licenses are returned to the Department of Licensing so they can be invalidated. If you have an expired out-of-state license, you must pass a written and driving test. The licensing office then issues a temporary license, which allows driving for 45 days. A permanent new Washington driver's license will be processed and mailed within five days. For a list of offices, go to www.dol.wa.gov.

i You may find the *Seattle Times* article "Leap of Faith: Shopping Around for a Place of Worship" interesting. Written by Joy Jernigan, this story is particularly interesting for someone searching for a new religious home in Seattle: http://seattletimes.nwsource.com/html/living/2004435067_church shopping240.html.

Utilities

Keep your move stress-free by dealing with your utilities well in advance of moving. This will prevent your having to experience the trauma of moving across town or across the country and arriving to find the phone line dead, the lights out, and no running water. Gas, electric, phone, sewage, water, trash, and cable companies each have their own recommended lead time for service start/stop notification; a good rule of thumb is to contact their customer service departments at least two weeks prior to the move for transfer of service, and a month prior for establishing new service. The **Northwest Newcomer** journal provides a list of all the utility companies and their contact information at http://nwnewcomer.com/moving.php#utilitycontact.

EDUCATION

Seattle is a city that prizes education. It has the highest percentage of citizens with a bachelor's degree or higher of any city in the United States, with more than 52 percent college graduates among residents age 25 and over (compared to a national average of 27 percent). More than nine out of 10 Seattle adults have graduated high school, also a number that is much higher than other cities. The U.S. Chamber of Commerce also ranked Washington among the top states in the nation in its first Education Report Card.

Washington's education system earned "A" grades in academic achievement, academic achievement of low-income and minority students, return on investment, 21st-century teaching force, and data quality.

The public school system had an enrollment of 45,933 as of October 2007, with just about the same number of students enrolled at the University of Washington. The four campuses of Seattle Community College aren't far behind, with a total student body of 39,600. The city also offers more than 300 private and parochial schools, including Seattle University, Seattle Pacific University, the Art Institute of Seattle, and Cornish College of the Arts.

Child Care and Preschool

For younger children who haven't yet started school, and for after-school and summer care, finding safe, quality care is paramount to most parents. Fortunately, several resources in the Seattle area can help you do just that.

Washington state has a licensing system to set basic standards of safety and quality in child care programs—including school-age care programs. The state issues licenses through the Department of Social and Health Services' (DSHS) Division of Child Care and Early Learning. Some types of care are not regulated by the state. These include part-day preschool programs, nanny and babysitting services in the child's home, care provided by relatives, community recreation programs, informal parent cooperatives, and playgroups.

CHILD CARE RESOURCES
1225 S. Weller, Suite 300
(206) 329-1011
www.childcare.org

Since 1990, nonprofit Child Care Resources (CCR) has been promoting school readiness, a stable community, and equity for children by building a quality child care system. CCR helps families in challenging situations find answers to child care questions. Parents who work evenings or weekends, children with special needs, families struggling to manage the cost of care, and homeless families can all find personalized and in-depth information, referrals, and help, including an Internet database of child care providers in King County that can be accessed 24 hours a day. You can also call the child care referral line at (206) 329-5544.

CITY OF SEATTLE HUMAN SERVICES DEPARTMENT'S CHILD CARE ASSISTANCE
700 5th Ave., Suite 5800
(206) 386-1050
www.seattle.gov/humanservices/
children_families/childcare/payment_
assistance.htm
The City of Seattle helps low- and moderate-income working families pay for child care for children ages one month to 13 years. Families can choose from more than approximately 145 licensed family child care homes and centers in Seattle, which contract with the city to provide high-quality and affordable child care. At the time of enrollment, the family receives a voucher that authorizes monthly payments to the child care home or center that they choose from the list provided. The amount of the payment from the city varies according to the income of the family, age of the child, and hours of care needed. The city typically pays between 40 percent and 90 percent of the cost, and the family is responsible for paying the difference. See the Web site for a chart of income guidelines and for more information.

PIKE MARKET CHILD CARE & PRESCHOOL
1501 Pike Place #313
(206) 625-0842
http://pikemarketkids.org

Pike Market Child Care & Preschool has been serving families of all income levels (particularly low- and moderate-income families) since Oct 1982. Pike Market Child Care & Preschool's overall goal is to make high-quality preschool available to all children (ages 18 months to six years), providing families with support and encouragement. Children receive healthy meals and excellent care, and build the social and learning skills necessary to succeed in kindergarten and beyond, while their parents have the opportunity to work, search for a job, or go to school confident with the knowledge that their children are safe and nurtured. About 75 percent of the center's families receive financial assistance. Pike Market Child Care & Preschool is a private, secular, nonprofit community-service corporation licensed to provide child care.

WASHINGTON STATE CHILD CARE RESOURCE & REFERRAL NETWORK
(800) 446-1114
www.childcarenet.org

Your local Washington State Child Care Resource & Referral Network member program can help you with any child care question, including licensing issues. To reach your local resource and referral program, call (800) 446-1114 and you will be connected with the agency serving your community. To inquire about a specific licensed program, discuss concerns, or file a complaint, call the DSHS Licensed Child Care Information Line at (866) 482-4325.

i Download a printable child care checklist by going to http://nwnewcomer.com/selectingchildcare.html.

Public School District

SEATTLE PUBLIC SCHOOLS
2445 3rd Ave. South
(206) 252-0000
www.seattleschools.org

Seattle Public Schools is the largest K–12 school system in Washington state, serving more than 45,000 students in 88 schools. Seattle is a city rich with neighborhoods, and concurrent with the development of those neighborhoods was the birth and development of neighborhood schools—some as far back as 1862, seven years before the city was incorporated. Three new elementary schools opened in fall 2010, as well as a new Science, Technology, Engineering & Mathematics (STEM) program at Cleveland High School.

Seattle Public Schools is governed by its board of directors, an elected body representing seven geographical regions, known as districts, within the city of Seattle. The mission of the school board is to enable all students to achieve their potential through quality instructional programs and a shared commitment to continuous improvement. The length of each member's term is four years. Board meetings are generally held at 6 p.m. on the first and third Wed of each month, with some exceptions. Board meetings are accessible to all members of the public.

The school system offers many resources for students and their parents, including bus transportation, assistance for homeless students, Head Start, family support workers, student health services, reduced-price meals, and even a GLBTQ (Gay, Lesbian, Bisexual, Transgender, Questioning) Advisory Committee.

The State of Washington only funds half-day kindergarten. This means that in Seattle schools, half-day kindergarten is free to all students at all schools, and about half of the elementary and K–8 schools offer free full-day kindergarten. However, at other schools there is a fee of about $200 per month for full-day kindergarten. For any students eligible for the free or reduced-price meal program, enrollment is free for full-day kindergarten at any Seattle public school.

To enroll your child in the Seattle Public School District, you must call or visit a Student Assignment Service Center for registration materials. The regular enrollment period is Feb for elementary school and Mar for middle and high school. Of course, new students to Seattle can enroll in school at any time. A recorded information line about enrollment can be reached at (206) 252-0760.

i Check out the school guide published by the *Seattle Times*. This is the most comprehensive report available on public and private schools in the greater Seattle area. The *Times* collects and analyzes information from a variety of sources to help you select a school: http://community.seattletimes.nwsource.com/schoolguide/.

Private Schools

The U.S. Census reports that a third of 1st through 12th graders participate in private education, and Seattle has the highest rate of private school attendance in the nation. The cost of attending a private school in the Northwest also ranks among the highest

in the country. According to the Washington Federation of Independent Schools, the state average annual private school tuition runs about $6,095 for 1st- through 4th-grade students, $7,109 for 5th through 8th graders, and $9,249 for 9th through 12th graders. These are statewide averages; figures tend to be even higher in Seattle. Tuition for at least three Puget Sound–area schools tops $20,000. Most schools offer some sort of financial aid, either through tuition breaks or scholarships based on financial need, academic merit, or a combination; in general the smaller the school, the fewer the scholarships available.

If you are interested in enrolling your child in private school, start the process as early as possible—a year in advance is not too soon. For many of the region's most competitive programs, the requirements can include tests, interviews, school tours, student essays, and mountains of paperwork. The application process runs from early Oct to mid-Nov. That's when required appointment-only school visits begin for many private high schools and competitive-enrollment elementary schools. Starting in Nov, applicants to fifth through eighth grades may take the required Independent School Entrance Exam. Open-house tours for students and families take place in Dec, as do tuition information meetings. Financial aid requests are due at this time, and by Jan most application paperwork and fees must be in for the following school year.

i A report card on area private schools can be found on the Northwest Newcomer Web site, http://nwnewcomer.com/education.php#private. You can also find a chart of all Washington private schools at http://nwnewcomer.com/education.php#104.

Higher Education

SEATTLE COMMUNITY COLLEGES
1500 Harvard Ave.
(888) 801-3607
www.sccd.ctc.edu

More than a million and a half students have advanced their educations and careers at the Seattle Community Colleges, the largest two-year system in Washington. All three colleges (central, north, and south campuses) offer programs in college transfer, professional-technical training, adult basic education, continuing education, and e-learning. In addition, the Seattle Vocational Institute provides short-term programs in basic skills and vocational and workforce training that help youth and adults attain education and employment. High school students can also take a variety of courses at the Seattle Community Colleges for college credit. Some of these programs provide dual credit that counts for both college credit and high school credit.

SEATTLE PACIFIC UNIVERSITY
3307 3rd Ave. West
(206) 281-2000
www.spu.edu

Founded in 1891, Seattle Pacific University has a long and distinguished history in Christian higher education of arts, sciences, and professional studies. About 3,800 students are enrolled each year at the campus just minutes from downtown, in SPU's undergraduate and graduate programs. High school students can take advantage of the Campus Preview, which includes classroom visits, financial aid workshops, overnight stays in a residence hall, and meals.

SEATTLE UNIVERSITY
901 12th Ave.
(206) 296-6000
www.seattleu.edu

Seattle University, founded in 1891, is a Jesuit Catholic university located on 48 acres on Seattle's Capitol Hill. More than 7,500 students are enrolled in undergraduate and graduate programs within eight schools. *U.S. News & World Report*'s "Best Colleges 2010" ranks Seattle University among the top 10 universities in the West that offer a full range of master's and undergraduate programs. Seattle is one of the world's greatest cities. Much of what makes it great—its global connectedness, natural beauty, environmental awareness, cutting-edge music scene, social entrepreneurism, and progressive civic ethic—is reflected in Seattle University, which makes the most of its energetic urban neighborhood.

UNIVERSITY OF WASHINGTON
Visitor Information Center, 022
   Odegaard
(206) 543-2100
www.washington.edu

Founded in 1861, the University of Washington is one of the oldest state-supported institutions of higher education on the West Coast and is one of the preeminent research universities in the world. Anyone can enjoy and be enriched by all UW has to offer, including world-class libraries, art, music, drama, sports, and the highest quality medical care in Washington state. UW is a multi-campus university in Seattle, Tacoma, and Bothell, with 17 colleges and schools, over 1,800 undergraduate courses offered each quarter, over 250 degree options, more than 70 languages to study, 500 student organizations to join, and over 7,000 undergraduate research opportunities.

More than 4,000 faculty—many who are renowned leaders in their field—are giving students a diverse learning experience in and out of the classroom. UW confers more than 12,000 bachelor's, master's, doctoral, and professional degrees annually. The Visitor Information Center is located on the ground floor of Odegaard Undergraduate Library and is open Mon through Fri from 8:30 a.m. to 5 p.m. (except for university holidays). Campus tours are led by UW undergraduates who combine knowledge of the historic campus with information about the student experience. Guided tours are offered Mon through Fri at 10:30 a.m. and 2:30 p.m. (except state holidays and some holiday weekends).

Specialty Colleges

ART INSTITUTE OF SEATTLE
2323 Elliott Ave.
(800) 275-2471
www.artinstitutes.edu/seattle

Founded in 1946 as the Burnley School for Professional Art, the Art Institute of Seattle (AIS) has a proud history as a part of the Seattle community and a contributor to the creative industries in the Northwest. In 1982 the Burnley School joined the Art Institute's system of schools and became the Art Institute of Seattle. In the next few years, AIS received accreditation from the Accrediting Commission for Career Schools and Colleges of Technology (1984), moved to its present location on Seattle's waterfront (1985), and grew from about 100 students to a fall 2008 enrollment of nearly 2,300. AIS achieved a major milestone in 1999 when it was granted regional accreditation by the Northwest Commission on Colleges and Universities. AIS offers programs in fashion, design, and culinary, and media arts. Every year the Art Institute admissions department hosts several events that allow prospective students and their families, high school teachers and counselors, and other interested groups to get information about the college and meet Art Institute faculty and staff. Open houses, college previews, and fairs are held frequently; check the Web site for dates.

CORNISH COLLEGE OF THE ARTS
1000 Lenora St.
(206) 726-5151
www.cornish.edu

Cornish College of the Arts is an exhilarating place to be. One of only three private, nonprofit performing and visual arts colleges in the nation, Cornish offers a distinctive blend of visual and performing arts grounded in a core curriculum of humanities and sciences. Cornish is a four-year college offering a bachelor of music degree and bachelor of fine arts degrees in art, dance, design, theater, and performance production. Cornish is a small college with 800 students in degree programs and another 150 in preparatory classes. The school is accredited by the Northwest Commission on Colleges and Universities and the National Association of Schools of Art and Design.

Other Specialty and Small Colleges in Seattle

Argosy University Seattle: www.argosy.edu

Antioch University Seattle: www.antiochsea.edu

City University: www.cityu.edu

DeVry University: www.sea.devry.edu

Gage Academy of Art: www.seattlefineart.org

International Academy of Design & Technology: www.iadtseattle.com
Seattle Vocational Institute: http://sviweb
.sccd.ctc.edu

> **i** For a full list of universities, colleges, and technical schools in Seattle and throughout Washington, go to www.seattle.gov/html/citizen/edu cate.htm#college.

HEALTH CARE AND WELLNESS

Seattle's health care system offers a variety of options, from private doctors, hospitals, and clinics to public health resources, as well as alternative and natural or holistic methods. In keeping with its progressive, change-leading nature, Seattle also has seen protests over health care issues and has implemented cutting-edge initiatives to the way the city addresses health care.

For example, in mid-2009 a new medical clinic opened up that was revolutionary—it completely cut insurance companies out of the picture. Qliance is run by doctors who are fed up with the fact that $1 of every $3 patients spend on health care goes to cover insurance processing costs, and so Qliance simply removed that factor from the mix. Qliance charges $99 to join, and between $44 and $129 per month. Its patients can receive medical care any time, seven days a week. KOMO 4 TV news said that the Qliance model "may change the face of health care."

Seattle is also home to a new breed of HMO providers: cooperative HMOs. This isn't surprising in a city that enthusiastically embraces cooperative grocery stores and utility companies. Group Health is owned, and its policies are determined by, the consumer members themselves. The plan received a lot of attention in the debate about health care reform, and PBS ran a

special report showing how it could offer a model nationwide.

As with almost every aspect of life, Seattle residents are highly vocal and involved with the issues. In May 2009 a peaceful health care rally convened downtown, creating a mellow parade to make the participants' views known to their representatives. This being Seattle, the parade also included belly dancers, drummers, air horns, bicycles, and lots of kids.

This section outlines some of the major health care providers and resources, to reference during your upcoming move to Seattle.

Alternative Care Clinics and Centers

BASTYR CENTER FOR NATURAL HEALTH
3670 Stone Way North
(206) 834-4100
www.bastyrcenter.org
Bastyr Center for Natural Health is the teaching clinic of Bastyr University, one of the world's leading centers of natural medicine education and research. Staffed by health care teams that include advanced students under the supervision of Bastyr's clinical faculty, the center provides a teaching vehicle for the university as well as quality health care. Bastyr Center is the largest natural medicine clinic in the Northwest and operates several clinics in the Seattle metro area, including Ballard, Central District, downtown, Capitol Hill, and South Seattle. Services offered include naturopathic medicine, acupuncture and Oriental medicine, herbal medicine, homeopathy, nutrition, and counseling services.

NORTHWEST NATURAL HEALTH
6135 Seaview Ave. NW, Suite 300
(206) 784-9111
www.nwnaturalhealth.com

The Northwest Natural Health Specialty Care clinic combines traditional natural therapies with the latest nutritional, botanical health sciences and technology. Clinic practitioners work with the patient's own physician to combine conventional therapy with the best of complementary and alternative medicine. Northwest Natural Health was founded in 1985 to provide safe, sensible, and scientific complementary therapies that respect and account for conventional treatments.

SEATTLE MEDFINDS
(415) 968-9938
http://seattle.medfinds.com
Seattle Medfinds.com is a comprehensive Web site for complementary and alternative medicine in Seattle. Its growing directory of local Seattle alternative health care providers, schools, and events is a simple gizmo for better health. You can easily find reliable information about Seattle holistic therapies, natural health remedies, and the latest health news in the site's Resource Center. From acupuncture to weight loss, Medfinds offers a good resource to find alternative options.

UNIVERSITY HEALTH CLINIC
5312 Roosevelt Way NE
(206) 525-8015
www.theuhc.com
The University Health Clinic was founded in 1983. From its founding, it has always focused on patient-centered, holistic health care. Over the past thirty years the UHC has helped pioneer the establishment of natural medicine as a recognized element of the integrated health care model not only in the greater Seattle area but also nationally. UHC integrates all forms of conventional and natural medicine, often with acupuncture

and East Asian medicine. UHC health care practitioners are credentialed with most insurance companies.

ℹ️ Check out the Alternative Health Care Review, a blog on the *Seattle Post–Intelligencer* Web site: http://blog .seattlepi.com/alternativehealth.

Referral Services

MEDCON EDUCATION AND REFERRAL SERVICE
(800) 326-5300
http://uwmedicine.washington.edu/ Patient-Care/Referrals/Pages/ MEDCON.aspx
MEDCON is a toll-free consultation and referral service of the UW School of Medicine and its academic medical centers, Harborview Medical Center and UW Medical Center. Special operators are available throughout the day to take providers' calls and to link them with an appropriate faculty physician with expertise in any particular area. The line is open 24 hours a day, seven days a week. After hours and on weekends, UW Medical Center operators will take your call.

SWEDISH PHYSICIAN REFERRAL SERVICE
(800) 833-8879
www.swedish.org/body.cfm?id=786
Swedish Health Services offers this online referral service to improve access to quality care and enhance relationships between physicians and patients in the Puget Sound region. This is a free community service that refers members of the public to physicians in good standing on the Swedish medical staff. You can search online or call the toll-free number.

WASHINGTON STATE MEDICAL ASSOCIATION
(800) 552-0612
www.wsma.org/patient_resources/tips-on-choosing-a-doctor.cfm

The WSMA offers this great resource for finding a physician anywhere in the state. The Web site includes searches into doctor credentials on the state Department of Health Web site, an online doctor-search tool, and a list of questions to think about when searching for a new physician. There are also a lot of tips, articles, and other resources available. An invaluable Web site for newcomers to the state.

Health Cooperatives

GROUP HEALTH COOPERATIVE OF PUGET SOUND
320 Westlake Ave. North, Suite 100
(888) 901-4636
www.ghc.org

Founded in 1947, Group Health Cooperative is a consumer-governed, nonprofit health care system that coordinates care and coverage. Based in Seattle, Group Health and its subsidiary health carriers serve more than half a million residents of Washington and Idaho. Care is provided by Group Health Permanente doctors and other clinicians at Group Health–operated medical facilities. In service areas where Group Health doesn't own facilities and for plans offering more choice, a network of nearly 9,000 community clinicians and 41 hospitals meets member health care needs.

Hospitals

SEATTLE CHILDREN'S HOSPITAL
4800 Sand Point Way NE
(866) 987-2000
www.seattlechildrens.org

Seattle Children's Hospital specializes in meeting the unique physical, emotional, and developmental needs of children from infancy through young adulthood. For more than 100 years, the hospital has been dedicated to providing top-quality care to every child in the region, regardless of the family's ability to pay. Seattle Children's Research Institute has nine major centers and is internationally recognized for its work in cancer, genetics, immunology, pathology, infectious disease, injury prevention, and bioethics. Seattle Children's is consistently ranked among the nation's best children's hospitals by *U.S. News & World Report* magazine. For nursing excellence, it received Magnet status in 2008—an honor bestowed on less than 4 percent of all hospitals in the United States.

SWEDISH MEDICAL CENTER
747 Broadway
(206) 386-6000
www.swedish.org

The year 2010 marked the 100th anniversary of Swedish Medical Center, opened by Swedish immigrant and surgeon Dr. Nils Johanson. Swedish is the largest, most comprehensive nonprofit health provider in the greater Seattle area and has been the region's hallmark for excellence in health care. In fact, in an independent research study conducted by the National Research Corporation, Swedish is consistently named the area's best hospital, with the best doctors, nurses, and overall care in a variety of specialty areas. There are several other Swedish Medical Centers as well, on 17th Avenue in Cherry Hill, in Ballard, and in Issaquah.

UW MEDICINE
(206) 543-2100
http://uwmedicine.washington.edu

The University of Washington medicine department operates several clinics, hospitals, and medical centers in Seattle. In 2008 Harborview Medical Center was ranked among the nation's top three hospitals in rehabilitation care by *U.S. News & World Report*. UW Medical Center is one of the nation's leading academic medical centers, which provides highly specialized medical care in areas such as cardiology, high-risk pregnancy, and neonatal intensive care, oncology, orthopedics, and organ transplantation. The newest entity in the UW Medicine Health System, Northwest Hospital & Medical Center is a full-service, acute-care community hospital offering comprehensive medical, surgical, and therapeutic services. With 281 beds, more than 1,900 employees, and a world-class medical staff, it provides some of the most innovative, technologically advanced care available. In addition, the UW Medicine Neighborhood Clinics have seven clinic locations throughout the greater Seattle area with nearly 70 health care providers. See the Web site for more information and locations of the various medical facilities offered by UW.

VIRGINIA MASON MEDICAL CENTER
1100 9th Ave.
(206) 223-6600
www.virginiamason.org
Virginia Mason Medical Center is an award-winning, private, not-for-profit organization offering a network of primary and specialty care clinics throughout the Puget Sound region and a hospital in Seattle. Established in 1920, Virginia Mason began as an 80-bed hospital with six physician offices. It was named after the daughters of James Tate Mason, MD, and John M. Blackford, MD, who

cofounded the clinic along with radiologist Maurice Dwyer, MD. The founders' vision was to provide a single place where patients could receive comprehensive medical care, a "one-stop-shopping" place for virtually any medical problem or need.

i For a complete list of area hospitals, go to www.seattle.gov/html/citizen/hospitals.htm.

Membership Health Care

QLIANCE
509 Olive Way
(877) 754-2623
www.qliance.com
Qliance is a monthly membership approach to health care, cutting out insurance to provide patients with the most comprehensive, high-quality primary care out there. The Qliance membership approach means you can see your doctor whenever you need to—even after work and on weekends. Traditionally, over 40 cents of every $1 you spend on health care goes toward insurance billing and overhead. This means your clinician must work harder and faster, seeing more patients each day just to make ends meet. As a patient, you experience longer wait times, shorter appointments, and higher costs. Qliance is like a health club membership, but for health care. Your membership gives you unrestricted access to your Qliance clinician and services for one monthly fee. There are two membership levels for patient care, and the monthly fees range from $44 to $129 depending on your age and which plan you choose. There is a one-time registration fee of $99 per family, and there are no long-term contracts—you may cancel at any time.

Mental Health

COMMUNITY PSYCHIATRIC CLINIC
1008 James St., Suite A
(206) 461-3209
www.cpcwa.org
Community Psychiatric Clinic is a dually licensed, state-certified, and nationally accredited nonprofit behavioral health care organization. CPC provides a comprehensive array of recovery-oriented mental health and chemical dependency services at six outpatient treatment sites and six staffed residential sites, in addition to a variety of housing locations in the community. Since 1953 CPC has helped thousands of individuals and their families.

NAVOS MENTAL HEALTH SOLUTIONS
2600 SW Holden St.
(206) 933-7000
www.navos.org
Navos is a consortium of various mental health facilities and resources, including a psychiatric hospital in West Seattle, two mental health center campuses, the Navos Housing Program of 24 properties that provide a home for more than 300 people with mental health issues, chemical dependency treatment, and special programs for children, immigrants, and the elderly.

SOUND MENTAL HEALTH
1600 E. Olive St.
(206) 302-2300
www.smh.org
Sound Mental Health provides a wide variety of mental health services, including counseling, chemical dependency services, crisis response, housing services, vocational assistance, and specialty services such as developmental disabilities, services for the deaf, and services for children and the elderly.

There are several locations throughout and beyond Seattle.

Public Health Resources

KING COUNTY PUBLIC HEALTH PROGRAMS
401 5th Ave., Suite 1300
(206) 296-4600
www.kingcounty.gov/healthservices/
   health/personal.aspx
The county offers a wealth of resources here, including free or low-cost health insurance, family planning clinics, HIV/AIDS programs, GLBT health resources, oral and dental health, WIC services, and public health centers.

Urgent Care/Emergency Clinics

GROUPHEALTH CAPITOL HILL CAMPUS URGENT CARE CLINIC
201 16th Ave. East
(206) 326-3175
www.ghc.org/locations/medcenters/3/
   index.jhtml
The GroupHealth cooperative includes a number of health care options, including this Capitol Hill campus, which offers an urgent care clinic. It is open 24 hours a day, seven days a week.

U.S. HEALTHWORKS MEDICAL CENTER
1151 Denny Way
(206) 682-7418
www.ushealthworks.com/Seattle
   (Denny)-CenterInfo.html
Serving the community since 1984, the Seattle Denny Way Medical Center offers urgent care treatment for non–life threatening injuries and illnesses, as well as comprehensive occupational health services to employers. There is also an urgent care medical center at 836 NE Northgate Way in North Seattle.

WEST SEATTLE CONVENIENT CARE

3623 SW Alaska St.

(206) 362-8671

www.westseattleconvenientcare.com

West Seattle Convenient Care provides easy, local, and rapid access to comprehensive medical care for acute illness or injury as an alternative to emergency room care. Walk-in hours are 6 to 9 p.m., Mon through Thurs; no appointment is necessary. This after-hours clinic does not provide routine or preventative care services, such as prescription refills or annual physical exams. Instead, it is here for the sudden onset of illness or injury, during the hours when a regular doctor's office is closed, to address basic urgent care issues without the lengthy waiting times and higher cost of an emergency room. The organization does offer a regular day clinic at Highline Medical Group, as well (see in section below).

Walk-in Clinics

COUNTRY DOCTOR COMMUNITY HEALTH CENTERS

2101 E. Yesler Way

500 19th Ave. East

(206) 299-1600

www.countrydoctor.org

Country Doctor Community Health Centers improves the health of the community by providing high-quality, caring, culturally appropriate primary health care that addresses the needs of all people regardless of their ability to pay. Two Seattle health centers are available, in the Central District and in Capitol Hill. CDCHC clinics are members of the Community Health Plan of Washington. Both clinics charge on a sliding fee scale and will accept medical coupons, Medicare, SSI, the Basic Health Plan, and most private insurance plans.

HIGHLINE MEDICAL GROUP WEST SEATTLE WALK-IN CLINIC

4744 41st Ave. SW, Suite 101

(206) 933-1041

www.highlinemedicalcenter.org/high line_medical_group/services/west-seattle-walk.htm

Highline's clinic offers both walk-in service as well as same-day appointments if you prefer. The clinic is open from 8 a.m. to 6 p.m. Mon through Fri, and 9 a.m. to 5 p.m. Sat. For care after those times, see the West Seattle Convenient Care clinic above.

NEIGHBORCARE HEALTH MEDICAL CLINICS

(206) 461-6935

www.neighborcare.org/index.php? page=Medical_Clinics

Neighborcare Health is the leading provider of primary medical and dental care to low-income and uninsured patients in Seattle. Neighborcare operates several walk-in medical clinics in Seattle, including locations on N. 45th, N. 85th, 35th Avenue SW, at Pike Market and Rainier Beach locations. Midwifery and women's health services are also available at the Rainier Park clinics.

RECREATION

There are nearly endless outdoor recreations and sports to take advantage of in the Seattle area. The following is a list of the major organized sports leagues available to adults and youth.

Adult Recreation and Sports Leagues

CITYWIDE ATHLETICS ADULT BASKET-BALL LEAGUES

(206) 684-7092

www.seattle.gov/parks/athletics/adult sports.htm

The competitive men's league offers men an opportunity to showcase their skills, sportsmanship, and passion for the game. League play begins in early Dec. Games take place at West Seattle High School and Delridge Community Center. For women, the basketball league is for ages 35 and older. Mon is ladies' night at Rainier Community Center. Women 35 and older with a competitive spirit can play and have fun in a structured basketball league. League play begins in Jan and is limited to eight teams. Visit the Web site for information on registration, season dates, and team placement.

i Team Seattle is a nonprofit organization that organizes and supports athletic teams for the LGBT community. Each team and league has a board for its own sport, and there are organized sports clubs for running, walking, swimming, bowling, soccer, softball, rugby, tennis, water polo, track, volleyball, biking, skiing, and snowboarding, and diverse outdoor hiking and camping activities. Team Seattle welcomes all ability levels, whether you are a beginner, advanced, or anywhere in between. (206) 367-4064, http://teamseattle.org.

CITYWIDE ATHLETICS ADULT SOFTBALL LEAGUES
(206) 684-7092
www.seattle.gov/parks/Athletics/softball.htm
In 2009 there were 86 men's teams, 106 co-ed teams, and 11 women's teams in this city league. Tentative league dates are late Apr through July, depending on the league.

A $200 nonrefundable deposit is due at the organizational meeting. Visit the Web site for information on registration, season dates, and team placement.

CITYWIDE ATHLETICS CO-ED VOLLEYBALL LEAGUE
(206) 684-7092
www.seattle.gov/parks/athletics/adultsports.htm
This recreation-level league is for players looking to enjoy volleyball without an intimidating atmosphere or attitude. The league consists of a minimum of three women and a maximum of three men. It uses double elimination play and gives players an opportunity to play volleyball in a fun and controlled environment in a spacious indoor facility. First- and second-place teams advance to the championship and receive uary and is limited to 10 teams. Visit the Web site for information on registration, season dates, and team placement.

CITYWIDE ATHLETICS DODGEBALL LEAGUES FOR ADULTS
(206) 684-7092
www.seattle.gov/parks/athletics/dodgeball.htm
Join the fastest-growing league in Seattle. The league consists of six matches followed by a single elimination tournament. A coed team must play games with no more than four players of the same gender with a total of six players per game. A team roster can have as few as six players, or as many as 15. Games are on Mon night, last 40 minutes, and are self-officiated. Visit the Web site for information on registration, season dates, and team placement.

CITYWIDE ATHLETICS FLAG FOOTBALL LEAGUES FOR ADULTS
(206) 684-7092
www.seattle.gov/parks/athletics/football.htm

This flag football city league is for men. Teams participate in league play during the fall season. Visit the Web site for information on registration, season dates, and team placement.

CITYWIDE ATHLETICS KICKBALL LEAGUES FOR ADULTS
(206) 684-7092
www.seattle.gov/parks/athletics/Kickball.htm

Players of all ability levels are welcome. Teams play with 10 players at time, with six men and four women on the field. You can bat/kick as many people as you want. Leagues include regular season games and one playoff game. All teams make the first round of playoffs. Leagues also typically include an umpire, T-shirts, and online schedules and standings. Visit the Web site for information on registration, season dates, and team placement.

DISCNW
(206) 781-5840
www.discnw.org

DiscNW is an educational, nonprofit organization established in 1995 to promote and support the sport of Ultimate Frisbee. DiscNW was incorporated with a mission to "serve as a regional resource, promoting growth in the sport of Ultimate and instilling the spirit of sportsmanship at all levels of play." It is intrinsic to DiscNW's mission to promote and teach mutual respect and fair play, demonstrate the value of team sports for health and social benefits, encourage women in coed recreation, and perform outreach in the community.

GREATER SEATTLE HOCKEY LEAGUE
(206) 523-PUCK
www.gshockey.com

Greater Seattle Hockey League is committed to providing fun, safe, recreational hockey for adult hockey players of all skill levels. Since the summer of 2001, GSHL has grown into the largest adult recreational ice hockey league in the Northwest and one of the largest in the country. The league offers two seasons to keep you busy on the ice throughout the year. The fall/winter season includes 22 games plus double-elimination playoffs and runs from Oct to Apr. The summer season consists of 12 games plus single-elimination playoffs and runs from May to Aug. GSHL also hosts two tournaments each year and welcomes new players of all skill levels.

GREATER SEATTLE SOCCER LEAGUE
(206) 782-6831
www.gssl.org

The Greater Seattle Soccer League is open to anyone of any age, although it consists primarily of adult men's teams (but there's no restriction on women playing on men's teams). All nationalities, backgrounds, and levels of skill are equally welcome. With as many as 20 skill divisions in four age groups, there is a place for almost anyone to play. Only an express lack of respect for the other members of the league, or for the game of soccer, will disqualify anyone from membership.

SEATTLE WOMEN'S FIELD HOCKEY CLUB
(206) 524-0968
www.seattlefieldhockey.org

The Seattle Women's Field Hockey Club comprises players from all around the world. The team plays year-round, and at a typical practice, players split into two teams and scrimmage. Visit the calendar for a detailed practice schedule. The club is more than 50 years old, formed by University of Washington alumnae in 1953. The team continues to grow and thrive, and active players range in age from 15 to 55.

UNDERDOG SPORTS LEAGUES
(206) 320-TEAM
www.underdogseattle.com

Underdog Sports Leagues was started with a simple idea: provide laid-back leagues for everyday players that are safe and fun. While USL never turns away real athletes or people who take sports seriously, most of its members are not superstars or blue-chippers, but rather everyday Underdogs who want to play a game or two, meet some people, and go talk about the game afterward at the local watering hole. Sports may be a way of life, a religion, or a huge business enterprise, but USL believes that sports should be enjoyable—the "agony of defeat" is for athletes with sponsorships, not everyday players. If you are a person who plays sports with a laid-back attitude and realizes that even if that cool-looking ref totally misses a call (rare) life will still go on—you sound like an Underdog. The league has teams for bowling, flag football, dodgeball, kickball, mini-golf, volleyball, and softball.

Youth Recreation and Sports Leagues

ARENA SPORTS
Magnuson Park, 7727 63rd Ave. NE
(206) 985-8990
www.arenasports.net

Arena Sports is all about fun, friendships, and having a great time playing the sports you love. Here you'll find all kinds of cool things like indoor and outdoor soccer for kids, cool birthday party packages, indoor and outdoor soccer camps and multi-sports camps, and the Fun Zone indoor inflatable playground. In addition to the Magnuson Park location, Arena Sports is also in South Seattle, Queen Anne, Mercer Island, Sammamish, and Redmond.

NORTHWEST CHRISTIAN SPORTS LEAGUE
(425) 743-3067
www.ncsl.cc

Northwest Christian Sports League is an independent, nonprofit organization. The nondenominational Christian youth sports leagues provide quality team sports and Christian outreach to kids and the community of Snohomish County, regardless of religion, ethnicity, or social class. Sports offered include baseball, softball, basketball, and soccer for ages 5–18.

SEATTLE PARKS & RECREATION YOUTH SPORTS TEAMS AND PROGRAMS
(206) 684-7138
www.seattle.gov/parks/Athletics/
  Ythsport.htm

Seattle Parks & Recreation provides a variety of seasonal sports for youth. All programs stress skill development, participation, and fun. Fall, winter, spring, and summer teams are available; team sports include flag football, Ultimate Frisbee, volleyball, cross country, basketball, track and field, softball, tennis, boating, and swimming instruction. All youth teams are coached by citizen volunteers, with officiating and program supervision provided by department staff. The sports are played at parks and community centers all over the city.

SEATTLE YOUTH SOCCER ASSOCIATION

520 NE Ravenna Blvd.
(206) 274-1318
www.sysa.org

This youth soccer league has teams and fields all over the city. In 1969 a group of soccer enthusiasts, including Walter Schmetzer, Rick Crudo, and Robin Chalmers, decided to teach the world's most popular sport to kids throughout the Seattle area. Their efforts led to the beginning of the Seattle Youth Soccer Association. Today over 11,000 young people play soccer in the association. The 13 member clubs cover every neighborhood in Seattle and Shoreline. For over 30 years Seattle Youth Soccer volunteers have brought soccer to kids and kids to soccer. They offer appropriate levels of play in recreational and competitive programs for young people from age five to 18. There are teams and try-outs for all ages, camps, training programs, and soccer schools.

STROUM JEWISH COMMUNITY CENTER

2618 NE 80th St.
(206) 232-7115
www.sjcc.org

The SJCC is a nonprofit organization that is open to everyone in the community. The SJCC offers two winter sports leagues for kids, Indoor Soccer League (ages four and five), and Dinky Dunkers kids' basketball league (K–third grade). There is also a fourth-grade basketball team. SJCC offers numerous summer camps, including sports camps, and the Spring Sports Spectacular provides a great introduction to learning various sports skills as well as teamwork and sportsmanship. Designed to be instructional and fun in a noncompetitive environment, the spring event may include baseball, T-ball, basketball, golf, soccer, and Frisbee.

WASHINGTON DISTRICT 8 LITTLE LEAGUE

(206) 789-4176
www.district8wa.org

Washington District 8 Little League serves the North Seattle area from the ship canal north to the King/Snohomish County line and from Puget Sound east to Lake Washington and through Woodinville. Boys and girls ages five to 18 participate in competitive and noncompetitive baseball and softball leagues in 14 leagues. District 8 also offers children the option to play in the Little League Challenger division, a separate program that provides a place for children with mental or physical disabilities to enjoy the game of baseball.

i Check out the Seattle Community Network for a comprehensive listing of all sports leagues and organized recreational activities in the Seattle area: www.scn.org/sports.

RETIREMENT

Money magazine put Seattle at number 10 on its list of the Best Places for a Healthy Retirement in 2009. Citing its bike-friendly climate, the Emerald City got high marks for its encouragement of ditching the car in favor of cycling and trekking on the 45 miles of urban trails available. *Money* also made mention of the fact that Seattle is one of the most literate U.S. cities, spending double the national average on books annually. Keeping the brain as well as the body healthy in retirement is important.

Housing

Seattle really has a lot of housing options for seniors and retirees. From luxury high-rise condominiums that cater to a clientele of a certain age, to independent and assisted living communities, there are dozens to choose from. Some of the top developments include **Mirabella,** offering larger apartment homes and cottages along with amenities and appointments like those found in the finest homes: slab granite countertops, walk-in closets, gas fireplaces, wine refrigerators, in-room safes, and full-size washers and dryers. Mirabella Seattle, in the South Lake Union neighborhood, is state-of-the-art in everything.

Aegis is another top senior living company that has a number of communities in various categories depending on interest. The Aegis Signature Living offers luxurious, resort-style retirement communities for those who seek independent living with discriminating tastes. Slightly more basic, less expensive communities are also offered, as well as assisted living and memory care facilities.

Horizon House is for assisted living, offering a continuing care retirement community designed to provide a spectrum of services and care for residents, from complete independence to individualized care. Supported living ranges from light assistance to daily living to 24-hour nursing care. A 5,000-book library, gardens, styling salon, activity rooms, and computer room are just some of the resident amenities.

And check out the interesting **Merrill Gardens** retirement community. Not only did it become the first such community to share space with college students, it also became the first retirement center to get its own liquor store! According to the *Seattle Times* story on the new state liquor store at Merrill Gardens, the students were mostly uninterested in the liquor sales, while the senior residents were much more enthusiastic. One even asked the reporters, hopefully, if there would be free samples (in case you're interested, the answer was no).

There are also several great resources to help you search for the right community, with online databases and personal assistance.

OPTIONS FOR SENIORS
(425) 827-0894
www.optionsforseniors.com
This is a senior housing placement service, offering personalized one-on-one service. Searching for a community on their Web site is easy. Simply enter a community name or select your search criteria from the drop-down menus.

SENIOR OUTLOOK
(800) 642-2429
http://seattle.senioroutlook.com
This resource offers a complete, searchable online database of senior housing and retirement communities in Seattle. The listings contain floor plans, virtual tours, maps, and photos, as well as information about amenities. Many properties have toll-free phone numbers and e-mail "guest cards," making it incredibly easy to get vacancy or other information. The company also prints a magazine called *After 55,* which is a terrific housing and retirement resource guide. Call the number above to order your copy; it's free, but you will need to pay $4 for shipping and handling.

SNAPFORSENIORS
1111 3rd Ave., Suite 1860
(206) 575-0728
www.snapforseniors.com/Housing.aspx

SNAPforSeniors offers a searchable database of listings for over 200,000 senior service providers in the United States, including hundreds in Seattle. The comprehensive listings include all licensed senior housing and Medicare-certified home health care providers across the country. It also lists continuing care retirement communities, independent living retirement communities, and facilities that provide assisted living, residential care, nursing, and rehabilitation.

Senior Centers

PIKE MARKET SENIOR CENTER
85 Pike St., Suite 200
(206) 728-2773
http://pikemarketseniorcenter.org
The Pike Market Senior Center is not only unique in its membership, but also its humble beginnings back in 1978. Its original location was a former biker bar, the Motherlode Tavern. Services include meals and nutrition, engagement and wellness, social services, and employment assistance. Membership is available to people age 55 and older; 85 percent are male and 15 percent female, with the female membership growing rapidly.

SEATTLE PARKS & RECREATION LIFELONG RECREATION
(206) 684-4951
www.seattle.gov/parks/seniors/index
.htm
Seattle Parks & Recreation Lifelong Recreation offers a wide range of fitness and social programs for people 50 and better that change each season. At the Web site you can download a PDF brochure of upcoming programs in spring and summer. Activities include lawn bowling, softball, games, and Sound Steps, a community-based walking program.

SENIOR SERVICES OF KING COUNTY
(206) 448-5757
www.seniorservices.org
Senior Services is the most comprehensive nonprofit agency serving older adults and their loved ones in Washington state. Senior Services assists and empowers more than 50,000 seniors and their families each year through an integrated system of quality programs and services. These programs include adult day centers, caregiver and fitness programs, Meals on Wheels, mobile markets, transportation, and senior activity centers throughout the city. These include locations in Central Seattle, Ballard, Southeast, and West Seattle.

Services

AREA AGENCY ON AGING FOR SEATTLE AND KING COUNTY
700 5th Ave., 51st Floor
(206) 684-0660
www.agingkingcounty.org
Aging and Disability Services plans, coordinates, and advocates for a comprehensive service delivery system for older adults, family caregivers, and people with disabilities in King County. Many services and resources are offered at the Web site, including a great calendar of events that are of interest to this community.

CHOICE ADVISORY SERVICES
(800) 361-0138
www.choiceadvisory.com
CHOICE is one of the most comprehensive, and user-friendly, database and referral services for older adults in the greater Puget Sound area. Search listings or call for referrals for housing, care, services, and products. CHOICE advisors are specially trained professionals, well versed in the topics you will

wish to discuss. You can also order a complimentary printed resource directory by calling or filling out the form online.

MAYOR'S OFFICE FOR SENIOR CITIZENS

810 3rd Ave., Suite 350
(206) 684-0500
www.seattle.gov/humanservices/
seniorsdisabled/mosc

The Mayor's Office for Senior Citizens supports healthy aging, independent living, and social and civic engagement, all to make a difference in the lives of older adults and adults with disabilities. The office does this with a wealth of services including referrals, employment resource center, utility assistance program, computer training classes, arts and special events, and the Gold Card that entitles cardholders to discounts on a variety of things around town.

SENIOR RESOURCE PAGE

www.krummefamily.org/pers/rares1
.html

This excellent resource was established as a public service and as a convenience to the community. Listings on this Web site do not infer an endorsement or recommendation of the businesses or agencies listed nor of the products and services they provide. It is an absolutely huge listing of all sorts of services, resources, and information for just about any topic having to do with seniors in the King County/Puget Sound area.

YMCA OF GREATER SEATTLE

(206) 382-5003
www.seattleymca.org/page.cfm?ID=
senior

The Seniors Program section of the YMCA has a multitude of offerings, from clubs and social events to education, conferences, and retreats. There are also group exercise classes, swimming and water fitness programs, and the Silver Sneakers, a great program that includes walking, yoga, and muscle-strengthening exercises. The YMCA of Greater Seattle has locations throughout the city.

i Check out Encore! a Seattle.gov web portal created for people 50+: www.seattle.gov/encore.

VOLUNTEER OPPORTUNITIES

Seniors are in great demand as volunteers with nonprofit organizations. They usually have more time to offer and bring a wealth of experience and knowledge. Volunteering is also a great way for seniors and retired people to be involved in their community and stay active.

One of the best places to find volunteer opportunities is at **Volunteer Match** (www.volunteermatch.org). Here you can search thousands of volunteer positions to find ones that suit your interests, abilities, skills, and geographic area.

United Way of King County also has a comprehensive online, searchable database of hundreds of nonprofit organizations and their volunteer needs. Go to www.uwkc.org/volunteer/default.asp to access it.

The **City of Seattle** also has a great resource page that lists and describes dozens of nonprofit organizations in the area, and the type of volunteer work that they need. You can access the city volunteer page at www.seattle.gov/html/citizen/volunteer.htm.

YMCA of Greater Seattle also offers a volunteer portal; simply select the location you are interested in, and the site will display

a list of YMCA volunteer opportunities: www
.seattleymca.org.

i Did you think that the Ameri-
Corps program was just for
students and young people? So did
Patti-lyn Bell, the volunteer program
coordinator for senior citizens at the
mayor's office. That is, until she became
a volunteer. Read about her reward-
ing experience here: www.poststat.net/
pwp008/pub.49/issue.743/article.3084.

MEDIA

The fact that Seattle is such a literate place—
there are more bookstores here than anywhere else in America—should make it no
surprise that we have a lot of intelligent,
quality media sources. Here are a few of the
major ones.

Magazines

ART ACCESS
(888) 970-9991
www.artaccess.com
The magazine for the arts scene in Seattle,
Art Access features directories of venues, galleries, curators and artists, as well as feature
stories and videos about what's going on in
the local arts.

OUTDOORS NW
(800) 935-1083
www.outdoorsnw.com
Outdoors NW magazine covers adventure,
travel, and recreation news and events for
the Seattle area. In addition to *Outdoors NW,*
Price Media also publishes the *Western Snow
Sports Guide,* the *Cascade Bicycle Club Event
and Activity Guide,* and *Therapeutic OUT-
LOOK magazine.* Your *Insiders' Guide to Seattle*
author has contributed to this magazine, on

subjects from area mountaineering and eco-
adventures to drinking our lovely Northwest
craft beer.

SEATTLE
(800) 637-0334
www.seattlemag.com
Seattle magazine call itself "the area's definitive city and regional magazine that helps
people get the most out of living in the
Puget Sound." Through award-winning photography and stories, *Seattle* magazine at
once celebrates the city's status as the birthplace of technology, innovation, and trends;
the surrounding natural beauty; and the
pioneering spirit that draws and keeps us all
here. Through in-depth stories about a civic,
political or newsy issue, or previews of new
hotspots, *Seattle* magazine keeps readers on
the pulse of restaurants, personalities, arts,
entertainment, and culture that reflect the
tapestry of our dynamic landscape.

SEATTLE DOG
(206) 913-2049
www.seattledogmagazine.com
Seattle Dog is a quarterly magazine that
reaches out to all Pacific Northwest dog
owners. This magazine is for every dog
owner in the Pacific Northwest, covering
all aspects from places to go, new products,
dog parks, day cares, grooming facilities,
treats, veterinarians, and people in the pet
industry. It has a readership of about 25,000.

SEATTLE HOMES & LIFESTYLES
(206) 322-6699
www.seattlehomesmag.com
Award-winning *Seattle Homes & Lifestyles* is
where Seattleites turn for high-end design—
architecture, interior design, public art—and
the lifestyle that surrounds it.

SEATTLE METROPOLITAN
(206) 957-2234
www.seattlemet.com

With a bold design, eye-catching photography, and an editorial voice that's at once witty and in-the-know, *Seattle Metropolitan* is our city's indispensable news, culture, and lifestyle magazine. From newsmakers to tastemakers, the publication canvases Washington's cultural capital for the people and trends that are changing the way Seattleites eat, play, dress, and think. Every month, in every issue, the magazine delivers its signature mix of in-depth news stories, provocative essays, and essential guides to the best of the city. Its singular goal is to inspire readers to get out and explore the vibrant and rapidly growing metropolis they call home.

SEATTLE WOMAN
(206) 784-5556
www.seattlewomanmagazine.com

Seattle Woman magazine recognizes that women crave stories and information that relate directly to them, and this groundbreaking magazine satisfies this hunger with intelligent, insightful, and involved coverage that supports local women in the many facets of their busy lives. Its goal is to print meaningful stories that inspire and empower local women, looking at careers, business, health, family, relationships, finances, and much more. It also helps readers connect with opportunities for professional growth, personal development, and community involvement. And by highlighting local poets, artists, and chefs, the magazine links them to the creative currents in the region. (Your *Insiders' Guide to Seattle* author has contributed to this magazine as well.)

SEATTLE'S CHILD
(206) 441-0191
www.seattleschild.com

Featuring everything about kids and parenting, *Seattle's Child* offers news and a calendar of events about the happenings concerning kids and parents in the Seattle area.

Newspapers

In addition to the more geographically broad newspapers below, Seattle also has several neighborhood newspapers. These include the **Ballard News-Tribune, Belltown Messenger, Capitol Hill Times, Madison Park Times, Mercer Island Reporter, North Seattle Herald Outlook, Queen Anne & Magnolia News, South Seattle Beacon,** and the **West Seattle News.** The **University of Washington Daily** also covers campus and University District news and happenings.

EAT THE STATE!
(206) 719-6947
http://eatthestate.org

Eat the State! is a shamelessly biased political journal seeking an end to poverty, exploitation, imperialism, militarism, racism, sexism, heterosexism, environmental destruction, television, and large ugly buildings. *Eat the State!* is published as a not-for-profit way of sharing information, resources, opinions, and hopefully inspiring action in the community. With no paid office staff, the publication is supported solely by volunteer labor, donations, subscriptions, in-kind donations, and ads from progressive groups and businesses. The newspaper is published on 40 percent postconsumer recycled newsprint, using soy-based ink.

PUGET SOUND BUSINESS JOURNAL
(206) 876-5500
http://seattle.bizjournals.com

At *Puget Sound Business Journal* you'll find the latest breaking business news on topics including small business, real estate, sales and marketing, the tech industry, and more. Special reports are also published throughout the year.

SEATTLE GAY NEWS
(206) 324-4297
www.sgn.org

Seattle Gay News is the third-oldest gay and lesbian newspaper publication in the United States and has proudly served the Pacific Northwest for more than 36 years. In addition to local, national, and international news stories, it also features arts and entertainment sections, an events calendar, business listings, and online classified ads.

SEATTLE STRANGER
(206) 323-7101
www.thestranger.com

The *Stranger* offers news, entertainment, and alternative information to the Seattle area. The *Stranger* has one of the city's most-read and -loved columns, *Savage Love* by Dan Savage. Read it. This newspaper is a member of the Association of Alternative Newsweeklies (AAN).

SEATTLE TIMES
(206) 464-2001
http://seattletimes.nwsource.com

Since 1896 the *Seattle Times* has been the Northwest's most trusted source of local news and information. As an independent, locally owned company with deep roots in the Pacific Northwest, it's committed to serving the community through quality journalism for many years to come. Today the Seattle Times Company Print and Online Network reaches more Northwest adults than any other local news media, with print and online products seen by seven out of 10 adults in King and Snohomish Counties. Your author has contributed to the *Seattle Times* real estate section in the past.

SEATTLE WEEKLY
(206) 623-0500
www.seattleweekly.com

Founded in 1976 by an arts-starved East Coast transplant named David Brewster, the award-winning *Seattle Weekly* has taken on as many faces as the city it covers through the course of time. But one thing has remained constant: stellar, engaging journalism that exposes municipal malfeasance just as often as it celebrates the wizards behind the city's civic curtain. Pair that with top-shelf music and arts coverage—as well as occasional (and welcome) doses of satire, such as the beloved advice column "Ask an Uptight Seattleite"—and it's no wonder Rainier drinkers and oenophiles alike have made picking up *Seattle Weekly* a priority every week for more than 30 years.

Online Newspapers

SEATTLE POST–INTELLIGENCER
(206) 448-8000
www.seattlepi.com

The *Seattle Post–Intelligencer* was founded in 1863 as the *Seattle Gazette*. Sadly, the last print edition of the *P-I* was published on March 17, 2009. At the time the newspaper's circulation was 127,584. The *P-I* continues to operate as an online-only news source for the Seattle area and is the nation's largest newspaper to shift to an entirely digital format. It remains an important source of news for Seattle.

Radio

KEXP FM 90.3
(206) 520-5800
www.kexp.org
KEXP first went on the air in 1972 as KCMU FM. It changed its name in 2001. The station offers listener-supported news and music radio and is owned by the University of Washington.

KING FM 98.1
(206) 691-2981
www.king.org
Broadcasting classical music in Seattle-Tacoma and the Puget Sound region, KING FM is moving to a listener-supported, public radio model in July 2011.

KMMT 103.7 FM
(206) 233-1037
www.kmtt.com
Known as The Mountain, KMMT plays folk, rock, and indie music, with a number of acoustic-based shows and cutting-edge international music.

KUBE 93 FM
(206) 494-2000
www.kube93.com
Seattle's hits and hip-hop radio station.

KUOW 94.9 FM PUGET SOUND PUBLIC RADIO
(206) 543-2710
www.kuow.org
The mission of KUOW is to create and serve an informed public, one challenged and invigorated by an understanding and appreciation of events, ideas, and cultures. KUOW is a founding member of NPR, and more than 89 percent of KUOW's applied revenue comes from individual and business support, while the Corporation for Public Broadcasting and the University of Washington provide 9 percent.

KZOK 102.5 FM
(206) 805-1025
http://kzok.radio.com
KZOK is Seattle's only classic rock station, playing everything from the Doobie Brothers to U2.

MY NORTHWEST
(206) 726-7000
www.mynorthwest.com
MyNorthwest.com is the home of Seattle radio stations News Talk 97.3 KIRO FM, 710 AM ESPN Seattle, and 770 AM KTTH The Truth.

Television

KCPQ 13
(206) 674-1321
www.q13fox.com
The local Fox station offers programming in news, weather, traffic, sports, health, lifestyle, and entertainment.

KCTS 9
(206) 728-6463
http://kcts9.org
KCTS 9 first went on the air December 7, 1954, broadcasting from the University of Washington. In 1970 National Educational Television was absorbed into the newly created Public Broadcasting Service. Under PBS affiliation, KCTS 9 began offering a vastly enhanced scope of programming for the general public, including British programming.

KING 5
(206) 448-5555
www.king5.com

KING5.com and local NBC affiliate KING 5 report the top local news, breaking news, entertainment news, local programming, national news, world news, weather, and sports.

KIRO
(206) 728-7777
www.kirotv.com
The local CBS affiliate provides local and national news coverage, and programming for sports, weather, and entertainment.

KOMO
(206) 404-4000
www.komonews.com
KOMO is the local ABC affiliate, providing local and network news and programming.

SEATTLE CHANNEL
(206) 684-8821
www.seattlechannel.org
The Seattle Channel is the award-winning local TV station that reflects, informs, and inspires the community it serves. The Seattle Channel presents programs on cable television (channel 21 on Comcast and Millennium) and via the Internet to help citizens connect with their city. Programming includes series and special features highlighting the diverse civic and cultural landscape of the Pacific Northwest's premier city.

UNIVERSITY OF WASHINGTON TV
(888) 616-UWTV
www.uwtv.org
As a service of the University of Washington, UWTV provides the people of Washington state and a worldwide audience with unique, high-quality educational programming. Offering a valuable antidote to commercial television and other mass media,

UWTV features the faculty and students from UW, and their collaborators from around the world. Together these world-class innovators explore the frontiers of knowledge and change the way we think, live, and work. UWTV programs show how UW responds to critical issues facing the region and the world: by being responsible and engaged global citizens, shaping a more sustainable future, driving innovations that serve society, and creating healthier lives at home and around the world.

LIBRARIES

The extensive Seattle Public Library system is quite good—as it should be, considering how much Seattleites like to read! The initial move to form a public library in Seattle came only 17 years after the first white settlers arrived on the shores of Puget Sound. It was July 30, 1868, when 50 residents of the rough-hewn logging town gathered to form a library association. The new public library opened in 1891 on the fifth floor of the Occidental Building in Pioneer Square. A lumber company vice president borrowed its first book, a brand-new copy of Mark Twain's *Innocents Abroad*.

Andrew Carnegie greatly influenced the library's later expansion and collection, by donating $200,000 in 1901—one of his largest library donations—with a notation to the city that read, "I like your pluck." Carnegie continued to donate more money in ensuing years, though the library went through many up-and-down years, including world wars and a depression.

Many years later, in 1998, Seattle voters approved what was at the time the largest library bond issue ever submitted in the United States. The landmark "Libraries for All" bond measure, which proposed a

$196.4 million makeover of the library system, garnered an unprecedented 69 percent approval rate at the polls.

Today the Seattle Public Library consists of the Central Library, 26 neighborhood branches, and mobile services. It has a total collection of 2.4 million books and other items. The Central Library downtown is the jewel of the bunch. One of the most dramatic buildings in Seattle, it was the first major work in the U.S. by renowned Dutch architect Rem Koolhaas. His 11-floor, 362,987-square-foot library, a dazzling avant-garde symphony of glass and form, has many innovative features, including a "Books Spiral" that displays the entire nonfiction collection in a continuous run; a towering "living room" along 5th Avenue that reaches 50 feet in height; and a distinctive diamond-shape exterior skin of glass and steel. The new Central Library's unorthodox shape, unlike any other building in Seattle, is the result of its use of five platform areas to reflect different aspects of the library's program.

Central Library tours are held Mon at 11 a.m., and architecture tours are Fri at noon. Besides the incredible collection of books, you can also check out DVDs at the library, take computer classes, get homework help, listen to award-winning authors speak, take your children to story time, and much more.

The Central Library is located at 1000 4th Ave. and is open from 10 a.m. to 8 p.m. Mon through Thurs. On Fri and Sat the hours are 10 a.m. to 6 p.m., and on Sun noon to 6 p.m. For other branches and information, call (206) 386-4636 or visit www.spl.org.

INDEX